Advanced Social Psychology

Advanced Social Psychology

Edited by
Heather Moore

Willford Press
www.willfordpress.com

Published by Willford Press,
118-35 Queens Blvd., Suite 400,
Forest Hills, NY 11375, USA

ISBN: 978-1-64728-366-7

Cataloging-in-Publication Data

Advanced social psychology / edited by Heather Moore.
p. cm.
Includes bibliographical references and index.
ISBN 978-1-64728-366-7
1. Social psychology. 2. Sociology. 3. Psychology. I. Moore, Heather.
HM1033 .A38 2021
302.14--dc23

For information on all Willford Press publications
visit our website at www.willfordpress.com

Willford Press

Contents

Preface

The scientific study of how the imagined, actual and implied presence of others influence an individual's feelings, behaviors and thoughts is referred to as social psychology. It studies and measures the psychological variables in humans. Social psychology explains human behavior as the result of the interaction of social situations and mental states. It focuses on the intrapersonal phenomena such as attitudes, persuasion, social cognition and self-concept as well as on the interpersonal phenomena including social influence, group dynamics and interpersonal attraction. Different approaches, evaluations, methodologies and advanced studies on social psychology have been included in this book. The topics covered herein deal with the core aspects of this discipline. This book aims to serve as a resource guide for students and experts alike and contribute to the growth of the discipline.

The researches compiled throughout the book are authentic and of high quality, combining several disciplines and from very diverse regions from around the world. Drawing on the contributions of many researchers from diverse countries, the book's objective is to provide the readers with the latest achievements in the area of research. This book will surely be a source of knowledge to all interested and researching the field.

In the end, I would like to express my deep sense of gratitude to all the authors for meeting the set deadlines in completing and submitting their research chapters. I would also like to thank the publisher for the support offered to us throughout the course of the book. Finally, I extend my sincere thanks to my family for being a constant source of inspiration and encouragement.

Editor

1

Facility for sustained positive affect as an individual difference characteristic

Nicola S. Schutte[1]* and John M. Malouff[1]

*Corresponding author: Nicola S. Schutte, Psychology, University of New England, Armidale, Australia
E-mail: nschutte@une.edu.au
Reviewing editor: Heather Lench, Texas A&M University, USA

Abstract: A series of studies investigated a proposed new individual difference characteristic or trait, facility for sustained positive affect, consisting of tendencies that allow individuals to maintain a high level of positive mood. Exploratory and confirmatory factor analyses resulted in the creation of a measure, the self-congruent and new activities (SANA) scale which identified two core aspects of sustainable positive affect, engaging in self-congruent activities and engaging in new activities. A higher level of facility for sustainable affect, as operationalized by the SANA scale, was associated with maintenance of positive mood for a month, fewer symptoms of depression and anxiety, less negative affect, and more life satisfaction, relationship satisfaction, work satisfaction, mindfulness, personal expansion and growth, and emotional intelligence. The results provided initial evidence that facility to maintain positive affect may be an emotion-related individual difference characteristic.

Subjects: Personality; Affect/Emotion; Personality Tests & Assessments

Keywords: sustainable positive affect; self-congruent and new activities (SANA) scale; affect; personality, trait; mental health; well-being; mindfulness; emotional intelligence

ABOUT THE AUTHORS

Nicola S. Schutte and John M. Malouff are both associate professors of psychology at the University of New England in Australia. Nicola Schutte's research focuses on positive psychology constructs such as positive affect, emotional intelligence, and self-efficacy. With regard to emotional intelligence, she is interested in exploring the ways in which high emotional intelligence may lead to positive outcomes and approaches to increasing emotional intelligence. The study of self-efficacy provides a promising avenue for facilitating beneficial outcomes in a variety of behavioural realms. Positive affect is linked to many desirable life outcomes and she is interested in exploring approaches to understanding and increasing positive affect. John Malouff's research also focuses on positive psychology constructs such as self-efficacy and emotional intelligence. He has a special interest in evaluating the effectiveness of approaches intended to increase quality of life, such as evaluation of self-help materials.

PUBLIC INTEREST STATEMENT

The ability to maintain positive emotion may be a unique emotion-related trait, termed facility for sustainable positive affect. This trait has two core components, engaging in activities that are consistent with one's values or goals and involvement in new activities. Facility for sustainable affect is associated with maintenance of positive mood over time, fewer symptoms of depression and anxiety, less negative affect, and more life satisfaction, relationship satisfaction, work satisfaction, mindfulness, personal expansion and growth, and emotional intelligence. Even though evidence suggests that facility for sustainable positive affect is a somewhat stable characteristic, it may be possible to increase individuals' levels of sustainable positive affect and related beneficial outcomes.

1. Introduction

Individuals who typically experience high levels of positive affect have better mental and physical health, have better relationships (Lyubomirsky, King, & Diener, 2005; Steptoe, Dockray, & Wardle, 2009), and live longer (Diener & Chan, 2011). Increasing positive affect can assist in maintaining and increasing mental health (Fredrickson, Cohn, Coffey, Pek, & Finkel, 2008; Lyubomirsky, King et al., 2005; Seligman, Steen, Park, & Peterson, 2005; Wood & Tarrier, 2010). An obstacle in maintaining the benefits associated with increasing positive affect is the hedonic treadmill effect, which involves adaptation to positive conditions, resulting in a return to the previous affect states (Diener, Lucas, & Scollon, 2006).

1.1. Facility for sustained positive affect as a proposed individual difference characteristic

The current project explored whether people can engage in behavioral and cognitive activities to offset hedonic adaptation, leading to sustained positive affect, and whether the tendency to engage in these activities is an individual difference that is related to well-being indices. The project set out to create an initial operationalization of facility for sustained positive affect to begin to place it in the nominological framework of personality traits and life functioning.

Results of empirical studies as well as theoretical approaches aimed at understanding the nature of the development and maintenance of positive affect provide information regarding which behavioral and cognitive approaches may be beneficial in maintaining positive affect. Qualities such as engagement with life (Livingstone & Srivastava, 2012) and typical antecedent-focused emotion regulation (Gross & John, 2003) are correlated with higher positive affect.

Some empirical research indicates that positive affect need not return to baseline (Fredrickson, 2001; Fredrickson & Losada, 2005; Fredrickson et al., 2008; Lyubomirsky, Sheldon, & Schkade, 2005) as suggested by the hedonic treadmill model (Diener et al., 2006). This research for the most part has focused on specific interventions designed to help individuals maintain heightened levels of positive affect. For example, Fredrickson et al. (2008) found that a meditation-based intervention resulted in continued increasing levels of happiness for weeks after the intervention ended. Lyubomirsky, Sheldon et al. (2005) presented evidence that certain aspects of activities lead to positive affect increases that remain after months of follow-up assessments. Positive affect that stems from intentional (volitional) activities, including cognitive and behaviorally based activities, is most likely to lead to sustained gains in positive affect (Lyubomirsky, Sheldon et al., 2005). Activities that can be varied and intentional activities that are congruent with personal goals, abilities, and interests may be especially likely to lead to long-term positive affect (Lyubomirsky, Sheldon et al., 2005).

Theoretical perspectives on motivation and growth processes offer additional reasons to expect that specific behaviors can contribute to sustained positive affect. Intentional activities congruent with intrinsic motivation may relate to self-determination as described by Deci and Ryan (2008) and may be especially effective in sustaining positive affect as these may contribute to the self-congruent activities identified by Lyubomirsky, Sheldon et al. (2005).

Positive appraisal of events is associated with more positive affect (Folkman & Moskowitz, 2000; Gross & John, 2003) and can be viewed as a cognitive activity. Mindfulness is associated with greater positive affect, and interventions that intended to increase mindfulness increase positive affect (Schroevers & Brandsma, 2010). The acceptance and non-judgmental evaluation that are part of characteristic, or trait, mindfulness (Baer, Smith, Hopkins, Krietemeyer, & Toney, 2006; Brown & Ryan, 2003) may facilitate the maintenance of positive affect.

The broaden-and-build process that is activated by high levels of positive affect (Fredrickson, 2001; Fredrickson & Losada, 2005) also may counter the hedonic treadmill effect and lead to sustained positive affect. The broaden-and-build theory proposes that high levels of positive affect lead to a broadening of cognition and behavior, resulting in more divergent and creative thoughts and more exploration. This broadening leads to more opportunities for building resources, such as personal resilience or social skills. These resources in turn lead to better life outcomes, such as better mental health or better relationships. Both the variety of cognitive and behavioral activity associated with broadening and resource building and the resulting positive life outcomes may lead to sustainable positive affect.

It may be that individuals naturally vary in an enduring way in the extent to which they engage in actions that tend to sustain positive affect. There are reasons to expect that actions that help sustain positive affect might be an individual difference characteristic. First, as well as being a state, positive affect may be an enduring individual difference characteristic (Diener & Chan, 2011; Diener et al., 2006; Diener & Seligman, 2002; Lyubomirsky, King et al., 2005; Lyubomirsky, Sheldon et al., 2005; Watson, Clark, & Tellegen, 1988). A large portion of variance in this individual difference characteristic may be due to biological set points for positive affect and life circumstances, but another portion of the variance may be explained by the activity of the individual (Lyubomirsky, Sheldon et al., 2005). One might expect that if such activities consistently contribute to characteristic positive affect, they might themselves comprise an identifiable individual difference characteristic or trait.

Other areas of research provide a model for conceptualizing a possible individual difference characteristic of capacity for sustainable positive affect leading to more experience of positive affect, which in turn leads to beneficial outcomes. The relationship between conscientiousness and key life outcomes (Conti & Heckman, 2014) provides an example of another individual difference characteristic creating a foundation for the development of beneficial outcomes.

If individuals vary with regard to the extent to which they show behaviors and thoughts that help sustain positive affect, it may be possible to assess these actions as an individual difference characteristic. The present project draws on the results of prior correlational and intervention research, as well as the theoretical perspectives reviewed above, to explore whether (a) actions leading to sustained positive affect comprise an individual difference characteristic and (b) this characteristic can be validly assessed.

1.2. Overview of operationalization of facility for sustained positive affect and analyses

We drew on theory and research relating to positive affect to create a pool of items that might describe actions that contribute to sustaining positive affect. We collected information from community samples, comprising a total of 863 Australian adults to further operationalize and then began to validate the characteristic of facility for sustaining positive affect. Participants in each sample responded to these items assessing the tendency to show actions that may contribute to sustained positive affect. Because including all validation measures for all the participants would have resulted in a study that would have fatigued respondents and led them to discontinue, different measures were included for the different samples. We first describe the operationalization of the proposed individual difference characteristic of facility for sustained positive affect through the self-congruent and new activities (SANA) scale. Next, we present exploratory and confirmatory factor analyses which provide information on the factor structure of behavioral and cognitive activities that may comprise actions facilitating sustainable positive affect. The factor analyses are based on the responses of a total of 787 participants, 185 not included in any other studies and the participants from four of the samples which form the basis of subsequently described studies were not included (samples also contributing to Studies 2, 3, 4, and 5). Studies 2–5 allowed us to examine the validity of the characteristic and explored its place in the structure of human functioning.

2. Study 1: nature and measurement of actions facilitating positive affect

If facility for sustaining positive affect is an individual difference characteristic, then identifying initial connected behaviors and thoughts that comprise the characteristic is a step towards operationalizing this individual difference characteristic. Several theories as well as empirical findings suggest types of thoughts and behaviors that may sustain positive affect.

2.1. Item pool

We created an initial pool of 27 items representing various possible components of behavioral and cognitive actions that may lead to sustainable positive affect. Providing the foundation for the items were (1) the results of intervention studies, such as ones that have found that activities that are congruent with personal goals, abilities, and interests, and activities that can be varied may be especially likely to lead to long-term positive affect (Lyubomirsky, Sheldon et al., 2005) and (2) theoretical approaches to understanding the development and maintenance of positive affect, such as positive appraisal of events (Folkman & Moskowitz, 2000), actions related to intrinsic motivation as described by Deci and Ryan (2008), and actions relating to the broaden-and-build process (Fredrickson, 2001). We attempted to phrase all items so that they would be focused on behavioral and cognitive patterns. We expected that responses to the items would be intercorrelated and that responses might separate to some extent into sub-factors. Appendix A shows the item pool and the basis for each item.

2.2. Factor structure

A community sample of 787 participants, from various regions of Australia, obtained through electronic announcements on community websites, Facebook, and snowball recruitment rated each of the 27 items on a five-point scale on which a "1" denoted strong disagreement and a "5" denoted strong agreement. Subsets of participants also completed other measures, described in a later section, of constructs logically related to actions resulting in sustainable positive affect. See below for age and gender information describing the participants.

2.2.1. Exploratory factor analysis of item pool

We randomly selected half of the participants for the exploratory factor analysis (EFA), a sample of 379 individuals, including 260 women, with a mean age for the sample of 41.59, SD = 11.04 (other demographic information is not available). The EFA, done with SPSS 19, used maximum likelihood as the extraction method to identify interpretable factors underlying sustainable positive affect as represented by the pool of 27 items.

The Kaiser–Meyer–Olkin measure of sampling adequacy was .85, and Bartlett's test of sphericity was significant at $p < .0001$, both results suggesting the sample was appropriate for EFA. The factor analysis produced eight eigenvalues of at least 1.0. These were 6.58, 1.95, 1.61, 1.41, 1.29, 1.22, 1.15, and 1.06. The approach of selecting the number of factors with eigenvalues of over 1 tends to suggest too many factors (Tabachnick & Fidell, 2007), and several of the eight factors had few high loading items, making identification of the nature of the factor difficult. According to Stevens (2002), a reasonable practice is to use a scree plot to select the number of factors, provided the sample size is greater than 200, as it was in the present sample. The scree plot suggested retaining two factors. A parallel analysis indicated eight factors. We tested two to seven factors and found that only the two-factor solution led to factors that had a number of high loading items and were interpretable.

An equamax rotation specifying two factors was used for the EFA. We hoped that this would result in factors different enough to lead to subscales that have differential validity and value. To allow the creation of a reasonably short scale with high loading items and to make factors as different as reasonably possible, we set the standard for a meaningful loading for an item at .45 or above, with the item not loading on the other factor at .30 or above.

Table 1 shows the loadings of items for the two factors. Labels for the factors are Factor 1 "Engaging in Self-Congruent Activities" and Factor 2 "Engaging in New Activities." Factor 1 seems to measure aspects of applying self-determination so as to engage in activities one values and that are congruent with one's sense of self. Factor 2 appears to measure engaging in new and varied activities. Each factor is consistent with a different theoretical view of actions that contribute to positive affect. For this two-factor solution, the amount of variance explained by each factor was 13.46 and 12.93, respectively.

Table 1. Factor loadings on items reflecting facilitation of sustainable positive affect

Items	Factor 1	Factor 2
Many of my activities have provided me with a sense of fulfillment year after year.	**.60**	.08
I do things that are important to me.	**.53**	.29
I think about how my activities bring me closer to my goals.	**.51**	.19
I think about how pointless it is to try to reach my goals.	**−.51**	−.19
Many of my activities draw on my talents.	**.50**	.27
Most of what I do is determined by me rather than by other people.	**.47**	.20
I try to vary how I do things to keep activities interesting.	.08	**.68**
To keep life interesting I make changes in my daily activities.	.06	**.64**
By being open to what is happening around me I keep life interesting.	.21	**.56**
I like to explore.	.23	**.51**
I try out new activities.	.21	**.49**
I seek out activities that give me a sense of fulfillment.	.46	.47*
I consider my strengths when deciding how I allocate my time.	.40	.28
Most of my activities are related to my goals.	.41	−.04
Most of my activities are consistent with my values.	.40	.27
I often find myself doing things in which I have little interest.	−.40	−.05
Many of my activities draw on my skills.	.39	.27
I seek out activities that make me happy.	.38	.30
I see new possibilities in the world around me.	.37	.43
I make the time to seek out activities that make me happy.	.36	.38
Many activities I enjoy at first bore me after a while.	−.34	.07
Most of what I do is determined by the situations in which I find myself rather than by me.	−.36	−.04
I make an effort to see the positive aspects of events.	.31	.44
Many of my activities focus on deepening my relationships with others.	.19	.28
I seek out individuals with whom I feel happy.	.17	.18
By being non-judgmental about what's happening around me I keep life interesting.	.13	.42
Once I find an activity I like, I stick to it without making changes.	.11	−.34

Note: Bold loadings indicate the factor and corresponding subscale to which an item was assigned.
*Because this item had high loadings on both factors, it was not used for either subscale.

A subscale consisting of items that loaded at over .45 on one factor but that did not load at over .30 on the other factor represented each of the two factors. The items comprising the subscales representing the two factors as shown in Table 1 were as follows: self-congruent activities (consisting of six items) and new activities (consisting of five items). The subscales were significantly correlated, $r(378) = .47$, $p = .001$, suggesting commonalities in the constructs assessed by the subscales. On the basis of these results, we computed a total scale score for the SANA scale, which comprised of the items from the two subscales. Table 2 shows the final scale. The total scale score consists of the average of the 11 items and the subscales consist of average of the items comprising the subscale.

2.2.2 Mean scores and Cronbach's alpha for the total scale and the subscales

Table 3 shows the mean scores for the scale and its subscales. For the EFA sample, Cronbach's alpha for the total scale consisting of 11 items was .80. Subscale Cronbach's alphas were .72 for self-congruent activities and .78 for new activities.

Table 2. SANA scale: please rate how much you agree with each of the following items	Strongly Disagree	Disagree	Neither Agree nor Disagree	Agree	Strongly Agree
1. I like to explore.	1	2	3	4	5
2. I do things that are important to me.	1	2	3	4	5
3. I try to vary how I do things to keep activities interesting.	1	2	3	4	5
4. I think about how pointless it is to try to reach my goals.	1	2	3	4	5
5. To keep life interesting I make changes in my daily activities.	1	2	3	4	5
6. Many of my activities draw on my talents.	1	2	3	4	5
7. I try out new activities.	1	2	3	4	5
8. Many of my activities have provided me with a sense of fulfillment year after year.	1	2	3	4	5
9. I think about how my activities bring me closer to my goals.	1	2	3	4	5
10. Most of what I do is determined by me rather than by other people.	1	2	3	4	5
11. By being open to what is happening around me I keep life interesting.	1	2	3	4	5

Scoring: Total scale: all item ratings summed with item 4 reverse coded, then divided by 11; Engaging in self-congruent activities subscale: items 2, 4 (reverse coded), 6, 8, 9, 10 summed, then divided by 6; Engaging in new activities subscale: items 1, 3, 5, 7, 11 summed, then divided by 5.

2.2.3. Age and gender

For this sample, there was no significant relationship between age and scale scores. The Pearson's *r* correlations with age were as follows: total SANA scale score, .04; engaging in self-congruent activities subscale, .02; and engaging in new activities subscale, .04. There were no significant differences between women and men as assessed by independent groups' *t*-tests. The non-significant *t* values were as follows: total SANA scale score, $t(378) = .96$; engaging in self-congruent activities subscale, $t(378) = .53$; and engaging in new activities subscale, $t(378) = 1.37$. Table 3 shows women's and men's mean scores and standard deviations.

Table 3. Means for facility for sustainable positive affect and subscales for each study

	Study	Measures			
	N (Number of women)	Age	Facility for sustainable positive affect	Self-congruent activities	New activities
			M (*SD*)	*M* (*SD*)	*M* (*SD*)
1 E*	379 (260)	41.59	3.75 (.49)	3.76 (.55)	3.70 (.65)
	Women	40.79	3.76 (.46)	3.79 (.85)	3.72 (.59)
	Men	42.37	3.73 (.47)	3.77 (.56)	3.10 (.65)
1 C*	408 (269)	41.10	3.78 (.46)	3.80 (.53)	3.76 (.57)
	Women	40.79	3.79 (.45)	3.81 (.53)	3.77 (.56)
	Men	44.38	3.77 (.46)	3.79 (.53)	3.76 (.57)
2	178 (129)	38.51	3.74 (.46)	3.78 (.55)	3.69 (.57)
3	162 (103)	42.99	3.82 (.45)	3.83 (.54)	3.80 (.57)
4	124 (94)	40.11	3.74 (.46)	3.78 (.56)	3.74 (.58)
5	138 (94)	45.78	3.78 (.41)	3.77 (.45)	3.73 (.55)

*E = exploratory factor analysis group; C = CFA group.

2.3. Confirmatory factor analysis

The confirmatory factor analysis (CFA) was based on the item responses of 408 (269 women; mean age of 41.10, SD = 11.89; other demographic information is not available) randomly selected participants whose responses did not contribute to the EFA. The purpose of the CFA was to evaluate with another sample the fit of the factor structure identified in the EFA. The CFA examined the model of observed items contributing to self-congruent and engaging in new activities as latent, correlated variables.

For various reasons, some experts recommend using parcel scores rather than individual items for CFA (Rae, 2008). These reasons include that parcels tend to be more normally distributed than individual items, they tend to have greater reliability, they are associated with better model fit, and they provide a lower ratio of indicator to sample size (Schmitt, Golubovich, & Leong, 2010). Other experts argue that researchers can lose interpretative value by using parcels, which could possibly mask item effects (Meade & Kroustalis, 2006). We conducted confirmatory factor analyses using parcels and not using parcels. First, following the suggestion of Schmitt et al. (2010), we randomly created parcels of two or three items for each subscale (three items and three items for self-congruent, and three items and two items for engaging in new activities). Summing the scores on the items in each parcel led to parcel scores. The model fit indices for the CFA using parcels were as follows: $\chi^2/df = 0.30$, $p = .29$, CFI = 1.00, TLI = 1.02, and RMSEA = .00 (.00, .12). Good fit is indicated by CFI and TLI values of .95 or higher, and a RMSEA of .05 or less; and acceptable fit is indicated by CFI and TLI values of .90 or higher and a RMSEA of .08 or less (McDonald & Ho, 2002). Thus, the parcel-based CFA showed a good fit for the two-factor model of sustainable positive affect. We also compared the two-factor model with a single-factor model, using the same parcels. The χ^2 difference was 59.57, significant at $p < .001$, indicating that the two-factor model was a significantly better fit to the data. Following the suggestions of Meade and Kroustalis (2006), we also conducted a CFA using items rather than parcels. The model fit indices were as follows: $\chi^2/df = 2.76$, $p = .01$, CFI = .91, TLI = .86, and RMSEA = .06 (.052, .08). Thus, the item-based CFA showed a marginally acceptable fit.

2.3.1. Mean scores, Cronbach's alpha for the total scale and the subscales, and correlation of subscales

Table 3 shows the mean scores for the scale and its subscales. For the CFA sample, Cronbach's alpha for the total scale consisting of 11 items was .80. Subscale Cronbach's alphas were .70 for self-congruent activities and .76 for new activities.

2.3.2. Age and gender differences

For this sample, there was also no significant relationship between age and scale scores. The Pearson's *r* correlations with age were as follows: total SANA scale score, −.01; engaging in self-congruent activities subscale, −.04; engaging in new activities subscale, .04. There were also no significant differences between women and men as assessed by independent groups *t*-tests. The non-significant *t* values were as follows: total SANA scale score, $t(407) = .27$; engaging in self-congruent activities subscale, $t(407) = .77$; engaging in new activities subscale, $t(407) = .97$. Table 3 shows women and men's mean scores and standard deviations.

3. Validation and exploration of the place of facility for sustainable positive affect in human functioning

3.1. Study 2: The relationship between of facility for sustainable positive affect, mood, and symptoms related to mental health

Individuals with a greater facility for sustainable positive affect should experience more positive affect, in general. As more positive affect has previously been found to be moderately associated with less negative affect (Watson et al., 1988), one might expect individuals with a greater facility for sustainable positive affect to score lower on negative affect. Low positive affect is related to symptoms of poorer mental health, including depression and anxiety (Clark & Watson, 1991) and more severe stress reactions (Folkman & Moskowitz, 2000). Thus, one might expect that individuals with a greater facility for sustainable positive affect would experience fewer symptoms of depression and anxiety and less severe stress reactions. The value of examining sustainable positive affect in relation to low positive affect and mental health is that it offers the possibility of insight into an alternative upward spiral that leads from sustainable positive affect, to more positive affect, to better mental health.

A community sample, recruited through electronic announcements and snowball recruitment, of 178 participants from different regions of Australia (129 women and 49 men, mean age = 38.51, SD = 11.20) completed the SANA measure, measures of positive and negative affect, and measures of symptoms of depression, anxiety, and stress online.

3.1.1. Measures

3.1.1.1. Facility for sustainable positive affect. Facility for sustainable positive affect was assessed by the 11-item SANA scale, the development of which is described in a previous section of this article. In the present sample, Cronbach's alpha for the total scale was .79. Subscale Cronbach's alphas were .71 for self-congruent activities and .74 for new activities.

3.1.1.2. Positive and negative affect. The positive and negative affect scales (PANAS; Watson et al., 1988) assessed positive and negative affects. The PANAS consists of emotion descriptors (such as "enthusiastic" for the positive affect scale and "guilty" for the negative affect scale). The PANAS has different instructions for different time periods, ranging from how the respondent feels at the moment (state affect) to how the respondent generally feels (trait affect). The general (trait) instructions were used. Internal consistency for the scales using the trait instructions has ranged from .85 to .88, eight-week test–retest reliability ranged from .68 to .71, and the scales have shown evidence of construct validity, including expected associations with other measures of mood (Watson et al., 1988). In the present sample, Cronbach's alpha for the positive affect scale was .84, and Alpha for the negative affect scale was .91.

3.1.1.3. Symptoms of depression, anxiety, and stress. The short-form Depression Anxiety and Stress Scale (DASS-21) assesses symptoms of depression, anxiety, and stress as separate dimensions (Henry & Crawford, 2005). Internal consistency of the scales as assessed by Cronbach's alpha has been reported at .94 for depression, .87 for anxiety, and .91 for stress, and the scales have evidence of construct validity (Antony, Bieling, Cox, Enns & Swinson, 1998; Henry & Crawford, 2005). In the present sample, Cronbach's alpha for the depression dimension was .86, alpha for the anxiety dimension was .76, and alpha for stress was .79.

3.1.2. Results

3.1.2.1. Descriptive statistics. Table 3 shows the mean scores for the SANA scale and its subscales. Mean scores for the other main variables were as follows: positive affect (Mean = 30.88, SD = 5.35), negative affect (Mean = 16.79, SD = 5.52), depression (Mean = 11.66, SD = 5.08), anxiety (Mean = 10.93, SD = 4.32), and stress (Mean = 15.33, SD = 5.09).

3.1.2.2. Validity analyses. Table 4 shows the intercorrelations of the main variables. As one would expect of the construct, higher scores on facility for sustainable positive affect were significantly associated with more positive affect and less negative affect. Higher scores on facility for sustainable positive affect were also associated with significantly fewer symptoms of depression and anxiety, but not with symptoms of stress. To assess construct validity through an expected pattern of relationships, we used a test recommended by Field (2013, p. 287) to test whether the correlation (.60) between facility for sustainable positive affect and positive affect was higher than the correlation (−.33) between facility for sustainable positive affect and negative affect. The difference was statistically significant, t (175) = 11.18, $p < .001$, showing the expected pattern of relationships. The correlations of the two subscales with the criterion measures were not significantly different from each other.

Table 4. Correlations between facility for sustainable positive affect, positive and negative affect, and symptoms of depression, anxiety, and stress (Study 2, *N* = 178)

Measures	Total facility for sustainable positive affect	Engaging in self-congruent activities	Engaging in new activities	Positive affect	Negative affect	Depression	Anxiety	Stress
Positive affect	.60**	.53**	.49**	–				
Negative affect	−.33**	−.32**	−.25**	−.07	–			
Depression	−.38**	−.36**	−.28**	−.37**	.50**	–		
Anxiety	−.25*	−.23**	−.19*	−.20*	.51**	.56**	–	
Stress	.02	.05	.05	−.10	.47**	.50**	.58**	–

*p = .05.

**p = .01.

Note: There were no significant differences between subscale (self-congruent activities and engaging in new activities) correlations and the criterion measures.

3.2. Study 3: The relationship between facility for sustainable positive affect and subjective well-being and the interaction between facility for sustainable positive affect and maintenance of positive affect over time

Individuals with a greater facility for sustainable positive affect should experience more subjective well-being. Greater life satisfaction as well as high positive affect and low negative affect are often used as indices of subjective well-being (Lyubomirsky, King et al., 2005). The present analysis examined the association between facility for sustained positive affect and life satisfaction and set out to replicate the relationships found in the previous sample regarding the association between greater facility for sustainable positive affect and positive and negative affect. This part of the project also examined the association between facility for sustainable positive affect and satisfaction in the life domains of relationships and work. The value of examining sustainable positive affect in relation to positive affect and satisfaction is that it offers the possibility of insight into what might prompt an upward spiral that leads from sustainable positive affect, to more positive affect, to satisfaction.

Finally, one would expect that individuals with a greater facility for sustainable positive affect would be more likely to maintain high positive affect over time. The premise underlying this prediction is that individuals with higher levels of sustainable positive affect as well as being more likely to experience positive affect would experience less of the hedonic treadmill effect (Diener et al., 2006) and be more likely to experience positive affect over time. Thus, this part of the project examined the interaction between facility for sustainable positive affect and maintenance of positive affect over a one-month period.

A community sample, recruited through electronic announcements and snowball recruitment, of 162 Australian residents (103 women and 59 men, mean age = 42.99, SD = 10.37) completed the SANA measure, measures of positive and negative affect, and measures of life satisfaction, relationship satisfaction, and work satisfaction online. Participants only completed the measure of relationship satisfaction if they were currently in a partner relationship (N = 119) and the measure of work satisfaction if they were currently participating in paid or volunteer work (N = 137). A subsample of 59 of the participants completed the SANA measure and the positive affect measure twice, with a one-month interval between completions.

3.2.1. Measures

3.2.1.1. Facility for sustainable positive affect. Facility for sustainable positive affect was assessed by the SANA scale, the development of which is described in a previous section of this article. In this sample, Cronbach's alpha for the total scale was .79. Subscale Cronbach's alphas were .68 for self-congruent activities and .78 for new activities.

3.2.1.2. Positive and negative affect. The PANAS (Watson et al.,1988) assessed positive and negative affects. This scale is described in the previous section. In the present sample, Cronbach's alpha for the positive affect scale was .84, and Alpha for the negative affect scale was .89.

3.2.1.3. Satisfaction with life. The satisfaction with life scale (Diener, Emmons, Larsen, & Griffin, 1985) is a measure of global life satisfaction. The internal consistency of the measure ranges from .82 to .87, and the scale shows evidence of construct validity through associations with theoretically related constructs, including other aspects of subjective well-being (Pavot & Diener, 1993). In the present sample, Cronbach's alpha was .90.

3.2.1.4. Relationship satisfaction. The relationship assessment scale (Hendrick, 1988) is a global measure of relationship satisfaction. The measure has good internal consistency ranging from .86 to .91 and evidence of validity through association with other indicators of relationship satisfaction (Hendrick, 1988; Vaughn & Matyastik-Baier, 1999). In the present sample, Cronbach's alpha was .95.

3.2.1.5. Work satisfaction. The abridged job in general scale (Russell et al., 2004) is a global measure of satisfaction with work. The scale has internal consistency of .85 and evidence of validity through correlations with related constructs in previous research (Russell et al., 2004). In the present sample, Cronbach's alpha was .89.

3.2.2. Results

3.2.2.1. Descriptive statistics. Table 3 shows the mean scores for the SANA scale and its subscales. Scores for the other main variables were as follows: positive affect (Mean = 31.056, SD = 5.08), negative affect (Mean = 15.32, SD = 5.00), general life satisfaction (Mean = 24.80, SD = 6.53), relationship satisfaction (Mean = 31.44, SD = 7.87), and work satisfaction (Mean = 19.88, SD = 3.72).

3.2.2.2. Test–retest reliability. Fifty-nine participants completed the SANA scale again after a one-month interval to provide information regarding the stability of facility for sustained positive affect as assessed by the scale. Test–retest reliability as assessed by Pearson's *r* was as follows: total facility for sustainable positive affect, .72; engaging in self-congruent activities subscale, .65; and engaging in new activities subscale, .69.

3.2.2.3. Validity analyses: Higher scores on facility for sustainable positive affect were significantly associated with more positive affect and less negative affect. As one would expect of the construct, higher scores on facility for sustainable positive affect were associated with significantly more global life satisfaction, greater relationship satisfaction, and greater work satisfaction (see Table 5).

To assess an expected divergent pattern of relationships, we used a test recommended by Field (2013) to test whether the correlation between facility for sustainable positive affect and positive affect was higher than the correlation between facility for sustainable positive affect and negative affect. The difference was statistically significant, t (159) = 11.27, $p < .001$, showing divergent validity.

The level of correlations with satisfaction measures was mostly higher for the self-congruent activities subscale than for the new activities subscale. Statistical comparisons using the test recommended by Field (2013) showed that the differences were significantly different for negative affect, life satisfaction, and work satisfaction, but not for positive affect or relationship satisfaction.

In a test of predictive validity, a regression-based moderation analysis examined whether high positive affect experienced by individuals with greater facility for sustainable positive affect was more likely to be maintained over a one-month period. After controlling for positive affect at pre -test, sustainable positive affect predicted positive affect one month later ($b = .41$, $SE_b = .14$, $\beta = .43$, $p = .04$) To further investigate this effect, after conversion to centered scores, an interaction term was

Table 5. Correlations between facility for sustainable positive affect and well-being measures (Study 3, *N* = 162)

Measures	Total facility for sustainable positive affect	Engaging in self-congruent activities	Engaging in new activities	Positive affect	Negative affect	Global life satisfaction	Relationship satisfaction	Work satisfaction
Positive affect	.63**	.55**	.49**	–				
Negative affect	−.34**	−.37**+	−.14	−.10	–			
Global life satisfaction	.51**	.57**++	.24**	.46**	−.60**	–		
Relationship satisfaction	.29**	.26**	.20*	.31**	−.36**	.61**	–	
Work satisfaction	.44**	.57**++	.18*	.47**	−.33**	.52**	.20*	–

*$p = .05$.

**$p = .01$.

+Self-congruent activities correlation higher than new activities correlation at $p = .05$.

++Self-congruent activities correlation higher than new activities correlation at $p = .01$.

created for the product of sustainable positive affect and positive affect at pre-test. This interaction predicted significant variance in positive affect one month later in addition to individual contributions of sustainable positive affect and positive affect as individual constructs ($b = 1.11$, $SE_b = .49$, $\beta = .21$, $p = .03$), indicating that those who at the start of the month scored high in facility for sustainable positive affect were more likely to maintain high positive affect at follow-up. A comparison of participants sorted into four groups (through a median split of positive affect scores both for pre- and post-test) showed a significant difference between groups, $F(3,56) = 17.30$, $p = .001$. Mean facility for sustaining positive affect scores and standard deviations were as follows for the four groups: low positive affect both pre- and post-test, 3.54 (.42); high positive affect pre- and post-test, 4.06 (.39); high positive affect at pre- and low positive affect at post-test, 3.74 (.27); and low positive affect at pre- and high positive affect at post-test, 4.02 (.36).

3.3. Study 4: The relationship between facility for sustainable positive affect and conceptually related characteristics

Though proposed to be a unique individual difference construct, facility for sustainable positive affect has components that may overlap with previously studied characteristics. These include mindfulness, agentic qualities of personal expansion and growth, and emotional intelligence. For example, the acceptance and non-judgmental evaluation of the self and world that are aspects of mindfulness (Brown & Ryan, 2003) may relate to individuals' ability to achieve adaptive perceptions that allow them to sustain positive affect. Tendencies toward growth and expansion may create variety and satisfaction that sustain positive affect. The ability to understand, utilize, and manage emotions in the self and others that are a hallmark of emotional intelligence (Neubauer & Freudenthaler, 2005; Mayer, Salovey, & Caruso, 2008) may be related to individuals' ability to sustain positive emotions. This part of the project examined the association between facility for sustainable positive affect and these characteristics to test the hypothesis that they would be related to but not redundant with facility for sustainable positive affect.

A community sample, recruited through electronic announcements and snowball recruitment, of 124 Australian residents (94 women and 30 men, with two individuals not reporting gender, mean age = 40.11, SD = 10.19) completed the SANA scale as well as measures of mindfulness, personal expansion, growth, and emotional intelligence online.

3.3.1. Measures

3.3.1.1. Facility for sustainable positive affect. Facility for sustainable positive affect was assessed by the SANA scale, the development of which is described in a previous section of this article. In this sample, Cronbach's alpha for the total scale was .85. Subscale Cronbach's alphas were .81 for self-congruent activities and .76 for new activities.

3.3.1.2. Mindfulness. The characteristic of mindfulness was assessed with the short form of the Freiburg mindfulness inventory (Kohls, Sauer, & Walach, 2009; Walach, Buchheld, Buttenmuller, Kleinknecht, & Schmidt, 2006). The scale assesses the extent to which individuals focus on the present in a non-evaluative manner. The measure has evidence of internal consistency, with a Cronbach's alpha of .86, and evidence of validity such as associations with years of practice of meditation (Kohls et al., 2009). In the present sample, Cronbach's alpha was .81.

3.3.1.3. Personal growth. The personal growth initiative scale (Robitschek, 1999) assesses active intentional personal growth. This is conceptualized as active and intentional involvement in changing and developing. Internal consistency ranges from .78 to .90 and the measure has evidence of validity (Robitschek, 1999). In the present sample, Cronbach's alpha was .88.

3.3.1.4. Personal expansion. The personal expansion questionnaire (Gordon & Luo, 2011) assesses individuals' tendency to grow through augmentation in both familiar and new domains of life. The measure has internal consistency of between .75 and .78 and has evidence of validity (Gordon & Luo, 2011). In the present sample, Cronbach's alpha was .66.

3.3.1.5. Emotional intelligence. The assessing emotions scale (Schutte et al., 1998; Schutte, Malouff, & Bhullar, 2009) measures trait emotional intelligence. The scale assesses how well respondents typically identify, understand, regulate, and harness emotions in themselves and others. In previous research, the scale has shown internal consistency of between .87 and .90, and evidence of construct validity through association with theoretically related constructs (Schutte et al., 1998; Schutte et al., 2009). In the present sample, Cronbach's alpha is .86.

3.3.2. Results

3.3.2.1. Descriptive statistics. Table 3 shows the mean scores for the scale and its subscales. Scores for the other main variables were as follows: mindfulness (Mean = 36.81, SD = 5.78), emotional intelligence (Mean = 126.94, SD = 10.84), personal growth (Mean = 38.73, SD = 8.19), and personal expansion (Mean = 39.60, SD = 4.31).

3.3.2.2. Validity analyses. Tests of convergent construct validity found that higher scores on facility for sustainable positive affect were significantly associated with greater mindfulness, more personal growth, more personal expansion, and higher emotional intelligence (see Table 6). Self-congruent activities' subscale scores were more highly related than new activities to growth and emotional intelligence.

3.4. Study 5: The relationship between facility for sustainable positive affect and the Big Five personality characteristics

The five personality dimensions of extraversion, agreeableness, conscientiousness, neuroticism, and openness underpin much human functioning (John & Srivastava, 1999; McCrae & Costa, 1997). To be optimally useful, a proposed new individual difference characteristic such as facility for sustainable positive affect will not substantially duplicate these five personality dimensions. Facility for sustainable positive affect might be related to extraversion, as extraversion is associated with experience of positive affect (McCrae & Costa, 1997). One might expect facility for sustainable positive affect also to be somewhat related to the Big Five characteristic of openness as this

Table 6. Correlations between facility for sustainable positive affect, growth, expansion, and emotional intelligence (Study 4, *N* = 124)

Measures	Total facility for sustainable positive affect	Engaging in self-congruent activities subscale	Engaging in new activities subscale	Mindfulness	Growth	Expansion	Emotional intelligence
Mindfulness	.49**	.47**	.38**	–			
Growth	.66**	.68**	.42**	.48**	–		
Expansion	.61**	.49**	.56**	.46**	.43**	–	
Emotional intelligence	.51**	.56**	.34**	.53**	.47**	.41**	–

*p = .05.
**p = .01.

characteristic is defined by willingness to engage with new ideas and experiences, and such engagement might facilitate sustained positive affect. Facility for sustainable positive affect might also be associated with lower levels of neuroticism as positive affect is to some extent inconsistent with neuroticism. This part of the project examined the relationship between facility for sustainable positive affect and each of the Big Five dimensions, and whether facility for sustained positive affect has variance not explained by the Big Five dimensions.

A community sample, recruited through electronic announcements and snowball recruitment of 138 Australian residents (94 women and 44 men; mean age = 45.78, SD = 10.32), completed the SANA scale as well as a measure of the Big Five personality dimensions online.

3.4.1. Measures

3.4.1.1. Facility for sustainable positive affect. Facility for sustainable positive affect was assessed by the 11-item SANA scale, the development of which is described in a previous section of this article. In this sample, Cronbach's alpha for the total scale was .72. Subscale Cronbach's alphas were .58 for self-congruent activities and .73 for new activities.

3.4.1.2. Big Five personality dimensions. The Big Five Inventory (John & Srivastava, 1999) assesses each of the Big Five personality dimensions. The average internal consistency for each of the five scales comprising the Big Five Inventory tends to be above .80, and validity evidence includes strong associations of scale scores with scales from other Big Five measures assessing the same personality dimensions and the association of scale scores with peer ratings of equivalent personality dimensions (John & Srivastava, 1999). In the present sample, Cronbach's alpha for each of the five dimensions was as follows: extraversion (.87), agreeableness (.78), conscientiousness (.79), neuroticism (.81), and openness (.77).

3.4.2. Results

3.4.2.1. Descriptive statistics. Table 3 shows the mean scores for the SANA scale and its subscales. Mean scores for the other main variables were: openness (Mean = 35.04, SD = 5.40), extraversion (Mean = 27.04, SD = 5.70), agreeableness (Mean = 34.36, SD = 4.21), conscientiousness (Mean = 33.62, SD = 4.71), and neuroticism (Mean = 21.56, SD = 4.94).

3.4.2.2. Validity analyses. Greater facility for sustainable positive affect was significantly associated with more openness, extraversion, agreeableness and conscientiousness, and with less neuroticism (see Table 7). The largest overlap in variance was between total facility for sustainable positive affect

Table 7. Correlations between facility for sustainable positive affect and the Big Five dimensions (Study 5, $N = 138$)

Measures	Total facility for sustainable positive affect	Engaging in self-congruent activities subscale	Engaging in new activities subscale	Openness	Extraversion	Agreeable-ness	Conscien-tiousness	Neuroticism
Openness	.44**	.25**	.48**	–				
Extraversion	.28**	.16	.31**	.14	–			
Agreeable-ness	.21*	.23*	.12	−.02	.08	–		
Conscien-tiousness	.24*	.37**	.02	−.02	.08	.23*	–	
Neuroticism	−.36**	−.39**	−.21*	−.10	−.25**	−.38**	−.27**	–

*$p = .05$.
**$p = .01$.

and openness, with 19% shared variance, and low neuroticism, with shared 13% shared variance. A multiple regression analysis examined how much common variance total facility for sustainable positive affect shared with all Big Five characteristics entered in one block as a predictor. The R of .59, with an R^2 of .35, indicated facility for sustainable affect shares only moderate variance with all Big Five dimensions combined.

The two subscales showed different patterns of correlations overall, and the difference in their respective correlations with conscientiousness and openness was statistically significant. Self-congruent activities correlated significantly more highly than new activities with conscientiousness, while new activities correlated significantly more highly with openness.

4. Discussion

The present research investigated whether there is an individual difference characteristic related to maintaining positive affect. The aims of the project were to begin to operationalize this characteristic and examine the relationship of the characteristic with functioning in realms such as mental health and well-being outcomes as well as other characteristics one might expect to be connected to the construct.

Findings from intervention studies designed to prolong the experience of positive affect (e.g. Lyubomirsky, Sheldon et al., 2005), theories relating to positive affect (Deci & Ryan, 2008; Fredrickson & Losada, 2005), and correlational studies of variables associated with positive affect (Livingstone & Srivastava, 2012) provided the basis for a pool of items representing behaviors and cognitions that may be related to maintaining high positive affect. These behaviors and cognitions represent paths potentially leading to positive affect rather than being themselves markers of positive affect.

Factor analyses of individuals' ratings of these items indicated that two related dimensions, labeled engaging in self-congruent activities and engaging in new activities, underlie the items. These two dimensions encompass many of the behaviors and cognitions that have been suggested by research (Livingstone & Srivastava, 2012; Lyubomirsky, Sheldon et al., 2005; Seligman et al., 2005) and theory (Deci & Ryan, 2008; Fredrickson & Losada, 2005) relating to maintaining positive affect.

On the basis of the results of EFA, we created a measure (the SANA scale) which comprised of 11 high loading items. CFA provided support for use of both total scale scores and scores on two subscales, engaging in self-congruent activities and engaging in new activities. The internal consistency of the total measure ranged from .80 to .85. Internal consistency of the engaging in self-congruent activities subscale ranged from .70 to .83 and internal consistency of the engaging in new activities subscale ranged from .76 to .84. One month test–retest reliability showed stability, with values of .72 for the total scale, .65 for the engaging in self-congruent activities subscale, and .69 for the engaging in new activities subscale. However, the test–retest reliability result was based on a small sample, providing limited information regarding stability over time (see Watson, 2004) and thus provides only preliminary information regarding the temporal stability and trait features of the total scale and the subscales.

The individual difference characteristic of facility for sustained positive affect, as assessed by the SANA scale, showed relationships with other constructs that one would expect of such an individual difference characteristic. These included associations with the following theoretically related constructs: (1) more experienced positive affect (Studies 2 and 3), (2) greater mindfulness, (3) more personal growth, (4) more personal expansion, (5) higher emotional intelligence, (6) greater life satisfaction, (7) greater work satisfaction, (8) greater relationship satisfaction, (9) lower negative affect, (10) fewer symptoms of depression, and (11) fewer symptoms of anxiety. The construct assessed by the SANA scale may indeed promote positive affect and may also encourage a general approach to life related to various good outcomes in addition to positive affect. Experienced positive affect may be a path from facility for sustained positive affect to these outcomes, but there may also be other paths from this facility to beneficial outcomes.

Facility for sustained positive affect shared variances of 36 and 40% with experienced positive affect across two studies. If facility for sustained positive affect is indeed a facilitator of positive affect, one would expect such overlap in variance. The percent of shared variance indicates that facility for sustained positive affect is related to but not redundant with actual experience of positive affect. The possible relationship between the individual difference characteristic of facility for sustained positive affect and experienced positive affect may be similar in nature to the Big Five individual difference characteristics underlying emotional, cognitive, and behavioral patterns that combine to give rise to psychopathology.

Individuals high in facility for sustained positive affect showed greater maintenance of positive affect over a one-month period. This finding suggests that facility for sustained positive affect may indeed facilitate experiencing positive affect. The broaden-and-build theory holds that positive affect may build resources. Facility for sustained positive affect may be one such resource. From the vantage point of the broaden-and-build theory, one can propose a bidirectional and synergistic relationship between positive affect and facility for sustained positive affect.

Evidence for the possible unique role of the proposed individual difference characteristic included the findings that scores on facility for sustained positive affect were more highly correlated with positive affect than with negative affect and were not so highly correlated with Big Five scores as to be redundant to the Big Five. The shared variance between the SANA scores and the combined Big Five dimensions was .35. Further, the shared variance of scores on facility for sustained positive affect with positive affect (.36 and .40) was not so high as to suggest that the two concepts are redundant. Also, conceptually, there is differentiation between the constructs as the focus of the items comprising the SANA scale are on actions, while the measure of positive affect focuses on internal experience.

These findings provide some initial evidence that facility for sustainable positive affect is a unique individual difference characteristic. However, not all of the findings were as hypothesized. For instance, sustainable positive affect, as operationalized by the SANA scale, was not significantly related to lower perceived stress, which as measured by the DASS (Henry & Crawford, 2005), indicates high arousal and irritability.

Among the Big Five characteristics, openness had the strongest association with sustainable positive affect. One might have expected extraversion to have that position because it is commonly found to have high association with positive affect (McCrae & Costa, 1997). One possible implication of the finding is that openness might contribute substantially to positive affect if the openness is directed toward openness to new experiences and to possibilities within oneself. The association with openness may have been due, in part, to similarity of items assessing openness and facility for sustained affect. Future research might explore further the overlap or integration of facility for sustained affect with personality as a whole, such as, for example, through the lens of a personality circumplex (Hofstee, de Raad, & Goldberg, 1992).

The factor analyses suggested that facility for sustainable positive affect may be comprised of two components, reflected by two subscales. The engaging in self-congruent activities and engaging in new activities subscales overall showed similar patterns of relationships with other constructs, with the engaging in self-congruent activities subscale, in general, showing stronger relationships with construct validation variables. In several analyses, however, the subscales showed differing patterns of associations, suggesting that the two components of sustainable positive affect may have somewhat different nature and utility. For example, engaging in self-congruent activities was strongly associated with work satisfaction, while the engaging in new activities was not. It could be that goal and interest-congruent activity at work is more relevant for work satisfaction than having the opportunity for variety in work life. Engaging in new activities was more strongly correlated with personal expansion through involvement in familiar and new domains than engaging in self-congruent activities. This finding is consistent with a conceptual interpretation that suggests that engaging in new activities leads to broadening. In the framework of the Big Five model, the engaging in self-congruent activities was more strongly associated with high conscientiousness, while engaging in new activities was more strongly associated with high openness. If similar differences are found in future studies, they might indicate important differences in effects of different types of behaviors that tend to sustain positive affect.

Facility for sustained positive affect was not significantly associated with either age or gender. Hence, one can draw a preliminary conclusion that the basic nature of the construct is about the same regardless of age or gender.

4.1. Limitations

A limitation of the studies involves the use of Australian community samples. The findings might not generalize to much different cultures. Most of the studies involved participants completing multiple measures; the resulting correlations may have been inflated to some extent by response biases. However, the comparison of scores of meditators and non-meditators provided a different type of validity not as likely to be affected by response biases, though expectancy effects may have influenced responding. A related limitation is that the studies relied on self-report data, which do not always correlate with other sources of information. On a conceptual level of limitations, some of the items comprising the sustainable affect measure may intertwine ratings of actions with outcomes.

4.2. Future directions

Future research might explore further the nature of facility for sustainable affect and its measurement and address possible limitations of the present research. The factor structure of the characteristic and its measure might be examined in further factor analyses. Future research might explore the connection between the characteristic and possibly related tendencies, such as goal concordance, perceiving purpose in life, broad-minded coping, and sensation seeking. Analyses of the factor structure of facility for sustainable affect might be explored with different samples. Future studies might explore whether sustainable affect can be increased through interventions and whether such increases are associated with increases in characteristics found to be associated with facility for sustainable affect in the present research. Outcomes that might change as a result of such interventions include positive affect, symptoms of depression, life satisfaction, and work satisfaction. Such research might also investigate what intervention strategies are most effective in increasing facility for sustainable positive affect. Future research might also include more behavioral outcomes. For example, just as the Big Five personality dimensions are related to behaviors with social significance (Paunonen, 2003), so might facility for sustained positive affect be related to such behavioral outcomes. Other research might address aspects of measurement of sustainable positive affect, for example, by asking close ones to rate behaviors and expressed thoughts of individuals. Future studies might examine the individual difference characteristic of sustainable positive affect in other populations, including other nations and specific groups, such as individuals who have been diagnosed with a disorder or who belong to a certain occupation.

Facility for sustainable positive affect is conceptualized as an individual difference characteristic with some temporal stability, but might be changeable through interventions. An analogy can be found in research on cognitive reappraisal interventions resulting in a change in characteristic pessimistic explanatory style, which in turn leads to decreases in symptoms of depression (Seligman et al., 1988). The sub-components found in the present research to comprise facility for sustainable affect may provide leads regarding how to increase the characteristic of sustainable positive affect in research exploring such intervention effects. Additionally, this proposed individual difference characteristic might provide insight into who might fully engage with interventions and who might need support to engage with interventions.

In conclusion, the results of the project provided initial evidence that facility to maintain positive affect may be an emotion-related individual difference characteristic. Its place in the framework of personality and life outcomes remains to be further explored.

Funding
The authors received no direct funding for this research.

Competing interests
The authors declare no competing interest.

Author details
Nicola S. Schutte[1]
E-mail: nschutte@une.edu.au
John M. Malouff[1]
E-mail: jmalouff@une.edu.au
[1] Psychology, University of New England, Armidale, Australia.

References
Antony, M. M., Bieling, P. J., Cox, B. J., Enns, M. W., & Swinson, R. P. (1998). Psychometric properties of the 42-item and 21-item versions of the Depression Anxiety Stress Scales in clinical groups and a community sample. *Psychological Assessment, 10*, 176–181.

Baer, R. A., Smith, G. T., Hopkins, J., Krietemeyer, J., & Toney, L. (2006). Using self-report assessment methods to explore facets of mindfulness. *Assessment, 13*, 27–45.

Brown, K. W., & Ryan, R. M. (2003). The benefits of being present: Mindfulness and its role in psychological well-being. *Journal of Personality and Social Psychology, 84*, 822–848.

Clark, L. A., & Watson, D. (1991). Tripartite model of anxiety and depression: Psychometric evidence and taxonomic implications. *Journal of Abnormal Psychology, 100*, 316–336.

Conti, G., & Heckman, J. J. (2014). Understanding conscientiousness across the life course: An economic perspective. *Developmental Psychology, 50*, 1451–1459.

Deci, E. L., & Ryan, R. M. (2008). Self-determination theory: A macrotheory of human motivation, development, and health. *Canadian Psychology/Psychologie canadienne, 49*, 182–185.

Diener, E., & Chan, M. Y. (2011). Happy people live longer: Subjective well-being contributes to health and longevity. *Applied Psychology: Health and Well-Being, 3*, 1–43.

Diener, E., Emmons, R. A., Larsen, R. J., & Griffin, S. (1985). The satisfaction with life scale. *Journal of Personality Assessment, 49*, 71–75.

Diener, E., Lucas, R. E., & Scollon, C. N. (2006). Beyond the hedonic treadmill: Revising the adaptation theory of well-being. *American Psychologist, 61*, 305–314.

Diener, E., & Seligman, M. E. P. (2002). Very happy people. *Psychological Science, 13*, 81–84.

Field, A. (2013). *Discovering statistics using IBM SPSS statistics.* Thousand Oaks, CA: Sage.

Folkman, S., & Moskowitz, J. T. (2000). Positive affect and the other side of coping. *American Psychologist, 55*, 647–654.

Fredrickson, B. L. (2001). The role of positive emotions in positive psychology: The broaden-and-build theory of positive emotions. *American Psychologist, 56*, 218–226.

Fredrickson, B. L., Cohn, M. A., Coffey, K. A., Pek, J., & Finkel, S. M. (2008). Open hearts build lives: Positive emotions, induced through loving-kindness meditation, build consequential personal resources. *Journal of Personality and Social Psychology, 95*, 1045–1062.

Fredrickson, B. L., & Losada, M. F. (2005). Positive affect and the complex dynamics of human flourishing. *American Psychologist, 60*, 678–686.

Gordon, C. L., & Luo, S. (2011). The personal expansion questionnaire: Measuring one's tendency to expand through novelty and augmentation. *Personality and Individual Differences, 51*, 89–94.

Gross, J. J., & John, O. P. (2003). Individual differences in two emotion regulation processes: Implications for affect, relationships, and well-being. *Journal of Personality and Social Psychology, 85*, 348–362.

Hendrick, S. S. (1988). A generic measure of relationship satisfaction. *Journal of Marriage and the Family, 50*, 93–98.

Henry, J. D., & Crawford, J. R. (2005). The short-form version of the Depression Anxiety Stress Scales (DASS-21): Construct validity and normative data in a large non-clinical sample. *British Journal of Clinical Psychology, 44*, 227–239.

Hofstee, W. K. B., de Raad, B., & Goldberg, L. R. (1992). Integration of the big five and circumplex approaches to trait structure. *Journal of Personality and Social Psychology, 63*, 146–163.

John, O. J., & Srivastava, S. (1999). The big five trait taxonomy: History, measurement, and theoretical perspectives. In L. A. Pervin, & O. P. John (Eds.), *Handbook of ersonality: Theory and research* (pp. 102–138). New York, NY: Guilford.

Kohls, S., Sauer, S., & Walach, H. (2009). Facets of mindfulness: Results of an online study investigating the Freiburg Mindfulness Inventory, *Personality and Individual Differences, 46*, 224–230. and well-being. *Current Psychology, 28*, 21–31.

Livingstone, K. M., & Srivastava, S. (2012). Up-regulating positive emotions in everyday life: Strategies, individual differences, and associations with positive emotion and well-being. *Journal of Research in Personality, 46*, 504–516.

Lyubomirsky, S., King, L., & Diener, E. (2005). The benefits of frequent positive affect: Does happiness lead to success? *Psychological Bulletin, 131*, 803–855.

Lyubomirsky, S., Sheldon, K. M., & Schkade, D. (2005). Pursuing happiness: The architecture of sustainable change. *Review of General Psychology, 9*, 111–131.

Mayer, J. D., Salovey, P., & Caruso, D. R. (2008). Emotional intelligence: New ability or eclectic traits? *American Psychologist, 63*, 503–517.

McCrae, R. R., & Costa, P. T. (1997). Personality trait structure as a human universal. *American Psychologist, 52*, 509–516.

McDonald, R. P., & Ho, M. H. R. (2002). Principles and practice in reporting structural equation analyses. *Psychological Methods, 7*, 64–82.

Meade, A. W., & Kroustalis, C. M. (2006). Problems with item parceling for confirmatory factor analytic tests of measurement invariance. *Organizational Research Methods, 9*, 369–403.

Neubauer, A. C., & Freudenthaler, H. H. (2005). Models of emotional intelligence. In R. Schultz, & R. D. Roberts (Eds.), *Emotional intelligence: An international handbook* (pp. 31–50). Cambridge, MA: Hogrefe.

Paunonen, S. (2003). Big five factors of personality and replicated predictions of behavior. *Journal of Personality and Social Psychology, 84*, 411–424.

Pavot, W., & Diener, E. (1993). Review of the satisfaction with life scale. *Psychological Assessment, 5*, 164–172.

Rae, G. (2008). A note on using alpha and stratified alpha to estimate the reliability of a test composed of item parcels. *British Journal of Mathematical and Statistical Psychology, 61*, 515–525.

Robitschek, C. (1999). Further validation of the personal growth initiative scale. *Measurement and Evaluation in Counseling and Development, 31*, 197–210.

Russell, S. S., Spitzmuller, C., Lin, L. F., Stanton, J. M., Smith, P. C., & Ironson, G. H. (2004). Shorter can also be better: The abridged job in general scale. *Educational and Psychological Measurement, 64*, 878–893.

Schmitt, N., & Golubovich, J., & Leong, F. T. (2010). Impact of measurement invariance on construct correlations, mean differences, and relations with external correlates: An illustrative example using big five and RIASEC measures. *Assessment, 18*, 412–427.

Schroevers, M. J., & Brandsma, R. (2010). Is learning mindfulness associated with improved affect after mindfulness-based cognitive therapy? *British Journal of Psychology, 101*, 95–107.

Schutte, N. S., Malouff, J. M., & Bhullar, N. (2009). The Assessing Emotions Scale. In J. D. A. Parker, D. Saklofske, & C. Stough (Eds.), *The Assessment of Emotional Intelligence* (pp. 119–134). New York, NY: Springer.

Schutte, N. S., Malouff, J. M., Hall, L. E., Haggerty, D. J., Cooper, J. T., Golden, C. J., & Dornheim, L. (1998). Development and validation of a measure of emotional intelligence. *Personality and Individual Differences, 25*, 167–177.

Seligman, M. E., Castellon, C., Cacciola, J., Schulman, P., Luborsky, L., Ollove, M., & Downing, R. (1988). Explanatory style change during cognitive therapy for unipolar depression. *Journal of Abnormal Psychology, 97*, 13–18.

Seligman, M. E. P., Steen, T. A., Park, N., & Peterson, C. P. (2005). Positive psychology progress: Empirical validation of interventions. *American Psychologist, 60*, 410–421.

Steptoe, A., Dockray, S., & Wardle, J. (2009). Positive affect and psychobiological processes relevant to health. *Journal of Personality, 77*, 1747–1776.

Stevens, J. (2002). *Applied multivariate statistics for the social sciences* (4th ed.). Mawwah, NJ: Erlbaum.

Tabachnick, B. G., & Fidell, L. S. (2007). *Using multivariate statistics* (5th ed.). New York, NY: HarperCollins.

Vaughn, M. J., & Baier, M. E. (1999). Reliability and validity of the relationship assessment scale. *The American Journal of Family Therapy, 27*, 137–147.

Walach, H., Buchheld, N., Buttenmüller, V., Kleinknecht, N., & Schmidt, S. (2006). Measuring mindfulness—the Freiburg Mindfulness Inventory (FMI). *Personality and Individual Differences, 40*, 1543–1555.

Watson, D. (2004). Stability versus change, dependability versus error: Issues in the assessment of personality over time. *Journal of Research in Personality, 38*, 319–350.

Watson, D., Clark, L. A., & Tellegen, A. (1988). Development and validation of brief measures of positive and negative affect: The PANAS scales. *Journal of Personality and Social Psychology, 54*, 1063–1070.

Wood, A. M., & Tarrier, N. (2010). Positive clinical psychology: A new vision and strategy for integrated research and practice. *Clinical Psychology Review, 30*, 819–829.

Appendix A

Pool of items of behaviors and thoughts facilitating sustainable positive affect with empirical or theoretical source of the concept underlying the item.

Item	Underlying concept
1. I seek out activities that make me happy.	1. Seeking positive affect, broaden-and-build theory
2. Most of what I do is determined by the situations in which I find myself rather than by me.*	2. Intentional activity, correlation/intervention studies; autonomy motivation, and SDT**
3. Most of my activities are related to my goals.	3. Goal-congruent activity, correlation, and intervention studies
4. I seek out individuals with whom I feel happy.	4. Seeking positive affect, broaden and build, relationship motivation, and SDT
5. I often find myself doing things in which I have little interest.*	5. Interest-congruent activity, correlation, and intervention studies
6. I see new possibilities.	6. Cognitive appraisal
7. Many of my activities draw on special skills I have.	7. Ability congruency, correlation/intervention studies, competency motivation, and SDT
8. I like to explore.	8. Engaging in new activities, correlation/intervention studies, and broaden and build)
9. I try to do things that are important to me.	9. Value-congruent activity, correlation, and intervention studies
10. Many activities I enjoy at first bore me after a while.*	10. Broaden and build, seeking positive affect
11. Most of my activities are consistent with my values.	11. Value-congruent activity, correlation, and intervention studies
12. I try to vary how I do things to keep activities interesting.	12. Engaging in new activities and intervention studies
13. By being non-judgmental about what's happening around me I keep life interesting.	13. Mindfulness
14. I make the time to seek out activities that make me happy.	14. Broaden and build, seeking positive affect
15. I make an effort to see the positive aspects of events.	15. Cognitive appraisal
16. To keep life interesting I make changes in my daily activities.	16. Engaging in new activities and intervention studies
17. I seek out activities that give me a sense of fulfillment.	17. Goal-congruent activity, correlation, and intervention studies; SDT
18. I think about how pointless it is to try to reach my goals.*	18. Cognitive appraisal, goal-congruent activity, correlation/intervention studies, and SDT
19. Many of my activities draw on my talents.	19. Ability-congruent activity, correlation/intervention studies; competency, and SDT
20. I consider my strengths when deciding how I allocate my time.	20. Ability-congruent activity, correlation/intervention studies, competency, and SDT
21. I try out new activities.	21. Engaging in new activities, intervention studies, and broaden and build
22. Once I find an activity I like, I stick to it without making changes.*	22. Engaging in new activities and intervention studies
23. Many of my activities have provided me with a sense of fulfillment year after year.	23. SDT
24. I think about how my activities bring me closer to my goals.	24. Cognitive appraisal, goal congruency, correlation/intervention studies, and SDT
25. Most of what I do is determined by me rather than by other people.	25. Intentional activity, intervention studies, autonomy motivation, and SDT
26. By being open to what is happening around me I keep life interesting.	26. Mindfulness
27. Many of my activities focus on deepening my relationships with others.	27. Relationship motivation and SDT

*Reverse coded.

**SDT = Self Determination Theory.

2

All we need is the candidate's face: The irrelevance of information about political coalition affiliation and campaign promises

Lucia Mannetti[1], Ambra Brizi[1]*, Jocelyn Belanger[2] and Ilaria Bufalari[1]

*Corresponding author: Ambra Brizi, Department of Social and Developmental Psychology, University of Rome La Sapienza, Via dei Marsi 78, 00185 Roma, Italy
E-mail: ambra.brizi@uniroma1.it

Reviewing editor: Traci Craig, University of Idaho, USA

Abstract: Recent research has indicated that judgments of competence based on very short exposure to political candidates' faces reliably predict electoral success. An unexplored question is whether presenting written information of the kind to which voters are typically exposed during an election alongside candidates' faces affects competence judgments. We conducted three studies using photographs of 16 pairs of competing politicians in 16 medium-sized towns of northeast Italy as stimuli. Study 1 confirmed the external validity of earlier research in which participants were exposed to candidates' faces without providing any other information. Study 2a showed that competence judgments were not subject to in-group favoritism: candidates' faces were presented alongside information about the political coalition to which they belonged (center left; center right) to participants who declared a left or right political orientation. Finally, Study 2c compared the competence inferences made in Study 1 (face-only condition) with those of Study 2a (face plus political coalition label) and with new inferences (Study 2b) based on candidates' faces plus information about campaign promises (greater equality; lower taxes). The results showed that automatic competence inferences are not substantially

ABOUT THE AUTHORS

Lucia Mannetti is a full professor of Social Psychology at Sapienza, University of Rome. Her research interests focus on epistemic motivations, group and intergroup processes, and persuasive communication.

Ambra Brizi is a post-doctoral fellow at Sapienza, University of Rome. She received her PhD in social psychology from Sapienza, University of Rome in 2011 and has research interests in intergroup relationship and motivation.

Jocelyn Belanger is an assistant professor of psychology at the New York University in Abu Dhabi. He received his PhD from the University of Maryland in 2013 and his research interests in social cognition, goal pursuit, and interpersonal relationships.

Ilaria Bufalari is an assistant professor of social psychology at Sapienza, University of Rome. She received her PhD in cognitive neuroscience from Sapienza, University of Rome in 2008. Her research interests focus on body representations and face perception.

PUBLIC INTEREST STATEMENT

Recent research has challenged the assumption of citizens, as rational actors, giving their votes on the basis of informed and systematic evaluation of candidates. Some recent studies point out that judgment of competence based on short exposure to political candidates' faces predicts success in political elections. Results of our study: (a) confirm validity of previous results in the Italian context; (b) show that there is no evaluative bias due to the fit between participants political preferences and candidate political affiliation, and (c) show that verbal information concerning political affiliation or campaign promises does not substantially modify fast inferences based on candidates' faces.
Our results suggest that, at least in the contemporary Italian context, political parties are not any more able to influence citizens' choices and that actual voters may neglect relevant information such as political coalition affiliations and candidates' main political goals, when casting their vote.

modified when relevant written information is presented alongside candidates' faces.

Subjects: Social Psychology; Non-verbal Communication; Political Psychology

Keywords: first impressions; political choices; candidate's face

1. Introduction

In order to explain voting behavior, modern political scientists have mostly assumed that citizens are rational actors, making choices based on relevant information, while being unaffected by irrelevant cues (Kuklinski & Quirk, 2000; Quattrone & Tversky, 1988). The assumption of rationality is, more or less explicitly, at the heart of citizens' trust in the democratic system, leaving everyone hoping that their fellow citizens are good at choosing the best leaders and the right policies.

However, this assumption has been challenged by research in cognitive psychology and behavioral economics (Ariely, 2009; Tversky & Kahneman, 1973, 1974, 1981). There is mounting evidence that in order to cope with the complexity of life human beings routinely rely on heuristics and automatic information processing and make relatively parsimonious use of more reflective ways of thinking (System 1s and 2; Kahneman, 2003; Kahneman & Frederick, 2002; Lieberman, McBratney, & Krovitz, 2002; Petty & Cacioppo, 1986; Sloman, 1986). Consistent with these notions, research in the political domain has revealed that voters are usually not well informed about policies (Converse, 1964; Zaller, 1992), do not understand economic issues (Bartels, 2005; Caplan, 2007), have idiosyncratic view of ideological differences (Conover & Feldman, 1981) and inconsistent preferences (Quattrone & Tversky, 1988), and largely predicate their evaluation of political candidates and political issues on emotions (Lodge & Taber, 2005).

Supporting the idea that people are often cognitive misers, recent research has indicated that judgments of competence based on very brief exposure to political candidates' faces reliably predict electoral success (Hall, Goren, Chaiken, & Todorov, 2009; Lenz & Lawson, 2007; Sussman, Petkova, & Todorov, 2013; Todorov, Mandisodza, Goren, & Hall, 2005). In fact, explicit instructions to make a judgment based on careful deliberations elicit competence judgments that are less predictive of electoral outcomes than those made rapidly and intuitively between 250 and 2,000 ms (Ballew & Todorov, 2007, Study 2).

If competence judgments based on candidates' faces were highly accurate, then the fact that they influence voting behavior would not be troublesome. Unfortunately, research on accuracy of social attributions based on images of faces (Todorov, Olivola, Dotsch, & Mende-Siedlecki, 2015) suggests that such inferences are rather inaccurate and that people are not aware of their degree of accuracy. In other words, individuals "may be better off ignoring subtle facial cues" and focusing on "other sources of information when they are presented with facial cues" (Todorov et al., 2015, p. 533). In the political domain, the accuracy of inferences based on faces has been examined by Olivola and Todorov (2010, Study 2), who asked participants to guess the political affiliation (Democrat or Republican) of US candidates both when participants had to make the inference only on the base of candidates' faces and when they were informed about the composition of the pool of candidates' photos (base rate information). Although participants performed significantly better than chance when they did not know the base rate, they were not able to integrate information from base rates and from photos properly; they over weighted appearances and underused information about base rate, thus confirming a well-known effect (base rate fallacy or neglect) in social attribution research (e.g. Borgida & Brekke, 1981; Borgida & Nisbett, 1977; Pennycook & Thompson, 2016). In another study, Olivola, Sussman, Tsetsos, Kang, and Todorov (2012, Study 1) examined the predictive impact of inferences about political affiliation based on facial features. They found that "candidates running in right-leaning states benefited from looking more stereotypically Republican than their rivals. In contrast, there was no relationship between political facial stereotypes and electoral success in liberal states" (pp. 607–608). The same pattern of results was replicated in the second experimental study: whilst right-leaning participants favored Republican-looking candidates, left-leaning participants did not show any political facial bias.

One critical question that has been left underexplored in previous studies is whether presenting more specific information alongside candidates' faces influences competence judgments and their utility as a predictor of electoral outcomes. This appears particularly important given that in real-life elections, voters are exposed to additional relevant information alongside candidates' faces. Indeed, the abundance of information surrounding candidates often competes with, and thus may reduce the effect of automatic inferences based on candidates' faces (Hall et al., 2009). To our knowledge, there is only one study that has tackled this, by showing participants video clips of a political debate with and without sound (Benjamin & Shapiro, 2009), and asking them which candidate they thought would win the election. Results of this study, beyond providing further supporting evidence of the predictive power of inferences of personal attributes based on "thin-slices", show that participants exposed to video clips with sound (in comparison to silent video clips) were better at guessing political positions of the candidates but less able to guess election outcomes.

One of the first pieces of information citizens received during electoral campaigns is the candidates' political affiliations. The relevance of this information is controversial as some political scientists believe that voters have become less loyal to political parties, a phenomenon which has been termed the "decline of the parties" (Wilson & DiIulio, 1995), whilst others (e.g. Bartels, 2000) have pointed out that parties still have a significant impact on voting behavior, and that party identity can be considered a "brand" that influences evaluations of candidates (Hoegg & Lewis, 2011). Another piece of information that is frequently associated with a candidate's face is his or her main campaign promises, that is, the main goals the candidate intends to pursue. These promises are frequently cited during electoral campaigns and are printed on campaign signs alongside the candidate's face. Information about political affiliation and campaign promises may appear weakly related to a candidate's competence in comparison with information about incumbency, previous experience in office, endorsements by third parties, the candidate's origins, or even socio-demographic information such as education and occupation; however, our aim was not to assess whether participants (and actual voters) would use relevant information to arrive at more accurate competence judgments. Our aim was simply to determine whether or not stimuli similar to actual political signs (i.e. consisting of candidates' faces plus political party or campaign promises) would induce inferences that differ from those based solely on images of candidates' faces. In other words, our aim was to assess what extent competence inferences based on faces might be influenced by verbal information about political categories that—for at least some citizens—functions as a group label (e.g. we (in-group) are leftwing, they (out-group) are rightwing). Olivola et al. (2012) demonstrated a political facial bias amongst right-leaning electors, which can be seen as another example, in the political domain, of classical in-group favoritism (Tajfel & Turner, 1979; Turner, 1985; more recently Eriksson & Funcke, 2015); however our aim was to assess whether brief verbal information—about political affiliation or campaign promises—positioned below an image of a candidate's face would influence left- and right-leaning participants' competence judgments. If participants' inferences were affected by in-group favoritism, competence judgments would be less predictive of actual election results. These results would suggest that in actual elections, when voters are frequently informed about—at the very least—candidates' political affiliations and main campaign promises, the impact of candidates' faces is reduced. If, however, information about political affiliation did not influence participants' competence judgments, this would support the suggestion that political parties are in decline (Wilson & DiIulio, 1995), showing that even individuals who declare a broad political orientation do not trust in-group members more than out-group ones. It is worth noting that this hypothesis is supported by a recent survey showing that only 5% of Italians trust political parties, although 70% trusts the police, the most trusted institution (Demos survey for the *La Repubblica* newspaper, 2013). In this paper, we present three studies. In the first study, we tested our first hypothesis, based on Todorov et al.'s results (e.g. 2005) that in the case of people from Central Italy competence judgments based solely on seeing political faces can predict the election outcomes in northeast Italy. The aim of this preliminary study was to provide further evidence for the external validity of previous results.

The aim of the Study 2a was to investigate whether competences judgments are influenced by the condition of fit or misfit between candidates' political affiliation and the participant's political preference. Based on the Italian political situation at the time of data collection, we used two political affiliation labels, "central left coalition" and "central right coalition", both including at least two parties.

Then, the aim of the Study 2b was to test the effect of another piece of information very often added to the candidate's photo on campaign signs, namely campaign promises.

Finally, the aim of Study 2c, was to compare the competence inferences made in Study 1 (face-only condition) with those of Study 2a (face plus political label) and Study 2b (faces plus campaign promises).

If participants' inferences were influenced by information about candidates' political affiliations and campaign promises, then competence judgments based solely on candidates' faces should differ from those based on candidates' faces plus information about political affiliation and from those based on candidates' faces plus information about campaign promises with respect to ability to predict election outcome. If, on the contrary, competence judgments based on short exposure to candidates' faces are made very quickly, they should be unaffected by further information requiring more cognitive elaboration such as political affiliation or campaign promises. In this case, competence judgments based on different information would all be equally predictive of actual electoral outcomes.

2. Study 1

2.1. Method

2.1.1. Participants

Seventy undergraduate students from Sapienza, University of Rome (*M* age = 24.20, *SD* age = 3.34) participated in the study on a voluntary basis.

The study was approved by the Ethics Committee of Psychology Research of Sapienza University (n°22-CED01).

2.1.2. Stimuli and procedures

To further test the external validity of previous results (e.g. USA: Sussman et al., 2013; Hall et al., 2009; Italy: Castelli, Carraro, Ghitti, & Pastore, 2009), we selected 16 pairs of politicians who competed in the elections of May 2011 in 16 cities in northeast Italy. All candidates were standing in medium-sized towns (between 15,000 and 21,000 inhabitants) in northeast Italy and were men with the same ethnic background who belonged to Civic Lists. We excluded very small towns as we assumed that in such cases, the voters were likely to have first-hand knowledge of local candidates. We also excluded major cities because the candidates' faces might have appeared on National TV programs or newspapers and could thus be familiar to our participants in Rome.

All 16 pairs of images of political candidates were presented on a computer screen, and participants indicated which of each pair they perceived as more competent. The positions of the candidates were counterbalanced across participants (see Figure 1).

All pictures were standardized: head shots, size 104 × 147 pixels, on a gray background. The pictures were 6 cm distant. The experiment was run using SuperLab software which randomized the location of presentation of the winning and losing candidates (right or left-hand side of the screen).

Figure 1. An example of a pair of faces used in the experiments with face only.

For each pair of politicians, participants were instructed to select the most competent candidate by pressing the "A" to select the candidate presented on the left or "L" key to select the candidate on the right. Before they left, the laboratory participants were asked if they had recognized any of the politicians during the experiment. None of the participants recognized any of the candidates and they were unaware that some had already been elected.

2.2. Results

Data were analyzed following the procedure described by Na, Kim, Oh, Choi, and O'Toole (2015). We counted the number of times participants chose the election winner as the most competent candidate of the pair and calculated a correct choice score (range: 0-16) for each participants and the percentage of successful candidates rated as more competent.

In order to assess whether judgments by people from central Italy based solely on candidates' faces predict election outcomes in northeast Italy, we correlated perceived competence judgments with the actual election outcome (dichotomous variable: 1 for winners; 0 for losers).

Perceived competence judgments were positively and significantly correlated with the actual results [$r = .56$, $p = .001$].

2.3. Discussion

In our first study, we replicated the Todorov's results in Italy such as in Castelli et al. (2009). The judgments about the competence of politicians from northeast Italy made by students in central Italy were positively correlated with actual election results.

2.4. Studies 2a, 2b and 2c

The general aim of this second set of studies was to assess whether judgments of competence were influenced by verbal information presented alongside candidate faces and whether such an effect would alter the predictive power of these judgments with respect to election outcome (percentage of votes). In Study 2a, the additional information was information about candidates' political affiliation, whereas in Study 2b, it was about campaign promises. Finally, in Study 2c, we compared the predictive power of all the different types of stimuli.

3. Study 2a

In this study, we not only assessed the impact of added information about candidates' political affiliation, but also whether judgments about competence were influenced by the fit between the candidates' political affiliations and the participant's political preference. For this purpose, we asked participants to indicate their political orientation.

As discussed in the introduction, an extended tradition of research on intergroup perceptions (Tajfel & Turner, 1979; Turner, 1985; more recently Eriksson & Funcke, 2015) strongly implies that people are prone to in-group favoritism when making inferences based on stable positive features of in-group and out-group members; in other words they tend to perceive in-group members in more positive terms than out-group members. In the context of this study this would manifest as

Figure 2. An example of a pair of faces used in the experiments with added information concerning candidate's political coalition.

left-leaning participants rating left-wing candidates as more competent than right-wing candidates and one would expect this bias to reduce the predictive power of their judgments. One could also hypothesize, based on the notion of the decline of parties, that participants do not really identify with the political coalition they favor and do not perceive candidates as belonging to their in-group or out-group. If this were the case, one would not expect information about political affiliation to bias competence inferences.

3.1. Method

3.1.1. Participants

The participants were 76 undergraduate students from Sapienza, University of Rome (*M* age = 25.15 years, *SD* age = 2.14).

3.1.2. Stimuli and procedures

Participants viewed 16 pairs of candidates, one candidate in each pair was tagged as belonging to the left-wing coalition and the other tagged as belonging to the right-wing coalition. All candidates' faces were presented in two conditions: once tagged with "central left coalition" and once tagged with "central right coalition"; half the participants viewed each candidate with one label and half with the other label (see Figure 2).

All 16 pairs of images of political candidates were presented on a computer screen and participants were asked to indicate which member of each pair they perceived as more competent.

In all conditions, the positions (left and right of the screen) of candidates' photographs were counterbalanced across participants.

All pictures were standardized as in Study 1. Participants were also asked to indicate their own political orientation ("centre right"; "centre left"; "other" [which had to be specified]). Before they left, the laboratory participants were asked if they had recognized any of the politicians during the experiment. None of the participants recognized any of the candidates and the participants were unaware that some had already been elected.

3.2. Results

The data were analyzed at the participant level. We used a 2 (candidate's political affiliation: centre right vs. central-left) × 2 (participant's political preference: centre right vs. centre left) ANOVA with percentage of cases in which the winner was selected as most competent as the dependent variable to assess whether participants' competence judgments were influenced by the fit between their political preference and the political affiliation of the candidates. Forty-two participants self-defined as left-wing, 26 as right-wing and 8 did not specify their political preferences and were excluded

Figure 3. An example of a pair of faces used in the experiments with added information concerning campaign promises.

from this analysis. Neither candidate's political affiliation ($F = 0.00$; $p = .99$, $\eta_p^2 = .00$) nor participant's political preference ($F = .64$, $p = .43$, $\eta_p^2 = .01$) had an effect on the percentage of winners selected as more competent. More interesting, however, is that the interaction also was not significant ($F = .27$, $p = .60$, $\eta_p^2 = .00$), which suggests that perceived competence judgments were not biased by the fit between the candidate's political affiliation and the participant's political preference. On average, participants selected the winner as the most competent in 9.04 out of 16 choices (56.52%), which replicates previous findings (e.g. Todorov et al., 2005) on the relationship between the perceived competence judgments and electoral success. This result supports the second hypothesis that is the equivalence of political signs with information concerning political coalition added to candidate's face to political signs with only candidate's face as far as the predictive power of competence inferences are concerned.

4. Study 2b

The aim of the this study was to test the effect of another piece of information very often added to the candidate's photo on campaign signs, namely campaign promises. The campaign promises used in the study were selected on the basis of a pilot investigation in which participants, who were drawn from the same population as those for the experimental study, were requested to indicate the extent to which they associated various campaign promises with the political left or right. We chose "greater equality" as the left-wing promise and "lower taxes" (see Figure 3) as the right-wing promise, as these were judged, respectively, as the most left- and right-wing (the other choices were "power to the people"; "faith and family"; "greater social justice"; "lower crime").

4.1. Method

4.1.1. Participants

The participants were 77 undergraduate students from Sapienza, University of Rome (*M* age = 23.17, *SD* age = 3.73), who were exposed to the stimuli: face plus campaign promise "greater equality" ($n = 38$) or "lower taxes" ($n = 39$).

4.1.2. Stimuli and procedures

Participant viewed 16 pairs of candidates, in which one candidate was tagged with the left-wing campaign promise ("greater equality") and the with the right-wing campaign promise ("lower taxes"). In all other respects, the procedure was as in Study 2a.

4.2. Results

As before, the data were analyzed at participant level. A one-way ANOVA with percentage of cases in which winner was chosen as most competent as the dependent variable showed that campaign promise did not affect competence inferences ($F(1,75) = .121$, $p < .729$, $\eta_p^2 = .002$). The mean number of cases in which the winner was selected as most competent was 9.18 when participants were exposed to the left-wing promise and 9.0 when they were exposed to the right-wing promise.

5. Study 2c

The final study consisted of a comparative analysis of the "accuracy" of competence inferences (i.e. the percentage of cases in which the winner was judged the more competent candidate) across the five conditions.

To summarize, 70 participants were exposed to the face-only (condition 1), 38 to the face plus "centre left" political label (condition 2), 38 to the face plus "centre right" political label (condition 3), 38 to the face plus "greater equality" promise (condition 4) and 39 to the face plus "lower taxes" promise (condition 5).

All pictures were standardized as in Study 1 and before they left the laboratory participants were asked if they had recognized any of the politicians during the experiment. None of the participants recognized any of the candidates and they were unaware that some had already been elected.

5.1. Results

On the basis of the results of Studies 2a and 2b, we hypothesized that all the additional information conditions would produce similarly successful predictions of electoral outcome to the face-only condition. This means to adopt the null hypothesis as the research hypothesis, or to test the equivalence of the different treatments (stimuli conditions). We are aware that this analytical procedure has been a subject of debate (e.g. Rouder, Speckman, Sun, Morey, & Iverson, 2009), but we think that in this instance, the reliability of the dependent measure (used in several previous studies) and the use of the different levels of analysis (participant and candidate) improves its reliability.

5.1.1. Analysis at participant level

We compared the predictive power of competence judgments based on candidates' faces across the five different conditions using a one-way ANOVA with the condition as the independent variable and the number of times in which each participant had chosen the winner as the most competent as the dependent variable. If the additional information presented alongside the faces influenced our participants' judgments of competence one would expect to see an effect of condition. On the contrary, if further information concerning political affiliation and campaign promises was not taken into account by participants, there would be no significant difference between conditions.

The results confirmed our second hypothesis: there was no effect of condition ($F(4, 220) = 1.22$; $p = .30$, $\eta_p^2 = .02$), indicating that in none of the four conditions in which additional relevant information was presented alongside the candidates' faces did judgments of competence differ from the face-only condition (condition 1). On average, participants selected the winner as the most competent in 9.45 out of 16 choices (59.08%), once again confirming previous results relating to the predictive power of citizens' perceived competence judgments with respect to observed electoral outcomes. We also ran an ANOVA in which the condition variable was dichotomized (face-only vs. face plus additional information conditions). In this analysis, the effect of condition just failed to reach significance ($F(1, 223) = 3.614$, $p < .06$, $\eta_p^2 = .016$), confirming again their predictive equivalence.

5.1.2. Analysis at candidate level

In this analysis, we followed the procedure described by Willis and Todorov (2006) and used the candidate as the unit of analysis; in other words, we counted the number of participants that had chosen each of the 32 candidates as the most competent in a pair, and then divided this number by the number of participants in that condition, thus obtaining five competence ratings for each candidate. As suggested by Rosenthal (2005), we used Cronbach's α coefficient to estimate the reliability of the five sets of competence ratings: face-only condition (condition1): Cronbach's $\alpha = .94$; face plus "centre left" label (condition 2): $\alpha = .80$; face plus "centre right" label (condition 3): $\alpha = .82$; face plus "greater equality" promise (condition 4): $\alpha = .92$; face plus "lower taxes" promise (condition 5): $\alpha = .89$. We had a data matrix consisting of five competence ratings for each of the candidates (derived from participants' selection of the most competent of the pair in the five different conditions) and the percentage of votes that each candidate had actually obtained in the election. We computed an average "face-plus" competence rating based on the four conditions with face plus relevant information and correlated this and the "face-only" competence rating with the percentage of votes obtained by each candidate in the election; both correlations were positive and significant. A comparison of the two coefficients (Fisher's $z = -.51, p < .61$) confirmed the participant level analysis results, showing that face-only competence ratings ($r(31) = .63, p < .01$) were as predictive of election outcomes as "face-plus" competence ratings ($r(31) = .54, p < .01$).

6. General discussion

The results of these studies provide further evidence of the predictive power of competence inferences based on brief presentations of electoral candidates' faces (Study 1) but they also provide some preliminary evidence for: (a) the absence of an in-group bias related to the fit between the candidate's political affiliation and the participant's political orientation (Study 2a) and (b) the absence of any interference from verbal information with competence inferences based on faces (Studies 2a, 2b, and 2c).

With regard to the predictive power of competence inferences based on brief exposures to political candidates' faces, the results of Study 1 are consistent with previous studies conducted in the USA (Hall et al., 2009; Lenz & Lawson, 2007; Sussman et al., 2013; Todorov et al., 2005) and in Italy (Castelli et al., 2009). They showed that the competence judgments expressed by young people in Rome based on presentations of candidates' faces were strongly related to actual election outcomes in medium-sized towns in northeast Italy.

Study 2a provided preliminary evidence for the absence of an in-group bias induced by providing information about the condition of fit or misfit between candidates' political affiliation and the participant's political orientation. Although these results are consistent with current Italian political debate and actual election outcomes characterized by strong growth, in support for a new movement that identifies itself as "non-partisan" (the "Five stars movement"), they are based on only one experimental study in which participants (potential voters) assessed a specific combination of information, namely the candidate's face and political affiliation.

The absence of an in-group bias (i.e. candidates who share the rater's ideological leaning are not rated more competent) seems to conflict with previous research, for example Jahoda (1954) found that "in judging other people, subjects tend to associate favorable personal characteristics with political attitudes of which they themselves approve" (p. 330) and Bull and Hawkes (1982) reported similar findings.

The present results can be explained in terms of the "halo effect" (Thorndike, 1920); similar findings were reported by Herrmann and Shikano (2015) who noted that participants were more likely to attribute their own political views to candidates they perceived as attractive and competent. Similarly, Riggle, Ottati, Wyer, Kuklinski, and Schwarz (1992) showed that in the absence of other information voters' judgments of politicians were affected by physical attractiveness; however these effects disappeared in presence of other specific indicators of candidates' political orientation.

One limitation of our experiments is that our stimuli consisted of candidates' faces with the political affiliation labels beneath the faces, which may have increased the impact of faces by making them the first information perceived by participants. Further research should be done to determine whether variables relating to the provision of information about political affiliation such as position, different size of it, or even the introduction of traditional party logos influences the extent to which such information affects participants' (and by implication voters') inferences. A further limitation of Study 2a is the young age for our participants: the absence of in-group bias in this Italian sample may be typical of the young population, but not of older people. Finally, it is also possible that forcing participants to choose between two candidates with opposite political affiliations alerted them to the research goal and prompted them to correct their bias. All these possibilities deserve further investigation.

Finally, the studies presented here provide the first empirical evidence that the predictive power of rapid inferences about competence (based only on faces) is not substantially modified by presentation of relevant written information along with candidates' faces. Neither information about political affiliation nor campaign promises appears to alter the predictive power of competence judgments. Although this study focused on competence judgments rather than guesses about election outcomes, our results appear very similar to those of Benjamin and Shapiro (2009): in both cases, in fact, added verbal information that should be relevant to the election outcome did not alter the predictive power of participants' judgments.

Although the verbal information added to the candidates' faces was very similar to that presented in actual campaign signs, the graphic format was different and not professional, so our finding that such information is largely irrelevant to potential voters' judgments should be replicated in studies based on stimuli consisting of a different combination of visual and verbal information.

The fact that the written information provided in our studies did not substantially modify the predictive power of competence judgments suggests that the people who actually voted in the elections concerned may also have neglected relevant information such as political affiliation and candidates' main political goals when casting their vote. This hypothesis should be tested empirically by interviewing actual voters.

While the rational voter model assumes that voters carry out an extended search for information relevant to choosing political representatives and process it in depth, our results suggest that contemporary voters might not have the minimal epistemic motivation required to process even very short labels stating political affiliation or campaign promises.

Further research should be conducted with samples more varied in terms of age and political orientation, using different stimuli and should include monitoring of visual observation (eye tracking) and physiological indices of emotional activation. Such research would improve our understanding of the processes underlying the predictive power of competence ratings derived from facial impressions. Does the power of such ratings derive from an attentional preference for faces relative to verbal stimuli? Do faces elicit greater affective reactions? These issues could be fruitfully probed in future research.

Funding
The research was founded by Sapienza University, 2014 [grant number C26A149HHJ].

Competing Interests
The authors declare no competing interest.

Author details
Lucia Mannetti[1]
E-mail: lucia.mannetti@uniroma1.it
Ambra Brizi[1]
E-mail: ambra.brizi@uniroma1.it
Jocelyn Belanger[2]
E-mail: jocelyn.belanger@gmail.com
Ilaria Bufalari[1]
E-mail: ilaria.bufalari@uniroma1.it
[1] Department of Social and Developmental Psychology, University of Rome La Sapienza, Via dei Marsi 78, 00185 Roma, Italy.
[2] New York University, Abu Dhabi, United Arab Emirates.

References

Ariely, D. (2009). The end of rational economics. *Harvard Business Review, 87*, 78–84.

Ballew, C. C., & Todorov, A. (2007). Predicting political elections from rapid and unreflective face judgments. *Proceedings of the National Academy of Sciences, 104*, 17948–17953. http://dx.doi.org/10.1073/pnas.0705435104

Bartels, L. M. (2000). Partisanship and voting behavior, 1952–1996. *American Journal of Political Science, 44*, 35–50. http://dx.doi.org/10.2307/2669291

Bartels, L. M. (2005). Homer gets a tax cut: Inequality and public policy in the American mind. *Perspectives on Politics, 3*, 15–31.

Benjamin, D. J., & Shapiro, J. M. (2009). Thin-slice forecasts of gubernatorial elections. *Review of Economics and Statistics, 91*, 523–536. http://dx.doi.org/10.1162/rest.91.3.523

Borgida, E., & Brekke, N. (1981). The base rate fallacy in attribution and prediction. *New Directions in Attribution Research, 3*, 63–95.

Borgida, E., & Nisbett, R. E. (1977). The differential impact of abstract vs. concrete information on decisions. *Journal of Applied Social Psychology, 7*, 258–271. http://dx.doi.org/10.1111/jasp.1977.7.issue-3

Bull, R., & Hawkes, C. (1982). Judging politicians by their faces. *Political Studies, 30*, 95–101. http://dx.doi.org/10.1111/j.1467-9248.1982.tb00522.x

Caplan, B. (2007). *The myth of the rational voter*. Princeton, NJ: Princeton University Press.

Castelli, L., Carraro, L., Ghitti, C., & Pastore, M. (2009). The effects of perceived competence and sociability on electoral outcomes. *Journal of Experimental Social Psychology, 45*, 1152–1155. http://dx.doi.org/10.1016/j.jesp.2009.06.018

Conover, P. J., & Feldman, S. (1981). The origins and meaning of liberal/conservative self-identifications. *American Journal of Political Science, 25*, 617–645. http://dx.doi.org/10.2307/2110756

Converse, P. E. (1964). The nature of belief systems in mass publics. *Critical Review, 18*, 1–74.

Eriksson, K., & Funcke, A. (2015). A below-average effect with respect to american political stereotypes on warmth and competence. *Political Psychology, 36*, 341–350. http://dx.doi.org/10.1111/pops.v36.3

Hall, C. C., Goren, A., Chaiken, S., & Todorov, A. (2009). Shallow cues and deep effects: Trait judgments from faces and voting decisions. In E. Borgida, C. M Federico, & J. L Sullivan (Eds.), *The political psychology of democratic citizenship* (pp. 73–99). Oxford: Oxford University Press. http://dx.doi.org/10.1093/acprof:o so/9780195335453.001.0001

Herrmann, M., & Shikano, S. (2015). Attractiveness and facial competence bias: Face-based inferences of candidate ideology. *Political Psychology, 37*, 401–417.

Hoegg, J., & Lewis, M. V. (2011). The impact of candidate appearance and advertising strategies on election results. *Journal of Marketing Research, 48*, 895–909. http://dx.doi.org/10.1509/jmkr.48.5.895

Jahoda, G. (1954). Political attitudes and judgments of other people. *The Journal of Abnormal and Social Psychology, 49*, 330–334. http://dx.doi.org/10.1037/h0062563

Kahneman, D. (2003). A perspective on judgment and choice: Mapping bounded rationality. *American Psychologist, 58*, 697–720. http://dx.doi.org/10.1037/0003-066X.58.9.697

Kahneman, D., & Frederick, S. (2002). Representativeness revisited: Attribute substitution in intuitive judgment. In T. Gilovich, D. Griffin, & D. Kahneman (Eds), *Heuristics and biases: The psychology of intuitive judgment* (pp. 49–81). New York, NY: Cambridge University Press.

Kuklinski, J. H., & Quirk, P. J. (2000). Reconsidering the rational public: Cognition, heuristics and mass opinion. In A. Lupia, M. D. McCubbins, & S. L. Popkin (Eds.), *Elements of reason: Understanding and expanding the limits of political rationality* (pp. 154–182). Cambridge: Cambridge University Press.

La Repubblica. (2013). Retrieved from www.repubblica.it/argomenti/demos

Lenz, G., & Lawson, C. (2007, August–September). *Looking the part: Television leads less informed citizens to vote based on candidates' appearance*. Paper presented at the meeting of the American Political Science Association, Chicago, IL.

Lieberman, D. E., McBratney, B. M., & Krovitz, G. E. (2002). The evolution and development of cranial form in Homo sapiens. *Proceedings of the National Academy of Sciences, 99*, 1134–1139. http://dx.doi.org/10.1073/pnas.022440799

Lodge, M., & Taber, C. S. (2005). The automaticity of affect for political leaders, groups, and issues: An experimental test of the hot cognition hypothesis. *Political Psychology, 26*, 455–482. http://dx.doi.org/10.1111/pops.2005.26.issue-3

Na, J., Kim, S., Oh, H., Choi, I., & O'Toole, A. (2015). Competence judgments based on facial appearance are better predictors of american elections than of korean elections. *Psychological Science, 26*, 1107–1113. http://dx.doi.org/10.1177/0956797615576489

Olivola, C. Y., & Todorov, A. (2010). Fooled by first impressions? Reexamining the diagnostic value of appearance-based inferences. *Journal of Experimental Social Psychology, 46*, 315–324. http://dx.doi.org/10.1016/j.jesp.2009.12.002

Olivola, C. Y., Sussman, A. B., Tsetsos, K., Kang, O. E., & Todorov, A. (2012). Republicans prefer republican-looking leaders: Political facial stereotypes predict candidate electoral success among right-leaning voters. *Social Psychological and Personality Science, 3*, 605–613. http://dx.doi.org/10.1177/1948550611432770

Pennycook, G., & Thompson, V. A. (2016). Base rate neglect. In R. F. Pohl (Ed.), Cognitive illusions (pp. 44–61), London: Routledge.

Petty, R. E., & Cacioppo, J. T. (1986). *Communication and persuasion*. New York, NY: Springer-Verlag. http://dx.doi.org/10.1007/978-1-4612-4964-1

Quattrone, G. A., & Tversky, A. (1988). Contrasting rational and psychological analyses of political choice. *The American Political Science Review, 82*, 719–736. http://dx.doi.org/10.2307/1962487

Riggle, E. D., Ottati, V. C., Wyer, R. S., Kuklinski, J., & Schwarz, N. (1992). Bases of political judgments: The role of stereotypic and nonstereotypic information. *Political Behavior, 14*, 67–87. http://dx.doi.org/10.1007/BF00993509

Rosenthal, R. (2005). Conducting judgment studies: Some methodological issues. In J. A. Harrigan, R. Rosenthal, & R. Scherer (Eds.), *The new handbook of methods in nonverbal behavior research* (pp. 199–234), . Oxford: Oxford Univeristy Press.

Rouder, J. N., Speckman, P. L., Sun, D., Morey, R. D., & Iverson, G. (2009). Bayesian t tests for accepting and rejecting the null hypothesis. *Psychonomic Bulletin & Review, 16*, 225–237. http://dx.doi.org/10.3758/PBR.16.2.225

Sloman, A. (1986). Did Searle attack strong strong or weak strong AI? In A. G. Cohn & J. R. Thomas (Eds.), *Artificial intelligence and its applications* (pp. 271–288). New York, NY: John Wiley and Sons.

Sussman, A. B., Petkova, K., & Todorov, A. (2013). Competence ratings in US predict presidential election outcomes in Bulgaria. *Journal of Experimental Social Psychology, 49*, 771–775. http://dx.doi.org/10.1016/j.jesp.2013.02.003

Tajfel, H., & Turner, J. (1979). An integrative theory of intergroup conflict. In W. Austin & S. Worchel (Eds.), *The social psychology of intergroup relations* (pp. 33–47). Monterey, CA: Brooks/Cole.

Thorndike, E. L. (1920). A constant error in psychological ratings. *Journal of Applied Psychology, 4*, 25–29. http://dx.doi.org/10.1037/h0071663

Todorov, A., Mandisodza, A. N., Goren, A., & Hall, C. C. (2005). Inferences of competence from faces predict election outcomes. *Science, 308*, 1623–1626. http://dx.doi.org/10.1126/science.1110589

Todorov, A., Olivola, C. Y., Dotsch, R., & Mende-Siedlecki, P. (2015). Social attributions from faces: Determinants, consequences, accuracy, and functional significance. *Annual Review of Psychology, 66*, 519–545. http://dx.doi.org/10.1146/annurev-psych-113011-143831

Turner, J. C. (1985). Social categorization and the self-concept: A social cognitive theory of group behavior. In E. J. Lawler (Ed.), *Advances in group process: Theory and research* (Vol. 2, pp. 77–122). Greenwich, CT: JAI Press.

Tversky, A., & Kahneman, D. (1973). Availability: A heuristic for judging frequency and probability. *Cognitive Psychology, 5*, 207–232. http://dx.doi.org/10.1016/0010-0285(73)90033-9

Tversky, A., & Kahneman, D. (1974). Judgment under uncertainty: Heuristics and biases. *Science, 185*, 1124–1131. http://dx.doi.org/10.1126/science.185.4157.1124

Tversky, A., & Kahneman, D. (1981). The framing of decisions and the psychology of choice. *Science, 211*, 453–458. http://dx.doi.org/10.1126/science.7455683

Willis, J., & Todorov, A. (2006). First impressions: Making up your mind after a 100-ms exposure to a face. *Psychological Science, 17*, 592–598. http://dx.doi.org/10.1111/j.1467-9280.2006.01750.x

Wilson, J. Q., & DiIulio, J. J. (1995). *American government* (6th ed.). Lexington, MA: D.C. Health and Company.

Zaller, J. R. (1992). *The nature and origins of mass opinion.* Cambridge: Cambridge University Press. http://dx.doi.org/10.1017/CBO9780511818691

3

Adult attachment style and beliefs about public affairs and scientific issues

Cecilie Gaziano[1]*

*Corresponding author: Cecilie Gaziano, Research Solutions, Inc., 4511 Fremont Avenue South, Minneapolis, MN 55419- 4744, USA
E-mails: cgaziano@prodigy.net,
cgaziano1@gmail.com

Reviewing editor: Justin Hackett, California University of Pennsylvania, USA

Abstract: As political polarization has rapidly increased since the 1970s in the United States, controversies about the facts of public affairs and scientific issues have also intensified. Disagreements occur especially between the most educated Democrats and the most educated Republicans. Concepts relevant to a relational variable that helps to explain differences in cognitive development in children, called attachment style, may illuminate differences in beliefs of adults about public affairs issues. National general population surveys were conducted online in 2013 and 2014, containing an adult attachment style self-report instrument with questions on beliefs about a number of public affairs topics. While several studies examine adult attachment and political ideology or partisanship, this paper is among the first to focus on adult attachment and specific contested political and scientific beliefs. The findings suggest that adult attachment styles may partly explain why belief gaps develop between more and less advantaged groups.

Subjects: Communication Theory; Mass Communication; Political Communication

Keywords: adult attachment style; political beliefs; belief gap; partisanship; religiosity; media trust

1. Political conflict and beliefs about issue facts

Until recently many researchers have assumed that perceptions of the facts about issues disseminated by mass media are widely shared among all groups receiving information about them. Upsurges in political polarization in the United States reveal, however, that different groups do not agree on the facts or their implications for many issues (Daves, White, & Everett, 2011; Gaines, Kuklinski, Quirk, Peyton, & Verkuilen, 2007; Garrett, Weeks, & Neo, 2016; Kull, Ramsay, & Lewis, 2003;

ABOUT THE AUTHOR

Cecilie Gaziano is a consultant at Research Solutions, Inc., in Minneapolis, Minnesota, USA. She holds Master's and Doctoral degrees in mass communication theory and methods from the University of Minnesota and is a fellow of the Midwest Association for Public Opinion Research. Her research interests include the knowledge gap and belief gap hypotheses, mass media and their audiences, and social science and medical research on parents, children, and families. She has authored or co-authored articles in journals of mass media, communication, public opinion, health, and medicine, as well as several chapters in edited books and entries in three international encyclopedias on media effects, communication, and survey research methods.

PUBLIC INTEREST STATEMENT

The paper "Adult attachment style and beliefs about public affairs and scientific issues" looks at a concept called adult attachment style in connection with political party and political beliefs in the United States. The research problem stems from findings that partisans on opposite sides of contested issues frequently define the issues in terms so different that coming to an agreement is difficult. Often there is a conflict between people who rely on scientific evidence and people who draw on religious convictions. Attachments may be secure or insecure. Secure attachments promote intellectual development in children and may do so in adults. On the whole, insecure attachment styles were related to conservative, or Republican, beliefs in about half the comparisons of beliefs about issues.

Nyhan & Reifler, 2010). Study of these changes led to a "belief gap hypothesis" that extends the "knowledge gap hypothesis" proposed by Tichenor, Donohue, and Olien (1970). The knowledge gap hypothesis states:

> As the infusion of mass media information into a social system increases, segments of the population with higher socioeconomic status [SES] tend to acquire this information at a faster rate than the lower status segments, so that the gap in knowledge between these segments tends to increase rather than decrease. (pp. 159–160)

Conflict, however, often brings issue knowledge to the attention of all social groups, leading to narrowing of knowledge differentials between more and less advantaged groups (Tichenor, Donohue, & Olien, 1980)—presuming that all are seeing the information in the same way.

The belief gap hypothesis states:

> Political ideology is a better predictor of the distribution of politically disputed beliefs than is education. As the infusion of mass media information into the system increases over time, the relationship between political ideology and politically disputed beliefs tends to strengthen. (Hindman, 2009, p. 794)

Principally, contested political beliefs tend to depend on whether the beliefs are held by liberals or conservatives, Democrats or Republicans (Garrett et al., 2016; Hindman, 2009, 2012; Hindman & Yan, 2015; Veenstra, Hossain, & Lyons, 2014; Veenstra, Lyons, & Fowler-Dawson, 2016).

The most educated citizens are often the most divided if they are partisans on the opposite sides of issues. Joslyn and Haider-Markel (2014, pp. 926–927) explain this:

> On the one hand, the cognitive development produced by education allows citizens to access an array of available information, process that information, and evaluate the alternatives. On the other, party identification narrows the information environment, attracting certain sources while ignoring others. Education provides a more thoughtful and effortful information search, whereas party identification engenders a biased use of information to arrive at a preferred conclusion.

Belief gap researchers conceive of knowledge as facts supported by scientific study and beliefs as views accepted without systematic scrutiny (Hindman, 2009, 2012). Perceived conflict between religion and science is often cited as the reason for political disputes between conservatives and liberals about issues (Gauchat, 2012; Hindman, 2009; McCright & Dunlap, 2011; Miller, Scott, & Okamoto, 2006). All knowledge can be thought of as a form of belief, however (Gaziano, 2013; Gaziano & Gaziano, 1999; McCright & Dunlap, 2011). In this paper, convictions about issues, whether based in science, religion, or other domains, will be treated as beliefs. Conflict may bring topics to the attention of a variety of social groups, who may take divergent views of those topics. They may disagree on what constitutes a fact or truth, and even if they agree on the facts, they may disagree on the interpretation of those facts (Gaines et al., 2007; Garrett et al., 2016; Hindman, 2009, 2012; Kull et al., 2003; Nyhan & Reifler, 2010).

The present paper reports on an exploratory study of political partisanship and beliefs in the context of a relational concept, adult attachment style. Concepts relevant to attachment may help to explain differences in beliefs of Republicans and Democrats. Previous researchers report mixed results for the relation of attachment and political ideology or partisanship (Koleva & Rip, 2009). Little, if any, research, however, has centered on adult attachment and specific contested public affairs and scientific beliefs.

2. Why adult attachment may affect beliefs

The attachment process influences variables pertinent to acquisition of beliefs and knowledge. The earliest relationships in life affect perceptions of power and authority (Barker & Tinnick, 2006; Feldman & Stenner, 1997; Lakoff, 2002) and may be the underpinnings of ideology and partisanship. These perceptions may derive from what is called attachment. The concept of adult attachment is receiving attention for its potential connection to ideology and partisanship (Dunkel & Decker, 2012; Gillath & Hart, 2010; Koleva & Rip, 2009; Thornhill & Fincher, 2007; Weber & Federico, 2007; Weise et al., 2008). Many researchers believe that adult attachment relationships derive from infant attachment, although theories and measurement of adult attachment style and infant attachment differ in many ways (Crowell & Treboux, 1995; Hazan & Shaver, 1987; Mikulincer & Shaver, 2003; Simpson, Rholes, & Phillips, 1996).

Infant attachments may be secure or insecure (Ainsworth, Blehar, Waters, & Wall, 1978; Mikulincer & Shaver, 2003). Secure attachment is fostered by the caregiver's ability to respond to the infant's emotional needs, anxiety, and distress with consistent comfort and reliability, so that the infant can trust the caregiver as a safe base from which to explore the environment (Ainsworth et al., 1978; Bowlby, 1988). Infants whose caregivers do not respond consistently to their emotional needs are more likely to develop insecure attachments. They have learned that the caregiver's ability to provide comfort and safety is unpredictable. They may feel powerless and fearful, have low self-esteem, and lack interest in new experiences. Their attachment system is hyperactivated in response to their anxiety (Ainsworth et al., 1978; Cassidy & Kobak, 1988; Main, 1990). This type of insecure attachment is called anxious-ambivalent. In more extreme cases where the infant learns that the caregiver consistently is unable to support the child emotionally, the child develops an insecure anxious-avoidant attachment. This child deactivates his or her attachment system in order to lower anxiety by restricting close relationships and emotional connections (Brennan, Clark, & Shaver, 1998; Griffin & Bartholomew, 1994; Mikulincer, 1998). Bowlby ([1969] 1982) theorized that children develop "working models" of relationships from these early experiences.

Individuals develop strategies to manage anxiety in relationships with others, based on their childhood experiences; however, they may be able to revise their coping strategies in response to later experiences. People with anxious-ambivalent attachment styles fear abandonment and often seek to merge with others. They may be approval-seeking, dependent, preoccupied, and self-critical (Collins & Read, 1990; Mikulincer & Florian, 1998; Simpson et al., 1996). Those with anxious-avoidant styles often seek emotional distance from others. They can construct a facade of self-reliance; they may be negative, cynical, and angry at perceived slights; and they can seek control over others (Brennan et al., 1998; Griffin & Bartholomew, 1994; Mikulincer, 1998; Mikulincer & Shaver, 2003). Securely attached individuals exhibit confidence in others, tolerance, capacity for intimacy, autonomy, and greater connections to others (Brennan et al., 1998; Hazan & Shaver, 1987; Mikulincer, 1998).

The quality of attachment in earliest life may impact cognitive development (Cassidy, 1986; De Ruiter & Van Ijzendoorn, 1993; Jacobsen, Edelstein, & Hofmann, 1994). This is because attitudes of trust and self-efficacy promote thinking, problem-solving, information processing, and attitudes toward learning. Attachment, therefore, may be an important factor in explaining development of political beliefs in adulthood. The objective of the present research was to determine if adult attachment is related to beliefs about scientific and public affairs issues.

There are several scales to measure attachment style in adults. Carver's (1997) Measure of Attachment Qualities (MAQ) was selected as suitable for a general population survey, as a result of examining results of several reports using this measure (Carver, 1997; Hollist & Miller, 2005; Roccato, 2008; Roccato & Ricolfi, 2005; Roccato, Russo, & Senestro, 2013; Segal, Needham, & Coolidge, 2009). Many self-report attachment measures treat security and avoidance as polar opposites. Carver (1997) thought of avoidance as a quality to be considered separately from security, even though these two variables were inversely related. Separate factor loadings for the items measuring the different scale components supported this contention (Carver, 1997; Hollist & Miller, 2005; Kim & Carver, 2007; Segal et al., 2009). Similarly, Carver's (1997) research found two types of anxious-ambivalent attachment: merger and worry, each of which expressed separate qualities according to factor loadings (Carver, 1997; Hollist & Miller, 2005; Segal et al., 2009). Ambivalent-worry captures fear of abandonment or relationship betrayal, positive view of self, and negative view of others. Ambivalent-merger denotes desire for closeness, preoccupation, negative view of self, and positive view of others. Although some other adult attachment scales contain one dimension that includes both the worry and merger forms of ambivalence, confirmatory factor analysis and other research validated separation into two constructs (Carver, 1997; Hollist & Miller, 2005; Roccato, 2008; Roccato & Ricolfi, 2005; Roccato et al., 2013; Segal et al., 2009).

3. Intervening variables

Variables that may affect the relationship between attachment and ideology, and also are pertinent to belief gaps were measured. These included trust, religiosity, and formal education.

3.1. Trust

Child development research identifies early attachment as a process of relationship experiences that enhance or restrict a child's development of trust, confidence, and interest in learning (Bowlby, [1969] 1982; De Ruiter & Van Ijzendoorn, 1993; Erickson & Egeland, 2004; Sroufe, Egeland, Carlson, & Collins, 2005). Because attachment styles tend to be stable throughout life, one may expect that more secure individuals will be higher in trust and interest when they reach adulthood (Ainsworth, 1991; Fraley, 2002; Fraley & Shaver, 2000; Hazan & Shaver, 1987; Simpson, Collins, Tran, & Haydon, 2007).

A type of trust relevant to belief gaps, ideology, and partisanship is trust in mass media to report news in an accurate, unbiased way (Gaziano, 2014; Hindman, 2009). In the US, many observers view media distrust as a serious problem for a democratic society, since media dissemination of news is an important element in the political process (Jones, 2004). Conservatives increasingly tend to distrust mainstream news media as too liberal and to favor news channels that cover news from a conservative point of view, such as Fox, and liberals are more disposed to choose CNN, MSNBC, and NPR (Hindman, 2009; Hindman & Yan, 2015; Jamieson & Cappella, 2009; Jones, 2004; Lee, 2010; Morris, 2005).

3.2. Religiosity

People often comprehend complicated or controversial public affairs and scientific issues such as abortion or global warming by using their value predispositions, such as religious values or heuristic cues from news media, religious institutions, and political elites (Brossard, Scheufele, Kim, & Lewenstein, 2009; Hindman, 2009; Ho, Brossard, & Scheufele, 2008). Being religious is often related to being conservative (Roccato, 2008) and is frequently a factor in conservatives' distrust of scientific information, for instance (Brossard et al., 2009; Gauchat, 2012; Ho et al., 2008).

3.3. Political orientations

Ideology and partisanship are major divisive factors among citizens today (Abramowitz & Saunders, 2005; Hindman, 2009; Layman, Carsey, & Horowitz, 2006; McCright & Dunlap, 2011; Shapiro & Bloch-Elkon, 2008). In the US, the primary political parties are Republicans and Democrats.

3.4. Demographic variables

Education, household income, gender, age, and race play roles in acquiring relevant information and defining its meaning. In particular, formal schooling may have a liberalizing effect on many people because of increased cognitive development, sophistication, abstract thinking, increased opportunity to meet people of varied backgrounds, and augmented political expertise and understanding of the importance of democratic principles (Altemeyer, 1981, 1996, 1998). On the other hand, education is a component of divisiveness in combination with ideology and political party identification (Joslyn & Haider-Markel, 2014; Pew Research Center, 2016).

4. Research question

Since the literature emphasizes the importance of secure attachments for cognitive development and since research conflicts as to whether attachment is related to political orientation, there is some question as to whether specific beliefs conditioned by political views may relate to attachment. The following research question, therefore, is proposed.

> RQ1. Is security of adult attachment style related to specific beliefs about public affairs and scientific issues?

5. Study 1

5.1. Data and method

A national general population survey in the United States was conducted online through SurveyMonkey during 27 September–1 October 2013 ($N = 330$). The response rate was 35.1% of persons invited to take part. The survey contained 50 questions and took about 10 minutes to complete. Its title was "Opinions about Topics in the News, Interpersonal, and Social Issues." SurveyMonkey recruits thousands of people to participate in its customers' surveys, who fill out personal profiles upon enrollment and who are compensated by donations to charitable organizations and entries in sweepstakes. The company says that it maintains benchmarking surveys to make sure that their panels are representative of the US population. Though Internet surveys are relatively inexpensive and quick, they also tend to over represent higher SES groups, compared with telephone and face-to-face surveys (Zickuhr & Rainie, 2013). A second study carried out in 2014 is described later in this report. Participants gave informed consent by registering in SurveyMonkey's panel and accepting the survey. No identifying information is in data provided by SurveyMonkey.

5.2. Independent variable: Adult attachment

Carver's (1997) MAQ is a self-report with 14 Likert-type categories that have endpoints of "disagree with the statement a lot" and "agree with the statement a lot." It yields four subscales of three to five items gauging secure attachment, avoidant attachment, and two types of ambivalent patterns—worry and merger. Examples include the following: "Being close to someone gives me a source of strength for other activities." "I often worry my partner will not want to stay with me." "I get uncomfortable when someone wants to be very close."

Three items were reverse coded, and the scales were averaged to be on the same metric. Internal consistency for Study 1 was: security, $\alpha = 0.71$; avoidance, $\alpha = 0.80$; ambivalent-worry, $\alpha = 0.77$; and ambivalent-merger, $\alpha = 0.75$. These results are congruent with other reports (Carver, 1997; Kim & Carver, 2007; Kim, Carver, Deci, & Kasser, 2008; Segal et al., 2009).

5.3. Dependent variables: Beliefs about issues

The belief answers supported by scientific research are shown in italics. These answers were coded as "0"; non-scientific belief answers were coded as "1." Categories were rotated.

5.3.1. Evolution

The question was:

> *Some people think that humans and other living things have evolved over time.* Others think that humans and other living things have existed in their present form since the beginning of time. Which of these comes closer to your view?

5.3.2. Global warming and its causes

Participants were asked: "From what you've read and heard, is there solid evidence that the average temperature on earth has been getting warmer over the past few decades, or not?" If they said "yes," they were asked: "Do you believe that the earth is getting warmer *mostly because of human activity such as burning fossil fuels* or mostly because of natural patterns in the earth's environment?"

5.3.3. Sexual orientation

> In your opinion, do you think that homosexuality is: (1) something that people are born with, (2) something that develops because of the way people are brought up, (3) or is it just the way that some people prefer to live?

There is no scientific consensus yet about causes of sexual orientation (Långström, Rahman, Carlström, & Lichtenstein, 2010; Osmundson, 2011; Sanders et al., 2015). Answer category (1) was coded "0" as a belief that homosexuality cannot be changed. The other two answer categories were combined and coded "1" as consistent with belief that it can be changed.

5.4. Intervening variables

5.4.1. Trust in media

Participants were asked, "How much of the time do you think you can trust the media to report the news fairly?" (five-point scale ranging from "always" to "never," recoded so 5 = high trust).

5.4.2. Religious value predispositions

Respondents were asked to evaluate the importance of religion in their lives and frequency of attending religious services on five-point scales. The end points were "extremely important" and "not important at all" for the first measure and "every week" to "never" for the second. Responses were combined to form a religiosity score and recoded so high scores meant very religious (Cronbach's $\alpha = 0.86$, Study 1 and Study 2).

5.4.3. Political party identification

Respondents were asked: "In politics today, which describes your views the best?" with a seven-point scale anchored by "strong Republican" and "strong Democrat" (with the option of "other, please specify"). "Don't know" and "other" responses were excluded in the analysis. Respondents also were asked about ideological identification on a seven-point scale arranged from "extremely liberal" to "extremely conservative." Ideology was not used in the regression analyses because it was highly correlated with partisanship at $r = 0.70$, $p < 0.001$) in the first study and 0.76 ($p < 0.001$) in the second study.

5.4.4. Demographics

Demographic control variables were gender, age, education, and household income. Gender was a dichotomous variable with male coded as "0" and female coded as "1." Age was continuous, computed from a question asking year of birth. Education was ordinal with five categories ranging from "less than high school" to "graduate degree." Household income was ordinal, concerning the total combined money earned by all household members during the previous year, with seven categories that had endpoints of "less than $20,000" and "$150,000 or more." Data were also collected on race and Hispanic ethnicity but excluded from analysis because there were too few cases of non-whites and Hispanics for analysis.

6. Results

In Study 1, the 2013 sample contained a larger share of women, people with higher education and incomes, and the middle-aged than national census data of the same period, shown in Table 1. (Tables 1 and 2 give results for Study 2 in 2014, which will be discussed later.) The 2013 sample also disproportionately represented whites and non-Hispanics, compared with the census (not shown).

The 2013 sample was more likely to be Democratic than the general population, as shown by a t-test comparison with the General Social Survey conducted by NORC in 2014, based on the same question about political party identification, but this difference was not statistically significant at 0.05 or better (Table 2). The 2014 samples will be considered later.

Table 1. Comparisons of 2013 and 2014 demographic data with national census data[a]

Variables	2013 general population sample (*N* = 330) (%)	2014 general population sample (*N* = 223) (%)	2014 conservative sample (*N* = 202) (%)	2013 American community survey (*N* = 163,663) (%)
Gender				
Males	45.5	44.8	55.4	48.6
Females	54.5	55.2	44.6	51.4
Education				
No high school degree	0.6	0.9	0.5	13.6[b]
High school degree	9.7	7.6	12.4	28.0
Some college	35.7	34.1	34.7	29.2
College degree	30.0	30.9	28.2	18.2
Graduate work/ degree	23.9	26.5	24.3	11.0
Household income				
Less than $20,000	9.4	13.5	7.9	18.8
$20,000–$34,999	11.6	13.0	11.4	16.0
$35,000–$49,999	10.6	15.2	14.9	13.7
$50,000–$74,999	23.7	13.0	20.3	18.1
$75,000–$99,999	17.9	15.7	15.3	11.8
$100,000–$149,999	17.6	17.9	13.9	12.4
$150,000 or more	9.1	11.7	16.3	9.2
Age				
18–24 years	7.9	14.3	7.4	12.8
25–34 years	16.1	17.9	11.4	17.6
35–44 years	22.4	17.5	14.9	16.8
45–54 years	20.3	23.3	16.3	18.3
55–64 years	20.3	16.6	25.7	16.2
65 years or older	13.0	10.3	24.3	18.3

[a]Some totals do not add to 100% because of rounding.

[b]Based on adults aged 25 years or older.

The four attachment variables and political party affinity were uncorrelated (Table 3). The only variables correlated with party were religiousness and media distrust. Interestingly, however, trust in media reporting and religiousness was unrelated. See Appendix A for descriptive statistics of continuous variables.

Secure attachment correlated negatively with anxious-avoidance, −0.45 ($p < 0.001$), and it was unrelated to anxiety-worry or anxiety-merger. Worry and merger were interrelated at 0.47 ($p < 0.001$). Avoidance was associated with both ambivalent-worry and ambivalent-merger at 0.27 ($p < 0.001$). These results were relatively congruent with previous work (Carver, 1997; Hollist & Miller, 2005; Kim & Carver, 2007; Kim et al., 2008; Segal et al., 2009).

Security was related to greater media trust and to higher household incomes. Avoidance was negatively related to religiousness, trust in media, and household income. Worry was negatively correlated with religiosity and age. Anxious-ambivalence-merger styles were not associated with

Table 2. *t*-tests on partisanship results for 2013 sample, 2014 samples, and 2014 national General Social Survey (GSS) sample obtained from the National Opinion Research Center at the University of Chicago, IL, USA

Partisan identification

	Mean	SD	Median	N
2013 general audience sample[a,b]	3.46	1.73	4	313
2014 general audience sample[b,c,d]	3.43	1.61	3	204
2014 conservative sample[c,e]	5.45	1.32	6	194
2014 GSS[a,d,e]	3.66	1.92	4	2,450

Notes: Partisanship was measured on a seven-point scale, where lowest = "strong Democrat," highest = "strong Republican," and 4 = "Independent." "Don't know" responses and identification with other parties excluded.

[a] $t = 1.75$, $df = 2{,}761$, $p = 0.10$.

[b] $t = 0.20$, $df = 515$, $p < 0.84$.

[c] $t = 13.65$, $df = 396$, $p < 0.001$.

[d] $t = 1.66$, $df = 2{,}652$, $p = 0.10$.

[e] $t = 12.72$, $df = 2{,}642$, $p = 0.001$.

Table 3. Pearson correlations for main variables in 2013 survey

	Party ID[a]	Security	Avoidance	Worry	Merger	Religiosity	Media trust	Education	Household income	Age
Party ID	–									
Security	−0.07	–								
Avoidance	−0.06	−0.45***	–							
Worry	−0.09	−0.01	0.27***	–						
Merger	−0.07	0.02	0.27***	0.47***	–					
Religiosity	0.25***	0.05	−0.23***	−0.15**	−0.00	–				
Media trust	−0.29***	0.23***	−0.14*	0.05	0.06	0.02	–			
Education	−0.04	0.10†	−0.08	−0.06	0.04	0.05	0.11*	–		
Household income	0.07	0.14*	−0.13*	−0.09†	−0.07	−0.04	0.11*	0.26***	–	
Age	0.06	0.07	−0.07	−0.14*	0.05	0.12*	0.17**	0.15**	0.07	–

Note: $N = 313$ (17 observations missing).

[a] High = Republican, low = Democrat.

† $p < 0.10$.

* $p < 0.05$.

** $p < 0.01$.

*** $p < 0.001$ (two-tailed).

other variables besides avoidance and worry attachment styles. Other researchers report that more people are securely attached than insecurely attached (Peterson & Park, 2007; Shallcross, Howland, Bemis, Simpson, & Frazier, 2011). The present study also found that a larger share of respondents scored highly on secure attachment style than the segments of respondents who scored highly on the insecure attachment styles.

Beliefs about evolution were regressed on main variables in a binary logistic procedure, first on a block containing education, household income, age, and gender, and in a second block including religiousness, trust in mass media as news sources, and political party identification (Table 4, left-hand side). Then came a third block for the four styles of adult attachment. Belief that evolution is not true was significantly associated with lower education, higher religiosity, and higher level of

Table 4. Binary logistic regression results for belief outcomes in 2013 and 2014 conservatives					
	2013 general population sample		2014 conservative sample		
	Evolution is untrue (=1)	Homosexuality can be changed (=1)	Government can't afford to help needy (=1)	Blacks are mostly responsible (=1)	Government is wasteful (=1)
Education	−0.668***	−0.390*	0.583†	−0.294	−0.265
Household income	0.036	−0.029	0.376*	−0.011	0.128
Age	0.006	0.020†	0.000	0.023	0.038**
Gender (1 = female)	0.323	−1.112***	0.178	0.592	0.982*
Block 1 χ^2	16.375**	26.149***	19.189***	6.020	13.421**
Religiosity	0.369***	0.262***	0.002	−0.423**	−0.151†
Media trust	−0.260	−0.186	−0.048	−0.168	−0.550*
Party ID°	0.141	0.401***	0.466*	0.634**	0.411*
Block 2 χ^2	63.750***	63.255***	10.514*	22.604***	14.322**
Secure	−0.051	−0.111†	0.140	0.082	−0.108
Avoidant	−0.082	−0.032	0.302*	−0.066	−0.090
Worry	0.096*	0.010	−0.234*	−0.119	−0.155*
Merger	−0.029	−0.011	0.174	0.174†	0.100
Block 3 χ^2	6.023	3.630	14.730**	5.695	5.162
Tests					
Model likelihood ratio test χ^2, $df = 11$	86.148***	93.034***	44.433***	34.319***	32.906***
Goodness of fit: Hosmer & Lemeshow $df = 8$	6.957	9.170	11.926	12.175	9.814
Nagelkerke R^2	0.346	0.401	0.388	0.308	0.261
N	313 (17 missing)	272 (58 missing)	194 (8 missing)	194 (8 missing)	194 (8 missing)

Notes: Entries are betas from binary logistic regressions. Republican, or more conservative, beliefs are coded = 1.

°High = Republican, low = Democrat.

†$p < 0.10$.

*$p < 0.05$.

**$p < 0.01$.

***$p < 0.001$ (two-tailed).

anxious-ambivalent-worry attachment style. Political party was not a predictor. The first two blocks were statistically significant, but as a block, attachment style scores were not significant. The Hosmer and Lemeshow test yielded a low chi-square that was not statistically significant, suggesting a well-fitting model. The likelihood ratio test indicated that the model did better than chance at predicting the dependent variable and was statistically significant.

Table 4 also presents a binary logistic regression in which beliefs about changeability of sexual orientation were regressed on the same blocks of variables as shown for evolution. Primary predictors of belief that sexual orientation can be changed were lower education, male gender, greater religiosity, and higher Republican party identification. Being older and scoring lower on secure attachment style may be important, also, but these variables were significant only at 0.10. Researchers may not accept significance levels of 0.10 as consequential; however, such levels are reported here as indications of relationships that could be explored more fully in future work. The model did well in this table, but the block of attachment variables was not significant.

Belief that global warming is not a real phenomenon was regressed on the same demographic, attachment, value, and attitude variables as the two previous belief variables (not shown). Here, however, neither the attachment styles nor the demographics were significant. The only statistically significant predictor was Republican partisanship, and model fit was poor. Belief that global warming is occurring because of human activity was regressed on the same blocks of variables (not shown). The only significant variable again was Republican party identification, and the model tests did not signify a well-fitting model.

These results did not satisfactorily answer the research question about adult attachment styles and beliefs, so additional research was needed.

7. Study 2

7.1. Data and method

Two new national samples were drawn from SurveyMonkey participants 23–24 September 2014. One sample was of the general population ($N = 223$), and the other was predominantly conservative ($N = 202$). The conservatives were sought because of a desire to compensate for the liberal skew of the sample in Study 1. Independent and intervening variables were the same as in Study 1, but new belief variables were added.

7.2. Dependent variables: Beliefs about issues

7.2.1. Obama's birthplace

> Which of the following statements expresses your opinion about where President Barack Obama was born? Do you think that President Barack Obama: (1) Definitely was born in the United States. (2) Probably was born in the United States. (3) Probably was born in another country. (4) Definitely was born in another country?

(Responses to the first two items were coded "0," as supported by Barack Obama's birth certificate, a position held by most Democrats, and responses to the last two items were coded "1," for Republican, more conservative, belief.)

7.2.2. Common Core

"A topic that sometimes has been controversial is Common Core standards in public education. Which of the two statements below best describes this issue, in your opinion?" [The first item is a Republican, or more conservative, response, coded "1," and the second is a Democratic, or more liberal, response, coded "0." Statement order was randomized in the survey.] (1) Common Core standards in public education were developed by the National Governors Association, working with an organization of state school superintendents, with the intent of advancing educational standards and identifying the math and literacy skills that every student at each grade level should have. (2) "Common Core standards in public education were developed by the Obama administration to teach values to children at an early age that appear to be anti-Christian, anti-American, and anti-family ideas."

Other public affairs issues

For the following beliefs, participants were instructed: "Please mark the statement that comes closer to your views." Questions are from Pew Research Center (2014) and were designed to separate Democrats and liberals from Republicans and conservatives. The Republican answer is shown as number "1" below, and the Democratic response is "2," although statement order was randomized in the survey.

7.2.3. Racial discrimination

(1) "Blacks who can't get ahead in this country are mostly responsible for their own condition." (2) "Racial discrimination is the main reason why many black people can't get ahead these days."

7.2.4. The needy

(1) "The government today can't afford to do much more to help the needy." (2) "The government should do more to help needy Americans, even if it means going deeper into debt."

7.2.5. The environment

(1) "Stricter environmental laws and regulations cost too many jobs and hurt the economy." (2) "Stricter environmental laws and regulations are worth the cost."

7.2.6. Government waste

(1) "Government is almost always wasteful and inefficient." (2) "Government often does a better job than people give it credit for."

7.2.7. Business

(1) "Government regulation of business usually does more harm than good." (2) "Government regulation of business is necessary to protect the public interest."

7.2.8. Government benefits

(1) "Poor people today have it easy because they can get government benefits without doing anything in return." (2) "Poor people have hard lives because government benefits don't go far enough to help them live decently."

7.2.9. Immigration

(1) "Immigrants today are a burden on our country because they take our jobs, housing and health care." (2) "Immigrants today strengthen our country because of their hard work and talents."

7.2.10. Ensuring peace

(1) "The best way to ensure peace is through military strength." (2) "Good diplomacy is the best way to ensure peace."

7.2.11. Profits

(1) "Most corporations make a fair and reasonable amount of profit." (2) "Business corporations make too much profit."

7.2.12. Homosexuality

(1) "Homosexuality should be discouraged by society." (2) "Homosexuality should be accepted by society."

7.2.13. Genetically modified organisms

GMO science belief scores on this issue were obtained by counting each answer supported by scientific research as "1" and summing those answers (Cronbach's $\alpha = 0.71$ for both the general population and conservative samples).

"We hear a lot in the news today about GMOs or 'genetically modified organisms.' Below are some possible definitions of genetic modification. Which of the following statements about genetic modification are true, and which are false?" [Questions below are labeled "T" (true) if supported by scientific research and "F" (false) if not supported by scientific study. For questions and answers, see: Hallman, Hebden, Cuite, Aquino, and Lang (2004); Legge and Durant (2010); Nicolia, Manzo, Veronesi, and Rosellini (2014)].

- "Genetic modification is a process by which scientists can change the genes in some food crops and farm animals to make them taste better and stay fresh longer." (F)
- "Genetic modification is a process by which scientists can change the genes in some food crops and farm animals to make them grow faster or bigger and be more resistant to bugs, weeds and disease." (T)
- "Genetic modification is a process by which scientists can change the genes in some food crops and farm animals so they can reproduce on their own and live longer creating everlasting yield." (F)
- "Most processed foods in the United States contain an ingredient from a GM crop." (T)
- "Human cells and human genes function differently from those in animals and plants." (F)
- "By eating genetically modified fruit, a person's genes may become altered." (F)
- "Ordinary tomatoes contain genes while genetically modified ones do not." (F)
- "Genetically modified animals are always bigger than ordinary ones." (F)
- "It is not possible to transfer animal genes into plants." (F)
- "The scientific research conducted so far has not detected any significant hazards directly connected with the use of GM crops." (T)

8. Results

The 2014 general population sample was similar in composition to the 2013 sample (turn back to Table 1). The 2014 conservatives sample over represented males, in contrast to the other two samples. Both the 2014 samples disproportionately represented higher SES individuals, whites and non-Hispanics, compared with the census. Race and Hispanic ethnicity were excluded from analysis, as in the 2013 investigation. The conservatives sample was significantly older, more religious, and less trusting of mass media, compared with the 2014 general population sample (not shown). The conservatives scored significantly higher than the general population group on security of attachment style, while the general population sample scored significantly higher on all the insecure styles (not shown).

The 2014 sample of the general public was not significantly different from the 2013 sample in partisanship (returning to Table 2), but like the 2013 sample, it was more Democratic that the General Social Survey ($p < 0.10$). The conservatives sample was considerably more Republican than the other two samples and the GSS, as would be expected.

For Study 2, internal consistency of the attachment variables in the general population sample was: security, $\alpha = 0.68$; avoidance, $\alpha = 0.83$; ambivalent-worry, $\alpha = 0.73$; and ambivalent-merger, $\alpha = 0.75$, similar to the 2013 results. The conservative sample's results were congruent, correspondingly 0.73, 0.78, 0.70, and 0.75.

8.1. The 2014 sample of conservatives

In the sample of conservatives, political party identification was weakly connected to security at a 0.10 level, and higher income made a significant difference in Republican identification (Table 5). The interrelationships of the attachment variables were similar to those in the other two samples. Trust in fairness of media reporting and being religious were weakly related.

Refer back to Table 4, right-hand side, for binary logistic results for the three belief variables that yielded significant findings in the conservative sample. Attachment variables helped to account for results in all three sets of beliefs, although the block for attachment variables was significant only in the case of helping the needy. Having an avoidant attachment style was a significant predictor of views about needy people. Lower level of anxious-ambivalent-worry style also significantly explained the beliefs about the role of government in aiding the poor, as well as government wastefulness. In the case of government help, it is possible that those with avoidant attachment styles

Table 5. Pearson correlations for main variables in 2014 survey of conservatives

	Party ID[a]	Security	Avoidance	Worry	Merger	Religiosity	Media trust	Education	Household income	Age
Party ID	–									
Security	0.13†	–								
Avoidance	0.02	−0.58***	–							
Worry	−0.09	−0.26***	0.31***	–						
Merger	−0.01	−0.07	0.28***	0.53***	–					
Religiosity	0.11	0.04	−0.13†	−0.04	0.08	–				
Media trust	−0.13†	0.09	−0.07	0.00	0.02	0.12†	–			
Education	0.07	0.05	−0.01	−0.08†	−0.08	0.06	−0.05	–		
Household income	0.44***	0.17*	−0.09	−0.08	−0.14*	−0.08	−0.06	0.22**	–	
Age	−0.04	0.05	−0.10	−0.13†	−0.14†	−0.02	0.10	0.16*	0.13†	–

Note: $N = 194$ (8 observations missing).

[a]High = Republican, low = Democrat.

†$p < 0.10$.

*$p < 0.05$.

**$p < 0.01$.

***$p < 0.001$ (two-tailed).

lowered their sense of worry in order to manage anxiety; however, this does not explain the lower degree of worry in the case of government waste.

Higher education (weakly) and higher household incomes (more strongly) predicted belief that the government cannot pay for aid to the needy but not the other two beliefs shown. Being older and/or female significantly accounted for belief that government is wasteful but not for the other two beliefs. Demographics did not predict belief that blacks who cannot get ahead in this country are mostly responsible for their condition. Being Republican was a consistent significant predictor of all three beliefs. Lower trust in media was significant only for belief that the government is wasteful and inefficient. Lower religiosity predicted belief that blacks are mostly responsible for their situation and weakly indicated belief that government is wasteful.

Lower level of worry attachment style also contributed significantly to the conservative sample's science belief scores on genetically modified organisms in a multiple regression analysis in which the same blocks of variables were entered in the same order as in the binary logistic regressions (Table 6). The third block of attachment variables did not reach significance at 0.05 or better, however. Higher education was the most powerful predictor of GMO science belief scores, entered in the first block of demographic variables. Political party and media trust were not predictors, and low religiosity was weakly related at $p < 0.10$.

Attachment variables did not sufficiently explain the conservative sample's awareness of nine other belief variables: Obama's birthplace, Common Core educational objectives, military strength, government benefits for poor people, immigrants, environmental protection costs, corporate profits, regulation of business, and whether or not homosexuality should be discouraged by society.

8.2. The 2014 general population sample

Partisanship showed no correlation with the attachment variables in the general population sample, according to Table 7. Republican affiliation was negatively related to education and positively related to religiosity in the general population group. Security was significantly associated with education and trust in media. Secure attachment and avoidant styles were correlated negatively, −0.51

Table 6. Multiple regression: GMO science belief scores for 2014 conservative sample

	Zero-order	Model 1	Model 2	Model 3
Block 1: Demographic variables				
Education	0.296***	0.255***	0.268***	0.255***
Household income	0.214**	0.140†	0.073	0.091
Age	0.055	−0.015	−0.002	−0.011
Gender (1 = female)	−0.157*	−0.102	−0.087	−0.075
Incremental R^2 (%)		12.1***		
Block 2: Heuristic cues				
Religiosity	−0.122†		−0.141*	−0.129†
Media trust	−0.092		−0.028	−0.024
Party ID[a]	0.173*		0.120	0.094
Incremental R^2 (%)			2.8	
Block 3: Attachment variables				
Secure	0.000			−0.006
Avoidant	0.096			0.134
Worry	−0.178*			−0.198*
Merger	−0.087			0.015
Incremental R^2 (%)				3.8†
Total R^2 (%)				18.7***
Adjusted R^2 (%)				13.8***
N				194 (8 missing)

Note: Cell entries are standardized regression coefficients.
[a]High = Republican, low = Democrat.
†$p < 0.10$.
*$p < 0.05$.
**$p < 0.01$.
***$p < 0.001$ (two-tailed).

Table 7. Pearson correlations for main variables in 2014 survey of general population

	Party ID[a]	Security	Avoidance	Worry	Merger	Religiosity	Media trust	Education	Household income	Age
Party ID	–									
Security	−0.03	–								
Avoidance	0.07	−0.51***	–							
Worry	−0.00	0.08	0.20**	–						
Merger	0.01	0.17*	0.19**	0.62***	–					
Religiosity	0.20**	0.07	−0.09	−0.01	−0.03	–				
Media trust	−0.11	0.15*	−0.10	−0.04	−0.06	0.05	–			
Education	−0.18**	0.18*	−0.05	−0.14*	−0.13†	0.00	−0.02	–		
Household income	0.06	0.11	−0.01	−0.19**	−0.16*	−0.04	0.11	0.37***	–	
Age	0.07	−0.08	−0.04	−0.14†	−0.07	0.19**	0.14*	0.10	0.30***	–

Note: *N* = 204 (19 observations missing).
[a]High = Republican, low = Democrat.
†$p < 0.10$.
*$p < 0.05$.
**$p < 0.01$.
***$p < 0.001$ (two-tailed).

Table 8. Binary logistic regression: Belief outcomes in 2014 general population sample

	2014 general population sample					
	Government can't afford to help needy (=1)	**Blacks are mostly responsible (=1)**	**Government is wasteful (=1)**	**Obama was not born in the US (=1)**	**Common Core is un-Christian, etc. (=1)**	**Environmental protection is too costly (=1)**
Education	0.361†	−0.125	−0.058	−0.712*	−0.327	−0.190
Household income	−0.031	0.085	0.026	−0.108	0.111	0.104
Age	−0.027*	0.032*	0.019	0.019	0.044†	−0.010
Gender (1 = female)	0.318	−0.410	0.550	0.508	0.238	−0.452
Block 1 χ^2	2.047	13.116*	5.512	17.052**	5.801	3.346
Religiosity	0.081	0.097	0.003	−0.018	0.236†	0.267***
Media trust	0.101	−0.579*	−0.790***	−0.638*	−0.914*	−0.344
Party ID[a]	0.694***	0.692***	0.577***	0.694***	0.602**	0.423***
Block 2 χ^2	43.852***	50.801***	42.867***	27.346***	21.563***	34.173***
Secure	−0.120†	0.047	−0.076	−0.097	0.009	−0.005
Avoidant	0.014	0.148*	−0.047	−0.074	−0.014	0.056
Worry	−0.055	−0.050	−0.068	0.165*	0.193†	−0.053
Merger	0.112†	0.074	0.214**	0.037	−0.073	0.174*
Block 3 χ^2	7.112	8.626†	12.065*	8.084†	3.148	9.621*
Tests						
Model likelihood ratio test χ^2, $df = 11$	53.012***	72.542***	60.444***	52.482***	30.513***	47.140***
Goodness of fit: Hosmer & Lemeshow $df = 8$	4.695	11.124	3.530	6.124	4.553	10.537
Nagelkerke R^2	0.307	0.401	0.346	0.394	0.353	0.309

Notes: $N = 204$ (19 observations missing, except for Obama's birthplace, where $N = 188$, 35 observations missing). Entries are betas from binary logistic regressions. Republican, or more conservative, beliefs are coded = 1.

[a]High = Republican, low = Democrat.

†$p < 0.10$.

*$p < 0.05$.

**$p < 0.01$.

***$p < 0.001$ (two-tailed).

($p < 0.001$). Worry and security were uncorrelated, but merger and security were modestly and significantly correlated. Worry and merger were strongly linked, however, and both related significantly to lower education and lower income. Avoidant style and lower trust in mass media were not connected. Religiosity and media trust were unrelated. Both of the 2014 samples contained larger proportions of securely attached individuals than insecurely attached individuals. Descriptive statistics of continuous variables are in Appendix A.

Moving now to results for binary logistic regressions with those beliefs in which attachment variables played some part, attachment variables explained some of the reasons for general population respondents' views of six of the 13 issues studied in 2014 (Table 8). Higher scores on ambivalent merger style may be related to agreement that government cannot afford to help the needy ($p < 0.10$). Those higher in avoidant attachment styles were significantly more likely to hold that blacks are mostly responsible for their condition. Lower scores on worry attachment style and belief that blacks are responsible were in the same direction as found for helping the needy in Table 4 but not statistically significant. Those higher in ambivalent-merger styles were significantly more likely to endorse the view that government is wasteful and that environmental protection hurts jobs and the economy. Those with higher levels of ambivalent-worry style were disproportionately more likely to believe that Obama was not born in the US ($p < 0.05$). The data suggested that higher scores on worry were related to the position that Common Core educational standards are anti-Christian and anti-family ($p < 0.10$). Attachment styles did not significantly predict beliefs of general population participants with regard to homosexuality, government benefits for the poor, immigration, ensuring peace, corporate profits, or government regulation of business.

Among demographic variables, lower education was a significant element in two cases (belief that Obama was not born in the United States, Table 8; immigrants are burdensome, data not shown); whereas higher education predicted higher GMO science belief scores (multiple regression results not shown). Possibly higher education was associated with belief that government cannot afford to help the needy ($p < 0.10$). Household incomes and gender mattered little for beliefs. Being younger was associated with believing that government cannot afford to help the needy, and being older was connected to belief that Blacks are mostly responsible for their condition. Age may also be linked to belief that Common Core standards are bad ($p < 0.10$).

Identifying with the Republican party was the strongest explanation for respondents' beliefs about the various issues in 12 of 13 cases for this sample (data not shown if attachment variables were not significant). The only topic with variance not explained by party was GMO science belief (data not shown), an issue different in character and measurement from the other issues. Distrust of media reporting significantly predicted six beliefs (data for two not shown); on the other hand, higher media trust explained GMO science belief scores (not shown). Higher religiosity accounted for significant results of three beliefs (costliness of environmental protection, discouragement of homosexuality (data not shown), and perceived burden of immigrants (not shown). Religiosity may have figured in lack of support for Common Core educational standards ($p < 0.10$) and maintaining military strength ($p < 0.10$, Table 8). Appendix B summarizes the results of logistic regressions in which attachment variables were significant at 0.10 or better with odds ratios, as an indication of effect sizes.

9. Limitations

Probability levels of 0.10 may not be accepted as meaningful, and most blocks of attachment variables in the binary logistic regressions did not reach significance. Readers may also be critical of significance levels because a number of significance tests were performed. These kinds of results were noted as signposts to potentially fruitful areas for future research. The study was cross sectional, not over time, which does not allow for assessing causes. More questions about interest in specific topics could be asked. The Internet samples in the current study can be criticized for being unrepresentative of the general population. The online samples over represented Caucasians, the more educated and well off financially and the middle aged. Democrats and liberals made up a larger proportion of the first sample than occurs in the general population. Future studies should be more representative of the general population, even if conducted on the Internet, and contain more variables that may further illuminate the relation of adult attachment to beliefs about public affairs and scientific issues.

10. Discussion and conclusions

Some form of adult attachment style, secure or insecure, was expected to be related to beliefs held by partisans, based on research that shows security to be linked to cognitive development in children. One component of Carver's (1997) MAQ assessed security of adult attachment style, and three components of the scale measured insecure attachment style: ambivalence-worry, ambivalence-merger, and avoidance. Worry and merger styles were not precisely the opposite of security, being uncorrelated with security in 2013 and yielding mixed results in 2014. Avoidance was correlated inversely with security ranging from −0.44 in 2013 to −0.53 for the 2014 general population sample and −0.59 in the 2014 conservatives sample, all at $p < 0.001$.

Taking into account results for all 30 belief comparisons (four beliefs, counting global warming and human causes as two issues, in the 2013 study and 13 beliefs in each of the 2014 samples), some form of adult attachment style accounted for results in 12 comparisons, although several of these were at $p < 0.10$, and blocks of attachment variables were not significant in many comparisons. Attachment did not predict results in another 18 comparisons. In 11 comparisons insecure attachment style significantly predicted beliefs associated with Republican political positions. Attachment was not correlated with party identification, indicating that when attachment was influential, its impact was in addition to partisanship, whereas religiosity and distrust of mass media were known correlates of partisanship. The pattern of findings supporting the role of attachment's contribution to beliefs is of consequence.

Although Republicans tended to be religious and not to trust media, compared with Democrats, media trust and religiousness were not especially interrelated in any of the three samples. In general, level of formal education and being religious made a difference in all the beliefs examined, except for climate change. Trust in news media reporting was less important overall in these particular samples. The relationship of insecure attachments to lower education or lower household incomes partly explains belief gaps between higher and lower SES groups. The results tend to support the belief gap hypothesis that political leanings are stronger predictors of politically disputed beliefs than education is. In Tables 4 and 8, political party significantly predicted beliefs and education did not in seven of 11 comparisons. Education was significant while party was not in one case. Both party and education mattered as predictors in three instances.

The results supporting the relation of partisanship to beliefs about causes of homosexuality, climate change, President Obama's birthplace, and school issues were relatively congruent with other research (Brossard et al., 2009; Gauchat, 2012; Hindman, 2009, 2012; Hindman & Yan, 2015). The relationship of religiousness and formal education to the kinds of beliefs studied supported outcomes of other investigations (Gaziano, 2013, 2014; Gauchat, 2012; McCright & Dunlap, 2011; Miller et al., 2006; Veenstra et al., 2014). Having lower education, higher religiosity, lower media trust, being a Republican, and holding beliefs that do not square with scientifically established facts also corresponded with previous research on other topics (Nyhan & Reifler, 2010; Veenstra et al., 2014).

Higher levels of ambivalence-worry, ambivalence-merger, and avoidance styles of attachment denote higher anxiety. Carver's (1997) comparisons of the MAQ scale with other kinds of scales revealed ambivalence-worry and ambivalence-merger to be more related to neuroticism than avoidance was. Neuroticism is one of the "big five" fundamental personality domains and is a principal component of dysfunctional coping mechanisms (Goldberg, 1993; Stöber, 2003). It includes anxiety, fear, worry, and emotional instability. Merger includes preoccupation, desire for close relationships but at the same time encompassing distrust of closeness, lower self-worth, lower self-efficacy, and higher emotional impulsiveness (Carver, 1997; Segal et al., 2009). Avoidance also includes fearfulness and worry, negative thinking, difficulty in creative problem-solving and handling stress (Carver, 1997; Mikulincer, Shaver, & Pereg, 2003; Segal et al., 2009). Ambivalent-worry was related moderately and inversely to conscientiousness in Carver's (1997) research. Characteristics of conscientiousness are achievement orientation, self-discipline, and being organized, all of which may be connected to higher SES. Future research should focus on lower SES groups, in whom attachment insecurity may be stronger, since one reason that attachment did not play a stronger role in shaping beliefs in the present research may be that the three samples overrepresented higher SES groups.

Funding
The author received no direct funding for this research.

Competing Interests
The author declares no competing interest.

Author details
Cecilie Gaziano[1]
E-mails: cgaziano@prodigy.net, cgaziano1@gmail.com
ORCID ID: http://orcid.org/0000-0002-8732-4491
[1] Research Solutions, Inc., 4511 Fremont Avenue South, Minneapolis, MN 55419-4744, USA.

Correction
When the above article was first published online, footnote b in Appendix B mistakenly referenced Table 7, instead of Table 6. This has now been corrected and the author apologizes for the error.

References

Abramowitz, A., & Saunders, K. (2005). Why can't we all just get along? The reality of a polarized America. *The Forum, 3*, 1–22. Retrieved from http://www.bepress.com/forum/vol3/iss2/art1

Ainsworth, M. D. S. (1991). Attachments and other affectional bonds across the life cycle. In C. M. Parkes, J. Stevenson-Hinde, & P. Marris (Eds.), *Attachment across the life cycle* (pp. 33–51). New York, NY: Routledge.

Ainsworth, M. D. S., Blehar, M. C., Waters, E., & Wall, S. N. (1978). *Patterns of attachment: A psychological study of the strange situation*. Hillsdale, NJ: Erlbaum.

Altemeyer, B. (1981). *Right-wing authoritarianism*. Winnipeg: University of Manitoba Press.

Altemeyer, B. (1996). *The authoritarian specter*. Cambridge, MA: Harvard University Press.

Altemeyer, B. (1998). The other "authoritarian personality". In M. Zanna (Ed.), *Advances in experimental social psychology, 30* (pp. 47–92). San Diego, CA: Academic Press.

Barker, D. C., & Tinnick, III, J. D. (2006). Competing visions of parental roles and ideological constraint. *American Political Science Review, 100*, 249–263. http://dx.doi.org/10.1017/S0003055406062149

Bowlby, J. ([1969] 1982). *Attachment and loss: Attachment* (Vol. 1, 2nd ed.). New York, NY: Basic Books.

Bowlby, J. (1988). *A secure base: Parent-child attachment and healthy human development*. New York, NY: Basic Books.

Brennan, K. A., Clark, C. L., & Shaver, P. R. (1998). Self-report measurement of adult romantic attachment: An integrative overview. In J. A. Simpson & W. S. Rholes (Eds.), *Attachment theory and close relationships* (pp. 46–76). New York, NY: Guilford Press.

Brossard, D., Scheufele, D. A., Kim, E., & Lewenstein, B. V. (2009). Religiosity as a perceptual filter: Examining processes of opinion formation about nanotechnology. *Public Understanding of Science, 18*, 546–558. http://dx.doi.org/10.1177/0963662507087304

Carver, C. S. (1997). Adult attachment and personality: Converging evidence and a new measure. *Personality and Social Psychology Bulletin, 23*, 865–883. http://dx.doi.org/10.1177/0146167297238007

Cassidy, J. (1986). The ability to negotiate the environment: An aspect of infant competence as related to quality of attachment. *Child Development, 57*, 331–337. http://dx.doi.org/10.2307/1130588

Cassidy, J., & Kobak, R. R. (1988). Avoidance and its relationship with other defensive processes. In J. Belsky & T. Nezworski (Eds.), *Clinical implications of attachment* (pp. 300–323). Hillsdale: Erlbaum.

Collins, N. L., & Read, S. J. (1990). Adult attachment, working models and relationship quality in dating couples. *Journal of Personality and Social Psychology, 58*, 644–663. http://dx.doi.org/10.1037/0022-3514.58.4.644

Crowell, J. A., & Treboux, D. (1995). A review of adult attachment measures: Implications for theory and research. *Social Development, 4*, 294–327. http://dx.doi.org/10.1111/sode.1995.4.issue-3

Daves, R. P., White, H. A., & Everett, S. E. (2011). *The belief gap: More than just one issue*. Paper presented at the annual meeting of the Midwest Association for Public Opinion Research, Chicago, IL.

De Ruiter, C., & Van Ijzendoorn, M. H. (1993). Attachment and cognition. *International Journal of Educational Research, 19*, 521–599. http://dx.doi.org/10.1016/0883-0355(93)90001-Z

Dunkel, C. S., & Decker, M. (2012). Using identity style and parental identification to predict political orientation. *Current Psychology, 31*, 65–78. http://dx.doi.org/10.1007/s12144-012-9131-8

Erickson, M. F., & Egeland, B. (2004). Linking theory and research to practice: The Minnesota longitudinal study of parents and children and the STEEP™ Program. *Clinical Psychologist, 8*, 3–10.

Feldman, S., & Stenner, K. (1997). Perceived threat and authoritarianism. *Political Psychology, 18*, 741–770. http://dx.doi.org/10.1111/pops.1997.18.issue-4

Fraley, R. C. (2002). Attachment stability from infancy to adulthood: Meta-analysis and dynamic modeling of developmental mechanisms. *Personality and Social Psychology Review, 6*, 123–151. http://dx.doi.org/10.1207/S15327957PSPR0602_03

Fraley, R. C., & Shaver, P. R. (2000). Adult romantic attachment: Theoretical developments, emerging controversies, and unanswered questions. *Review of General Psychology, 4*, 132–154. http://dx.doi.org/10.1037/1089-2680.4.2.132

Gaines, B. J., Kuklinski, J. H., Quirk, P. J., Peyton, B., & Verkuilen, J. (2007). Same facts, different interpretations: Partisan motivation and opinion on Iraq. *The Journal of Politics, 69*, 957–974.http://dx.doi.org/10.1111/j.1468-2508.2007.00601.x

Garrett, R. K., Weeks, B. F., & Neo, R. L. (2016). Driving a wedge between evidence and beliefs: How online ideological news exposure promotes political misperceptions. *Journal of Computer-Mediated Communication, 21*, 331–348. http://dx.doi.org/10.1111/jcc4.2016.21.issue-5

Gauchat, G. (2012). Politicization of science in the public sphere. *American Sociological Review, 77*, 167–187. http://dx.doi.org/10.1177/0003122412438225

Gaziano, C. (2013). Knowledge gaps, belief gaps, ideology, and culture wars. *Open Journal of Political Science, 3*, 116–130. http://dx.doi.org/10.4236/ojps.2013.34017

Gaziano, C. (2014). Components of the belief gap: Ideology and education. *Sage Open, 4*, 1–18.

Gaziano, E., & Gaziano, C. (1999). Social control, social change, and the knowledge gap hypothesis. In D. Demers & K. Viswanath (Eds.), *Mass media, social control and social change: A macrosocial perspective* (pp. 117–136). Ames, IA: Iowa State University Press.

Gillath, O., & Hart, J. (2010). The effects of psychological security and insecurity on political attitudes and leadership preferences. *European Journal of Social Psychology, 40*, 122–134.

Goldberg, L. R. (1993). The structure of phenotypic personality traits. *American Psychologist, 48*, 26–34. http://dx.doi.org/10.1037/0003-066X.48.1.26

Griffin, D. W., & Bartholomew, K. (1994). Models of the self and other: Fundamental dimensions underlying measures of adult attachment. *Journal of Personality and Social Psychology, 67*, 430–445. http://dx.doi.org/10.1037/0022-3514.67.3.430

Hallman, W. K., Hebden, W. C., Cuite, C. L., Aquino, H. L., & Lang, J. T. (2004). *Americans and GM food: Knowledge, opinion and interest in 2004 (University Research News RR-1104-007)*. New Brunswick, NJ: Food Policy Institute, Cook College, Rutgers University.

Hazan, C., & Shaver, P. R. (1987). Romantic love conceptualized as an attachment process. *Journal of Personality and Social Psychology, 52*, 511–524. http://dx.doi.org/10.1037/0022-3514.52.3.511

Hindman, D. B. (2009). Mass media flow and differential distribution of politically disputed beliefs: The belief gap hypothesis. *Journalism & Mass Communication Quarterly, 86*, 790–808. http://dx.doi.org/10.1177/107769900908600405

Hindman, D. B. (2012). Knowledge gaps, belief gaps, and public opinion about health care reform. *Journalism & Mass Communication Quarterly, 89*, 585–605. http://dx.doi.org/10.1177/1077699012456021

Hindman, D., & Yan, C. (2015). The knowledge gap versus the belief gap and abstinence-only sex education. *Journal of Health Communication, 20*, 949–957. http://dx.doi.org/10.1080/10810730.2015.1018571

Ho, S. S., Brossard, D., & Scheufele, D. A. (2008). Effects of value predispositions, mass media use, and knowledge on public attitudes toward embryonic stem cell research. *International Journal of Public Opinion Research, 20*, 171–192. http://dx.doi.org/10.1093/ijpor/edn017

Hollist, C. S., & Miller, R. B. (2005). Perceptions of attachment style and marital quality in midlife marriage. *Family Relations, 54*, 46–57. http://dx.doi.org/10.1111/fare.2005.54.issue-1

Jacobsen, T., Edelstein, W., & Hofmann, V. (1994). A longitudinal study of the relation between representations of attachment in childhood and cognitive functioning in childhood and adolescence. *Developmental Psychology, 30*, 112–124. http://dx.doi.org/10.1037/0012-1649.30.1.112

Jamieson, K. H., & Cappella, J. N. (2009). *Echo chamber: Rush Limbaugh and the conservative media establishment*. New York, NY: Oxford University Press.

Jones, D. A. (2004). Why Americans don't trust the media: A preliminary analysis. *The Harvard International Journal of Press/Politics, 9*, 60–75. http://dx.doi.org/10.1177/1081180X04263461

Joslyn, M. R., & Haider-Markel, D. P. (2014). Who knows best? Education, partisanship, and contested facts. *Politics & Policy, 42*, 919–947. http://dx.doi.org/10.1111/polp.2014.42.issue-6

Kim, Y., & Carver, C. S. (2007). Frequency and difficulty in caregiving among spouses of individuals with cancer: Effects of adult attachment and gender. *Psycho-Oncology, 16*, 714–723. http://dx.doi.org/10.1002/(ISSN)1099-1611

Kim, Y., Carver, C. S., Deci, E. L., & Kasser, T. (2008). Adult attachment and psychological well-being in cancer caregivers: The mediational role of spouses' motives for caregiving. *Health Psychology, 27*, S144–S154. http://dx.doi.org/10.1037/0278-6133.27.2(Suppl.).S144

Koleva, S. P., & Rip, B. (2009). Attachment style and political ideology: A review of contradictory findings. *Social Justice Research, 22*, 241–258. http://dx.doi.org/10.1007/s11211-009-0099-y

Kull, S., Ramsay, C., & Lewis, E. (2003). Misperceptions, the media, and the Iraq war. *Political Science Quarterly, 118*, 569–598. http://dx.doi.org/10.1002/j.1538-165X.2003.tb00406.x

Lakoff, G. (2002). *Moral politics* (2nd ed.). Chicago, IL: University of Chicago Press. http://dx.doi.org/10.7208/chicago/9780226471006.001.0001

Långström, N., Rahman, Q., Carlström, E., & Lichtenstein, P. (2010). Genetic and environmental effects on same-sex sexual behavior: A population study of twins in Sweden. *Archives of Sexual Behavior, 39*, 75–80. http://dx.doi.org/10.1007/s10508-008-9386-1

Layman, G. C., Carsey, T. M., & Horowitz, J. M. (2006). Party polarization in American politics: Characteristics, causes, and consequences. *Annual Review of Political Science, 9*, 83–110. http://dx.doi.org/10.1146/annurev.polisci.9.070204.105138

Lee, T.-T. (2010). Why they don't trust the media: An examination of factors predicting trust. *American Behavioral Scientist, 54*, 8–21. http://dx.doi.org/10.1177/0002764210376308

Legge, Jr., J. S., & Durant, R. F. (2010). Public opinion, risk assessment, and biotechnology: Lessons from attitudes toward genetically modified foods in the European union. *Review of Policy Research, 27*, 59–76. http://dx.doi.org/10.1111/ropr.2010.27.issue-1

Main, M. (1990). Cross-cultural studies of attachment organization: Recent studies, changing methodologies, and the concept of conditional strategies. *Human Development, 33*, 48–61. http://dx.doi.org/10.1159/000276502

McCright, A. M., & Dunlap, R. E. (2011). The politicization of climate change and polarization in the American public's views of global warming, 2001–2010. *Sociological Quarterly, 52*, 155–194. http://dx.doi.org/10.1111/tsq.2011.52.issue-2

Mikulincer, M. (1998). Attachment working models and the sense of trust: An exploration of interaction goals and affect regulation. *Journal of Personality and Social Psychology, 74*, 1209–1224. http://dx.doi.org/10.1037/0022-3514.74.5.1209

Mikulincer, M., & Florian, V. (1998). The relationship between adult attachment styles and emotional and cognitive reactions to stressful events. In J. A. Simpson & W. S. Rholes (Eds.), *Attachment theory and close relationships* (pp. 143–165). New York, NY: Guilford Press.

Mikulincer, M., & Shaver, P. R. (2003). The attachment behavioral system in adulthood: Activation, psychodynamics, and interpersonal processes. In M. P. Zanna (Ed.), *Advances in experimental social psychology* (Vol. 35, pp. 53–152). San Diego, CA: Academic Press.

Mikulincer, M., Shaver, P. R., & Pereg, D. (2003). Attachment theory and affect regulation: The dynamics, development, and cognitive consequences of attachment-related strategies. *Motivation and Emotion, 27*, 77–102. http://dx.doi.org/10.1023/A:1024515519160

Miller, J. D., Scott, E. C., & Okamoto, S. (2006). Science communication: Public acceptance of evolution. *Science, 313*, 765–766. http://dx.doi.org/10.1126/science.1126746

Morris, J. S. (2005). The Fox News factor. *The Harvard International Journal of Press/Politics, 10*, 56–79. http://dx.doi.org/10.1177/1081180X05279264

Nicolia, A., Manzo, A., Veronesi, F., & Rosellini, D. (2014). An overview of the last 10 years of genetically engineered crop safety research. *Critical Reviews in Biotechnology, 34*, 77–88. http://dx.doi.org/10.3109/07388551.2013.823595

Nyhan, B., & Reifler, J. (2010). When corrections fail: The persistence of political misperceptions. *Political Behavior, 32*, 303–330. http://dx.doi.org/10.1007/s11109-010-9112-2

Osmundson, J. (2011). "I was born this way": Is sexuality innate, and should it matter? *LGBTQ Policy Journal at the Harvard Kennedy School, 1*, 15–27.

Peterson, C., & Park, N. (2007). Attachment security and its benefits in context. *Psychological Inquiry, 18*, 172–176. http://dx.doi.org/10.1080/10478400701512752

Pew Research Center. (2014). Political polarization in the American public: How increasing ideological uniformity and partisan antipathy affect politics, compromise and everyday life. Retrieved from http://www.people-press.org/2014/06/12/political-polarization-in-the-american-public/

Pew Research Center. (2016). A wider ideological gap between more and less educated adults: Political polarization update. Retrieved from http://www.people-press.org/2016/04/26/a-wider-ideological-gap-between-more-and-less-educated-adults/

Roccato, M. (2008). Right-wing authoritarianism, social dominance orientation, and attachment: An Italian study. *Swiss Journal of Psychology, 67*, 219–229. http://dx.doi.org/10.1024/1421-0185.67.4.219

Roccato, M., & Ricolfi, L. (2005). On the correlation between right-wing authoritarianism and social dominance orientation. *Basic and Applied Social Psychology, 27*, 187–200. http://dx.doi.org/10.1207/s15324834basp2703_1

Roccato, M., Russo, S., & Senestro, S. (2013). Adult attachment styles, life experiences, right-wing authoritarianism, and social dominance orientation. *Psicologia Sociale, 2*, 249–265.

Sanders, A. R., Martin, E. R., Beecham, G. W., Guo, S., Dawood, K., Rieger, G., ... Bailey, J. M. (2015). Genome-wide scan demonstrates significant linkage for male sexual orientation. *Psychological Medicine, 45*, 1379–1388. http://dx.doi.org/10.1017/S0033291714002451

Segal, D. L., Needham, T. N., & Coolidge, F. L. (2009). Age differences in attachment orientations among younger and older adults: Evidence from two self-report measures of attachment. *The International Journal of Aging and Human Development, 69*, 119–132. http://dx.doi.org/10.2190/AG.69.2.c

Shallcross, S. L., Howland, M., Bemis, J., Simpson, J. A., & Frazier, P. (2011). Not "capitalizing" on social capitalization interactions: The role of attachment insecurity. *Journal of Family Psychology, 25*, 77–85. http://dx.doi.org/10.1037/a0021876

Shapiro, R. Y., & Bloch-Elkon, Y. (2008). Do the facts speak for themselves? Partisan disagreement as a challenge to democratic competence. *Critical Review, 20*, 115–139. http://dx.doi.org/10.1080/08913810802316373

Simpson, J. A., Collins, W. A., Tran, S. S., & Haydon, K. C. (2007). Attachment and the experience and expression of emotions in romantic relationships: A developmental perspective. *Journal of Personality and Social Psychology, 92*, 355–367. http://dx.doi.org/10.1037/0022-3514.92.2.355

Simpson, J. A., Rholes, W. S., & Phillips, D. (1996). Conflict in close relationships: An attachment perspective. *Journal of Personality and Social Psychology, 71*, 899–914. http://dx.doi.org/10.1037/0022-3514.71.5.899

Sroufe, L. A., Egeland, B., Carlson, E. A., & Collins, W. A. (2005). *The development of the person: The Minnesota study of risk and adaptation from birth to adulthood*. New York, NY: Guilford.

Stöber, J. (2003). Self-pity: Exploring the links to personality, control beliefs, and anger. *Journal of Personality, 71*, 183–220. http://dx.doi.org/10.1111/1467-6494.7102004

Thornhill, R., & Fincher, C. L. (2007). What is the relevance of attachment and life history to political values? *Evolution and Human Behavior, 28*, 215–222. http://dx.doi.org/10.1016/j.evolhumbehav.2007.01.005

Tichenor, P. J., Donohue, G. A., & Olien, C. N. (1970). Mass media flow and differential growth in knowledge. *Public Opinion Quarterly, 34*, 159–170. http://dx.doi.org/10.1086/267786

Tichenor, P. J., Donohue, G. A., & Olien, C. N. (1980). Conflict and the knowledge gap. In P. J. Tichenor, G. A. Donohue, & C. N. Olien (Eds.), *Community conflict and the press* (pp. 175–203). Beverly Hills, CA: Sage.

Veenstra, A. S., Hossain, M. D., & Lyons, B. A. (2014). Partisan media and discussion as enhancers of the belief gap. *Mass Communication and Society, 17*, 874–897. http://dx.doi.org/10.1080/15205436.2013.855791

Veenstra, A. S., Lyons, B. A., & Fowler-Dawson, A. (2016). Conservatism vs. conservationism: Differential influences of social identities on beliefs about fracking. *Environmental Communication, 10*, 322–336. http://dx.doi.org/10.1080/17524032.2015.1127851

Weber, C., & Federico, C. M. (2007). Interpersonal attachment and patterns of ideological belief. *Political Psychology, 28*, 389–416. http://dx.doi.org/10.1111/pops.2007.28.issue-4

Weise, D. R., Pyszczynski, T., Cox, C. R., Arndt, J., Greenberg, J., Solomon, S., & Kosloff, S. (2008). Interpersonal politics: The role of terror management and attachment processes in shaping political preferences. *Psychological Science, 19*, 448–455. http://dx.doi.org/10.1111/j.1467-9280.2008.02108.x

Zickuhr, K., & Rainie, L. (2013, November 29). 7 things to know about offline Americans. Pew Research Center. Retrieved from http://www.pewresearch.org/fact-tank/2013/11/29/7-things-to-know-about-offline-americans/

Appendix A

Descriptive statistics

	M	SD	N
2013 study			
Education	3.67	0.966	330
Household income	4.18	1.760	330
Age	46.58	14.767	330
Secure	16.44	3.009	330
Avoidant	10.37	3.465	330
Ambivalent-worry	8.76	3.878	330
Ambivalent-merger	9.58	3.537	330
Political party identification	3.46	1.726	313
Ideology	3.74	1.669	330
Religiosity	5.53	2.927	330
Media trust	2.67	0.884	330
2014 study, general population			
Education	3.74	0.964	223
Household income	4.05	1.955	223
Age	43.67	15.372	223
Secure	16.44	3.108	223
Avoidant	10.60	3.461	223
Ambivalent-worry	9.14	3.730	223
Ambivalent-merger	9.76	3.627	223
Political party identification	3.43	1.606	204
Ideology	3.52	1.494	223
Religiosity	5.14	2.870	223
Media trust	3.01	0.872	223
2014 study, conservatives			
Education	3.63	1.000	202
Household income	4.31	1.849	202
Age	51.31	16.311	202
Secure	17.10	2.740	202
Avoidant	9.97	3.211	202
Ambivalent-worry	8.08	3.404	202
Ambivalent-merger	9.26	3.391	202
Political party identification	5.45	1.319	194
Ideology	5.80	0.904	202
Religiosity	7.22	2.747	202
Media trust	2.63	0.867	202

Appendix B

Summary of findings about attachment style and beliefs

Type of belief	Attachment style	β^{a}	Odds ratio exp (B)	Direction of relationship
General population 2013				
Evolution	Worry	0.096*	1.101	Higher worry and did not believe in evolution
Changing homosexuality	Security	−0.111†	0.895	Lower security and belief that homosexuality could be changed
General population 2014				
Helping needy	Security	−0.120†	0.887	Lower security and/or higher merger and belief that helping the needy is too expensive
	Merger	0.112†	1.119	
Blacks responsible	Avoidance	0.148*	1.159	Higher avoidance and belief that blacks are responsible for their condition
Government waste	Merger	0.214**	1.238	Higher merger and belief that government is wasteful
Obama's birthplace	Worry	0.165*	1.180	Higher worry and belief Obama was not born in USA
Common Core	Worry	0.193†	1.213	Higher worry and belief that Common Core is bad
Environment	Merger	0.174*	1.190	Higher merger and belief protection is too costly
Conservatives 2014				
Helping needy	Avoidance	0.302*	1.352	Higher avoidance and/or lower worry and belief that helping the needy is too expensive
	Worry	−0.234*	0.791	
Blacks responsible	Merger	0.174†	1.190	Higher merger and belief that blacks are responsible for their condition
Government waste	Worry	−0.155*	0.856	Lower worry and belief that government is wasteful
GMO belief-knowledge[b]	Worry	−0.198*	$d = -0.40$	Lower worry and more knowledgeable about scientific facts

†$p < 0.10$.
*$p < 0.05$.
**$p < 0.01$ (two-tailed).
[a]From logistic regressions in Tables 4 and 8.
[b]Measured as a continuous variable. Result is from the multiple regression in Table 6.

4

Work-family life balance in a Nigerian banking sector setting

Fabian O. Ugwu[1], Lawrence O. Amazue[2]* and Nneoma G. Onyedire[2]

*Corresponding author: Lawrence O. Amazue, Faculty of the Social Sciences, Department of Psychology, University of Nigeria, Nsukka, Nigeria

E-mails: Lawrence.amazue@unn.edu.ng, okwychimgift@yahoo.com

Reviewing editor: Justin Hackett, California University of Pennsylvania, USA

Abstract: This study examined work-family life in a Nigerian banking sector setting. One hundred and twenty-one (121) commercial bank employees from the North Central region of Nigeria were the participants (females = 37.5%; age range = 29–56 years). The employees completed measures of work life and work-interference with family conflict (WIFC). The results of the regression analyses showed that work organizational citizenship behaviour was a significant predictor of WIFC ($\beta = .46$, $p < .001$) and contributed 31% of the variance in WIFC. The result further revealed that work-role overload significantly predicted WIFC ($\beta = .33$, $p < .001$) and contributed 47% of the variance in work interference with family conflict. Job stress significantly predicted WIFC ($\beta = .36$, $p < .001$) and contributed 57% of the variance in WIFC. Based on the scarcity hypothesis, the findings of the study suggest that when employees invest resources in their jobs as a result of OCB, work overload and job stress, they tend to experience work-interference with their family lives due to fewer resources allocated to their family roles.

Subjects: Development Studies, Environment, Social Work, Urban Studies; Social Sciences; Behavioral Sciences

Keywords: organizational citizenship behaviour; role overload; job stress; work-interfering with family conflict

ABOUT THE AUTHORS

The authors of this paper have similar research interests and their research activities centre especially on positive organizational behaviour, extra role behaviour and work-family interface. This is evident in that our key publications revolve around these areas of research. Studies in these areas are still lacking and we have been concerned at looking more at the sunny side of organizational behaviour. We still see ourselves publishing in this area for many years to come. Organizational citizenship behaviour for instance, has been continuously linked to organizational effectiveness but not without a price on the employees. Family issues are usually sensitive in that what is going on in our families determine how effective employees may be in the work domain. However, the results of this study is significant in many respects particularly, its exposition that employees perception of excessive work pressures have dire consequences of destabilizing the family harmony in the form of engendering family conflict and this may be counterproductive for the industries.

PUBLIC INTEREST STATEMENT

This study examined work-family life in a Nigerian banking sector setting. One hundred and twenty-one bank employees participated in the study. The results of the regression analyses showed that employees that engage in organizational citizenship behavior (OCB) were more likely to experience work-interference with family conflict compared to those that do not engage in OCB. The results further revealed that employees with high perception of work role-overload were more likely to experience work-interference with family conflict compared to those with low perception of work role-overload. The results of the study equally showed that employees with high perception of job stress were more likely to experience work-interference with family conflict compared to those with low perception of job stress. The findings of the study suggest that when employees invest resources in their jobs they tend to experience work-interference with their family lives due to fewer resources allocated to their family roles.

1. Introduction

Work forms a significant fraction of most people's activities and is an important aspect of their lives (Ilies et al., 2007). Work has been described as the best form of welfare (Deacon, 1997; King & Wickham-Jones, 1999; Mead, 1997) and is the most efficient way to improve the well-being of individuals. However, most jobs are designed as if workers have no family responsibilities resulting in inter-role conflict. When an individual finds it difficult to balance work and family roles work-family conflict may arise (Greenhaus & Beutell, 1985). Work-family conflict is an important issue because it is an indicator for health, well-being, quality of life and duration of self-employment (Williams, 2004). For instance, role ambiguity, role overload, time demands and work centrality may hinder performance of family roles or deplete resources needed for participation in family activities. This study investigated work-to-family conflict (WFC), from the perspective of relationship resourcing in the Nigerian banking sector.

1.1. The Nigerian banking sector

The Nigerian banking sector has undergone a wide range of reforms in recent years leading to increased demands from customers and regulators with regard to the availability and quality of worker service delivery. These reforms were brought about by bank deregulations policy, unstable monetary policy, new competitive repositioning, innovation in communication and information processing resulting in a rapid change in Nigeria's business environment.

These changes have also affected banking work and may have increased the challenges of balancing work and family roles among bank workers. The Nigerian banking sector is noted for its long hour culture and high work loads of employees in the sector which seem to result in the neglect of other areas of life as spending enough time with one's family. This trend could have a negative influence on the individuals because Nigeria places some values on the family system. Thus, the failure of a family system is termed as a failure on the individual's part which tends to affect success of the individual (Ojo, Salau, & Falola, 2014).

The scarcity hypothesis (Edwards & Rothbard, 2000) proposes that individuals possess limited and fixed amounts of resources (e.g. time and energy). Managing multiple roles, such as engagement in in-role and extra-role behaviour, in employee and spouse interaction and involvement in domestic roles could deplete these scarce resources as these activities draw on them. In other words, when employees invest resources in jobs that are beyond their call of duty, perceive their workload to be more than they can handle or appraise the demand of their work as exceeding their resources, they are likely to experience interference from their work with their family lives due to fewer resources left to allocate to their family roles (Ng, Sorensen, & Feldman, 2007).

Long working hours, work time pressure and strict supervision characterizes work life in the Nigerian commercial banking sector. The organizational citizenship behaviours (OCBs) might increase customer satisfaction (Grant & Mayer, 2009) but they also may come at a cost to employees through more effort from increased work hours (e.g. Bond, Galinsky, & Swanberg, 1997; Hochschild, 1997). Majority of research evidence suggest that OCB is significantly related to work-family conflict (Bolino, Turnley, & Niehoff, 2004). However, a few other studies have indicated no significant relationship between OCB and work-interference with family conflict (WIFC) (Beham, 2010; Klein, 2007).

Research evidence also suggests that work-related variables such as role overload and job stress are significantly related to the experience of work-family conflict. Role overload results from too many responsibilities expected of employees with little time available to deliver on those expectations and are overwhelmed (Yip, Rowlinson, & Siu, 2008) and can lead to job stress or unpleasant work-related emotional experience that could time away from spousal and family responsibilities (Hochschild, 1997; Lingard & Francis, 2006).

Several studies (e.g. Michel, Kotrba, Mitchelson, Clark, & Baltes, 2011) have pointed to the importance of the characteristics of work domain as antecedents of work-family conflict, but majority of these studies have been conducted in Europe and America. Far less attention has been given to this area of research in the developing economies like Nigeria (Oludayo, Gberevbie, Popoola, & Omonijo, 2015). Besides, only a few studies have investigated work-family conflict in the banking industry in Nigeria (Adekola, 2010; Amazue & Onyishi, 2015; Ojo et al., 2014; Oludayo et al., 2015). Many of these studies investigate work-life balance and demonstrate that some demographics, coping strategies, work-life initiatives and work-life policies of organizations are related to employees' experience of work-life balance. However, Adekola's (2010) study with business executives in Nigeria is one of the few studies that attempts to relate job demand factors to WIFC and found that career salience, hours of work and work involvement were associated with work interference with family conflict.

In line with Ng et al. (2007), when employees invest resources in jobs that are beyond their call of duty, perceive their workload to be more than they can handle or appraise the demand of their work as exceeding their resources, they may likely experience WFC. The present study therefore attempts to advance the literature in this area of research by examining extra-role behaviours and the work life of Nigerian bank employees in relation to the scarcity of resources model.

1.2. Goal of the study

The present research sought to determine Nigerian bank employees' perceptions of influences of OCB, role overload and job stress on WIFC. The following research question guided the study: Would OCB, work-role overload and job stress significantly influence work interference with family conflict of Nigerian bank employees?

We hypothesized that:

OCB will significantly predict work interference with family conflict (H1).
Role overload will significantly predict work interference with family conflict (H2).
Job stress will significantly predict work interference with family conflict (H3).

2. Method

2.1. Sample

The sample for the study consisted of a convenience sample of 121 commercial bank employees from commercial banks in the North Central region of Nigeria (females = 37.5%; age range of 29 to 56 years) with a mean age of 43.5 years; with standard deviation of 5.98. Eighty-three (83) of the respondents were full time and senior staff, 23 of them were on contract appointment, and 15 were on managerial positions. The highest and lowest academic qualifications of the respondents were university masters' degree and Ordinary National Diploma. Their organizational tenure ranges from 3 to 7 years, with average tenure of 2.93 years, whereas their job tenure ranged from 1 to 5 years, with mean job tenure of 2.54 years.

2.2. Measures

Employees completed the Organizational Citizenship Behaviour Scale (OCBS: Lambert, Hogan, & Griffin, 2008) and the Role Overload scale (ROS: Bolino & Turnley, 2005), Job Stress Scale (JSS: Motowidlo, Packard, & Manning, 1986), and the Work-interfering with Family Conflict Scale (WIFC: Gutek, Searle, & Klepa, 1991). They also provided data on their demographics.

The OCBS is an 8-item scale to measure employees' engagement in extra role behaviour. A sample of self-report items on the scale include: "I frequently volunteer to do things without being asked". The peer report sample items include: "He/She frequently volunteers to do things without being asked". Responses are scored from 1 (*strongly disagree*) to 5 (*strongly agree*). The Cronbach's alpha for the self-report scale in the present study was .73 whereas the Cronbach's alpha for the peer report of the OCB scale was .77.

The ROS is a 3-item measure and includes items such as: "The amount of work I am expected to do is too great". The scale is scored on a 5-point Likert-type response (1 = *strongly disagree*; 5 = *strongly agree*). The Cronbach's alpha for the scale in the present study was .89.

The JSS is a 4-item measure. Sample items from the scale include: "My job is extremely stressful", "Very few stressful things happen to me at work" (reverse scored), "I feel a great deal of stress because of my job" and "I almost never feel stressed because of my work" (reverse-scored). Responses were made on a 5-point scale ranging from 1 = strongly disagree to 5 = strongly agree. The Scale's Cronbach's alpha for the present study was .84.

The WIFC comprised 4-items. Sample item of the scale is: "After work, I come home too tired to do some of the things I'd like to do". It is a 5-point Likert response format that ranged from 1 (*strongly disagree*) to 5 (*strongly agree*). Cronbach's alpha of the scale for the present study was .70.

2.3. Procedure

A total of 133 copies of the questionnaires were administered to the participants in their places of work. In all the banks visited for this study, the Operations Manager gave approval for the study and designated a staff to distribute and collect completed questionnaires. Participants consented to the study. They were informed of the goal of the study (research purpose) and also that participation was optional. The participants were promised anonymity and confidentiality of their responses and the data was analysed at aggregate level.

3. Data analysis

The data were controlled for the impact of demographic variables: Gender, Education, Job status, job tenure, organizational tenure, age, and number of children at home. The demographic variables were coded as follows: gender (male = 1, female = 2); education (high = 1, low = 2); job status (senior = 1, junior = 2); job tenure, organizational tenure, age (1 = below 40 years, 2 + 40 years and above), number of children (1 = none, 2 = at least 1).

Hierarchical multiple regression statistics was used to analyse the data. We entered all the control variables as a block in the first model. Secondly, the OCB self-report data were entered in model 2, followed by OCB peer-report. After this data on role overload were entered in the third model. Furthermore, data on job stress were entered in model 4 and finally we entered data on work-interfering with family conflict in model.

4. Results

Tables 1 and 2 present the descriptive statistics and inter-correlations among studied variables and Hierarchical regression results, respectively.

The results of the correlational analysis showed that level of education had a significant positive relationship with work interference with family conflict ($r = .17$, $p < .05$). Organizational tenure was negatively related to WIFC ($r = -.14$, $p < .05$). Age was also negatively related to WIFC ($r = -.14$, $p < .05$); younger bank employees reported higher scores on WIFC than older employees. Number of children was positively related to WIFC ($r = .18$, $p < .05$); employees who had many children reported higher scores on WIFC than those with fewer children. However, the following demographic variables (gender, job status and job tenure) were not shown to be related to WIFC. OCB as self reported by the employees was shown to be positively related to WIFC ($r = .49$, $p < .001$). Also OCB as reported

Table 1. Means (*M*), standard deviations (SD) and Pearson's correlations of control variables, OCB, role overload, job stress and WIFC

Variables	*M*	SD	1	2	3	4	5	6	7	8	9	10	11	12
1. WIFC	12.30	1.80	–											
2. Gender	1.60	.49	.09	–										
3. Education	1.65	.48	.17*	.53***	–									
4. Job status	1.34	.4	−.02	−.05	.16*	–								
5. Job tenure	2.54	1.25	−.08	−.04	−.10	−.07	–							
6. Organizational tenure	2.93	1.19	−.14*	−.04	−.16*	−.06	.86***	–						
7. Age	43.48	5.98	−.14*	.20**	.33***	.34***	−.20**	−.22**	–					
8. Number of children	2.61	1.16	.18*	.13	.04	.07	−.04	−.12	.48***	–				
9. OCB self-report	24.87	4.20	.49***	.08	.13	−.01	.15*	.12	−.06	−.06	–			
10. OCB peer report	23.83	3.37	.55***	.10	.14*	.01	.11	.13	−.10	−.07	.59***	–		
11. Role overload	10.71	1.33	.51***	.01	−.02	−.03	.04	.12	−.06	−.18*	.44***	.34***	–	
12. Job stress	11.71	2.04	.54***	.26**	−.32***	−.00	−.03	.01	.04	−.05	.20**	.29**	.27**	–

Notes: A total number of 121 commercial bank employees participated in the study. Gender (male = 1, female = 2); education (high = 1, low = 2); job status (senior = 1, junior = 2); job tenure, organizational tenure, age, number of children at home, OCB self-report, OCB peer report, role overload and job stress were coded such that higher scores indicated higher report of the behaviours.

$*p < .05$.

$**p < .01$.

$***p < .001$.

Table 2. Hierarchical multiple regression model of contributions of organizational citizenship behaviours, role overload and job stress to WIFC

Variables	Steps				
	1	2	3	4	5
Gender	.00	−.01	−.01	−.28**	−.06
Education	.25*	.18	.14	.20*	.08
Job status	.00	−.00	−.01	−.00	.01
Job tenure	−.19	−.28**	−.22	−.09	−.09
Organizational tenure	.30***	.32**	.25*	.13	.12
Age	−.16	−.12	−.08	−.09	−.11
Number of children	−.08	−.07	−.08	−.05	−.02
OCB self-report		.46***	.26**	.13	.15
OCB peer report			.36***	.32***	.25*
Role overload			.33***	.24**	.25*
Job stress				.35***	.36***
R^2	.05	.26	.34	.42	.53
$R^2\Delta$	.11	.31	.39	.47	.57
$F\Delta$	1.96	32.63	14.57	16.27	25.96
F Value	1.96	6.27	7.87	9.68	13.16

$*p < .05$.

$**p < .01$.

$***p < .001$.

by employees' peers was positively related to work interference with family conflict ($r = .55, p < .001$). Role overload was related to work interference with family conflict ($r = .51, p < .001$). Job stress was also related to work interference with family conflict ($r = .54, p < .001$).

The results of the hierarchical regression analyses revealed that all the control variables explained a significant 11% of the variance in WIFC. However, among all the control variables only education ($\beta = .25, p < .05$) and organizational tenure ($\beta = .30, p < .001$) predicted WIFC. Gender, job status, job tenure, age and number of children were not predictors of work interference with family conflict.

OCB explained 31% of the variance in WIFC over and above the control variables. In the regression equation, OCB positively predicted WIFC ($\beta = .46$, $p < .001$), which is consistent with H1 in that OCB will significantly predict WIFC.

Role overload explained 47% of the variance in WIFC. In the regression equation, role overload positively predicted WIFC ($\beta = .33$, $p < .001$), which is consistent with H2 that role overload will significantly predict WIFC.

The result also revealed that job stress explained 57% of the variance in WIFC over and above role overload F change (1, 109) = 25.96, $p < .001$). In the regression equation, job stress positively predicted WIFC ($\beta = .36$, $p < .001$), which is consistent with H3 that job stress will significantly predict WIFC.

5. Discussion

As expected OCB predicted WIFC. The result of the current study indicated that bank employees who invest resources in their jobs beyond their call of duty are more likely to experience WIFC than those who do not invest much resource. This result is consistent with previous studies (e.g. Bolino & Turnley, 2005; Halbesleben, Harvey, & Bolino, 2009) that found OCBs to be associated with higher levels of work interference with family. This result could be explained with the scarcity hypothesis which suggests that as employees expend a great deal of energy on behalf of their organizations, they are likely to run short of energy to commit to their spousal and family responsibilities (Hochschild, 1997). This finding is however inconsistent with some earlier studies that found no significant relationship between OCB and WIFC (e.g. Beham, 2010; Klein, 2007). These authors for instance, studied American and European samples in a university context and various industries that have different work culture from Nigerian bank employees who are involved in wide variety of extra-role behaviours in their workplace to earn their supervisors'/management recommendations. The present finding thus suggests that, although organizations benefit when their employees willingly contribute to the organization above and beyond the definition of their job requirements (OCB), such employees suffer loss of energy resource for allocation to family responsibilities and hence experience WIFC.

The perception of work-role overload predicted WIFC. This result supported the hypothesis that perceived work role overload will significantly predict work interference with family conflict (H2). The result is in agreement with Lingard and Francis (2006) who found that employees that perceive their workload as more than they can cope successfully, experienced greater work-family conflict than those who perceive lesser workload (see also Byron, 2005; Greenglass, Burke, & Moore, 2003). Again, this finding could be explained from the scarcity hypothesis point of view which suggests that individuals who perceive their work load to be more than they can handle are likely to experience exhaustion and fatigue, which may negatively influence the individual's energy and motivation to respond to the demands of the family domain.

Job stress was significantly related to work-family conflict. This result supports our hypothesis that job stress will significantly predict work interference with family conflict. The result seems to be in line with some earlier studies (e.g. Allen, Herst, Bruck, & Sutton, 2000; Byron, 2005; Noor, 2002) which in their separate studies demonstrated that job stress is significantly related to WIFC. Stress places huge emotional and physical demands on individual employees and in the process saps many energy resources meant to cope with family responsibilities and hence leading to the experience of work-family conflict. Among the study variables, job stress seems to have contributed the highest percentage (57%) to the variance in the WIFC, suggesting that bank employees who experience job stress seem to be more emotionally drained and hence experience greater conflict between work and family roles.

5.1. Strengths and limitations of the study

The findings of the present study indicate that to understand work interference with family better attention should be paid to work demand variables. Such work pressures as experienced in OCB, work-role overload and job stress may explain why Nigerian bank employees experience work interference with their family roles. While recent research in Nigeria has found relationship between coping strategies, organizational work-life policies and initiatives and work-life balance, the present results indicate that work OCB, work-role overload and job stress could lead to squandering of personal resources and hence experience of WIFC. The present study, however, has some limitations. First, the sample focused on commercial bank employees thus the findings may not represent employees from other sectors of the economy. Extending this study to other sectors of Nigerian economy and increasing the sample size in future studies is recommended. Another limitation of the study is that the data were collected at one point in time making it difficult to establish causal relationships. Longitudinal studies are needed to replicate the findings reported here.

In addition, work demand variables as examined in this study seem to drain employees' resources but may vary between individuals. Thus, future studies should consider individual differences as additional factors, by examining whether personality factors such as self-efficacy, self-esteem and big five may moderate the relationship between OCB, work-role overload, job stress and WIFC.

6. Conclusion

The findings of the present study indicate that OCB, role overload and job stress are strong predictors of WIFC. In line with previous studies, the present findings suggest that Nigerian bank employees who engage in extra role behaviours (e.g. OCB) may likely experience WIFC. In addition, the findings indicate that bank employees who perceive their job roles as beyond their capacities and more than they can handle may likely experience WIFC. Finally, the present findings suggest that bank employees who may be stressed as a result of work pressures that are beyond their capabilities and resources for meeting them may likely experience WIFC. Although, studies have pointed to several work-related antecedents of WFC, very few of such studies have explored OCB, work-role overload and job stress in a developing economy like Nigeria. It is therefore, hoped that the present research findings will not only validate these earlier studies in the developed countries of America and Europe, but also be useful to human resource management in the Nigerian banking industry. It is concluded that Nigerian bank organizations should initiate policies that will enable employees to spend moderate resources (energy and time) on their work, bearing in mind that when greater resources are invested in one role it tends to have negative impact on the employee by reducing his/her ability to attend to the other role. This in turn will enhance employees' chances of balancing work and family responsibilities.

Funding
The authors received no direct funding for this research.

Competing Interests
The authors declare no competing interest.

Author details
Fabian O. Ugwu[1]
E-mail: fabian.ugwu@gmail.com
Lawrence O. Amazue[2]
E-mails: Lawrence.amazue@unn.edu.ng, okwychimgift@yahoo.com
Nneoma G. Onyedire[2]
E-mail: nneoma.obi@unn.edu.ng
[1] Department of Psychology, Federal University Ndufu-Alike, Ikwo Nigeria, Abakiliki, Nigeria.
[2] Faculty of the Social Sciences, Department of Psychology, University of Nigeria, Nsukka, Nigeria.

References

Adekola, B. (2010). Interference between work and family among male and female executives in Nigeria. *African Journal of Business Management, 4*, 1069–1077.

Allen, T. D., Herst, D. E. L., Bruck, C., & Sutton, M. (2000). Consequences associated with work-to-family conflict: A review and agenda for future research. *Journal of Occupational Health Psychology, 5*, 278–308. http://dx.doi.org/10.1037/1076-8998.5.2.278

Amazue, L. O., & Onyishi, I. E. (2015). Stress coping strategies, perceived organization support and marital status as predictors of work-life balance among Nigerian bank employees. *Social Indicators Research*. doi:10.1007/s11205-015-1023-5

Beham, B. (2010). Work-family conflict and organizational citizenship behaviour: Empirical evidence from Spanish employees. *Community, Work and Family, 14*, 63–80.

Bolino, M. C., & Turnley, W. H. (2005). The personal costs of citizenship behavior: The relationship between individual initiative and role overload, job stress, and work-family conflict. *Journal of Applied Psychology, 90*, 740–748. http://dx.doi.org/10.1037/0021-9010.90.4.740

Bolino, M. C., Turnley, W. H., & Niehoff, B. P. (2004). The other side of the story: Reexamining prevailing assumptions about organizational citizenship behavior. *Human Resource Management Review, 14*, 229–246.

Bond, J. T., Galinsky, E., & Swanberg, J. E. (1997). *The 1997 national study of the changing workforce* (Vol. 2). New York, NY: Families and Work Institute.

Byron, K. (2005). A meta-analytic review of work-family conflict and its antecedents. *Journal of Vocational Behavior, 67*, 169–198. http://dx.doi.org/10.1016/j.jvb.2004.08.009

Deacon, A. (1997). *From welfare to work: Lessons from America.* London: Institute of Economic Affairs, Health & Welfare Unit.

Edwards, J. R., & Rothbard, N. P. (2000). Mechanisms linking work and family: Clarifying the relationship between work and family constructs. *Academy of Management Review, 25*, 178–199.

Grant, A. M., & Mayer, D. M. (2009). Good soldiers and good actors: Prosocial and impression management motives as interactive predictors of affiliative citizenship behaviors. *Journal of Applied Psychology, 94*, 900–912. http://dx.doi.org/10.1037/a0013770

Greenglass, E. R., Burke, R. J., & Moore, K. A. (2003). Reactions to increased workload: Effects on professional efficacy of nurses. *Applied Psychology, 52*, 580–597. http://dx.doi.org/10.1111/apps.2003.52.issue-4

Greenhaus, J. H., & Beutell, N. J. (1985). Sources of conflict between work and family roles. *Academy of Management Review, 10*, 76–88.

Gutek, B. A., Searle, S., & Klepa, L. (1991). Rational versus gender role explanations for work-family conflict. *Journal of Applied Psychology, 76*, 560–568. http://dx.doi.org/10.1037/0021-9010.76.4.560

Halbesleben, J. R. B., Harvey, J., & Bolino, M. C. (2009). Too engaged? A conservation of resources view of the relationship between work engagement and work interference with family. *Journal of Applied Psychology, 94*, 1452–1465. http://dx.doi.org/10.1037/a0017595

Hochschild, A. R. (1997). *The time bind: When work becomes home and home becomes work.* New York, NY: Metropolitan.

Ilies, R., Schwind, K., Wagner, D. T., Johnson, M. D., DeRue, D. S., & Ilgen, D. R. (2007). When can employees have a family life? The effects of daily workload and affect on work-family conflict and social behaviors at home. *Journal of Applied Psychology, 92*, 1368–1379. http://dx.doi.org/10.1037/0021-9010.92.5.1368

King, D., & Wickham-Jones, M. (1999). From Clinton to Blair: The democratic (party) origins of welfare to work. *The Political Quarterly, 70*, 62–74. http://dx.doi.org/10.1111/poqu.1999.70.issue-1

Klein, R. H. (2007). *The "dark side" of OCB: Examining the relationship between citizenship behaviour and work-to-family conflict* (Graduate Theses and Dissertations). Retrieved from http://scholarcommons.usf.edu/etd/2247

Lambert, E. G., Hogan, N. L., & Griffin, M. L. (2008). Being the good soldier. *Criminal Justice and Behavior, 35*, 56–68. http://dx.doi.org/10.1177/0093854807308853

Lingard, H., & Francis, V. (2006). Does a supportive work environment moderate the relationship between work-family conflict and burnout among construction professionals? *Construction Management and Economics, 24*, 185–196. http://dx.doi.org/10.1080/14697010500226913

Mead, L. M. (1997). *The new paternalism: Supervisory approaches to poverty.* Washington DC: Brookings Institute Press.

Michel, J. S., Kotrba, L. M., Mitchelson, J. K., Clark, M. A., & Baltes, B. B. (2011). Antecedents of work–family conflict: A meta-analytic review. *Journal of Organizational Behavior, 32*, 689–725. doi:10.1002/job.695

Motowidlo, S. J., Packard, J. S., & Manning, M. R. (1986). Occupational stress: Its causes and consequences for job performance. *Journal of Applied Psychology, 71*, 618–629. http://dx.doi.org/10.1037/0021-9010.71.4.618

Ng, T. W., Sorensen, K. L., & Feldman, D. C. (2007). Dimensions, antecedents, and consequences of workaholism: A conceptual integration and extension. *Journal of Organizational Behavior, 28*, 111–136. http://dx.doi.org/10.1002/(ISSN)1099-1379

Noor, N. M. (2002). Work-family conflict, locus of control, and women's weil-being: Tests of alternative pathways. *The Journal of Social Psychology, 142*, 645–662. http://dx.doi.org/10.1080/00224540209603924

Ojo, I. S., Salau, O. P., & Falola, H. O. (2014). Work-life balance practices in Nigeria: A comparison of three sectors. *Journal of Competitiveness, 6*, 3–14. http://dx.doi.org/10.7441/joc

Oludayo, O. A., Gberevbie, D. E., Popoola, D., & Omonijo, D. O. (2015). A study of multiple work-life initiatives in banking industry in Nigeria. *International Research Journal of Finance and Economics, 133*, 108–125.

Williams, D. R. (2004). Effects of childcare activities on the duration of self-employment in Europe. *Entrepreneurship Theory and Practice, 28*, 467–485. http://dx.doi.org/10.1111/etap.2004.28.issue-5

Yip, B., Rowlinson, S., & Siu, O. L. (2008). Coping strategies as moderators in the relationship between role overload and burnout. *Construction Management and Economics, 26*, 869–880.

5

Predictors of sexual abstinence: A prospective study of college women in the United States

Hazel Spears[1,2]*, John B. Jemmott III[1,3] and G. Anita Heeren[4]

*Corresponding author: Hazel Spears, Center for Health Behavior and Communication Research, Annenberg School for Communication, University of Pennsylvania, 3901 Walnut Street Suite 503, Philadelphia, PA 19104, USA; Department of Social and Behavioral Sciences, Cheyney University of Pennsylvania, Cheyney, PA, USA
Email: dr.hazel.spears@gmail.com
Reviewing editor: Ross Wilkinson, University of Newcastle, Australia

Abstract: *Purpose*: Using the theory of reasoned action (TRA), this research examined predictors of sexual intercourse among first- and second-year college women. *Methods*: Participants completed a confidential self-administered questionnaire on their attitude, subjective norm, and intention regarding sexual intercourse and their behavioral beliefs about the consequences of abstinence and sexual intercourse. *Results*: At baseline, 58 (34%) of the 172 participants (mean age = 18.2; SD = 0.56) reported ever having sexual intercourse, and 41 (24%) reported having sexual intercourse within the last three months. Proportional-odds analysis on baseline data revealed that attitude and subjective norm were associated with a greater intention to have intercourse, as was relationship status (i.e. being in a relationship), a variable external to the TRA. Three-month follow-up questionnaires were completed by 165 (96%) of the participants. Logistic regression indicated that baseline intention and relationship status predicted self-reported sexual intercourse three months later. Examination of the relation of behavioral beliefs to attitude revealed that beliefs about the positive consequences of abstinence were associated with a negative attitude toward intercourse, whereas beliefs about the negative consequences of intercourse were unrelated to attitude toward intercourse. Being in a relationship and alcohol use were also related to positive attitude toward intercourse. *Conclusions*: These results suggest that, for college women, the TRA is a useful model of sexual

ABOUT THE AUTHORS

How messages move people has been a focus of Dr Spears teaching and research interests, whether in the acceptance of disabled others, minority pursuit of higher education, or adoption of a healthful lifestyle. Her co-authors are long-time researchers in the area of interventions to reduce sexual risk behaviors among young people both in the United States and in South Africa. Given the rise of STIs on college campuses, closed communities that can foster the spread of illnesses, they are an ideal setting for the dissemination of health behavior messages. Accordingly, the identification and design of effective behavior change interventions for young people, including college students, remain the motivation and goals of these researchers.

PUBLIC INTEREST STATEMENT

Annually, 10 million new sexually transmitted infections (STIs) occur among college-aged youth (15-24 year olds). Consider too that almost half of college students think they can tell if a person has an STI just by looking at them, and it is clear that sexual health among college women is deserving of attention and intervention. This study found that as many as two-thirds of young women entering college are not yet sexually active, which indicates that they may be receptive to messages about abstinence. The study also found that, over time, it is not beliefs about the negative consequences of sexual engagement that influences women's behavior, but beliefs about the benefits of abstinence. The important implication is that focusing on the positive side of abstaining from sex could prove a useful tool for college health centers to employ in their continuing quest to keep their charges safe and healthy.

behavior and that abstinence interventions may be a viable risk-reduction approach if the abstinence message is framed to emphasize the positive consequences of abstinence rather than the negative consequences of sexual intercourse.

Subject: Behavioral Sciences

Keywords: sexual abstinence; college women; human immunodeficiency virus; sexually transmitted diseases; sexual intercourse; risk-reduction; theory of reasoned action

1. Introduction

HIV and other sexually transmitted diseases (STD) are a major health threat for adolescents and young adults in the US. Among developed countries, US teenagers have the highest STD rates (Panchaud, Singh, Feivelson, & Darroch, 2000). Over half of the STDs in the US occur among people 15–24 years of age (Centers for Disease Control & Prevention, 2013a), and one-fifth of all new HIV infections occur in this same age group (Centers for Disease Control & Prevention, 2013b). The risk of HIV/STD is tied to unprotected sexual intercourse. Two strategies can be used to reduce unprotected sexual intercourse: condom use and abstinence (Jemmott, Jemmott, & Fong, 1998). Interventions can utilize either of these strategies exclusively or can use both to varying degrees. The sexual risk-reduction intervention literature reveals two dominant approaches: interventions focused on abstinence-only and interventions focused on both abstinence and condom use, which are called comprehensive interventions (Zhang, Jemmott, & Jemmott, 2015).

Considerable research has been conducted on condom use, and several successful theory-based comprehensive interventions to increase condom use have been identified (DiClemente et al., 2004; Heeren, Jemmott, Ngwane, Mandeya, & Tyler, 2013; Jemmott, Jemmott, Fong, & Morales, 2010). In contrast, little is known about abstinence, and few successful abstinence intervention studies have been published (Chin et al., 2012; Jemmott et al., 1998; Jemmott, Jemmott, & Fong, 2010; Sather & Zinn, 2002; Thomas, 2000; Tortolero et al., 2010). In the recent past, governmental policy focused on funding "abstinence-only until marriage" sex education. However, identifying the factors that predict sexual involvement can provide important information for designing more effective safer-sex and abstinence interventions (Santelli et al., 2006).

By senior year in high school, approximately 57.2% of adolescent girls in the US have had sexual intercourse (Kann et al., 2016). Among college women aged 18–24, almost 67% become sexually experienced during their college years (March & Serdar Atav, 2010). Some of the demographic factors associated with being sexually active are prior sexual experience, being older, being Black, lower income, lower parental education, poorer academic performance, and general tendency to participate in high risk behaviors, including cigarette smoking, drug use, and alcohol use (Aten, Siegel, Enaharo, & Auinger, 2002; Goodson, Evans, & Edmundson, 1997; Kohler, Manhart, & Lafferty, 2008; McCave, Azulay Chertok, Winter, & Haile, 2013; Raine et al., 1999). Some of the modifiable factors related to sexual involvement are attitude, subjective norm, and the behavioral and normative beliefs that form those attitudes and subjective norms (Goodson et al., 1997; Jemmott, 2012).

Studies of sexual abstinence interventions have been hampered by lack of long-term follow-up (Christopher & Roosa, 1990), lack of any follow-up (Goodson et al., 1997), lack of power due to small samples (Jorgensen, Potts, & Camp, 1993) or too few participants initiating sexual activity (Thomas, 2000), high attrition rates (Christopher & Roosa, 1990), and lack of a theoretical framework (Thomas, 2000).

In an effort to address some past limitations, the research presented here is a prospective, theory-based study. This study examines sexual abstinence among college women. We considered two themes regarding abstinence: (1) abstinence is good, or (2) sex outside of marriage is bad (Kempner, Amberg, & Bracksmajer, 2000), two divergent orientations, one emphasizing the positive aspects of abstinence, the other the negative aspects of unmarried sex. Programs to promote abstinence could use either or both of these themes (Zhang et al., 2015). For instance, Department of Health and Human Services guidelines for abstinence-until-marriage education programs funded under Title V Section 510 of the Social Security Act include "teaching the social, psychological, and health gains to be realized by abstaining from sexual activity," and that "sexual activity outside of the context of marriage is likely to have harmful psychological and physical effects" (Title V Section 510 of the Social Security Act, n.d.). Research on framing of health message appeals (Detweiler, Bedell, Salovey, Pronin, & Rothman, 1999; Garcia-Retamero & Cokely, 2013; Rothman & Salovey, 1997) suggests that although negative framing works well for predicting diagnostic behavior (e.g. breast self exams), positive framing will more effectively predict preventative behavior, such as condom use or abstinence. Using the findings from message framing research, one would predict that positive messages would be more effective in convincing young women to remain abstinent.

2. Theoretical framework

This research was guided by the theory of reasoned action (TRA) (Ajzen & Fishbein, 1980; Fishbein & Ajzen, 1975). According to this theory, specific behavioral intentions are the determinants of behaviors, and intentions are determined by attitudes and subjective norms regarding the behavior. Thus, for example, women will intend to practice abstinence when they evaluate that behavior positively and believe significant others think they should practice abstinence. A valuable feature of the TRA is that it directs attention to the basis of people's attitudes and subjective norms. Attitudes toward behavior are seen as reflecting behavioral beliefs about the consequences of performing the behavior. Subjective norms are seen as reflecting normative beliefs about whether specific reference persons or groups would approve or disapprove of the behavior.

In the case of sexual intercourse, perhaps the most widespread behavioral beliefs are that sexual intercourse increases the risk of pregnancy and HIV infection. Other key considerations are beliefs about the social consequences of sexual activity, such as the impact on educational or career goals, self-respect, and parental respect if one engages in sexual intercourse. Important referents for young women's normative beliefs include romantic partners, parents, and friends (DiClemente et al., 2001; Meston & Ahrold, 2010).

The TRA predicts that attitudes and subjective norms have independent and direct effects on intentions and that intentions predict subsequent behavior. We examined the TRA as a model of sexual abstinence in college women collecting data on two occasions three months apart to test these predictions using a prospective design. In addition, we examined whether beliefs about the positive consequences of sexual abstinence and beliefs about the negative consequences of sexual intercourse were associated with attitudes toward sexual intercourse.

3. Methods

3.1. Participants

Participants were female undergraduates recruited for a study of STD prevention, sexual health, alcohol use, nutrition, and exercise among college women. Participants received $20 for completing the baseline questionnaire and $20 for completing the follow-up questionnaire 3 months later.

3.2. Procedure

The Institutional Review Board of the University of Pennsylvania approved the study. Written informed consent was required to participate. Based on information from participants in focus groups, a questionnaire was designed to measure college women's sexual behavior, marijuana use, alcohol consumption, and attitudes and beliefs about such behavior. All first- and second-year women on a list of undergraduates supplied by the registrar's office were sent, via campus mail, a letter inviting them to participate in a study concerning drinking, dating, exercise, and nutrition behavior among college women. This procedure was done to enhance the representativeness of the sample, by giving all members of the target population a chance to participate, as opposed to recruiting from dining halls, sororities, or limited enclaves. Potential participants were invited to attend a data-collection session to complete the baseline questionnaire sessions and to return three months to complete the follow-up questionnaire.

We took several steps to increase the validity of self-reported behavior. To reduce potential memory problems, we asked participants to report their behaviors over a three-month period (and wrote the dates bracketing that period on the whiteboard in the questionnaire-administration room). Before completing the questionnaire, the participants signed a "survey agreement" form that emphasized the importance of responding honestly, a procedure that has been shown to yield more valid self-reports on sensitive issues (Shu, Mazar, Gino, Ariely, & Bazerman, 2012) and served to reduce socially desirable responding. This form let participants know that their responses would be used to develop programs for other undergraduate women and that the programs would be successful only if they answered the questions truthfully. In this sense, we attempted to arouse the "social responsibility motive" to counteract any possible social desirability motive. Participants were also assured that their responses were confidential and that code numbers rather than names would be used on the questionnaires.

3.3. Measures

The questionnaire included measures of basic demographic information, sexual attitudes, self-reported sexual behavior, relationship status, and alcohol and drug use. Tendency to engage in socially desirable responding was measured using the Marlowe–Crowne Social Desirability Scale (Crowne & Marlow, 1964).

3.3.1. Self-reported sexual intercourse

Participants were asked whether they had sex in the past 3 months, with sex defined as "a man's penis inserted into your vagina."

3.3.2. Intention to have sexual intercourse

Respondents were asked, on a 5-point scale ranging from 1 (*very unlikely*) to 5 (*very likely*), "How likely is it that you will decide to have sex in the next 3 months?" In a randomized controlled trial, an abstinence-based intervention reduced scores on this single-item measure of intention compared with the control group, whereas an intervention emphasizing condom use did not (Jemmott et al., 1998).

3.3.3. Attitude toward and behavioral beliefs about having sexual intercourse

Attitude toward having sex was measured by asking "How do you feel about having sex in the next 3 months?" which participants rated on 5-point scales ranging from 1 (*very bad idea*) to 5 (*very good idea*). In a randomized controlled trial, an abstinence-based intervention reduced scores on this single-item measure of attitude compared with the control group, whereas an intervention emphasizing condom use did not (Jemmott et al., 1998) To measure behavioral beliefs toward having sex, participants responded to items on scales ranging from 1 (*disagree strongly*) to 5 (*agree strongly*). Behavioral beliefs about the positive consequences of sexual abstinence ($\alpha = 0.90$) were assessed by asking participants whether they thought that not having sex would help them focus on their education, maintain their emotional health, increase their chances of having a good marriage, be proud of themselves, and maintain their parents' respect. Behavioral beliefs about the negative consequences of having sex ($\alpha = 0.81$) were assessed by asking participants whether they thought having sex would result in failing to graduate from college, failing to have the career they desired, getting pregnant, or getting infected with the HIV.

3.3.4. Subjective norms regarding sexual intercourse

Subjective norms regarding sexual intercourse ($\alpha = 0.79$) were assessed using four items concerning participants' ratings of how much their sexual partner, friends, mother, and father "would approve of your having sex in the next 3 months?" The ratings were made on 5-point scales ranging from 1 (disapprove strongly) to 5 (approve strongly).

3.3.5. Substance use

Alcohol use was assessed by asking, "In the past 30 days, on how many days did you drink alcohol?" Marijuana use was assessed by asking, "In the past 30 days, on how many days did you use marijuana?"

3.4. Statistical analysis

Chi square and t-tests were performed to analyze attrition. Zero-order correlations were computed using Pearson product-moment correlation coefficients for the continuous variables, and point-biserial correlation coefficients for the dichotomous variables. Two dummy variables were created to represent race/ethnicity with White as the default. One dummy variable was coded 1 if the person was Asian, and 0 for all others. The second dummy variable was coded 1 if the person was African-American, Latina, or Native American, and 0 for all others. Relationship status was coded so that 1 = no steady relationship, 2 = steady relationship. To test the predictions of the TRA hierarchical proportional-odds analysis was used. The first step focused on the predictors of intention, an ordinal variable, and included attitude and subjective norm. In the second step, relevant external variables were added to the model to determine if they had direct effects on intention, behavior, or attitudes. Logistic regression was used to examine whether intention predicted the dichotomous variable of self-reported sexual intercourse in the past 3 months.

4. Results

A total of 1,390 letters were mailed inviting undergraduate women to participate, and 172 women completed the baseline questionnaire. They ranged in age from 16 to 20 years (mean = 18.2; SD = 0.56). About 56% were White, 24% were Asian, 8% were African-American, and 5% were Latina. Approximately 83% reported that their mother and 88% reported that their father had a 4-year college degree or more education. Fifty-eight participants (34%) reported ever having coitus, and 41 (24%) reported having coitus in the previous three months. Fifty-eight participants (34%) reported being in a steady relationship (median length = 9 months). Only one student reported having more than one partner, and none reported having intercourse with a person of their own gender or with both genders.

4.1. Attrition/missing data analyses

There were no missing data at baseline on any of the study variables of interest with the exception of one participant who did not indicate whether she had sexual intercourse in the past 3 months at baseline. Of the 172 participants, 165 (96%) completed the three-month follow-up questionnaire. None of the 165 who returned had any missing data. No differences were found on any of the theoretical or external variables of interest, sexual experience, or recent coitus at baseline between those who attended the follow-up, as compared with those who did not.

4.2. Correlations among variables of interest

Table 1 presents zero-order correlations among key variables examined. It can be seen that intention to have sex is positively correlated with the TRA constructs, attitude, and subjective norm. Negatively correlated with intention are two other variables the TRA encompasses, abstinence behavioral beliefs (beliefs about positive consequences of abstinence), and coitus behavioral beliefs (beliefs about the negative consequences of sex). Relationship status, alcohol use, and marijuana use also emerge as being significantly and positively correlated to intention.

4.3. Proportional-odds analyses testing the TRA on the prediction of intention

The TRA states that attitudes and subjective norms affect intention, and any effect of external variables will be mediated through attitudes and subjective norms. In step one in Table 2 of the analyses, intention was regressed on attitude and subjective norm regarding sexual intercourse, all measured at baseline. Both attitude (OR = 8.75; 95% CI = 5.40, 14.17; $p < 0.0001$), and subjective norm (OR = 2.22; 95% CI = 1.26, 3.91; $p < 0.0056$) were significantly related to intention. Women expressing more favorable attitudes toward having sex and perceiving more normative support for

Table 1. Means, standard deviations (SD), and correlations among analysis variables

Variable	1	2	3	4	5	6	7	8	9	10	Mean	SD
1. 3-month follow-up coitus	–										1.27	0.45
2. Intention	0.76****	–									2.41	1.43
3. Attitude	0.61****	0.85****	–								2.63	1.32
4. Subjective norm	0.44****	0.66****	0.70****	–							2.44	0.82
5. Abs behavioral beliefs	−0.40****	−0.64****	−0.73****	−0.76****	–						3.02	1.08
6. Coitus behavioral beliefs	−0.29****	−0.42****	−0.49****	−0.50****	0.63****	–					1.99	0.72
7. Relationship status	0.57****	0.54****	0.39****	0.32****	−0.19**	−0.18*	–				1.34	0.47
8. Alcohol use	0.27***	0.35****	0.43****	0.34****	−0.43****	−0.40****	−0.00	–			4.07	3.62
9. Marijuana use	0.20**	0.18*	0.17*	0.20**	−0.21**	−0.22**	0.02	0.32****	–		0.55	1.48
10. Asian	−0.14	−0.17*	−0.18*	−0.35****	0.28***	0.29***	−0.08	−0.25***	−0.17*	–	0.24	0.43
11. Other minority	0.13	0.05	−0.00	0.00	0.12	−0.01	0.11	−0.01	−0.06	−0.28***	0.20	0.40

Notes: Abs behavioral beliefs = beliefs about the positive consequences of sexual abstinence. Coitus behavioral beliefs = beliefs about the negative consequences of sexual intercourse. Relationship status is coded "2" if the person has a steady boyfriend and "1" if the person does not have a steady boyfriend. Alcohol use is sum of the self-reported number of days on which they consumed alcohol in the past 30 days. Marijuana use is sum of the self-reported number of days on which they consumed marijuana in the past 30 days. Asian is a dummy variable where 1 = Asian and 0 = not Asian. Other minority is a dummy variable where 1 = Black, Latina, or Native American and 0 = White or Asian.

*$p < 0.05$.

**$p < 0.01$.

***$p < 0.001$.

****$p < 0.0001$.

Table 2. Hierarchical proportional-odds analysis of predictors of baseline intention to have sexual intercourse ($n = 172$)

Predictors	Step 1: Theory of reasoned action		Step 2: Adding external variables	
	OR (95% CI)	*p*-value	OR (95% CI)	*p*-value
Attitude	8.75 (5.40, 14.17)	<0.0001	8.84 (5.24, 14.92)	<0.0001
Subjective norm	2.22 (1.26, 3.91)	0.0056	2.10 (1.13, 3.85)	0.0174
Relationship status	–		6.21 (2.84, 13.56)	<0.0001
Alcohol use	–		1.02 (0.92, 1.14)	0.6493
Marijuana use	–		1.13 (0.91, 1.40)	0.2614
Asian	–		1.21 (0.49, 3.03)	0.6809
Other minority	–		1.36 (0.52, 3.55)	0.5317

Notes: Relationship status is coded "2" if the person has a steady boyfriend and "1" if the person does not have a steady boyfriend. Alcohol use is sum of the self-reported number of days on which they consumed alcohol in the past 30 days. Marijuana use is sum of the self-reported number of days on which they consumed marijuana in the past 30 days. Asian is a dummy variable where 1 = Asian and 0 = not Asian. Other minority is a dummy variable where 1 = Black, Latina, or Native American and 0 = White or Asian.

engaging in sex, express stronger intentions to have sex within the next 3 months than do those holding less favorable attitudes toward having sex or perceiving less favorable normative support.

As shown in Table 1, several external variables were strongly correlated with intention and behavior. Their direct effects were examined in a second step of the proportional-odds analysis. External variables, including relationship status, frequency of alcohol use, frequency of marijuana use, and race/ethnicity were added to the model containing attitude and subjective norm. Only relationship status (OR = 6.21; 95% CI = 2.84, 13.56; $p < 0.0001$) appears to have a direct effect on intention to have sex.

4.4. Logistic regression analyses testing the TRA on the prediction of behavior

Predictors of intercourse were examined, first by examining the effect of intention to have sex on self-reported sexual intercourse at 3-month follow-up, and then by adding the TRA and external variables.

In step 1 in Table 3, self-reported sex at 3-month follow-up was regressed on baseline intention to have sex. This revealed that women who had stronger intentions to have sexual intercourse at baseline were more likely to report having sexual intercourse at 3-month follow-up (OR = 5.71; CI = 3.45, 9.45; $p < 0.0001$), than were those with less strong intentions. In step 2, attitude and subjective norm measured at baseline, as well as the external variables of relationship status, alcohol use, marijuana use, and the race dummy variables were added to the model. The coefficients for attitude and subjective norm were not significant, indicating they did not have direct effects on behavior. Only relationship status was a significant predictor of having sexual intercourse in the 3 months preceding follow-up, (OR = 8.42; CI = 2.08, 33.99; $p < 0.0028$). Therefore, the 2-step hierarchical analysis suggests that intention to have sex and being in a relationship have direct effects on having sexual intercourse three months later.

4.5. Proportional-odds analyses examining the effect of behavioral beliefs on attitude

Additional analyses were performed to identify specific behavioral beliefs that predicted attitude because attitude predicted intention, consistent with the TRA. To examine the effects of specific behavioral beliefs on attitude, attitude toward sex at baseline was regressed on the two types of behavioral beliefs about sex. As shown in step 1 in Table 4, women who hold stronger behavioral beliefs about the positive consequences of abstinence have a more negative attitude toward sexual intercourse (OR = 0.17; CI = 0.11, 0.27; $p < 0.0001$) than do women who hold less favorable abstinence beliefs. In contrast, behavioral beliefs about the negative consequences of engaging in sexual intercourse were not related to attitude toward sex.

Step 2 of the analysis examined whether external variables had direct effects on attitude toward sex. As shown in Table 4, relationship status (OR = 5.35; CI = 2.74, 10.45; $p < 0.0001$, and alcohol use (OR = 1.15; CI = 1.04, 1.26; $p < 0.0044$,) are significant predictors of attitude toward sex. Using alcohol and having a steady boyfriend were related to having a favorable attitude toward sex.

Table 3. Hierarchical logistic regression analysis of self-reported coitus at 3-month follow-up (*n* = 165)

	Step 1: Intention		Step 2: Adding TRA variables and external variables	
Predictors	**OR (95% CI)**	***p*-value**	**OR (95% CI)**	***p*-value**
Intention	5.71 (3.45, 9.45)	<0.0001	4.54 (1.84, 11.24)	0.0011
Attitude	-		1.13 (0.42, 3.07)	0.8040
Subjective norm	-		0.62 (0.21, 1.82)	0.3879
Relationship status	-		8.42 (2.08, 33.99)	0.0028
Alcohol use	-		1.13 (0.95, 1.36)	0.1668
Marijuana use	-		1.23 (0.94, 1.61)	0.1256
Asian race	-		0.91 (0.16, 5.23)	0.9150
Other race	-		1.85 (0.39, 8.78)	0.4387

Notes: Relationship status is coded "2" if the person has a steady boyfriend and "1" if the person does not have a steady boyfriend. Alcohol use is sum of the self-reported number of days on which they consumed alcohol in the past 30 days. Marijuana use is sum of the self-reported number of days on which they consumed marijuana in the past 30 days. Asian is a dummy variable where 1 = Asian and 0 = not Asian. Other minority is a dummy variable where 1 = Black, Latina, or Native American and 0 = White or Asian.

Table 4. Hierarchical proportional-odds analysis of predictors of baseline attitude toward sexual intercourse (*n* = 172)

	Step 1: Behavioral beliefs		Step 2: Adding external variables	
Predictors	**OR (95% CI)**	***p*-value**	**OR (95% CI)**	***p*-value**
Abstinence behavioral belief	0.17 (0.11, 0.27)	<0.0001	0.16 (0.10, 0.26)	<0.0001
Coitus behavioral belief	0.67 (0.38, 1.16)	0.1516	0.78 (0.43, 1.41)	0.4117
Relationship status	-		5.35 (2.74, 10.45)	<0.0001
Alcohol use	-		1.15 (1.04, 1.26)	0.0044
Marijuana use	-		0.98 (0.80, 1.20)	0.8384
Asian	-		1.68 (0.76, 3.69)	0.1985
Other minority	-		1.62 (0.71, 3.68)	0.2538

Notes: Abstinence behavioral beliefs = beliefs about the positive consequences of sexual abstinence. Coitus behavioral beliefs = beliefs about the negative consequences of sexual intercourse. Relationship status is coded "2" if the person has a steady boyfriend and "1" if the person does not have a steady boyfriend. Alcohol use is sum of the self-reported number of days on which they consumed alcohol in the past 30 days. Marijuana use is sum of the self-reported number of days on which they consumed marijuana in the past 30 days. Asian is a dummy variable where 1 = Asian and 0 = not Asian. Other minority is a dummy variable where 1 = Black, Latina, or Native American and 0 = White or Asian.

5. Discussion

The results of this prospective study suggest that the TRA is appropriate for understanding abstinence among college women. Consistent with the TRA, baseline attitude toward having sexual intercourse and subjective norms regarding sexual intercourse predicted intention, and intention measured at baseline predicted self-reported sexual intercourse 3 months later. In addition, behavioral beliefs about the benefits of abstinence predicted attitude and intention, whereas beliefs about the adverse consequences of sexual intercourse did not. These findings have implications for interventions with college women.

The TRA holds that the relative predictive power of attitudes and subjective norms will vary depending on the behavior and the population in question. This study suggests that attitudes and subjective norms are important in predicting sexual intention among college women, but that attitudes are particularly important. Accordingly, interventions to reduce college women's intention to have sexual intercourse might be more efficacious if they focus on attitude toward sexual intercourse.

The TRA holds that external variables will not have direct effects on the theorized mediators and outcome measures. In this study, however, two external variables were found to have such direct effects. Relationship status and alcohol use had direct effects on attitude toward sex. Relationship status also had direct effects on intention to have sex when attitude and subjective norms were in the model. Finally, relationship status and alcohol use had direct effects on subsequent self-reported sexual intercourse. There are two possible explanations for these findings. It is possible that the relevant beliefs were not measured. Or it may be that some external variables supersede mediation by attitude, norm, or intention as predicted by the TRA model. For the prediction of intention, descriptive norm and self-efficacy, which are components of the reasoned action approach (Fishbein & Ajzen, 2010), an extension of TRA not assessed in this study, may explain the effects of relationship status and using alcohol. On the other hand, relationship status and alcohol use may be part of a constellation of situational factors that make it more likely an individual will have sex (Kempner et al., 2000) without the predisposing attitude, norm or intention of doing so. Their presence constitutes more of a vulnerability to an event than an active seeking out of an event. Since these findings are consistent with earlier findings that associate relationship status (Sanderson & Jemmott, 1996) and substance use (Rosenbaum & Kandel, 1990) with more active and more risky sexual behavior, research testing these two possible explanations in one design would help clarify the boundaries of the TRA. Adding more items tapping behavioral beliefs in the areas of hedonistic beliefs about sex, substance use associated with sexual intercourse, and how being in a relationship might affect attitude toward sex would address this question.

The findings, however, do suggest that certain avenues can be fruitful for interventions to influence sexual intercourse in college women. This prospective study suggests that encouraging abstinence may be a viable approach with college women. First, a large percentage of the college women (67%) were sexually inexperienced; in fact, only 24% of the whole sample reported having sexual intercourse in the previous 3 months. Second, behavioral beliefs about the benefits of abstinence predicted attitudes, these attitudes predicted intentions, which, in turn, predicted sexual intercourse 3 months later. The influence of positive beliefs about abstinence is particularly noteworthy because behavioral beliefs about the adverse effects of sexual intercourse were not related to intentions or behaviors. Although "abstinence-only" approaches may focus on both the positive consequences of abstinence and the negative consequences of sexual activity, the finding suggests focusing on the benefits of abstinence might be a more effective sexual risk reduction strategy than is emphasizing the negative consequences of sexual intercourse. This suggestion is consistent with a recent mediation analysis of a theory-based abstinence-only intervention reporting that beliefs about the positive consequences of abstinence mediated the intervention's efficacy in reducing sexual initiation over a 24-month period whereas beliefs about the negative consequences of sexual intercourse did not (Zhang et al., 2015). Similar to Detweiler et al.'s (1999) sunbathers, who responded more to messages emphasizing the benefits of protecting their healthy skin than to messages warning of the dire consequences of failing to protect their skin, the college women in this study seemed more focused on preserving benefits they have, rather than avoiding negative consequences in the future when it comes to remaining sexually abstinent. Determining the influence of gain versus loss framing for the promotion of abstinence may be an effective manipulation for increasing the efficacy of such programs, of particular import given the widespread prescription and funding of abstinence-only intervention by government agencies. Further research should test whether this finding holds in populations of different ages, socioeconomic status, and education.

The findings also suggest that it may be efficacious for risk reduction efforts to focus on certain subpopulations, such as those who have a steady partner or are alcohol users. These characteristics were shown to have an unmediated effect on being sexually active and/or attitude toward sexual intercourse.

One of the study's strengths is its prospective design, which allows it to predict and measure behavior in relation to prior attitude and intention, which a cross-sectional design examining intention and behavior at a time point would not. Additionally, it was able to maintain very low attrition and few missing data. This study also showed that the rate of abstinence among college women is substantially higher than that of the general non-college female population, which is in keeping with the findings for those with high cognitive functioning (Halpern, Joyner, Udry, & Suchindran, 2000). The limitations of this study should also be considered. The participants were predominantly White and Asian and from an Ivy League university where only 12% of those invited enrolled; therefore future research should examine the generalizability of findings to other college female populations. The study used single-item measures of attitude and intention; the use of multi-item measures in future research would increase statistical power. Although the primary analysis was prospective, some analyses were cross-sectional (e.g. attitude-intention), which does not preclude the possibility of reverse causality. Future studies might address causal relationships by directly manipulating theoretical variables and examining the effects on outcomes. The study did not include measures of descriptive norm and self-efficacy, which might help understand abstinence in college women and should be examined in future studies.

Despite these limitations, the results of this study suggest that, for college women, the TRA is a useful model of sexual abstinence. Attitude and subjective norm predicted intention and intention predicted self-reported sexual intercourse three months later. The finding that beliefs about positive consequences of abstinence, but not negative consequences of intercourse, predict attitude, suggests that abstinence interventions may be a viable risk-reduction approach if the abstinence message is framed to emphasize the positive consequences of abstinence rather than the negative consequences of sexual intercourse. Future research using a randomized controlled trial design directly comparing the efficacy of these two abstinence messages would address an important research question about the best approach to encouraging abstinence.

Implications and contributions

Beliefs about positive consequences of abstinence, but not negative consequences of intercourse, predict attitude, suggesting abstinence messages be framed positively. The theory of reasoned action is a useful model of college women's sexual abstinence: attitude and subjective norm predict intention to have intercourse, and intention predicts self-reported intercourse three months later.

Acknowledgments

The authors wish to thank all participants for their time.

Funding

This research was supported by grant R03 MH60584 from the National Institute of Mental Health (NIMH). This sponsor had no role in the study design, the collection, analysis, and interpretation of data, the writing of the report, or the decision to submit this manuscript for publication. The first author, Dr. Hazel Spears, wrote the first draft of the manuscript. None of the authors received an honorarium, grant, or other form of payment to produce the manuscript.

Competing Interest

The authors declare no competing interests.

Author details

Hazel Spears[1,2]
E-mail: dr.hazel.spears@gmail.com
John B. Jemmott III[1,3]
E-mail: jjemmott@asc.upenn.edu
G. Anita Heeren[4]
E-mail: gheeren@sju.edu
ORCID ID: http://orcid.org/0000-0001-7376-1132

[1] Center for Health Behavior and Communication Research, Annenberg School for Communication, University of Pennsylvania, 3901 Walnut Street Suite 503, Philadelphia, PA 19104, USA.
[2] Department of Social and Behavioral Sciences, Cheyney University of Pennsylvania, Cheyney, PA, USA.
[3] Department of Psychiatry, Perelman School of Medicine, University of Pennsylvania, 3901 Walnut Street, Philadelphia, PA 19104, USA.
[4] Health Services, St. Joseph's University, Philadelphia, PA, USA.

References

Ajzen, I., & Fishbein, M. (1980). *Understanding attitudes and predicting social behavior*. Englewood Cliffs, NJ: Prentice-Hall.

Aten, M. J., Siegel, D. M., Enaharo, M., & Auinger, P. (2002). Keeping middle school students abstinent: Outcomes of a primary prevention intervention. *Journal of Adolescent Health, 31*, 70–78. http://dx.doi.org/10.1016/S1054-139X(02)00367-1

Centers for Disease Control and Prevention. (2013a). Summary of notifiable diseases, United States, 2011. *Morbidity and Mortality Weekly Report, 60*, 1–120.

Centers for Disease Control and Prevention. (2013b). Rates of diagnoses of HIV infection among adults and adolescents, by area of residence, 2011–United States and 6 dependent areas. *HIV Surveilance Report, 23*, 1–84.

Chin, H. B., Sipe, T. A., Elder, R., Mercer, S. L., Chattopadhyay, S. K., Jacob, V., ... Chuke, S. O. (2012). The effectiveness of group-based comprehensive risk-reduction and abstinence education interventions to prevent or reduce the risk of adolescent pregnancy, human immunodeficiency virus, and sexually transmitted infections: Two systematic reviews for the Guide to Community Preventive Services. *American Journal of Preventive Medicine, 42*, 272–294. http://dx.doi.org/10.1016/j.amepre.2011.11.006

Christopher, F. S., & Roosa, M. W. (1990). An evaluation of an adolescent pregnancy prevention program—Is just say no enough. *Family Relations, 39*, 68–72. http://dx.doi.org/10.2307/584951

Crowne, D. P., & Marlow, D. (1964). *The approval motive: Studies in adaptive dependence*. New York, NY: Wiley.

Detweiler, J. B., Bedell, B. T., Salovey, P., Pronin, E., & Rothman, A. J. (1999). Message framing and sunscreen use: Gain-framed messages motivate beach-goers. *Health Psychology, 18*, 189–196. http://dx.doi.org/10.1037/0278-6133.18.2.189

DiClemente, R. J., Wingood, G. M., Crosby, R., Sionean, C., Cobb, B. K., Harrington, K., ... Oh, M. K. (2001). Parental monitoring: Association with adolescents' risk behaviors. *Pediatrics, 107*, 1363–1368. http://dx.doi.org/10.1542/peds.107.6.1363

DiClemente, R. J., Wingood, G. M., Harrington, K. F., Lang, D. L., Davies, S. L., Hook III, E. W., ... Hardin, J. W. (2004). Efficacy of an HIV prevention intervention for African American adolescent girls. *JAMA, 292*, 171–179. http://dx.doi.org/10.1001/jama.292.2.171

Fishbein, M., & Ajzen, I. (1975). *Belief, attitude, intention and behavior*. Boston, MA: Addison-Wesley.

Fishbein, M., & Ajzen, I. (2010). *Predicting and changing behavior: The reasoned action approach*. New York, NY: Taylor and Francis Group.

Garcia-Retamero, R., & Cokely, E. T. (2013). Simple but powerful health messages for increasing condom use in young adults. *The Journal of Sex Research, 52*, 30–42.

Goodson, P., Evans, A., & Edmundson, E. (1997). Female adolescents and onset of sexual intercourse: A theory-based review of research from 1984 to 1994. *Journal of Adolescent Health, 21*, 147–156. http://dx.doi.org/10.1016/S1054-139X(97)00004-9

Halpern, C. T., Joyner, K., Udry, J. R., & Suchindran, C. (2000). Smart teens don't have sex (or kiss much either). *Journal of Adolescent Health, 26*, 213–225. http://dx.doi.org/10.1016/S1054-139X(99)00061-0

Heeren, G. A., Jemmott III, J. B., Ngwane, Z., Mandeya, A., & Tyler, J. C. (2013). A randomized controlled pilot study of an HIV risk-reduction intervention for Sub-Saharan African university students. *AIDS and Behavior, 17*, 1105–1115. http://dx.doi.org/10.1007/s10461-011-0129-2

Jemmott III, J. B. (2012). The reasoned action approach in HIV risk-reduction strategies for adolescents. *The ANNALS of the American Academy of Political and Social Science, 640*, 150–172. http://dx.doi.org/10.1177/0002716211426096

Jemmott III, J. B., Jemmott, L., & Fong, G. T. (1998). Abstinence and safer sex HIV risk-reduction interventions for African American adolescents: A randomized controlled trial. *JAMA, 279*, 1529–1536. http://dx.doi.org/10.1001/jama.279.19.1529

Jemmott III, J. B., Jemmott, L. S., Fong, G. T., & Morales, K. H. (2010). Effectiveness of an HIV/STD risk-reduction intervention for adolescents when implemented by community-based organizations: A cluster-randomized controlled trial. *American Journal of Public Health, 100*, 720–726.

Jemmott III, J. B., Jemmott, L. S., & Fong, G. T. (2010). Efficacy of a theory-based abstinence-only intervention over 24 months: A randomized controlled trial with young adolescents. *Archives of Pediatrics & Adolescent Medicine, 164*, 152–159.

Jorgensen, S. R., Potts, V., & Camp, B. (1993). Project taking charge: Six-month follow-up of a pregnancy prevention program for early adolescents. *Family Relations, 42*, 401–406. http://dx.doi.org/10.2307/585340

Kann, L., McManus, T., Harris, W. A., Shanklin, S. L., Flint, K. H., Hawkins, J., ... Stephanie, Z. (2016). Youth risk behavior surveillance–United States, 2015. *Morbidity and Mortality Weekly Report Surveillance Summaries, 65*(6), 1–174.

Kempner, M., Amberg, D., & Bracksmajer, A. (2000). Fact sheet on opponents of comprehensive sexuality education. *Siecus Reports, 28*, 19–27.

Kohler, P. K., Manhart, L. E., & Lafferty, W. E. (2008). Abstinence-only and comprehensive sex education and the initiation of sexual activity and teen pregnancy. *Journal of Adolescent Health, 42*, 344–351. http://dx.doi.org/10.1016/j.jadohealth.2007.08.026

March, A. L., & Serdar Atav, A. S. (2010). Social environment and problem behavior: Perceived school safety, gender, and sexual debut. *The Journal of School Nursing, 26*, 121–130. http://dx.doi.org/10.1177/1059840509343112

McCave, E. L., Azulay Chertok, I. R. A., Winter, V. R., & Haile, Z. T. (2013). Sexual health behaviors in a random sample of students at a Mid-Atlantic university: 2010–2011. *Journal of Community Health, 38*, 310–319. http://dx.doi.org/10.1007/s10900-012-9616-2

Meston, C. M., & Ahrold, T. (2010). Ethnic, gender, and acculturation influences on sexual behaviors. *Archives of Sexual Behavior, 39*, 179–189. http://dx.doi.org/10.1007/s10508-008-9415-0

Panchaud, C., Singh, S., Feivelson, D., & Darroch, J. E. (2000). Sexually transmitted diseases among adolescents in developed countries. *Family Planning Perspectives, 32*, 24–32. http://dx.doi.org/10.2307/2648145

Raine, T. R., Jenkins, R., Aarons, S. J., Woodward, K., Fairfax, J. L., El-Khorazaty, M. N., & Herman, A. (1999). Sociodemographic correlates of virginity in seventh-grade black and Latino students. *Journal of Adolescent Health, 24*, 304–312. http://dx.doi.org/10.1016/S1054-139X(98)00109-8

Rosenbaum, E., & Kandel, D. B. (1990). Early onset of adolescent sexual-behavior and drug involvement. *Journal of Marriage and the Family, 52*, 783–798. http://dx.doi.org/10.2307/352942

Rothman, A. J., & Salovey, P. (1997). Shaping perceptions to motivate healthy behavior: The role of message framing. *Psychological Bulletin, 121*, 3–19. http://dx.doi.org/10.1037/0033-2909.121.1.3

Sanderson, C. A., & Jemmott III, J. B. (1996). Moderation and mediation of HIV prevention interventions: Relationship status, intentions, and condom use among college students. *Journal of Applied Social Psychology, 26*, 2076–2099. http://dx.doi.org/10.1111/jasp.1996.26.issue-23

Santelli, J., Ott, M. A., Lyon, M., Rogers, J., Summers, D., & Schleifer, R. (2006). Abstinence and abstinence-only education: A review of U.S. policies and programs. *Journal of Adolescent Health, 38*, 72–81. http://dx.doi.org/10.1016/j.jadohealth.2005.10.006

Sather, L., & Zinn, K. (2002). Effects of abstinence-only education on adolescent attitudes and values concerning premarital sexual intercourse. *Family & Community Health, 25*(2), 1–15. http://dx.doi.org/10.1097/00003727-200207000-00003

Shu, L. L., Mazar, N., Gino, F., Ariely, D., & Bazerman, M. H. (2012). Signing at the beginning makes ethics salient and decreases dishonest self-reports in comparison to signing at the end. *Proceedings of the National Academy of Sciences, 109*, 15197–15200. http://dx.doi.org/10.1073/pnas.1209746109

Thomas, M. H. (2000). Abstinence-based programs for prevention of adolescent pregnancies. *Journal of Adolescent Health, 26*, 5–17. http://dx.doi.org/10.1016/S1054-139X(98)00126-8

Title V Section 510 of the Social Security Act. (n.d.). Retrieved from https://www.ssa.gov/OP_Home/ssact/title05/0510.htm

Tortolero, S. R., Markham, C. M., Peskin, M. F., Shegog, R., Addy, R. C., Escobar-Chaves, S. L., & Baumler, E. R. (2010). It's your game: Keep it real: Delaying sexual behavior with an effective middle school program. *Journal of Adolescent Health, 46*, 169–179. http://dx.doi.org/10.1016/j.jadohealth.2009.06.008

Zhang, J., Jemmott III, J. B., & Jemmott, L. S. (2015). Mediation and moderation of an efficacious theory-based abstinence-only intervention for African American adolescents. *Health Psychology, 34*, 1175–1184. http://dx.doi.org/10.1037/hea0000244

6

Conditions and constraints of political participation among Turkish students in Germany

Frank Reichert[1]*

*Corresponding author: Frank Reichert, Faculty of Education, The University of Hong Kong, Room 217, 2/F, Runme Shaw Building, Pok Fu Lam Road, Hong Kong, Hong Kong SAR
E-mail: reichert@hku.hk

Reviewing editor: Natasha Tidwell, Fort Lewis College, USA

Abstract: What motivates conventional and unconventional participation in the political realm? Specifically, what are the facilitators and constraints of political participation in the views of Turkish migrants? The present study explored these conditions using semi-structured interviews with a small number of university students of Turkish descent in Germany, as these may be more likely to become spokespersons of the Turkish people in Germany than other members of their ethnic minority in-group. The interviewees draw attention to characteristics of different kinds of political activities, linking them to a lack of trustworthiness, frustration, disappointment, and reflection. Most of these factors can be related to rational actor approaches of political behavior; hence, the findings are discussed with respect to rational choice theory and with regard to the importance of sociopolitical and emotional integration of Turkish migrants. The role of political trust is discussed as that of a potential moderating force in the facilitation of political participation.

Subjects: Political Behavior and Participation; Political Psychology; Racial & Ethnic Politics; Political Sociology; Race & Ethnic Studies; Social Psychology; Multiculturalism

Keywords: Germany; migrant; political participation; political trust; rational choice; Turkish

ABOUT THE AUTHOR

Frank Reichert, Dr Phil, is a postdoctoral fellow at the Faculty of Education, University of Hong Kong, Hong Kong SAR, and has received the award of 2016 NAEd/Spencer Postdoctoral Fellow from the National Academy of Education in Washington, DC, USA. He studied educational science, political science, and psychology and received his doctorate in Germany. He has worked in the disciplines of education, political science, psychology, and sociology, doing research on youth development, political behavior, citizenship education, and immigration. His research in progress investigates citizenship norms and their relationship to political behavior, civic communication and its impact on political knowledge and behavior, and how education policy influences civic learning, with a particular focus on the Asia-Pacific region. The research reported in the present article reflects Dr Reichert's interest in political psychology, and it is a good example of his interest in the conditions of political participation, and youth and other minorities in general.

PUBLIC INTEREST STATEMENT

The discrimination of immigrants and social inequities can pose serious threats to social peace and the health of a nation, and are therefore pressing challenges for many Western societies. The Turkish community forms the largest migrant group in Germany, whose social and political discrimination has been of ongoing public interest. Such discrimination can be challenged through the co-shaping of public policies. This requires the members of the Turkish community to get politically active, because others may be unaware of or uninterested in overcoming existing inequalities. However, educational and language barriers can prevent minorities from co-shaping the public. Highly educated members of the Turkish minority may therefore be most influential in promoting the interests of the Turkish community. This research interviewed university students of Turkish descent to identify obstacles to their active participation in the co-shaping of public policies, which can help us to address existing inequities and to encourage them to help co-shaping our shared communities.

1. Introduction

For modern democracies, the participation of citizens in the political realm is an important characteristic of legitimate political decision-making. As many modern democracies face the challenge of the social and political integration of immigrants, the participation of immigrants and their descendants is of particular significance. This requires us to know how we can effectively stimulate political participation and, as a consequence, the political integration of immigrants.

This paper employs a qualitative approach to explore the motives and facilitators of, and obstacles to, unconventional and conventional political activities among Turkish migrants[1] in Germany. The focus is on Turkish migrants as these represent the largest group of immigrants in Germany (17.4% of all immigrants; Statistisches Bundesamt (Destatis), 2015, p. 7). Hence, their integration into political life is a significant challenge, in particular as Germany for a long time did not define itself as a country of immigrants (Bommes, 2010; Joppke, 1999; Santel, 2006). Although the present study does not give a representative account of that population, this study aims to provide insights into conditions and intervening variables that may be of relevance in the facilitation of political action in addition to those conditions and constraints that were examined in a standardized survey, which focused on cognitive political mobilization as well as collective identity.

2. Conceptual background

2.1. Political participation

"Political participation" consists of every voluntary activity a person performs in their role as a citizen to influence authoritative regulations and decisions of the political system or political processes (van Deth, 2014, p. 351f.). "Political action" and "political behavior" are often used as synonyms, and intentions to participate in politics are frequently understood as political participation, too. Based on existing literature (Barnes et al., 1979; Steinbrecher, 2009), we may distinguish four kinds of political participation: *Electoral* participation—voting—does not require intense effort, nor is it bound by a strong commitment. Voting is only constrained by formal regulations (e.g. citizenship). *Conventional* political activities are traditional, party-related forms of participation, and are sometimes called "party politics." These activities are often institutionalized and require a certain degree of commitment as well as a higher investment of time by the activists (e.g. supporting an election campaign). *Unconventional* activities refer to a broad range of less time-intensive or committed political activities outside the realm of political parties. In fact, these activities have a long tradition in many Western countries and are nowadays often referred to as "protest activities" (e.g. signing a petition, distributing leaflets). Finally, *non-normative*, illegal political activities are located outside the legal framework (e.g. attending a violent demonstration).

2.2. Key concepts of the present study

The present study is a follow-up to a panel survey which focused on the distinctive role of political knowledge, interest in politics, and political self-efficacy as precursors of different kinds of political participation (Reichert, 2013). These core concepts were defined with reference to common conceptualizations in the field. That is, political knowledge was defined "as the range of factual information about politics that is stored in long-term memory" (Delli Carpini & Keeter, 1996, p. 10). Political interest was understood as the "degree to which politics arouses a citizen's curiosity" (van Deth, 1990, p. 278). This includes citizens' awareness of and attention to political issues (Zaller, 1992). Political self-efficacy was defined as the feeling of being politically powerful on one's own. That is, political self-efficacy was conceptualized as an individual's perception of being capable to understand political facts and processes, and to take political influence (Almond & Verba, 1963; Balch, 1974; Campbell, Gurin, & Miller, 1954). This conceptualization aligns with psychological concepts of internal efficacy (Bandura, 1977) and the concept of perceived behavioral control in the *Theory of Planned Behavior* (Ajzen, 2012), and it is a key variable that has been used in empirical tests of rational choice models (e.g. Lüdemann, 2001) (cf. *2.3 Political Participation: A Rational Decision?*). Finally, political trust turned out as an important concept. It was loosely defined as the belief that politicians and political institutions would not treat people unjustly (Newton, 2007).

2.3. Political participation: A rational decision?

Typically, political participation is explained by demographic variables (e.g. age, gender), resources (e.g. status, income), or social capital (esp. social networks); by the political values and attitudes of individuals; and by political interest, internal and external political efficacy, and other political competences (Steinbrecher, 2009; Verba, Schlozman, & Brady, 1995). At the individual level, biological variables such as personality traits (Mondak, Hibbing, Canache, Seligson, & Anderson, 2010; Quintelier, 2012) or genetics (Fowler, Baker, & Dawes, 2008; Hatemi, Medland, Morley, Heath, & Martin, 2007) have also been taken into consideration to explain political participation.

Rational choice approaches often utilize some of the variables identified and introduced above—values, norms, attitudes, motivations—to explain political behavior (Steinbrecher, 2009, p. 67). Rational choice models generally assume that "individuals engage in political activity to pursue particular goals, and they decide to participate when the benefits of such activity outweigh the costs" (Leighley, 1995, p. 192). Essentially, this thesis comprises three basic assumptions (Opp, 2009, p. 2ff.): (1) Individuals engage in political activity to pursue particular goals and to satisfy their own needs (*preference hypothesis*). (2) The probability that their goals are achieved and/or that their needs are satisfied depends not only on themselves, but it is constrained by contextual factors, hence the likelihood that an individual will engage in a certain political activity also depends on those external factors (*constraint hypothesis*). (3) Rational actors will not act if the costs of action outweigh the returns. More specifically, rational actors try to satisfy their needs to the highest possible extent and at the same time try to keep their own costs of acting at a minimum (*maximization hypothesis*).

However, decisions that result from participation in the political arena are almost always the consequence of the political acts of many individuals. That is, making politics is a form of collective action to define common rules (e.g. making laws) and to achieve the common good, and thus political participation is often irrational if it is seen from such an economic rational actor perspective.

> Indeed, unless the number of individuals in a group is quite small, or unless there is coercion or some other special device to make individuals act in their common interest, *rational, self-interested individuals will not act to achieve their common or group interests*. In other words, even if all of the individuals in a large group are rational and self-interested, and would gain if, as a group, they acted to achieve their common interest or objective, they will still not voluntarily act to achieve that common or group interest. (Olson, 1965, p. 2)

In quite many situations, one individual cannot make a huge difference and the effect of an individual's act remains extremely small (e.g. one vote out of several million votes). In addition, if all group members benefit from a specific political decision, it is more rational to let others engage in the decision-making process: in fact, free riders act more rationally than those who actively contribute to the making of politics. Consequently, nobody would engage in political action if everyone acted entirely rational; yet individuals do participate in politics. This "paradox of participation" has struggled researchers for decades, but most research in the rational actor framework has examined voter turnout, which (at least in consolidated democracies) is a very low-cost activity and not well-suited for examination in this framework (Leighley, 1995).

"Incentives" have been proposed as the solution of the paradox of participation, such as psychological selective incentives, policy dissatisfaction, feelings of personal influence and group success (i.e. internal, external and group efficacy), and a sense of duty to participate (Leighley, 1995). Arguably, diffuse trust in political institutions can be one of these incentives and its effect may depend on the political goals to be achieved. A recent study showed that a lack of such trust is positively associated with non-institutionalized political participation, whereas diffuse trust in political institutions is not only positively associated with electoral and institutionalized participation, but the latter effects cumulate with higher levels of political awareness (Hooghe & Marien, 2013). Leighley (1995) also emphasized the role of group membership and that participation might be expressive rather than instrumental (e.g. to express dissatisfaction about policies), and that expressing political opinions could be a motivating benefit in itself.

One rational approach that combines some of those suggested variables to explain participation is the *Theory of Planned Behavior* (Ajzen, 2012; Eckstein, Jugert, Noack, Born, & Şener, 2015; Jugert, Eckstein, Noack, Kuhn, & Benbow, 2013). It assumes that

> human action is guided by three kinds of considerations: beliefs about the likely outcomes of the behavior and the evaluations of these outcomes (behavioral beliefs), beliefs about the normative expectations and actions of important referents and motivation to comply with these referents (normative beliefs), and beliefs about the presence of factors that may facilitate or impede performance of the behavior and the perceived power of these factors (control beliefs). (Ajzen, 2012, p. 18)

Recent studies have expanded that framework in the political realm to account for political knowledge as an additional condition, or precursor of individuals' beliefs of internal control (i.e. internal political self-efficacy, see above) (Reichert, 2016). Yet despite supporting evidence for these approaches, debate remains about the applicability of rational actor models. One question is about the behaviors that are supposed to be rational, as partially planned or unplanned behavior might be automatically activated (Bargh, 1997; Fazio, 1990; Kahneman, 2003; Strack & Deutsch, 2004). Also, as was mentioned earlier, it is challenging to solve the paradox of political action using such a framework. In addition, the measures used in (quantitative) studies on rational actor theory have been criticized (Leighley, 1995), because the incentives, benefits, and costs that are associated with political participation may vary largely between individuals.

The reflective-impulsive model (RIM), which was proposed by Strack and Deutsch (2004), might provide a solution to this paradox: These researchers have developed a dual process model, according to which two pathways lead to behavior. "The reflective system generates behavioral decisions that are based on knowledge about facts and values, whereas the impulsive system elicits behavior through associative links and motivational orientations." (Strack & Deutsch, 2004, p. 220) Moreover, the RIM assumes that both systems operate simultaneously: On the one hand, affective processes are always involved in the initiation of behavior and are dominant in spontaneous activities. On the other hand, reflective processes are only activated in addition to impulsive processes when reasoned action is required. Thus, the reflective system has precursors that are considered in rational actor models, but it is only active if the "stakes are high," i.e. when the consequences are not immediately clear or when the costs of an activity are quite high. However, this system is also more prone to disruption than the impulsive system, because the former depends on the available capacities of our working memory. On the other hand, the impulsive path depends on particular habits and the satisfaction of basic needs as well as motivational orientations which ease information processing and behavior.

The RIM has not been applied to political theory, and it is questionable whether political participation could be entirely impulsive. Still, it would be helpful to learn whether differential pathways that might represent highly reflective vs. less reflective processes can be explored for political participation. More specifically, questions that need to be answered are: What are the goals and the expected benefits of those who decide to participate in politics? Do the expected costs and benefits of, as well as the reasons for participation in party-political activities differ from those that are linked to participation in protest activities? Can we identify, in fact, two different pathways to political action, of which one is more rational than the other in that costs and benefits are weighed against each other more explicitly (completely unreasoned political action might be less common though)? Finally, can we link these pathways to differences in the types of political activity as well as to differences in political interest and political self-efficacy?

2.4. The present study

The present study was part of a larger project which examined the role of collective identities among highly educated Turkish migrants (Simon, Reichert, & Grabow, 2013; Simon, Reichert, Schaefer, Bachmann, & Renger, 2015). For migrants, the costs of participation are usually higher than for non-migrants, which makes Turkish migrants a particularly interesting population. Given lower levels of participation among Turkish migrants, we had chosen university students as our population, due to the well-known positive correlation between education and political participation, and because those migrants were more likely to become spokespersons of their own minority group and, thus, to initiate change. Results from the standardized survey suggest that political interest directly predicts unconventional political participation, but it needs to translate into the explicit intention to participate with respect to electoral and conventional political participation. Political interest appeared as the more proximal predictor of political action compared with political self-efficacy. However, the latter was almost as important as political interest in the prediction of conventional political participation (Reichert, 2013). Moreover, identification with both their minority in-group and the German majority appeared to promote normative political participation among Turkish migrants, a group that reported a significant level of collective grievances (i.e. they perceived being treated unfairly because of their Turkish origin, or being discriminated against as members of the Turkish community) (Simon et al., 2015).

It seems plausible to assume that other conditions and additional intervening variables may be relevant in the prediction of political behavior, however. The present study presents results from a small number of qualitative interviews with participants of that panel survey. These interviews were analyzed with respect to additional conditions that may or may not relate to individuals' interest in politics, political self-efficacy, and their knowledge and skills in the political realm. The aim of this analysis was to gain insights that are not constrained by a standardized questionnaire, and to gather qualitative, open responses on study participants' decisions to participate, or not to participate, in politics, and to link these responses to their political interest, self-efficacy, and costs and benefits of participation. Therefore, this research focuses on individual (and not collective) participation, and it tries to explore further rational and non-rational "conditions" of political participation (for more details, see Section 4). An important feature is its focus on Turkish migrants, who represent the largest group of immigrants in Germany (Statistisches Bundesamt (Destatis), 2015, p. 7), as they may experience higher hurdles to participation in politics than native Germans.

3. Turkish migrants in Germany

3.1. The situation of Turkish migrants in Germany

With almost three million Turkish migrants, this group represents the majority among migrants in Germany (Statistisches Bundesamt (Destatis), 2015). The first Turks arrived in Germany in the 1950s, and due to political regulations, the immigration of Turks increased in the 1960s, and Germany became the home for many Turkish families in the 1970s (Böcker & Groenendijk, 2006; Joppke, 1999; Meier-Braun, 2007; Şen & Faruk, 2002; Thränhardt, 1999, 2004). Although Germany abandoned the *ius sanguinis* in 2000 in favor of the *ius solis*, so that newborns can acquire the citizenship of their country of their parents' citizenship, Germany still does not fully accept dual citizenship. Hence, the offspring of Turkish immigrants have to choose between the German and the Turkish citizenship when they are adults. Those who choose to keep their Turkish citizenship will be excluded from electoral participation.

Many Turkish migrants have been living in Germany for more than two decades (Babka von Gostomski, 2008). Although most of them are Muslims (Haug, Müssig, & Stichs, 2009), Turkish immigrants are by no means a homogenous group—and this not merely because Muslims are a diverse group or because some Turks may be Muslims in name only (Halm, 2013). Yet despite the vibrant social life and a vast number of club activities in the Turkish communities, they are actually disadvantaged and perceive being deprived: compared to children without migration background, Turkish migrants perform much worse in skills assessments even after controlling for other influences (Diehl

& Fick, 2016). No other migrant group counts a relatively higher number of members without a secondary school qualification and with fewer members who have received a university entrance certificate (see also Avcı, 2006; Woellert, Kröhnert, Sippel, & Klingholz, 2009). Only among Turkish migrants is it possible to explain their lower position in the German labor market not almost exclusively by differences in education (Granato & Kalter, 2001). Youths from (Turkish) immigrant families are significantly disadvantaged with respect to vocational training and job search compared to their German peers—even if they have equivalent school leaving degrees (Goldberg, Mourinho, & Kulke, 1995; Granato, 2003; Hunkler, 2016; Kaas & Manger, 2010). Yet Turkish youth are more likely than Germans to enter tertiary education, which could be due to their unfamiliarity with the German system of vocational training (Kristen, Reimer, & Kogan, 2008).

Turkish migrants also experience rejection in everyday life, and politics and fellow citizens refuse to treat them equally (Böltken, 2000; Sachverständigenrat Deutscher Stiftungen für Integration und Migration, 2014; Şener, 2007; Wasmer & Koch, 2000), in particular if they are Muslims (Brettfeld & Wetzels, 2008). As Germans seem to have a more critical perspective on Turkish immigration compared to immigration of other populations (Yavçan, 2013),[2] Turkish migrants feel more disadvantaged and pessimistic compared to other migrant groups in Germany (Fassmann & İçduygu, 2013; Sachverständigenrat Deutscher Stiftungen für Integration und Migration, 2014). Therefore, the basic premise of active participation in politics clearly exists; which is: to complain about social deficiencies and to demand political change, and therefore to get involved in the political process. Social psychological theory and research on intergroup behavior indeed suggests that the perception of illegitimate injustice of one's own in-groups, such as the ethnic collective, compared to other groups within the same society can trigger grievances that are shared among in-group members (e.g. Simon & Klandermans, 2001). If in-group members attribute the causes for their perceived injustice to other groups within the wider society, and if these out-groups do not accept responsibility for that injustice, then in-group members may become politically active in order to obtain a more just situation (Simon & Klandermans, 2001). Clearly, these conditions are present in the case of Turkish migrants in Germany.

3.2. Political participation of migrants in Germany

The few existing studies on migrant political participation in Germany indicate that legally existing opportunities for political participation correspond with an ineffective advocacy of migrants (Diehl, 2002; Ergi, 2000; Wiedemann, 2006). Accordingly, migrants usually lobby for political, cultural, and social rights (Rucht & Heitmeyer, 2008), and Turkish migrant organizations address both the situation of Turks in Germany and political developments in Turkey (Sezgin, 2010). Although there exist many opportunities to individual political participation even without the possession of German citizenship (Diehl, 2002), citizenship is important for the alignment of political participation of migrants in Germany (de Wit & Koopmans, 2005; Koopmans & Statham, 1999).

Related to a lack of legal requirements is a significantly lower level of political interest among migrants, which is higher among Turkish migrants though, compared with other migrant groups (Diehl & Blohm, 2001; Diehl & Urbahn, 1998; Wächter, 2005; Wüst, 2003). However, the patterns of political participation among young migrants differ only little from native Germans if it is accounted for the legal framework—participation rates are merely at a lower level, and these differences disappear almost completely when controlling for education (Gaiser & de Rijke, 2006; Gille, Krüger, & de Rijke, 2000; Heß-Meining, 2000; Wiedemann, 2006). Yet people of Turkish origin are less connected with German society, and previous research found that they report the lowest willingness to participate in politics as well as the lowest propensity to participate in politics (Glatzer, 2004; Wiedemann, 2006). This also applies to the electoral participation of naturalized Turks who have the lowest turnout rates compared with almost all other naturalized citizens (Wüst, 2007). Probably due to their lower levels of education, Turkish migrants also prefer to participate in Turkish associations rather than German associations. However, more recent works found indication that young immigrants may be more active than non-immigrant youth (Eckstein et al., 2015), and particularly Turkish migrants might be more active than Russian migrants, and potentially also compared to non-migrant Germans (Jugert et al., 2013; Simon et al., 2015).

4. Methodology

The present, qualitative study was conducted as a follow-up to a longitudinal survey study which focused on the cognitive political mobilization of highly educated Turkish migrants (Reichert, 2013). Given lower levels of participation among Turkish migrants, we had chosen university students as our population, due to the well-known positive correlation between education and political participation, and because those people were more likely to become spokespersons of their own minority group and, thus, to initiate change. This was an important choice, because well-educated migrants are more likely to have the skills to influence and convince members of their own minority group. In addition, less well-educated migrants would be less likely to engage with the German society and, hence, to address the perceived injustice of their in-group. At the same time, there might be a higher risk for highly educated migrants to feel aggrieved if they sense discrimination despite their high level of education, which might turn their grievances into unproductive forms of participation.[3] On the other hand, this selection also means that the findings may disregard to some extent the role of Turkish associations, which are commonly used by Turkish migrants as a means of addressing their political claims. The present explorative study aims to give our respondents a voice and to enrich the findings from the quantitative study with qualitative insights from the respondents. The primary goal of the qualitative interview study was to gain deeper insights on the factors that motivate or hinder political participation among our participants, for the purpose of a more thorough interpretation of our quantitative findings. Thereby, this analysis intends to yield additional insights into constraints and further variables that may or may not be relevant to facilitate different kinds of political participation.

Semi-structured interviews were conducted in order to broaden our survey results by inviting some of the survey respondents to speak on their own, without the standardized format of a survey questionnaire. For this purpose, individuals who had previously participated in the online panel survey were selected for interview participation using a criteria-based case selection based on our quantitative data (Reichert, 2013). This specific sampling plan leads to a heterogeneous sample, which has the power to identify typical patterns (Merkens, 2005; Schreier, 2010). More specifically, the larger project on identity, within which the current study was conducted, aimed to conduct interviews with

Table 1 Characteristics of the interviewees

ID	Gender	Age	Citizenship[b]	Political interest[c]	Political self-efficacy[c]	V[d]	C[d]	U[d]	N[d]
A	Male	27[a]	Dual	4.00	3.33	1	0	1	0
B	Male	27	Turkish	1.50	1.67	0	1	1	0
C	Female	24	Turkish	2.00	1.78	–[e]	0	2	0
D	Female	38[a]	German	3.33	3.45	1	1	4	0
E	Male	26	Dual	3.00	3.11	1	0	1	0
F	Female	29	Turkish	3.33	3.11	–[e]	0	0	0
G	Female	38[a]	Dual	3.50	3.84	1	1	3	0
H	Female	26	German	2.33	2.44	1	0	3	0
I	Female	23	Turkish	3.33	1.66	–[e]	0	2	0
J	Female	29	German	3.17	3.89	1	1	3	1

[a]Not born in Germany (immigrated to Germany in childhood or early childhood).

[b]"Dual" means the possession of both the German and the Turkish citizenship.

[c]Range is from 0 = little interest/efficacy to 4 = high interest/efficacy.

[d]Self-reported political participation since the first survey. *V* = Voting (0 = no; 1 = yes), *C* = Conventional participation (0 = no activity; 1 = at least one of the following: contacted a politician, actively supported a political party campaign, membership in a political party, or participation in a political committee or working group), *U* = Unconventional participation (sum index of the following activities: signed a petition, distributed political leaflets, consumer boycott, participated in a legal demonstration, and participated in a citizens' initiative), *N* = non-normative political action (0 = no activity; 1 = at least one of the following: wrote a political slogan on a public wall, participated in an illegal demonstration, blocked a road for political reasons, occupied houses or offices, participated in a violent demonstration, damaged other people's property).

[e]According to self-report, there was no opportunity/legal right to participate in elections between the first and the last survey.

an equal number of (1) respondents who self-identified as both Turkish and German, and those who did not identify as both; (2) respondents who thought there was vs. was not an incompatibility between being both; and (3) male and female respondents. In a second step, for this present study and after the interviews had been conducted, interviewees were selected according to their participation in conventional and unconventional political activities, as they had reported it themselves in the online surveys before the conduct of the qualitative interviews. These patterns were then linked to the key variables of the quantitative analysis, that is, respondents' self-reported interest in politics and their political self-efficacy. This procedure ensured that these interviewees covered the entire range from low to high political interest and self-efficacy, and it enables the comparison of the quantitative and qualitative data. Table 1 shows the composition of the interviewees.

Interviewees were assured anonymity and written consent was obtained from all interviewees at the end of the interview, allowing us to use the data obtained during the interview for our research purposes. No incentive for participation was offered to motivate respondents to participate in the interview study. However, those respondents who participated in the interview received either a book voucher or cash (each worth ten Euro) after the interview. The present study analyzed 10 interviews that were collected by either a female or a male interviewer in German language. These interviews were 92 min long on average (ranging from 74 to 128 min), and all interviews were transcribed and analyzed after data collection.

The interviews always started with a standardized introduction before the interviewees were asked to talk about several issues. Here interviewees were informed that there were no "correct" or "incorrect" answers to our questions, and that they could take all the time they needed to talk about everything they would associate with the questions, or consider relevant for answering our questions. The interview guideline itself was structured around three key questions: (1) "What does it mean for you that you have Turkish roots on the one hand, and live in Germany on the other?" (2) "How do you integrate the different aspects of your 'self'?" (3) "What do you think of the fact that people who live in Germany and have Turkish roots are politically engaged in Germany?" The guideline also contained additional questions in case that narrative flow did not come about. Those most relevant for the present analysis were listed under the third key question and covered the topics of competence, efficacy, engagement, motivation and obstacles, duty, goals, and significance. Examples are: "Some people think it is much too complicated to understand what is going on in politics. What do you think?"; "What motivates you to engage in the public?"; or "What are the goals of your public engagement?" Finally, continuative keywords were only used when no flow of conversation came about or when it had stalled. Some examples of these keywords are: "importance of politics for you;" "effects of participation;" "influence;" "risks;" etc.

The following analysis focuses on subjective complexity, the interviewees' understanding of and interest in politics, and statements on political behavior. These narrations were meant to enable us to draw conclusions about the interviewees' political activities, and the specific nature of these political activities, as well as particular motives or action conditions underlying their political participation that our standardized survey may have missed. That is, the goal of this analysis was to examine the three "types" of participants (no participation—only unconventional participation—conventional and unconventional participation) with respect to their qualitative understandings of political participation, their motivations to or not to participate, and how the qualitative reports "match" the quantitative self-reports on interviewees' interest in politics and political self-efficacy. The expectation was that the resulting narratives might provide further insights into the specific kinds of and motivations behind actual political participation, or subjective conditions of participation. It seemed reasonable that this would help to expand our understanding of the conditions and constraints of political participation.

The steps that guided the analysis of the qualitative data were driven by content analysis as suggested by Mayring (2003), and case-based data exploration similar to qualitative evaluation as described in Kuckartz (2007). Each case was explored individually in the first place, before a more systematic analysis of the interviews was conducted based on five categories: motives of political participation; conventional political participation; unconventional political participation; political interest; and political efficacy. All texts were analyzed with the aim to draw generalizations based on "typical" statements of the interviewees, to explore correlations between the mentioned categories, and to identify statements that are potentially inconsistent within the interviewees or in relation to the quantitative data. The following section summarizes the qualitative interview findings.

5. Results

5.1 Politically inactive interviewee

The guided conversation with the only person who had participated in neither conventional nor unconventional political activities (*ID F*) was not very informative, and the interviewee reported a somewhat contradictory attitude. The interviewee expresses "unfortunately" to have a basic interest in politics, which essentially is an interest in everyday politics ("politically charged topics", "panel discussions" on television). However, the respondent also claims to be in a position to critically question current political events: she deliberately does not call herself "politically informed," but rather means to have a "political awareness." She clarifies this by stating that she no longer can inform herself about politics (as this is too time-consuming, such as reading a daily newspaper), but is only aware of the political events without having a deeper knowledge of the details. At the same time, this person shows little appreciation of conventional, party-political activities: "I get too irritated. [...] Particularly about these party-political conflicts; and this party-political demeanor is beastly unnerving." This interviewee explains her political inactivity by the absence of political goals. In her opinion, the prerequisite for political action is to have a specific objective, as well as the individual need to contribute to social change and "to be a help" to other people or society. However, none of these two prerequisites were met in her case, according to herself; instead, the interviewee claimed to lack of interests and objectives, "because I myself do not know what is stopping me now. Yes, maybe because I cannot accumulate for myself any interests that are so important to me that I would now bother to be politically active." She can still imagine being politically active, though, if a particular political topic would become "so politically charged that it is impossible for me not to do it" or if she was not required to develop her own agenda, but if she was told specific political objectives—such as in the form of a party programme, for example. Also, this interviewee does not believe in political violence: "I would not have the balls for that."

In summary, this person watches political events suspiciously though she endorses political activity in general. However, although she reports an interest in politics, this does not lead to political activity—in her opinion, her interest does not yield a sufficient level of cognitive involvement in the sense of a productive reflection on how the alleged weaknesses of the political process can be eliminated by her own contribution. Her interest rather appears to be a manifestation of her distrust in the polity. This person simply seems to be uninterested in making an active contribution to political life herself. Instead she is satisfied with the current division of responsibilities and her own role as a "critic of political events," for she leaves political work to other people.

5.2. Interviewees who participated only in unconventional political activities

These interviews (*IDs A, C, E, H,* and *I*) suggest that the respondents participate in unconventional ways because they do not trust conventional structures which they think are nontransparent and inefficient. "Actually, I was always very interested and then I realized, 'Oh, they get the money and do anything to boost the media and the like.' I just realized that this is not my world. I do not know any true, reasonable politician who really wants the best for their country." (*H*) Thus, politics is considered a "dirty deal" (*H*). One of the interviewees explains his distrust in political parties, "because I have such an attitude that I do not trust politics so much and so on, and I would rather prefer to have direct access and not to rely on someone else." (*A*)

Moreover, these interviewees do not feel sufficiently politically competent and efficacious themselves. Hence, these students might either indeed be not as competent as necessary for participation in conventional politics, or they do not put enough effort in making politics transparent to themselves. One of the interviewees justifies this by her "sciolism," and she further notes: "I think I have other interests [than politics and political participation]. I do not know if it has ever interested me or I do not know. I guess I have just left it to others. [...] I mean if you want to be politically active, you should have a firm political stance." (*C*) Conditions for political participation that are mentioned by this interviewee are time, political interest, and perseverance, owing to the perception that individuals and small groups have no influence: politics "is decided elsewhere. As a small group? I do not know." (*C*)

Most of the respondents who participated in unconventional political behavior, but not in conventional activities, really want to reap the fruits of their labor directly. Thus, they prefer possibilities of direct democratic participation—activities that "can really have a direct impact on society" (*A*) and activities in non-governmental organizations (*A, I*). These people also talk about the realization of "projects" instead of persistent, "ideologically" coined party politics (*A*), and they want to recognize the results of their political activities immediately. They aim to "support the community" (*E*), "give something back to society" (*E*), "show solidarity with other people" (*I*) and promote a just society. Hence, it comes without surprise that these interviewees also suggest that social awareness and the individual's need to bring about social change are necessities. Political action is also considered to be a "hobby" (*E*) and should be anchored in the living environment, everyday life and day-to-day needs. For interviewee *I*, for example, political action "is a very personal matter," because she feels excluded and "does not feel to be free" in her own daily life. It is for this reason that she prioritizes the fight for freedom and justice in her own engagement. Though at the same time, she reports that she deliberately decided to participate in an *international* nongovernmental organization, because people in Germany would have a good life. Yet this emphasizes her concern about social justice, and her interest in freedom and justice further explains why her activities are at the international level.

Those interviewees' unconventional political participation whose political interest is relatively low are likely to be encouraged by fellow activists. "I guess I have just left it to others. [...] If someone would come and say, 'Well we do this and that and do you want to work with us, help us?' I think that would be the way where I would say yes, gladly, so what can I do? Then I would be helpful of course." (*C*) If an opportunity to express one's own political concerns opens up and one is not alone, you just participate, in particular spontaneously and on short notice, by going on a political demonstration, for example. Personal interests are supposed to reflect the activities of those interviewees, and short-term, well-defined commitments are often preferred. These, in turn, are characteristic of unconventional political activities. The concise statement of interviewee *H* puts it succinctly: "If you are interested, then go ahead." This suggests a direct link between political interest and issue-related political action (see also earlier, interviewee *C*).

Particularly interesting and somewhat different is interviewee *E*, who clearly prefers conventional ways of participation, though not yet being actively engaged in these. In his opinion, political decisions can only be influenced by elections and direct contact: "You talk until you are blue in the face, so to speak. I always think that people are demonstrating against a wall, because politics can only be influenced by elections." His level of political self-efficacy is relatively above his interest in politics, and he does not think that politics is complicated: "One does not have to have studied politics to become a politician." Moreover, he has already plans to further political participation using conventional means in the future.

Overall, it is amazing that those migrants who had participated in many unconventional activities simultaneously tend to report lower levels of political self-efficacy, and sometimes also lower levels of political interest, compared with those interviewees who had performed only one of the unconventional activities that we tapped in our survey. Whether this is because the interviewees understand "political interest" as an interest in traditional or conventional politics could not be clarified.

5.3. Interviewees who participated in conventional and unconventional political activities

The interviews with those who additionally participated in conventional political activities (*IDs B, D, G,* and *J*) suggest that conventional political action requires carefully planned decision-making and a consideration of costs and benefits. All four interviewees point out that political action requires organization, planning, and a long-term commitment—things that other interviewees had also mentioned. Interviewee *B*: "An individual cannot achieve that much. If you manage to organize yourself and collect a few votes, be it a signatory campaign or a demonstration, you can achieve a lot more."

Conventional, particularly party-political activities are described as tedious; our interviewees emphasize that persistence is actually a personal requirement. They suggest that one needs to refrain from the desire to recognize immediate success of political actions, since doing successful politics is quite time-consuming and proceeds in small steps. Interviewees say that one has to be "deathly cold" (*J*) and should have a "thick skin" (*G*). Acting in a conventional way is considered as a kind of "self-flagellation" (*J*). *J* further clarifies that she has "given up" and is now "depoliticized," because people would always talk but not act, and even in those groups that she worked in, hierarchies persisted with no societal change in sight. According to the interviews, one clearly needs to be able to emotional distancing, and has to accept social exclusion. For example, interviewee *G* reports a clear example when she describes that her circle of acquaintances shows a lack of understanding and appreciation of her participation in the German Social Democratic Party. This is because the party is seen as the wrong place to advocate for Turkish people, as it dithered and eventually did not exclude Thilo Sarrazin, who wrote the book "Germany is abolishing itself." In his book, he argued that Muslim immigrants—and particularly those from Turkey—are hard to integrate into society, and that this is due to those immigrants' attitudes. This interviewee characterizes herself as a "warrior by nature," because she has not given up her conventional participation despite her enormous frustration about the "cliquing" in her own party (as well as "lobbying," as *B* puts it) and about the fact that politics "always operates on a very short-term basis and always just survive the next election."

Another thing that individuals may need to engage in conventional action, according to these interviews, is to overestimate their own contribution. This might result in frustration though. Like previous interviewees, social change is an important objective, but most of the interviewees who report conventional political participation confirm that it is a conscious decision to participate that accounts for the costs of conventional participation. "I cannot save the whole world, but at least I have this ideal to change something and improve something." (*G*)

Finally, the interviewees also talk about political competence in a broad sense, and objectively incorrect knowledge appears to be an obstacle to conventional political action for one of the interviewees: "I would also like to get involved in politics, but I lack the German nationality. [...] According to German law, I believe that one must be a German citizen to get active in a party and unfortunately, God forbids me to move up to the Federal Chancellor. I might have had that ambition." (*B*) In fact, non-German citizens can legally participate in a political party. However, this interviewee is not just unaware of this fact, but he possesses incorrect knowledge, which seems to prevent him from more conventional participation. Unsurprisingly, a lack of participation is attributed to a lack of political knowledge and political skills, and this does not only concern the knowledge of political rights and opportunities to participate, but linguistic skills such as the knowledge of technical terms, completing forms or writing political proposals are discussed as well. The command of the German language is also meant to be important, in particular when it comes to conventional political participation. An instance reported by interviewee *G* makes this very clear: During a meeting of district delegates, her friend—who had no university degree, as emphasized by *G*—asked her about the meaning of the word "pragmatic," which she could not make sense of. All these aspects show the significance of being conscious of your activity, your aims and the time frame until you will succeed, which skills you need and what you might have to spare meanwhile. This actually corresponds to the high levels of political self-efficacy among these interviewees.

Unconventional political activities were carried out by all of these interviewees, too, which also matches their high political interest. As noted earlier, the aims of participation, and particularly of unconventional participation, are similar to those mentioned by the interviewees who only participated in unconventional activities, are related to social change and justice. "When I see something unjust, I try to get it right as quickly as possible." (*D*) This interviewee strives for a community that is "worth living in:" "So if you can change something in their lives, this is politics for me. [...] For me, politics is to change the active life here in Germany—with the rights one has got." Similar is interviewee G: "I cannot save the whole world, but at least I have this ideal to change something and improve something." These interviewees believe that change can be achieved by multiple means—conventional and unconventional.

One exception is interviewee *B* though, who has the lowest levels of political interest and efficacy among the 10 interviewees, which might correlate with his distrust in German politics. It should also be noted that immigrants and their descendants are often excluded from the political process so that they do not know their options to participate, and interviewee *B* is apparently unaware of his right to participate in political parties (see above). Thus political knowledge *is* important.

6. Discussion

The explorative interviews analyzed here followed a survey study which examined political interest and political self-efficacy as precursors of different kinds of political action. This qualitative study focused on a well-educated subpopulation of Turkish migrants in Germany, and the results may not be generalizable across the entire population of Turkish migrants. The presented interviews draw attention to the characteristics of the different kinds of political action and they shed light on further processes and conditions of political participation beyond interest and efficacy. In particular, among the interviewees political inactivity was associated with distrust in (conventional) politics. Instead of active participation, primarily criticism was practiced and a rather individualistic strategy was pursued. In this study, political distrust and dissatisfaction with politics also did not necessarily pose an incentive to get politically active, although dissatisfaction was consistently associated with the wish for a better society.

Resignation and a lack of credibility of political parties and politicians were linked to the lack of conventional political activity, but as indicated, unconventional participation was frequently reported by the interviewees who indicated that they were unsatisfied with conventional politics. A lack of confidence in their political self-efficacy and skills, which are often considered to be prerequisites for reasoned, rational, reflective behavior, also prevented some interviewees from engaging in conventional political participation. On the other hand, a basic level of distrust and possibly a moderate interest in political issues were associated with increased unconventional activity among the Turkish migrant interviewees. Other research has shown that despite the often positive ramifications of political trust, more trust does not necessarily implicate more participation in any political activity (Torney-Purta, Barber, & Richardson, 2004; Torney-Purta & Richardson, 2004).

Recent research has provided a more nuanced answer to the role of political trust and suggested that more institutional trust might be positively correlated with more electoral and conventional political participation, whereas less political trust might trigger unconventional participation (Hooghe & Marien, 2013). That study also found a cumulative effect of political trust and political self-efficacy with respect to electoral and conventional participation. The findings of the present study align well with that (see below). In terms of rational choice theory, electoral and conventional political activities are probably instrumental forms of participation that serve a specific goal. On the other hand, unconventional or "protest" participation might be regarded as more expressive in nature, so that dissatisfaction and distrust in political institutions might primarily serve the purpose of expressing one's dissatisfaction, which then would provide instant gratification. Major societal changes were indeed rarely the primary purpose of respondents' unconventional acts, rather, they wanted to see immediate results and help their local and immediate environment(s).

Also, we could speculate that political trust might influence outcome beliefs and the perceived power of impeding factors to the successful execution of a particular behavior; hence, participation within the traditional system may be believed to be costlier, and combined with limited political self-efficacy, this type of political participation might be less common. If trust took the role of a switching point that facilitated conventional participation, whereas distrust triggered unconventional participation, a pronounced withdrawal from conventional politics could be the consequence: Turkish migrants are disadvantaged in German society, which arguably could promote distrust in the established institutions. In return, this could consolidate their disengagement with conventional politics, a means of participation that is more likely to produce authoritative and binding decisions and regulations. Consequently, that development might have the potential to promote a democratic deficit, if our study findings would be generalizable across the whole population of Turkish migrants.

An important task for future research will be the examination of the relationships between political trust, political self-efficacy, and political participation among different groups in society, of which some might be more disadvantaged than others, to learn whether the mentioned mechanism is conditional of social disadvantage of a (minority) in-group. For example, as Muslims—who are "dominated" by the Turkish population in Germany (Halm, 2013; Haug et al., 2009)—are more politically trusting than non-Muslims (Doerschler & Irving Jackson, 2011), it is worth examining how this trust may moderate the intensity of political participation between Turkish migrants and Germans without any immigration background, as well as between different migrant groups. An additional question that needs to be answered is about the role of religiousness in general, and whether the strength of religious belief is a moderator that works above and beyond the pure membership in the Muslim community.

In addition, in a time when "fake news" has become a serious threat to society, it is also essential to connect trust, efficacy, and actual knowledge about politics, and to study whether correct and incorrect knowledge of politics (and the degree of certainty about the correctness of the knowledge one beliefs to have) make a difference in how trust and efficacy relate to different types of political participation. Although prior research has suggested that political knowledge has indirect effects on political participation (Reichert, 2016), it would be useful to study the interactions between the three mentioned variables. Arguably, respondents' confidence in the accuracy of their political knowledge might affect the level of their trust or distrust in politics, which then should affect the strength of the relationship between political trust and the different types of participation.

Furthermore, the interviewees found it important consciously and deliberately to opt for participation in conventional political activities: Those who were, are, or plan to get active in conventional ways reported about well-planned decisions regarding their political participation, and that their choices were made despite the acknowledgement of significant "costs" (emotional distancing, social exclusion). These respondents weighed the costs of participation, although some also mentioned that the cost is quite high and that their participation does not provide immediate benefits. Individuals may (initially) need to overestimate their own contribution to politics in order to get involved in conventional activities (Opp, 2009), but this might also increase the risk of political resignation. In any instance, participation in conventional activities always was a highly reflective decision, not primarily an affective "impulse." Although unconventional activities were not always as strongly thought through and might be related primarily to specific political issues, interests and current topics, these more expressive activities also required reflection.

Another inevitable aspect that is linked to reflective decision-making is political competence, which comprises the skills that are required for successful participations (e.g. knowledge, behavioral skills, language skills): In particular linguistic skills to articulate political concerns, the knowledge of certain political concepts and practices within legal structures were understood as necessary conditions of political activity; the lack of communication competence was even considered to be a cause of political violence. Communication scholars also argue that communication competence, understood as the capacity to interpersonal communication and the adequate use and interpretation of news media, is an essential requirement for political activism (Shah, McLeod, & Lee, 2009). Developing such competences may be more demanding and difficult for (Turkish) migrants, however, as they are disadvantaged with respect to their educational achievement. Moreover, their families and peers might prefer to speak Turkish at home or to discuss Turkish politics.

Members of the Turkish community also do not feel accepted in German society (Sachverständigenrat Deutscher Stiftungen für Integration und Migration, 2014). Hence, non-participating peers or acquaintances may find it hard to understand why, and to accept that, a member of their ethnic in-group would engage in conventional politics and, thus, become part of the political establishment. This would raise the psychological costs of participation. In fact, research suggests that norms of significant others such as family and peers can play a major role in motivating behavior (Ajzen, 2012), and it seems that for young Turkish migrants, significant others' views are indeed relevant for offline participation (Jugert et al., 2013). Being surrounded by people who do not understand or accept such an involvement in the established political processes, resignation or frustration could be likely consequences. Such undesirable attitudes might be even more likely to develop the less the expected outcomes are achieved.

In particular, if participation is not backed by the support (in form of acceptance) by those significant others and at the same time the expected outcomes are not achieved within a given timeframe, it is reasonable to expect that this will affect political self-efficacy or the perceived influence as a collective of Turkish migrants, which rational actor theory has identified as important predictors of intended and actual behavior (Ajzen, 2012; but see Eckstein et al., 2015; who found significant influences of political self-efficacy only among non-immigrant youth—yet their measure of participation comprised no conventional activities; Jugert et al., 2013; Opp, 2009). That is, the incentives that rational actor theory has identified (Leighley, 1995) would not be present in order to balance the costs that are associated with an engagement in political action. Consequently, behavioral beliefs, normative beliefs, and control beliefs would be negative and no participation would be the likely consequence (Ajzen, 2012). Our study provides some evidence that political self-efficacy is in fact a requirement for political participation, in particular regarding conventional activities (Reichert, 2013). The interviewees of the present study furthermore pointed out the significance of other factors that theory has found to be important precursors of (reasoned) action.

Yet it is an undeniable truth that the marginal position of Turkish migrants in Germany requires them to tackle higher hurdles to engage in a conventional manner than, for instance, native Germans without a migration history. Therefore, weighing costs and benefits could be more significant compared to other populations such as native Germans and other migrant groups. Recall, for instance, that some of the obstacles that the interviewees mentioned included, for instance, experiences of exclusion (also from their own social group), but also missing opportunities to participate in general, or an absence of a lobby within their own minority in-group in Germany.

In addition, experiences of exclusion and the absence of a lobby within their own minority in-group indicate little approval for such participation, that is, a lack of norms of participation among the interviewees' significant others. It is worth mentioning that interviewee *B* also suggests a need to identify yourself with your representatives in order to develop an interest in politics. Such identification can be regarded as an important aspect of normative beliefs, which provide directions for action (Ajzen, 2012). The absence of the mentioned factors, however, could reduce an individuals' collective efficacy and, eventually, their political self-efficacy. That is, if political participation is not valued among members of the minority in-group, and if there is no lobby that advocates for the goals and needs of that group, then the expectation of group success may be limited—even if all group members share a sense of injustice against their group and even if they attribute the responsibility to another group (which are conditions in the model proposed by Simon & Klandermans, 2001). However, the interrelationships between collective and self-efficacy need more attention in future research: If the group cannot achieve the goals as a group, how would an individual feel (externally and internally) efficacious to do so, in particular if there are no role models that would show

how to perform political action successfully? Apparently, significant contextual conditions for participation, especially participation in conventional politics, would not be met, and only little incentives to engage in politics would prevail.

In such a context, respondents would probably have two options to justify their political participation: either they raise the value of the expected outcome of participation, or they value less the opinions of their significant others (cf. Ajzen, 2012). This could cause issues of incompatibility between being a member of the disadvantaged minority in-group and participation within the majority society. Recent research has shown that such an incompatibility can become a liability in that it might increase the readiness for radical political action (Simon et al., 2013). Therefore, future research needs to identify the specific conditions and how these would enable migrants to channel their feelings of disadvantage, unacceptance of participation by other minority in-group members, and the aim to improve society toward the use of legitimate means, rather than to give up or turn to radical forms of participation.

In particular, interviewees mentioned needs such as bringing about social change, an anchoring of political participation in the living environment, and an immediate recognition of action results. These needs are not easily satisfied through conventional means of participation. Those interviewees who utilized unconventional means of participation reported that in their opinion an engagement in these activities demands social awareness, some distrust in "traditional" politics, and a need for immediate change (or "improvement") of social or political conditions. "If you are interested, then go ahead," was the slogan of these interviewees, without bothering about institutionalized means of participation and all the hassle that seems to be associated with them (see also the above discussion on expressive behaviors). We may note here that scholars have argued that younger cohorts may be driving a value change and generally prefer unconventional political activities instead of traditional ways of participation.[4] It would be worthy to examine whether this development is more pronounced among migrant youth.[5]

7. Conclusion

The present study used a selective sample of well-educated university students with a Turkish migrant background. Although it does not allow us to draw general conclusions, it explored and confirmed further conditions and variables that may be required in addition to political interest and self-efficacy to promote political participation of Turkish migrants. This paper did not *test* any theory, but building on a survey study, we were more prone to identify variables that may be considered in rational actor theories. The results could be easily linked to rational choice models and the *Theory of Planned Behavior* (Ajzen, 2012), as we found that normative beliefs were important conditions of conventional participation among our study participants—or at least were these constraints taken into consideration by the interviewees. Control beliefs, defined by political self-efficacy and actual political skills (e.g. communication competence) were positively associated with political participation and, again, primarily with conventional activities among the respondents. Motivations such as a just society or positive contributions to society were easily identified by all interviewees. Apparently, striving for a just society, potentially an expressive goal, was the major incentive for political participation, although it was mingled with (a lack of) trust in politics, political self-efficacy and skills.

In conclusion, this study has confirmed the role of several incentives and conditions of participation, as these were identified in rational actor and action theoretic models, among a small and unrepresentative group of highly educated Turkish migrants. However, future research is needed to examine the specific relationships that we tentatively identified. (1) Future research should study the relationship(s) between political trust, political self-efficacy, (objective and subjective) political knowledge and participation among different groups with different levels of (perceived and actual) disadvantage. (2) The relationships between collective and self-efficacy deserve more attention in future research and should be examined with samples from different ethnic groups. (3) Finally, future research needs to examine how feelings of disadvantage, the rejection of participation and participants by other minority in-group members, and the wish to improve society work together, and under which conditions members of the minority group will opt for legitimate forms of participation, radical means of participation, or no participation.

As for the Turkish migrants in our study, we may conclude that due consideration of their legitimate interests as a collective is important for their social integration and their readiness to participate in political life. This seems crucial to make the political game also their game, and not just the game of the majority. Otherwise, and if the findings of this study apply to the majority of Turkish migrants in Germany, the liberal democratic society would remain a hollow promise. As European societies are faced with large numbers of immigrants, we have to keep that promise in order not to cultivate disenchanted, distrustful, and frustrated immigrants. Otherwise, democracy may as well abolish itself. If our societies fail to integrate young migrants socially and politically, these young people could endorse authoritarian or totalitarian forms of government, and only then would they become actual threats to democracy.

Acknowledgement
This article summarizes selected findings that have been published by Oldenbourg in German language. The author is grateful to Oldenbourg for the permission to publish these findings in English.

Funding
This research was supported by research grants from the Deutsche Forschungsgemeinschaft (DFG) to Bernd Simon, Christian-Albrechts-Universität Kiel [grant numbers SI 428/13-3 and SI 428/13-4].

Competing Interests
The authors declare no competing interest.

Author details
Frank Reichert[1]
E-mail: reichert@hku.hk
[1] Faculty of Education, The University of Hong Kong, Room 217, 2/F, Runme Shaw Building, Pok Fu Lam Road, Hong Kong, Hong Kong SAR.

Notes

1. The term "migrant" is used to refer to both first-generation immigrants and their descendants (i.e. immigrant-origin individuals).
2. Although recent Muslim immigration towards Germany could possibly advance the relative position of Turkish migrants.
3. In fact, a high percentage of the 9/11 and other significant terror attacks were highly educated (Bergen & Pandey, 2005). Hence, understanding successful pathways to legitimate political participation of well-educated migrants is particularly worthwhile.
4. Dalton (2008) is probably the most salient proponent of this view.
5. Eckstein et al. (2015) and Jugert et al. (2013) provide some indication that this could be the case, especially among Turkish migrants.

References

Ajzen, I. (2012). Martin Fishbein's Legacy: The reasoned action approach. *The ANNALS of the American Academy of Political and Social Science, 640*, 11–27. doi:10.1177/0002716211423363

Almond, G. A., & Verba, S. (1963). *The civic culture. Political attitudes and democracy in five nations.* Princeton: Princeton University Press. https://doi.org/10.1515/9781400874569

Avcı, G. (2006). Comparing integration policies and outcomes: Turks in the Netherlands and Germany. *Turkish Studies, 7*, 67–84.

Babka von Gostomski, C. (2008). *Türkische, griechische, italienische und polnische Personen sowie Personen aus den Nachfolgestaaten des ehemaligen Jugoslawien in Deutschland: Erste Ergebnisse der Repräsentativbefragung "Ausgewählte Migrantengruppen in Deutschland 2006/2007" (RAM)* [Turkish, Greek, Italian and Polish persons as well as persons from the successor states of the former Yugoslavia in Germany: First results of the representative survey "Selected migrant groups in Germany 2006/2007" (RAM)] (Working paper der Forschungsgruppe des Bundesamtes: Vol. 11). Nürnberg: Bundesamt für Migration und Flüchtlinge.

Balch, G. I. (1974). Multiple indicators in survey research: The concept of 'sense of political efficacy'. *Political Methodology, 1*(2), 1–43.

Bandura, A. (1977). Self-efficacy: Toward a unifying theory of behavioral change. *Psychological Review, 84*, 191–215. https://doi.org/10.1037/0033-295X.84.2.191

Bargh, J. A. (1997). The automaticity of everyday life. In R. S. Wyer (Ed.), *Advances in social cognition: X. The automaticity of everyday life* (pp. 1–61). Mahwah, NJ: Erlbaum.

Barnes, S. H., Kaase, M., Allerbeck, K. R., Farah, B. G., Heunks, F., Inglehart, R., & Rosenmayr, L. (1979). *Political action: Mass participation in five western democracies.* Beverly Hills, London: Sage.

Bergen, P., & Pandey, S. (2005, June 14). The madrassa myth. *The New York Times.* Retrieved from https://nyti.ms/2lgWx2y

Böcker, A., & Groenendijk, K. (2006). Die sichtbare Hand der Politik oder die unsichtbare Hand des Marktes: Eine Analyse der türkischen Migration nach und aus Deutschland und den Niederlanden [The visible hand of politics or the invisible hand of the market: An analysis of the Turkish migration to and from Germany and the Netherlands]. In S. Baringhorst, J. F. Hollifield, & U. Hunger (Eds.), *Herausforderung Migration – Perspektiven der vergleichenden Politikwissenschaft. Festschrift für Dietrich Thränhardt* [Challenge migration - Perspectives of comparative political science: Festschrift for Dietrich Thränhardt] (pp. 167–194). Berlin: LIT.

Böltken, F. (2000). Soziale Distanz und räumliche Nähe – Einstellungen und Erfahrungen im alltäglichen Zusammenleben von Ausländern und Deutschen im Wohngebiet [Social distance and spatial proximity – Attitudes and experiences in the everyday coexistence of foreigners and Germans in the residential district]. In R.

Alba, P. Schmidt, & M. Wasmer (Eds.), *Blickpunkt Gesellschaft: Vol. 5. Deutsche und Ausländer. Freunde, Fremde oder Feinde? Empirische Befunde und theoretische Erklärungen* [Focus society: Vol. 5. Germans and foreigners: Friends, strangers or enemies? Empirical findings and theoretical explanations] (pp. 147–194). Wiesbaden: Westdeutscher Verlag. https://doi.org/10.1007/978-3-322-86615-8

Bommes, M. (2010). Migration research in Germany: The emergence of a generalised research field in a reluctant immigration country. In D. Thränhardt & M. Bommes (Eds.), *IMIS-Schriften: Vol. 13. National Paradigms of Migration Research* (pp. 127–185). Göttingen: V&R unipress.

Brettfeld, K., & Wetzels, P. (2008). *Muslime in Deutschland – Integration, Integrationsbarrieren, Religion sowie Einstellungen zu Demokratie, Rechtsstaat und politisch-religiös motivierter Gewalt: Ergebnisse von Befragungen im Rahmen einer multizentrischen Studie in städtischen Lebensräumen* [Muslims in Germany - integration, integration barriers, religion and attitudes towards democracy, the rule of law and political-religious violence: Results of surveys within a multicentric study in urban habitats] (2nd ed.). Berlin, Hamburg: Bundesministerium des Innern.

Campbell, A., Gurin, G., & Miller, W. E. (1954). *The voter decides.* Evanston; White Plains: Row, Peterson and Company.

Dalton, R. J. (2008). Citizenship norms and the expansion of political participation. *Political Studies, 56*, 76–98. doi:10.1111/j.1467-9248.2007.00718.x

Delli Carpini, M. X., & Keeter, S. (1996). *What Americans know about politics and why it matters.* New Haven, CT: Yale University Press.

de Wit, T. D., & Koopmans, R. (2005). The integration of ethnic minorities into political culture: The Netherlands, Germany and Great Britain compared. *Acta Politica, 40*, 50–73. doi:10.1057/palgrave.ap.5500096

Diehl, C. (2002). *Die Partizipation von Migranten in Deutschland: Rückzug oder Mobilisierung?* [The participation of migrants in Germany: Retreat or mobilization?]. Opladen: Leske + Budrich.

Diehl, C., & Blohm, M. (2001). Apathy, adaptation or ethnic mobilisation? On the attitudes of a politically excluded group. *Journal of Ethnic and Migration Studies, 27*, 401–420. doi:10.1080/136918301200266149

Diehl, C., & Fick, P. (2016). Ethnische Diskriminierung im deutschen Bildungssystem [Ethnic discrimination in the German education system]. In C. Diehl, C. Hunkler, & C. Kristen (Eds.), *Ethnische Ungleichheiten im Bildungsverlauf. Mechanismen, Befunde, Debatten* [Ethnic inequalities in education: Mechanisms, findings, debates] (pp. 243–286). Wiesbaden: Springer VS. https://doi.org/10.1007/978-3-658-04322-3

Diehl, C., & Urbahn, J. (1998). *Die soziale und politische Partizipation von Zuwanderern in der Bundesrepublik Deutschland. Gesprächskreis Arbeit und Soziales* [The social and political participation of immigrants in the Federal Republic of Germany]. Bonn: Forschungsinst. der Friedrich-Ebert-Stiftung, Abt. Arbeits- und Sozialpolitik. Retrieved from https://library.fes.de/fulltext/asfo/00258toc.htm

Doerschler, P., & Irving Jackson, P. (2011). Do muslims in Germany really fail to integrate? Muslim integration and trust in public institutions. *Journal of International Migration and Integration, 13*, 503–523. doi:10.1007/s12134-011-0220-6

Eckstein, K., Jugert, P., Noack, P., Born, M., & Şener, T. (2015). Comparing correlates of civic engagement between immigrant and majority youth in Belgium, Germany, and Turkey. *Research in Human Development, 12*, 44–62. doi:10.1080/15427609.2015.1010346

Ergi, I. (2000). *Lebenssituation und politische Beteiligung von ArbeitsimmigrantInnen in der Bundesrepublik Deutschland: Möglichkeiten, Probleme und Formen, dargestellt am Beispiel von TürkInnen* [Life situation and political participation of labor immigrants in the Federal Republic of Germany: Possibilities, problems and forms, by the example of Turks] (2nd ed.). Marburg: Tectum.

Fassmann, H., & İçduygu, A. (2013). Turks in Europe: Migration flows, migrant stocks and demographic structure. *European Review, 21*, 349–361. doi:10.1017/S1062798713000318

Fazio, R. H. (1990). Multiple processes by which attitudes guide behavior: The MODE model as an integrative framework. In M. P. Zanna (Ed.), *Advances in experimental social psychology* (Vol. 23, pp. 75–109). New York, NY: Academic Press.

Fowler, J. H., Baker, L. A., & Dawes, C. T. (2008). Genetic variation in political participation. *American Political Science Review, 102*, 233–248. doi:10.1017/S0003055408080209

Gaiser, W., & de Rijke, J. (2006). Gesellschaftliche und politische Beteiligung [Social and political participation]. In M. Gille, S. Sardei-Biermann, W. Gaiser, & J. de Rijke (Eds.), *Jugendsurvey: Vol. 3. Jugendliche und junge Erwachsene in Deutschland. Lebensverhältnisse, Werte und gesellschaftliche Beteiligung 12- bis 29-Jähriger* [Youth survey: Vol. 3. Adolescents and young adults in Germany: Living conditions, values and social participation of 12- to 29-year-olds] (pp. 213–275). Wiesbaden: VS.

Gille, M., Krüger, W., & de Rijke, J. (2000). Politische Orientierungen [Political orientations]. In M. Gille, & W. Krüger (Eds.), *DJI-Jugendsurvey: Vol. 2. Unzufriedene Demokraten. Politische Orientierungen der 16- bis 29jährigen im vereinigten Deutschland* [Youth survey: Vol. 2. Dissatisfied democrats: Political orientations of 16- to 29-year-olds in unified Germany] (pp. 205–265). Opladen: Leske + Budrich.

Glatzer, W. (2004). *Integration und Partizipation junger Ausländer vor dem Hintergrund ethnischer und kultureller Identifikation: Ergebnisse des Integrationssurveys des BiB. Materialien zur Bevölkerungswissenschaft: 105c* [Integration and participation of young foreigners against the background of ethnic and cultural identification: Results of the integration survey of the BiB. Materials for population science: 105c]. Wiesbaden: Bundesinstitut für Bevölkerungsforschung.

Goldberg, A., Mourinho, D., & Kulke, U. (Eds.) (1995). *Arbeitsmarkt-Diskriminierung gegenüber ausländischen Arbeitnehmern in Deutschland* [Labor market discrimination against foreign workers in Germany]. (International Migration Papers: Vol. 7). Geneva: ILO.

Granato, M. (2003). Jugendliche mit Migrationshintergrund – auch in der beruflichen Bildung geringere Chancen? [Youths with a migration background - less opportunities in vocational education and training too?] In G. Auernheimer (Ed.), *Interkulturelle Studien: Band 16. Schieflagen im Bildungssystem. Die Benachteiligung der Migrantenkinder* [Imbalances in the education system: The disadvantage of migrant children] (pp. 113–135). Opladen: Leske + Budrich. https://doi.org/10.1007/978-3-322-97594-2

Granato, N., & Kalter, F. (2001). Die Persistenz ethnischer Ungleichheit auf dem deutschen Arbeitsmarkt: Diskriminierung oder Unterinvestition in Humankapital? [The persistence of ethnic inequality on the German labor market: Discrimination or under-investment in human capital?] *Kölner Zeitschrift für Soziologie und Sozialpsychologie, 53*, 497–520. https://doi.org/10.1007/s11577-001-0076-4

Halm, D. (2013). The current discourse on Islam in Germany. *Journal of International Migration and Integration, 14*, 457–474. doi:10.1007/s12134-012-0251-7

Hatemi, P. K., Medland, S. E., Morley, K. I., Heath, A. C., & Martin, N. G. (2007). The genetics of voting: An Australian twin study. *Behavior Genetics, 37*, 435–448. doi:10.1007/s10519-006-9138-8

Haug, S., Müssig, S., & Stichs, A. (2009). *Muslimisches Leben in Deutschland. Forschungsbericht: Vol. 6.* [Muslim life in Germany. Research report: Vol. 6]. Nürnberg: Bundesamt für Migration u. Flüchtlinge.

Heß-Meining, U. (2000). Interesse an politischem Engagement und Formen gesellschaftlich-politischer Beteiligung [Interest in political engagement and forms of socio-political participation]. In A. Weidacher (Ed.), *In Deutschland zu Hause. Politische Orientierungen griechischer, italienischer, türkischer und deutscher junger Erwachsener* [At home in Germany: Political orientations of Greek, Italian, Turkish and German young adults] (pp. 191–224). Opladen: Leske + Budrich.

Hooghe, M., & Marien, S. (2013). A comparative analysis f the relation between political trust and forms of political participation in Europe. *European Societies, 15*, 131–152. doi:10.1080/14616696.2012.692807

Hunkler, C. (2016). Ethnische Unterschiede beim Zugang zu beruflicher Ausbildung [Ethnic differences in access to vocational training]. In C. Diehl, C. Hunkler, & C. Kristen (Eds.), *Ethnische Ungleichheiten im Bildungsverlauf. Mechanismen, Befunde, Debatten* [Ethnic inequalities in education: Mechanisms, findings, debates] (pp. 597–641). Wiesbaden: Springer VS. https://doi.org/10.1007/978-3-658-04322-3

Joppke, C. (1999). *Immigration and the nation-state: The United States, Germany, and Great Britain.* Oxford: Oxford University Press. https://doi.org/10.1093/0198295405.001.0001

Jugert, P., Eckstein, K., Noack, P., Kuhn, A., & Benbow, A. (2013). Offline and online civic engagement among adolescents and young adults from three ethnic groups. *Journal of Youth and Adolescence, 42*, 123–135. doi:10.1007/s10964-012-9805-4

Kaas, L., & Manger, C. (2010). *Ethnic discrimination in Germany's labour market: A field experiment.* Retrieved from https://www.econstor.eu/dspace/bitstream/10419/36152/1/61883852X.pdf

Kahneman, D. (2003). Maps of bounded rationality: Psychology for behavioral economics. *American Economic Review, 93*, 1449–1475. https://doi.org/10.1257/000282803322655392

Koopmans, R., & Statham, P. (1999). Challenging the liberal nation-state? Postnationalism, multiculturalism, and the collective claims making of migrants and ethnic minorities in Britain and Germany. *American Journal of Sociology, 105*, 652–696. doi:10.1086/210357

Kristen, C., Reimer, D., & Kogan, I. (2008). Higher education entry of turkish immigrant youth in Germany. *International Journal of Comparative Sociology, 49*, 127–151. doi:10.1177/0020715208088909

Kuckartz, U. (2007). *Qualitative evaluation. Der Einstieg in die Praxis* [Qualitative evaluation: Getting into practice]. Wiesbaden: VS.

Leighley, K. E. (1995). Attitudes, opportunities and incentives: A field essay on political participation. *Political Research Quarterly, 48*, 181–209. https://doi.org/10.1177/106591299504800111

Lüdemann, C. (2001). Politische Partizipation, Anreize und Ressourcen. Ein Test verschiedener Handlungsmodelle und Anschlußtheorien am ALLBUS 1998 [Political participation, incentives and resources: A test of different action models and associated theories using ALLBUS 1998]. In A. Koch, M. Wasmer, P. Schmidt (Eds.), *Politische Partizipation in der Bundesrepublik Deutschland: Empirische Befunde und theoretische Erklärungen* [Political participation in the Federal Republic of Germany: Empirical findings and theoretical explanations] (pp. 43–71). Opladen: Leske + Budrich. https://doi.org/10.1007/978-3-322-99341-0

Mayring, P. (2003). *Qualitative Inhaltsanalyse. Grundlagen und Techniken* [Qualitative content analysis. Basics and techniques] (8th ed.) Weinheim; Basel: Beltz.

Meier-Braun, K.-H. (2007). Der lange Weg ins Einwanderungsland Deutschland [The long way to immigration country Germany]. In S. Frech, & K.-H. Meier-Braun (Eds.), *Die offene Gesellschaft. Zuwanderung und Integration* [The open society: Immigration and integration] (pp. 21–39). Schwalbach/Ts.: Wochenschau Verlag.

Merkens, H. (2005). Auswahlverfahren, Sampling, Fallkonstruktion [Selection, sampling, case construction]. In U. Flick, E. v. Kardorff, & I. Steinke (Eds.), *Qualitative Forschung. Ein Handbuch* [Qualitative research: A handbook] (4th ed., pp. 286–299). Reinbek bei Hamburg: Rowohlt.

Mondak, J. J., Hibbing, J. R., Canache, D., Seligson, M. A., & Anderson, M. R. (2010). Personality and civic engagement: An integrative framework for the study of trait effects on political behavior. *American Political Science Review, 104*, 85–110. doi:10.1017/S0003055409990359

Newton, K. (2007). Social and political trust. In R. J. Dalton, & H.-D. Klingemann (Eds.), *The Oxford handbook of political behavior* (pp. 342–361). Oxford, New York: Oxford University Press.

Olson, M. (1965/2002). *The logic of collective action. Public goods and the theory of groups.* Cambridge: Harvard University Press.

Opp, K.-D. (2009). *Theories of political protest and social movements: A multidisciplinary introduction, critique, and synthesis.* New York, NY: Routledge.

Quintelier, E. (2012, December). *The effect of personality on political participation among adolescents: Self reports of children and observer ratings from their parents.* Oldenburg: MSW Research Seminar. Retrieved from https://lirias.kuleuven.be/bitstream/123456789/369646/1/PaperOldenburg.pdf

Reichert, F. (2013). *Kognitive Politisierung bei Studierenden mit türkischer Migrationsgeschichte. Zum Einfluss von politischem Interesse und politischen Kompetenzen auf politisches Handeln sowie zur Rolle kollektiver Identitäten im Prozess kognitiver Politisierung* [Cognitive politicization among university students with Turkish migration history. On the influence of political interest and political competences on political action, and the role of collective identities in cognitive politicization]. München: De Gruyter Oldenbourg.

Reichert, F. (2016). How internal political efficacy translates political knowledge into political participation. *Europe's Journal of Psychology, 12*, 221–241. https://doi.org/10.5964/ejop.v12i2.1095

Rucht, D., & Heitmeyer, W. (2008). Mobilisierung von und für Migranten [Mobilization of and for migrants]. In R. Roth & D. Rucht (Eds.), *Die sozialen Bewegungen in Deutschland seit 1945. Ein Handbuch* [The social movements in Germany since 1945: A handbook] (pp. 573–592). Frankfurt: Campus.

Sachverständigenrat Deutscher Stiftungen für Integration und Migration. (2014). *Deutschlands Wandel zum modernen Einwanderungsland: Jahresgutachten 2014 mit Integrationsbarometer* [Germany's transition to a modern country of immigration: Annual report 2014 with integration barometer]. Berlin: SVR.

Santel, B. (2006). In der Realität angekommen: Die Bundesrepublik Deutschland als Einwanderungsland [Arrived in reality: The Federal Republic of Germany as a country of immigration]. *Politische Bildung., 3*, 9–25.

Schreier, M. (2010). Fallauswahl [Case selection]. In G. Mey & K. Mruck (Eds.), *Handbuch Qualitative Forschung in der Psychologie* [Handbook qualitative research in psychology] (pp. 238–251). Wiesbaden: VS. https://doi.org/10.1007/978-3-531-92052-8

Şen, & Faruk (2002). Türkische Minderheit in Deutschland [Turkish minority in Germany]. *Informationen zur politischen Bildung., 277*, 53–61.

Şener, T. (2007). Civic engagement of Turkish youth in Germany. *Journal of Social Science Education, 6*, 59–66.

Sezgin, Z. (2010). Türkische Migrantenorganisationen in Deutschland - Zwischen Mitgliederinteressen und institutioneller Umwelt [Turkish migrant organizations in Germany - Between members' interests and institutional environment]. In L. Pries, & Z. Sezgin (Eds.), *Jenseits von 'Identität oder Integration'. Grenzen überspannende Migrantenorganisationen* [Beyond 'identity or integration'. Cross-border migrant organizations] (pp. 201–232). Wiesbaden: VS. https://doi.org/10.1007/978-3-531-92280-5

Shah, D. V., McLeod, J. M., & Lee, N.-J. (2009). Communication competence as a foundation for civic competence: Processes of socialization into citizenship. *Political Communication, 26*, 102–117. doi:10.1080/10584600802710384

Simon, B., & Klandermans, B. (2001). Politicized collective identity. A social psychological analysis. *American Psychologist, 56*, 319–331.

Simon, B., Reichert, F., & Grabow, O. (2013). When dual identity becomes a liability: Identity and political radicalism among migrants. *Psychological Science, 24*, 251–257. doi:10.1177/0956797612450889

Simon, B., Reichert, F., Schaefer, C. D., Bachmann, A., & Renger, D. (2015). Dual identification and the (De-)politicization of migrants: Longitudinal and comparative evidence. *Journal of Community & Applied Social Psychology, 25*, 193–203. doi:10.1002/casp.2206

Statistisches Bundesamt (Destatis). (2015). *Bevölkerung und Erwerbstätigkeit: Bevölkerung mit Migrationshintergrund - Ergebnisse des Mikrozensus. 2014. Fachserie 1 Reihe 2.2* [Population and employment: Population with migration background - Results of the microcensus. 2014. Subject series 1 Series 2.2]. Wiesbaden: Statistisches Bundesamt.

Steinbrecher, M. (2009). *Politische Partizipation in Deutschland* [Political participation in Germany]. Baden-Baden: Nomos. https://doi.org/10.5771/9783845212838

Strack, F., & Deutsch, R. (2004). Reflective and impulsive determinants of social behavior. *Personality and Social Psychology Review, 8*, 220–247. https://doi.org/10.1207/s15327957pspr0803_1

Thränhardt, D. (1999). Integrationsprozesse in der Bundesrepublik Deutschland [Integration processes in the Federal Republic of Germany]. In Forschungsinstitut der Friedrich-Ebert-Stiftung (Ed.), *Gesprächskreis Arbeit und Soziales: Vol. 91. Integration und Intergrationsförderung in der Einwanderungsgesellschaft* [Working group labor and social affairs: Vol. 91. Integration and its promotion in the immigration society] (pp. 13–46). Bonn: FES.

Thränhardt, D. (2004). Immigrant cultures, state policies and social capital formation in Germany. *Journal of Comparative Policy Analysis: Research and Practice, 6*, 159–183. doi:10.1080/1387698042000273460

Torney-Purta, J., Barber, C. H., & Richardson, W. K. (2004). Trust in government-related institutions and political engagement among adolescents in six countries. *Acta Politica, 39*, 380–406. doi:10.1057/palgrave.ap.5500080

Torney-Purta, J., & Richardson, W. K. (2004). Anticipated political engagement among adolescents in Australia, England, Norway and the United States. In J. Demaine (Ed.), *Citizenship and political education today* (pp. 41–58). New York, NY: Palgrave Macmillan. https://doi.org/10.1057/9780230522879

van Deth, J. W. (1990). Interest in politics. In Jennings, K. M., van Deth, J. W., Barnes, S. H., Fuchs, D., Heunks, F. J., Inglehart, R., & Kaase, M., ... Thomassen, J. J. A., (Eds.), *Continuities in political action. A longitudinal study of political orientations in three western democracies* (pp. 275–312). Berlin: de Gruyter.

van Deth, J. W. (2014). A conceptual map of political participation. *Acta Politica, 49*, 349–367. doi:10.1057/ap.2014.6

Verba, S., Schlozman, K. L., & Brady, H. E. (1995). *Voice and equality: Civic volunteerism in American politics*. Cambridge: Harvard University Press.

Wächter, F. (2005). *EUYOUPART, WP 8/D15: National report: Germany*. Retrieved from https://www.sora.at/fileadmin/images/content/Pages/euyoupart_nationalreport-germany.pdf

Wasmer, M., & Koch, A. (2000). Ausländer als Bürger zweiter Klasse? Einstellungen zur rechtlichen Gleichstellung von Ausländern [Foreigners as second class citizens: Attitudes to the legal equality of foreigners]. In R. Alba, P. Schmidt, & M. Wasmer (Eds.), *Blickpunkt Gesellschaft: Vol. 5. Deutsche und Ausländer. Freunde, Fremde oder Feinde? Empirische Befunde und theoretische Erklärungen* [Focus society: Vol. 5. Germans and foreigners: Friends, strangers or enemies? Empirical findings and theoretical explanations] (pp. 255–293). Wiesbaden: Westdeutscher Verlag. https://doi.org/10.1007/978-3-322-86615-8

Wiedemann, C. (2006). Politische Partizipation von Migranten und Migrantinnen [Political participation of migrants]. In B. Hoecker (Ed.), *Politische Partizipation zwischen Konvention und Protest. Eine studienorientierte Einführung*[Political participation between convention and protest: A study-oriented introduction] (pp. 261–286). Opladen: Budrich.

Woellert, F., Kröhnert, S., Sippel, L., & Klingholz, R. (2009). *Ungenutzte Potenziale: Zur Lage der Integration in Deutschland* [Unused potentials: On the state of the art of integration in Germany]. Berlin: Stiftung Berlin-Institut für Bevölkerung und Entwicklung.

Wüst, A. M. (2003). Das Wahlverhalten eingebürgerter Personen in Deutschland [The voting behaviour of naturalised persons in Germany]. *Aus Politik und Zeitgeschichte., 52*, 29–38.

Wüst, A. M. (2007). Wahlverhalten und politische Repräsentation von Migranten [Voting behaviour and political representation of migrants]. In S. Frech, & K.-H. Meier-Braun (Eds.), *Die offene Gesellschaft. Zuwanderung und Integration* [The open society: Immigration and integration] (pp. 145–173). Schwalbach/Ts.: Wochenschau Verlag.

Yavçan, B. (2013). Public opinion toward immigration and the EU: How are Turkish immigrants different than others? *Turkish Studies, 14*, 158–178. doi:10.1080/14683849.2013.766990

Zaller, J. (1992). *The nature and origins of mass opinion*. Cambridge: Cambridge University Press. https://doi.org/10.1017/CBO9780511818691

7

Self-referent upward counterfactuals and depression: Examining regret as a mediator

Anne Gene Broomhall[1]* and Wendy J. Phillips[1]

*Corresponding author: Anne Gene Broomhall, School of Behavioural, Cognitive and Social Sciences of University of New England, Armidale, NSW, 2351 Australia
E-mail: abroomha@myune.edu.au
Reviewing editor: Peter Walla, University of Newcastle, Australia

Abstract: Previous research has found that self-referent upward counterfactuals are associated with depression. However, empirical evidence regarding the way self-referent upward counterfactuals exert their influence on depression remains scarce. This study examined whether regret intensity mediates the relationship between self-referent upward counterfactuals and depression. This possibility is in line with a sequential negative cognitions-to-affect theoretical framework, given that self-referent upward counterfactuals that blame the self for not bringing about desired outcomes may elicit feelings of regret. Adding to the limited number of studies involving Asian samples about counterfactual-related depression, the study was conducted on 147 university-educated residents of the Philippines (M_{age} = 28.28, *SD* = 9.23; Range = 18–62) who completed an online survey. Mediation analysis using multiple regression found that regret intensity fully mediated the relationship between self-referent upward counterfactuals and depression, after controlling for the effects of three variables related to regret regulation (self-deceptive enhancement, other-referent upward and nonreferent downward counterfactual thinking).

ABOUT THE AUTHORS

Anne Gene Broomhall is currently a PhD student from University of New England, Australia. She holds a post-graduate diploma in Psychology, and has worked as a tutor in Psychology subjects such as Psychological Medicine and Human Development (Developmental Psychology) and Statistics at James Cook University, Australia. She is also an Associate Member of the Australian Psychological Society (APS). Her research interests include counterfactuals, depression and Philippine culture. The findings reported in this paper may inform psychotherapy techniques for counterfactual-related depression in the Philippines.

Wendy J. Phillips is currently a senior lecturer in Psychology at the University of New England, Australia. Her research interests include mental health and psychological well-being, and cognitive models of behaviour, risk perception and decision-making in applied contexts. She is particularly interested in the relative influence of implicit (automatic, affective, fast, experiential) vs. explicit (deliberate, rule-based, slow, rational) processes involved in regulating emotions, managing problems or making decisions.

PUBLIC INTEREST STATEMENT

People may imagine ways in which an unfortunate event should not have happened. This mental exercise is called counterfactual thinking, as people think of scenarios contrary to reality. They may generate self-referent upward counterfactuals, which involve blaming oneself for not doing something that could have made the situation better. This counterfactual type has been linked to depression, but little is known about how this association occurs. The current study investigated whether this relationship depends on the emotional experience of regret that may be felt in response to self-referent upward counterfactual thinking. University-educated Filipino residents completed an online survey assessing various counterfactual thinking tendencies, depression and self-deceptive enhancement. The results indicated that more frequent generation of self-referent upward counterfactuals was associated with more intense regret, which in turn was associated with more depression symptoms.

Specifically, greater tendencies to generate self-referent upward counterfactuals were associated with greater regret intensity which, in turn, was associated with higher levels of depression symptoms. This finding suggests that depressed individuals who report more frequent self-referent upward counterfactuals may benefit from treatment strategies that lower regret intensity.

Subjects: Mental Health; Psychological Disorders - Adult; Mood Disorders in Adults - Depression

Keywords: counterfactual thinking; self-referent upward counterfactuals; regret; depression; self-enhancement

1. Introduction

Various cognitive models of depression suggest that engaging in negative self-referential cognitions evokes negative affect, which is an essential element in the development and maintenance of depression (Beck, Rush, Shaw, & Emery, 1979; Wisco, 2009). A cognitive activity that is associated with high levels of depression symptoms is self-referent upward counterfactual thinking (Rye, Cahoon, Ali, & Daftary, 2008). When people generate *self-referent upward counterfactuals*, they compare a factual negative outcome with an imagined better outcome and blame themselves for their wrongful action and for failing to take the action required to produce the better outcome (Howlett & Paulus, 2013; Rye et al., 2008). They also experience *regret* – the negative emotional concomitant of self-referent upward counterfactual thinking (Epstude & Roese, 2008). Landman, Vandewater, Stewart, and Malley (1995) suggested that depression could be a consequence of too much negative affect arising from personally relevant counterfactuals. However, there is a paucity of studies explicating how generating self-referent upward counterfactuals is related to depression tendencies. A possible indirect pathway through which self-referent upward counterfactuals could influence depression is the experience of intense regret. Examining this possibility is an important research aim of the current study.

1.1. Counterfactuals, regret and depression

Counterfactuals may be upward (imagining better outcomes) or downward (imagining worse off outcomes) in direction (Markman, Gavanski, Sherman, & McMullen, 1993), and may or may not involve blame attributions for the negative event (Byrne, 2016). Researchers often specify the referent in upward counterfactuals, which represents individual tendencies to externalise and internalise blame for the negative event (Callander, Brown, Tata, & Regan, 2007; Catellani & Bertolotti, 2014; Rye et al., 2008), whereas downward counterfactuals often do not involve blame attributions because these are irrelevant when people consider themselves lucky to have avoided a much bigger misfortune (Mandel, 2003). Rye et al. (2008), factor-analytically identified four distinct types of counterfactuals that differ in direction and attribution of blame: self-referent upward, other-referent upward, nonreferent upward and nonreferent downward counterfactuals. As alluded to earlier, more frequent self-referent upward counterfactuals are generated when people blame themselves for not bringing about the imagined desired results, whereas more frequent other-referent upward counterfactuals are generated when blame is deflected on others. More frequent nonreferent upward counterfactuals and nonreferent downward counterfactuals are generated when imagining better and worse off alternatives without blame for the negative event, respectively. These orthogonal counterfactual types are often assessed by the Counterfactual Thinking for Negative Events Scale (CTNES; Rye et al., 2008). While validating the CTNES, Rye and colleagues found that generated self-referent upward and nonreferent upward counterfactuals were significantly positively associated with depressive symptoms, but only self-referent upward counterfactuals were also significantly positively correlated with regret. In contrast, nonreferent downward counterfactuals and other-referent upward counterfactuals were neither associated with depression nor with regret.

On functional grounds, Epstude and Roese (2008) suggested that amongst all counterfactual types, self-referent upward is the most beneficial in facilitating behavioural change because people realise how their decisions or actions could have contributed to the unfavourable result. Consequently, the insights derived from imagining what one could have done differently may serve a preparative function (Sirois, Monforton, & Simpson, 2010). Several studies have demonstrated that counterfactual insights facilitate behavioural intentions in participants (e.g. Morris & Moore, 2000; Quelhas, Power, Juhos, & Senos, 2008; Smallman, 2013; Smallman & McCulloch, 2012; Smallman & Roese, 2009). For example, after engaging in upward counterfactual thinking following a failed exam (i.e., "I wouldn"t have failed if I had worked harder"), student participants expressed greater intentions to work harder in preparation for future exams (Quelhas et al., 2008; Study 2), suggesting that counterfactual insights can serve as behavioural guides to prevent the same negative outcomes from happening in the future ("content-specific pathway"; Epstude & Roese, 2008; Roese & Epstude, 2017). Consequently, counterfactual insights have been found to yield favourable effects on performance (e.g. Kray, Galinsky, & Markman, 2009; Kray, Galinsky, & Wong, 2006; Myers, McCrea, & Tyser, 2013). However, this learning function could backfire if an individual incessantly dwells on the past and excessively blames oneself for the undesirable event (Branscombe, Wohl, Owen, Allison, & N'gbala, 2003). To this extent, depression is hypothesised to ensue given the excessive negative affect associated with the contrast between reality and the imagined better alternative, and the blame attributions focused on the self (Epstude & Roese, 2008). Quelhas et al. (2008) also identified this potential dysfunctional consequence, since the preparative effect of upward counterfactual thinking was not observed in their student participants who were subsequently classified as depressed.

The experience of regret is contingent on personal responsibility for undesired outcomes (Zeelenberg & Pieters, 2007). A large body of literature has theoretically discussed and empirically demonstrated the self-referential characteristic of underlying upward counterfactuals in the experience of regret (Mandel, 2003; Roese & Hur, 1997). Regret has also been found to be associated with self-agency (i.e. attributing cause to the self) (Bossuyt, Moors, & De Houwer, 2014; Contractor & Kumar, 2013; Zeelenberg, van Dijk, Pieters, & van den Bos, 2002) and self-attacking cognitions (Schmidt, Renaud, & Van Der Linden, 2011). Thus, evidence suggests that one cannot feel regret without some heightened self-blame (Roese & Morrison, 2009; Roese et al., 2009) over one's inactions and/or actions that led to the undesirable result (Gilovich & Medvec, 1995; Gilovich, Medvec, & Kahneman, 1998). Accordingly, several studies have found significant associations between generating self-referent upward counterfactuals and regret (Mandel, 2005; Rye et al., 2008).

Since regret is a distressing emotion (Landman, 1995), its influence on depression has been extensively documented in the literature. These studies have demonstrated that regret is a significant predictor of high levels of current and future depressive symptoms across various research themes including surgery-related decision-making (e.g. Harcourt et al., 2011; Sheehan, Sherman, Lam, & Boyages, 2007), grief and bereavement (Torges, Stewart, & Nolen-Hoeksema, 2008), life outcomes in various stages of adulthood (e.g. Lecci, Okun, & Karoly, 1994; Schmidt et al., 2011; Wrosch, Bauer, & Scheier, 2005), and experienced stigma (e.g. Gore-Felton et al., 2008; Kissane et al., 2013). Notably, a study by Roese et al. (2009) found that regret predicted current depression, and its combined effect with repetitive thoughts explained more variance in distress. Thus, regret experienced in response to relentless cognitions in the form of self-referent upward counterfactuals may play an important role in increasing depression symptoms.

1.1.1. Counterfactual-related depression

Individuals may become distressed if they brood over their failure and imagine the ways in which they could have prevented their misfortune; a process which may outweigh any lessons from the experience that could be useful for future behavioural change ("spinning their wheels"; Kray et al., 2010). Indeed, a maladaptive internal attributional style has been implicated in one's vulnerability for depression (Abramson, Metalsky, & Alloy, 1989; Alloy, Lipman, & Abramson, 1992; Beck, 1967, 1987; Phillips, Hine, & Thorsteinsson, 2010; Wisco, 2009) because it triggers or sustains negative affect (Shaver & Drown, 1986; Teasdale, 1988; Wisco, 2009), particularly amongst those who are self-blaming (Zahn et al., 2015). A considerable number of studies have demonstrated that self-blaming emotions are associated with heightened depression, such as shame and guilt (e.g. Luby et al., 2009; Martin, Gilbert, McEwan, & Irons, 2006; Tilghman-Osborne, Cole, Felton, & Ciesla, 2008; Zahn et al., 2015). In a study conducted on patients with major depressive disorder, Zahn et al. (2015) found that the majority experienced heightened feelings of inadequacy, which coincided with their depressed mood and depressive symptoms, such as hopelessness and anhedonia.

With regards specifically to regret, a recent study by Kraines, Krug, and Wells (2017) demonstrated that depressed individuals experience greater self-blame for regrettable decisions compared to their never depressed counterparts. The study corroborates past findings about depressed individuals experiencing more regret (e.g. Monroe, Skowronski, MacDonald, & Wood, 2005) and adds to the literature that has examined depression as a determinant of upward counterfactual thinking tendencies (e.g. Chase et al., 2010; Feng et al., 2015; Markman & Miller, 2006; Monroe et al., 2005). However, to the best of our knowledge, no previous studies have investigated the facilitating influence of regret in the relationship between self-referent upward counterfactuals and depression. More research is therefore needed to demonstrate if a sequential negative cognitions-to-affect framework is relevant to the counterfactual-depression link. Given that self-referent upward counterfactuals are cognitions that reflect a negative internal attributional style (Rye et al., 2008) which cause one to feel regret (Epstude & Roese, 2008; Howlett & Paulus, 2013), the latter may represent the negative affect that may lead to depressive moods. If depression is believed to be a consequence of negative self-views and biases impairing one's ability for emotion regulation (Phillips et al., 2010), then the unsettling emotion of regret may serve as a link to an individual's depression risk related to self-referent upward counterfactuals.

1.2. The lost opportunity principle

Beike, Markman, and Karadogan (2009) proposed the notion of the *lost opportunity principle*. This concept is a refinement of Roese and Summerville's (2005) "opportunity principle", which states that regret is more intense for outcomes wherein future opportunities for change are perceived to be available. Beike et al. (2009) reformulated this concept by demonstrating that regret is more intense for negative outcomes that could have been avoided in the past – at a time when there was still an opportunity to do so – but is no longer changeable. They argued that hope stems from perceived available future opportunities which could lead to the achievement of one's goals, but with regards to lost opportunities, regret is more intense because an individual is no longer afforded the chance to prevent what went wrong, and is now suffering the consequences of this mistake. A study by Contractor and Kumar (2013) supported the lost opportunity tenet. They found that regret is amplified by personal agency when the superior outcome is made salient and the undesired outcome is irreversible.

There are two reasons why the lost opportunity principle is relevant to the experience of depression according to Beike et al. (2009). First, hopelessness becomes more intense given the minute chance of reversing one's misfortune. Second, a sense of low psychological closure regarding the life event is experienced (see also the Zeigernik effect, Zeigarnik, 1927), which indicates that resolution is still needed, and memories of the event could still evoke emotional responses (Beike, Adams, & Wirth-Beaumont, 2007; Beike et al., 2009; Beike & Wirth-Beaumont, 2005). Beike et al. (2009) argued that an indication of low psychological closure is when people engage in finding meaning in the face of traumatic and unexpected experiences, even though it brings them greater distress (e.g. Davis, Lehman, Wortman, Silver, & Thompson, 1995). The lack of closure is also associated with unattained goals (e.g. Jokisaari, 2004; Lecci et al., 1994); thus, they persist in the mind and evoke disquiet (Robbins & Stanley, 2012) because people are reminded of incomplete tasks (Epstude & Roese, 2008). In line with the above evidence, Landman et al. (1995) found that middle-aged women who had experienced missed opportunities reported significantly higher levels of depression than middle-aged women who had not experienced missed opportunities.

Over the years, a substantial number of studies have linked upward counterfactuals, regret and depression, which appeared to be informed by the lost opportunity principle (Broomhall, Phillips, Hine, & Loi, 2017). These studies involved participants facing irreversible life events such as their impending death (e.g. Reker & Woo, 2011; Schmidt et al., 2011) and the death of their loved ones (e.g. Eisma et al., 2015; Torges et al., 2008). However, to our knowledge, past research has not provided evidence about how counterfactual thinking and regret explicitly couched within the lost opportunity framework by Beike et al. (2009) may relate to high depression symptoms.

2. The current study

Most previous studies that have assessed the relationship between upward counterfactual thinking and depression have not explicitly indicated the object of reference (Broomhall et al., 2017). The current study addressed this lack of research by specifically focusing on self-referent upward counterfactuals. We aimed to examine whether the intensity of regret experienced in response to a lost opportunity plays a pivotal role in the relationship between tendencies to generate self-referent upward counterfactuals and depression symptoms. We hypothesised that greater self-referent upward counterfactual thinking tendencies would be associated with greater regret intensity which, in turn, would be associated with higher levels of depression symptoms.

A great body of literature has examined the relationship between upward counterfactual thinking and depression, in general, in Western cultures (Broomhall et al., 2017; Stroebe et al., 2014), suggesting the need for studies involving people from Asian backgrounds. The limited number of existing studies involving Asian samples largely involved Chinese and Japanese samples, and these studies were not explicitly informed by Epstude and Roese's (2008) theory of counterfactual-related depression (e.g. Akiyama, Numata, & Mikami, 2010; Feng et al., 2015; Lam et al., 2014). Hence, we chose to conduct our study on a Philippine sample because: (1) there is an apparent lack of studies about counterfactual thinking and depression conducted in this cultural group, and (2) Filipinos have a past temporal orientation that compels them towards retrospection (Ligo-Ralph, 1990), which may make them particularly likely to generate counterfactuals and to experience regret. Although previous studies have examined regret in Filipinos that may reflect lost opportunities, these studies did not investigate depression as a possible negative mental health outcome (e.g. Maximo, Berlanga, Aquisay, Valencia, & Daoen, 2012; Osorio et al., 2012). Therefore, it is not known whether the same positive relationships between upward counterfactual thinking and depression exist in this population. One aim of the current study is to provide initial information about these relationships in this relatively under-investigated population.

We limited our sample to university-educated Filipinos given past findings that higher education may serve as a buffer against regret-related depression (Roese et al., 2009), as highly-educated individuals may find it easy to rationalise their regrettable outcomes. Hence, limiting our sample to university-educated individuals should provide a conservative estimate of the proposed model, while still capturing culturally specific values and propensities.

In this study, we controlled for the effects of other-referent upward, nonreferent downward counterfactual thinking and self-deceptive enhancement variables. Other-referent upward and nonreferent downward counterfactual thinking tendencies were used as statistical controls because blaming others for one's misfortune and engaging in downward-oriented comparisons are techniques for regret regulation (Markman et al., 1993; Pieters & Zeelenberg, 2007; Roese & Olson, 2007; Zeelenberg & Pieters, 2007), and thus, could provide a buffering effect against depression. Self-deceptive enhancement was also statistically controlled because this pertains to participants' tendencies to give positive appraisals of themselves (Paulhus, 1991a, 1991b). Since recalling negative events may pose a challenge to one's self-views, participants may be inclined to make unrealistic portrayals of themselves, which could influence the truthfulness of their self-reports.

3. Method

3.1. Participants

The sample comprised of 147 (51 males and 96 females) individuals who had commenced or completed university education and currently resided in the Philippines. A minimum required sample size of 116 was calculated *a priori* using a power analysis, based on achieving power of 90%, with an alpha value of .05, and an expected medium effect size of .15. The final sample size was therefore more than enough to address the main research aim. The age range of participants was between 18 and 62, with a mean age of 28.23 (*SD* = 9.23). The mean number of years of Philippine-residence was 27.48 (*SD* = 9.12). No incentives were received for participation. Almost all participants were born in the Philippines (99%). Regarding educational background, 44% of participants had completed a Bachelor's degree, 15% had completed a postgraduate qualification (Master-level degree, *n* = 18; Doctoral degree, *n* = 4) and 41% had some university education (freshmen, *n* = 7; sophomores, *n* = 7; juniors, *n* = 23; and seniors, *n* = 23). The current sample was composed of university students (33%), and people working in the education (17%), managerial (12%), health sciences (3%), information technology (3%), arts and design (3%), business (3%), finance (3%) and legal (2%) sectors. Other occupations were related to engineering, entertainment, food, hospitality, property and housing, research and social work (each less than 2%). There were also unemployed participants (12%), one retired, and one who did not provide information.

3.2. Procedure and measures

Participant recruitment was conducted by posting an invitation and Qualtrics (Qualtrics, Provo, UT) survey link on Filipino social groups on Facebook. Participants were also encouraged to share the survey link to their networks to generate more participants (snowballing technique). Using the custom validation options of Qualtrics, potential participants who indicated they were below the age of 18 and had no university education were excluded. The measures were administered in English (one of the official languages in the Philippines) given that it is the language of academic instruction (Bernardo, 2004, 2007). Moreover, the current study specifically targeted highly-educated Filipinos, whereby English is deemed more fitting to use than the vernacular Tagalog/Filipino (Bernardo & Estrellado, 2014). Past researchers who have investigated university-educated Filipinos have successfully used psychological assessments in their original English form without the need for assessment in fluency (e.g. Bernardo, Clemente, & Nalipay, 2016).

First, participants answered demographic questions. Given the recent trend of including religiosity when investigating negative mental health outcomes (Cruz et al., 2016), and that religious beliefs are important to Filipinos (Bernardo et al., 2016), participants were also asked to rate their perceived level of religiosity on a scale ranging from 1 (*not religious*) to 7 (*very religious*). Participants were then asked to complete the following assessments as described below. After completing the assessments, participants were provided with the number of a free counselling service in the Philippines to call if they felt distress because of participation. The study was approved by the Human Research Ethics Committee of the university where the two authors are affiliated.

3.2.1. Depression symptoms

Participants completed the 7-item depression subscale of the Hospital Anxiety and Depression Scale (HADS-D: Zigmond & Snaith, 1983). The HADS-D assesses cognitive and emotional symptoms of depression (Smarr & Keefer, 2011) and has been used in previous research on upward counterfactual thinking and depression (e.g. Eisma et al., 2015; van Tol-Geerdink et al., 2015) and depression in Filipinos (e.g. Aherrera, Abrahan, Racaza, Train, & Jara, 2015; de Guzman, 2013; Tay, Cheung, & Mak, 2015). Using a 4-point Likert scale, participants indicated how often they have been experiencing each described feeling (e.g. "I feel as if I am slowed down".) in the past week. Cronbach's alpha for the HADS was .74. Scores were summed, in which a higher score corresponds to more experienced depression symptoms. The HADS-D was especially appropriate for the current study because of its brevity, as keeping the survey short was needed to minimise attrition due to the slow and intermittent internet connection in the Philippines (Marasigan, 2015).

3.2.2. Counterfactuals

Specific counterfactuals generated were assessed by the subscales of the CTNES (Rye et al., 2008). The CTNES was constructed in such a way that it could be adapted to assess counterfactuals instigated by a specific stimulus (Rye et al., 2008). In the current study, participants were prompted to generate counterfactual thoughts using the following instruction of the CTNES which reflected the tenet of the lost opportunity principle by Beike et al. (2009): "*Please think of an event that occurred recently which had a negative impact on you. This event should have an undesirable outcome which could have been prevented at the time of its occurrence but can no longer be resolved at the present time*". Participants indicated their agreement on the four orthogonal measures of counterfactual thinking tendencies from 1 (*never*) to 5 (*very often*), each with four items: self-referent upward (e.g. "I think about how much better things would have been if I had acted differently"; $\alpha = .80$), other-referent upward (e.g. "If only another person (or other people) had not been so selfish, this whole mess could have been avoided"; $\alpha = .89$), nonreferent upward (e.g. "I feel sad when I think about how much better things could have been") and nonreferent downward (e.g. "I think about how much worse things could have been"; $\alpha = .68$). Item scores were summed to obtain a score for each subscale. Higher scores indicate more tendencies to engage in each counterfactual thinking type. Following preliminary factor analyses (reported in the results), the nonreferent upward counterfactuals subscale was not used in this study, and one nonreferent downward item was removed from the subscale.

3.2.3. Regret

Participants rated their regret intensity as a response to the recalled negative event following this instruction adapted from Beike et al. (2009): "*Rate the intensity of regret you currently experience regarding your choices or decisions in relation to the negative event using the scale below*". They indicated their agreement on a 6-point Likert scale ranging from 1 (*not at all*) to 6 (*intensely*). A single-item regret assessment has been successfully employed in previous studies (e.g. East, Chien, & Barber, 2012; Newall, Chipperfield, Daniels, Hladkyj, & Perry, 2009; Stewart & Vandewater, 1999; Towers, Williams, Hill, Philipp, & Flett, 2016).

3.2.4. Nature of the negative event

Participants also indicated the nature of the negative event they experienced by selecting one of the 12 life domains identified by Roese and Summerville (2005): education, career, romance, parenting, self-improvement, leisure, finance, family, health, friends, spirituality and community.

3.2.5. Self-deceptive enhancement

Participants' inclination for making excessive positive self-appraisals was measured by the 20-item Self-Deceptive Enhancement (SDE) subscale of the Balanced Inventory for Social Desirable Responding (Paulhus, 1991b). Each item (e.g. "My first impressions of people usually turn out to be right") was rated on a 7-point Likert scale ranging from 1 (*not true*) to 7 (*very true*). Following its scoring procedure (Paulhus, 1991a), after reverse-scoring negatively worded items, an additional point was added for each highest possible response (6 or 7). Scores were summed to obtain an overall score of self-deceptive enhancement, with higher scores indicating higher tendencies. In the current study, reliability for this scale was satisfactory ($\alpha = .75$).

4. Results

4.1. Structure of the CTNES

To our knowledge, this is the first time the CTNES has assessed counterfactual thinking in a Filipino sample. We therefore conducted a preliminary confirmatory factor analysis in AMOS 23.0 (Arbuckle, 2015) to assess whether the four factors identified by Rye et al. (2008) also fitted our data-set. Based on Kline (2005), we defined good fit as a comparative fit index (CFI) and goodness-of-fit index (GFI) greater than .90, a root mean square error of approximation (RMSEA) less than .08 and a standardised root mean square residual (SRMR) of less than .10. After allowing the four latent factors to covary, the model provided a marginally satisfactory fit to the data: CFI = .91; GFI = .85; RMSEA = .09;

SRMR = .08. However, a very high correlation ($r = .89$) between the latent factors for self-referent upward and non-referent upward counterfactuals indicated that the two subscales were not independent.

A subsequent principal axis factoring analysis in SPSS 24, with oblimin rotation, indicated a three-factor solution in which nonreferent upward counterfactual items and self-referent upward counterfactual items loaded on the same factor. As our study specifically aimed to address self-referent upward counterfactuals arising from lost opportunities, we elected to exclude items that assessed nonreferent upward counterfactuals from the study. Excluding these four items resulted in a three-factor structure that explained 65.4% of the variance in the data-set, which assessed self-referent upward counterfactuals, other-referent upward counterfactuals and nonreferent downward counterfactuals. Eleven items loaded between .47 and .96 on their respective factors, with no cross-loadings above .30. However, one nonreferent downward item ("I count my blessings when I think about how much worse things could have been") loaded at only .37 and was removed from the subscale. The removal of this nonreferent downward item increased that subscale's alpha from .68 to .73.

4.2. Descriptives

We did not find normative data for the HADS in Filipinos. However, applying cut-off scores recommended by Zigmond and Snaith (1983), 65% of our participants scored within the normal range on depression (between 0 and 7), 22% were mildly depressed (8 and 10) and 12%[1] were severely depressed (≥11). Following Roese and Summerville (2005), we also ranked the frequency of life domains associated with participants' regret (Figure 1). The majority of regrets pertained to issues concerning romance, followed by family, career, education and self-improvement (both ranked 4th), finance and friends. The current study corroborated past findings by Morrison, Epstude, and Roese (2012) that the most intense regrets experienced are about close relationships (i.e. romance and family) rather than those that are less socially relevant (e.g. career, education).

Given that the depression scores had a positively skewed distribution, they were transformed using the square root transformation formula to improve the non-normality of the regression residuals. All other assumptions of multiple linear regression were met, and no missing values were observed. Table 1 shows the Pearson's correlations, means, and standard deviations of the study variables. Significant medium to large correlations were observed amongst variables of primary interest.

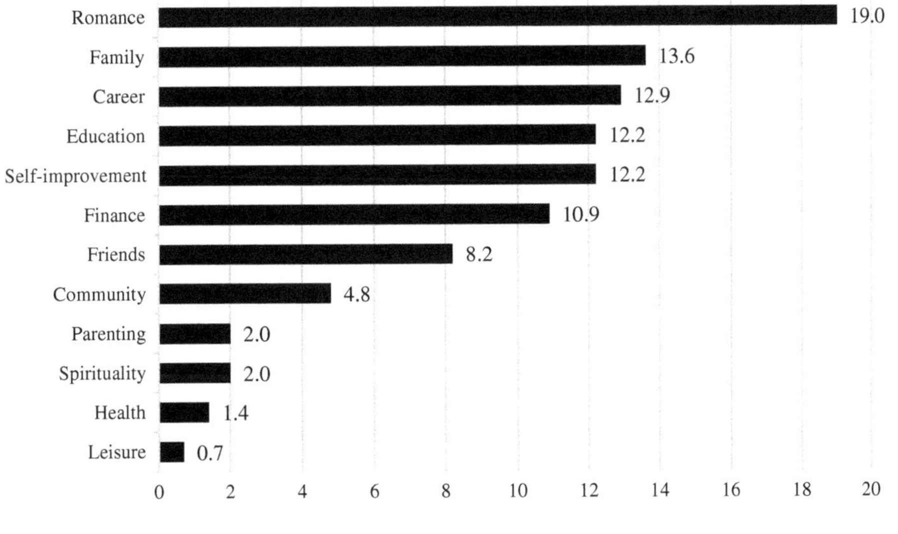

Figure 1. Percentage of negative events recalled across different life domains.

Table 1. Summary statistics of study variables										
Variables	**1**	**2**	**3**	**4**	**5**	**6**	**7**	**8**	**9**	**10**
1. Depression	1	.34**	.30**	.30**	−.01	−.26**	−.07	−.12	−.14	−.33**
2. Regret		1	.57**	.31**	.24**	−.26**	.07	−.17*	.05	−.23**
3. Self-referent upward			1	.35**	.20*	−.27**	−.01	−.18*	.05	−.28**
4. Other-referent upward				1	.31**	−.16	.18*	−.03	.03	−.08
5. Nonreferent downward					1	−.01	.19*	−.02	.18*	.12
6. Self-deceptive enhancement						1	.07	.27**	−.04	.23**
7. Religiosity							1	.02	.20*	.06
8. Age								1	−.09	.49**
9. Gender									1	.12
10. Educational attainment										1
Mean	2.32	3.81	12.87	12.51	8.83	100.97	3.99	28.23	1.65	6.37
SD	0.74	1.39	3.74	4.26	2.49	13.01	1.64	9.23	0.48	1.35

Note: $n = 147$. Gender, Male = 1, Female = 2.
$^{*}p < .05$.
$^{**}p < .01$.

4.3. Mediation analysis

Multiple linear regressions were conducted to examine the possible mediating function of regret in the relationship between self-referent upward counterfactuals (independent variable) and depression (dependent variable), after controlling for other-referent upward counterfactuals, nonreferent downward counterfactuals and self-deceptive enhancement tendencies. The mediational analysis was conducted using the SPSS macro called PROCESS, with a recommended bootstrap of 5,000 samples using 95% confidence intervals to determine the significance of the indirect effect (Hayes, 2013). The bootstrapping method increases statistical power to detect an indirect effect and minimises the likelihood of a type II error (Hayes, 2013; Preacher & Hayes, 2008). To facilitate interpretation of effects, the mediation analysis was repeated using *z*-scores to generate standardised beta coefficients (values are shown in Figure 2). A hierarchical regression was also conducted on the raw

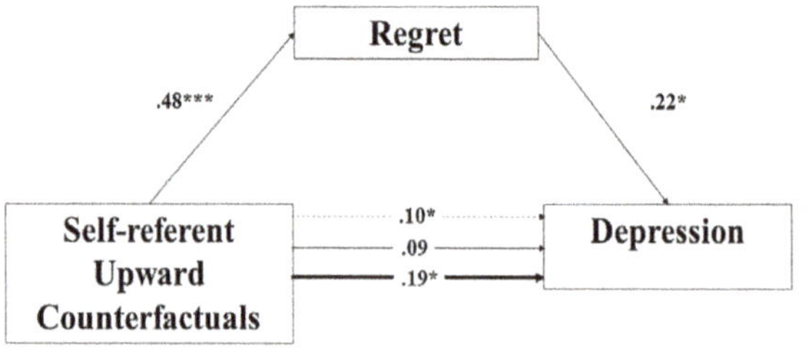

Figure 2. Mediational model representing the direct pathway (solid line) and indirect pathway (dotted line) from self-referent upward counterfactuals to depression via regret, while controlling for other-referent upward counterfactuals, nonreferent downward counterfactuals, and self-deceptive enhancement.

Notes: The total effect is in boldface. Standardised beta coefficients are reported.
$^{***}p < .001$, $^{*}p < .05$.

scores using SPSS 22 to obtain semi-partial correlations (*sr*) because these are not generated by PROCESS.

Model statistics, unstandardised coefficients and semi-partial correlations are shown in Table 2, and standardised coefficients are presented in Figure 2. The mediation model explained 20.5% of the variance in depressive symptoms. Together, self-referent upward counterfactuals and the three covariates explained a significant 17.4% of the variance in depressive symptoms, and intensity of regret explained an additional and significant 3.0% of the variance. Examination of the total effect revealed that, after controlling for the effects of the three covariates, generating self-referent upward counterfactuals significantly predicted heightened depression symptoms. Self-referent upward counterfactuals also significantly predicted intense regret.

Table 2. Regret as mediator of the relationship between self-referent upward counterfactual thinking and depression

		Regret					Depression				
Variable	**Effect**	***B***	***SE***	***p***	**95% CIs**	***sr***	***B***	***SE***	***p***	**95% CIs**	***sr***
Self-referent upward	Total						0.04	0.02	.03	0.01 to 0.07	.17
Covariates											
Other-referent upward							0.04	0.02	.00	0.01 to 0.07	.22
Nonreferent downward							−0.04	0.02	.13	−0.09 to 0.01	−.12
Self-deceptive enhancement							−0.01	0.01	.04	−0.02 to −0.00	−.16
Model							F (4, 142) = 7.50, $p < .001$, $R^2 = .17$				
Self-referent upward		0.18	0.03	<.001	0.13 to 0.23	.44					
Covariates											
Other-referent upward		0.03	0.02	.23	−0.02 to 0.08	.08					
Nonreferent downward		0.06	0.04	.12	−0.02 to 0.14	.11					
Self-deceptive enhancement		−0.01	0.01	.09	−0.03 to 0.00	−.11					
Model		F (4, 142) = 19.92, $p < .001$, $R^2 = .36$									
Regret							0.12	0.05	.02	0.02 to 0.22	.17
Self-referent upward	Direct						0.02	0.02	.37	−0.02 to 0.05	.07
Covariates											
Other-referent upward							0.04	0.02	.01	0.01 to 0.07	.20
Nonreferent downward							−0.04	0.02	.07	−0.09 to 0.00	−.14
Self-deceptive enhancement							−0.01	0.01	.07	−0.02 to 0.00	−.14
Model							F (5, 141) = 7.26, $p < .001$, $R^2 = .21$				
Self-referent upward	Indirect						0.02	0.01		0.00 to 0.05	

Note: Unstandardised beta coefficients are reported.

As hypothesised, regret mediated the relationship between self-referent upward counterfactuals and depression, as evidenced by a significant indirect effect (based on the 95% bootstrap confidence intervals that did not include zero) and a direct effect that was not significant.[2] The results indicate that generating highly frequent self-referent upward counterfactuals was associated with greater regret intensity, which in turn were associated with high levels of depressive symptoms; and that generating self-referent upward counterfactuals was no longer directly associated with depression after regret was added to the model. Amongst the covariates entered, only other-referent upward counterfactuals contributed significantly to the mediation model by yielding a positive relationship with depression. This relationship was unexpected, as it is contrary to previous observations (Rye et al., 2008).

4.4. *Post hoc mediation analysis*

Given the significant positive relationship between other-referent upward counterfactuals and depression, we conducted a *post hoc* analysis to determine whether regret also mediated this relationship. A mediation analysis using PROCESS, with generated self-referent upward counterfactuals, nonreferent downward counterfactuals and self-deceptive enhancement as covariates, indicated that the indirect effect was not significant, $B = 0.00$ ($\beta = .02$), $SE = 0.00$, 95% $CI = -0.00$ to 0.01.

5. Discussion

The current study investigated regret as a mediator of the association between self-referent upward counterfactual thinking and depression. As hypothesised, the more participants frequently generate self-referent upward counterfactuals, the more intense regret over a lost opportunity they experienced which, in turn, was associated with higher levels of depression symptoms. Further, after including regret in the model, self-referent upward counterfactual thinking was no longer significantly associated with depression. This pattern of results, and a significant indirect effect, indicate that regret fully mediated the relationship between self-referent upward counterfactual thinking and depression. This finding is consistent with previous research that has demonstrated significant associations between generated self-referent upward counterfactuals and regret (Rye et al., 2008) and between regret and depression (Bruine de Bruin, Dombrovski, Parker, & Szanto, 2016; Roese et al., 2009; Schwartz et al., 2002). Our results also indicate that the same positive relationships between self-referent upward counterfactuals, regret and depression that have been observed in Western populations (e.g. Rye et al., 2008) are also evident in a Filipino sample.

Our results are also consistent with one theoretical explanation for depression, which underscores the role of negative affect arising from upward counterfactual thinking activity; that is, upward counterfactual thinking activity may bring about negative emotions, which may pave the way for depressive episodes (Davis & Lehman, 1995; Landman et al., 1995; Roese & Olson, 1997). In relation to the current findings, generating maladaptive thoughts in the form of self-referent upward counterfactuals may evoke feelings of regret, and this emotional response may negatively impact one's depression risk (Epstude & Roese, 2008). Regret may likely link self-referent upward counterfactual thinking and depression, given that this emotion makes one feel responsible for the misfortune. This is because regret is a distressing emotion (Landman, 1995); it involves beating oneself up for not being able to do the right thing, whilst wishing to rectify wrongdoings (Zeelenberg & van Dijk, 2005) when there is no more opportunity to do so – reflecting the tenet of the lost opportunity principle (Beike et al., 2009). To this extent, depression may possibly ensue as a consequence of the intense regret experienced. The current results correspond to classic cognitive theories of depression that underscore the role of self-referential cognitions that induce negative responses, thereby leading to increased depression risk (Abramson et al., 1989; Beck, 1987; Teasdale, 1988).

Although the literature suggests that downward counterfactual thinking activity may serve as a strategy for emotional regulation (Markman et al., 1993; Roese, 1994; Sanna, Turley-Ames, & Meier, 1999; White & Lehman, 2005; Zeelenberg & Pieters, 2007), our results indicate that generated nonreferent downward counterfactuals did not significantly predict decreased depression symptoms, which is inconsistent with past findings suggesting that people often imagine worse off situations following adverse events (e.g. Sanna & Turley-Ames, 2000; Teigen & Jensen, 2011). This is a surprising finding because when individuals reflect over lost opportunities, they are often motivated to employ strategies to regulate their emotions, such as seeking downward-oriented comparisons (Roese & Epstude, 2017). A possible explanation for this non-significant relationship is the inability or lack of desire to lighten one's mood that is commonly associated with depression (White & Lehman, 2005). Further, some experiences can be so traumatic and distressing that seeking downward-oriented comparisons, so the current situation looks better could hardly induce positive moods (Rye et al., 2008; White & Lehman, 2005). Our result, nevertheless, is consistent with a few previous findings in the literature, whereby downward counterfactuals were neither related to decreased distress (Gilbar & Hevroni, 2007) nor less depression symptoms (Rye et al., 2008). It is also important to note that we examined nonreferent downward counterfactuals in aggregation with other distress-buffering variables that may have cancelled out its impact. Past findings suggest that imagining worse off alternatives to regulate one's emotions can be attenuated if such negative moods are externally attributed (Sanna, Meier, & Turley-Ames, 1998). Hence, it is reasonable to suspect that other-referent upward counterfactuals (which represents externalisation) may have rendered nonreferent downward counterfactuals irrelevant in the model given that it significantly predicted depression.

5.1. Other-referent upward counterfactuals

Notably, we observed an unexpected significant positive relationship between other-referent upward counterfactuals and depression, which was not mediated by regret. The direct relationship is inconsistent with previous findings that generating other-referent upward counterfactuals is unrelated to depression in samples sourced from Western cultures (e.g. Markman & Miller, 2006; Rye et al., 2008), and contradicts previous assumptions about blame shifting as a strategy to regulate regret (Zeelenberg & Pieters, 2007), in order to lessen distress and depression (e.g. Rye et al., 2008; Wrosch et al., 2005).

A possible explanation for the current finding is that Filipinos may perceive that their social environment influences the favourability of their outcomes given their collectivist outlook (for extensive discussions see, Church, 1987; Church & Katigbak, 2000). More specifically, people from collectivist cultures are more predisposed to social conformity than their individualist (less collectivist) counterparts (Bond & Smith, 1996; Chen et al., 2006; Fukushima, Sharp, & Kobayashi, 2009). Hence, it is not uncommon in collectivist cultures to blame others when an outcome is unsatisfactory (Carpenter, 2000). This may be because, for Filipinos, achieving the outcome they want may depend upon the outputs and decisions of others. For instance, they are likely to compromise their own needs and give in to societal expectations in order to maintain harmonious interpersonal relationships and interactions (Lynch, 1973). If they do not compromise, however, their despondency may further increase given that social harmony is an important condition in order to achieve happiness in a collectivist environment (Datu, King, & Valdez, 2016; Markus & Kitayama, 1991). To this extent, the lack of control over one's outcomes may represent the helplessness involved in the experience of depression (Seligman, 1975).

5.2. Therapeutic implications

Our results suggest that regret plays a crucial role in the link between self-referent upward counterfactuals and depression. That is, the current framework indicates that generating self-referent upward counterfactuals in response to lost opportunities may not necessarily lead to depression, but their concomitant negative affect may become a catalyst for developing depression. This provides support to the view that depression could be a negative mental health consequence if individuals are not adept in regulating their emotions (Ehring, Fischer, Schnülle, Bösterling, & Tuschen-Caffier, 2008; Ehring, Tuschen-Caffier, Schnülle, Fischer, & Gross, 2010; Kring & Werner, 2004). Hence, inhibiting negative emotional reactivity is an important strategy for therapy.

Several intervention approaches may successfully reduce regret arising from self-referent upward counterfactuals. For example, Cognitive Behavioural Therapy (CBT) targets and corrects information processing that is biased against oneself (Beck & Dozois, 2011; Beck et al., 1979; Beck & Weishaar, 2005). In CBT, individuals are helped to identify and curb their negative automatic thoughts and maladaptive assumptions, examine the validity of these cognitions, reframe their thinking towards a more reasonable interpretation of their circumstances, and recognise that their thoughts may impact on their feelings and behaviours (Beck & Weishaar, 2005). CBT has been found to be an effective psychotherapy in the treatment of depression in adults (Cristea et al., 2015; Cuijpers et al., 2013), not just in the developed world but also in developing countries (Vally & Maggott, 2015). With regards to individuals who tend to generate frequent self-referent upward counterfactuals, CBT can be used to make them aware that such thoughts could result in distressing feelings. Specifically, a reattribution cognitive technique is highly recommended to modify their strong beliefs that they brought misfortune to themselves. Awareness about the link between cognitions and affect will empower individuals to take control over their emotional reactions so they can refocus their attention to finding solutions to recover from their hardships.

CBT could also be modified by incorporating self-compassion. Interventions based on self-compassion have been found to help individuals regulate negative emotions arising from difficult experiences (Diedrich, Grant, Hofmann, Hiller, & Berking, 2014; Diedrich, Hofmann, Cuijpers, & Berking, 2016). Neff (2003b) defined self-compassion as a positive self-attitude that involves accepting one's pain, shortcomings, or failures in a non-judgemental manner, and viewing a negative life episode as something that others also experience (Neff, 2003a). Self-compassion has been found to be negatively associated with depression (Krieger, Altenstein, Baettig, Doerig, & Holtforth, 2013; MacBeth & Gumley, 2012), and a lack of self-compassion is a predictor of subsequent depression (see also, Krieger, Berger, & Holtforth, 2016; Krieger et al., 2013). Practicing self-compassion may also serve as a catalyst for self-improvement associated with learning from regrettable experiences, because it helps people to adapt to their circumstances and embrace acceptance and self-forgiveness (Zhang & Chen, 2016). It has also been associated with the effective selection of healthy life goals and intentions to engage in success-facilitating behaviours to achieve these goals (Neely, Schallert, Mohammed, Roberts, & Chen, 2009; Neff, Ya-Ping, & Dejitterat, 2005; Terry & Leary, 2011). Consequently, individuals will be more likely to eschew the temptation to constantly look back and engage in self-referent upward counterfactual thinking. They could easily move forward with their lives by seeking opportunities that could eventually result in better outcomes.

Another therapeutic intervention that helps to regulate negative emotions is Emotion-Focused Therapy (EFT; Greenberg & Watson, 2005; Lafrance Robinson, McCague, & Whissell, 2014). In EFT, the client's negative emotions are accessed, and their underlying meanings are uncovered in order to convert them into useful and adaptive emotions (Greenberg, 2008; Timulak, 2014). Individuals also become adept at accessing useful insights embedded in these negative emotions which may assist them to live with flexibility under difficult circumstances (Pos & Greenberg, 2007) and to respond adaptively to future similar situations (content-specific) or more general situations (content-neutral) (Epstude & Roese, 2008). Such an approach to regret corresponds with the view that its primary purpose is behavioural regulation (Roese, Summerville, & Fessel, 2007; Saffrey, Summerville, & Roese, 2008; Zeelenberg, 2007).

The observed direct positive relationship between other-referent upward counterfactuals and depression suggests that blaming others when imagining better outcomes is not protective against depression in the current sample. Although we primarily recommend CBT to reduce depression risk associated with frequent self-referent upward counterfactuals, it may also assist Filipino individuals who tend to generate highly frequent other-referent upward counterfactuals. CBT instils awareness in individuals of how their unduly negative thoughts about others could influence their feelings and behaviours (Beck & Dozois, 2011). In CBT, the therapist helps individuals to examine the truthfulness of their beliefs and change their behaviours (Hollon & Dimidjian, 2014). For example, the therapist may challenge the validity of the helplessness narrative in other-referent upward counterfactuals (e.g. If only my parents could afford to send me to university ...) and highlight other options to achieve desired outcomes.

Interpersonal Psychotherapy (IPT) may also be useful to mitigate depression risk associated with frequent other-referent upward counterfactuals. IPT addresses difficulties arising from social interactions across four life issues: grief, role transition due to major life changes, relationship disputes and interpersonal deficits (e.g. social isolation) (Klerman, Weissman, Rounsaville, & Chevron, 1984; Lipsitz & Markowitz, 2013; Weissman, Markowitz, & Klerman, 2007). IPT aims to enhance an individual's social support and social skills, minimise interpersonal stress and facilitate in the processing of negative emotions (Lipsitz & Markowitz, 2013). It has been found to be an effective psychotherapy in the treatment of depression (Cuijpers, Donker, Weissman, Ravitz, & Cristea, 2016; Cuijpers et al., 2011, 2013). IPT is premised on the view that current stressors are caused by interpersonal problems, so the therapist's goal is to lessen the impact of these stressors on the individual (Lipsitz & Markowitz, 2013). For example, the therapist may decrease helplessness associated with a culturally stifling environment by allowing their clients to freely talk about their feelings and come up with ways to become assertive. In the same way as grief, lost opportunities can be emotionally processed to facilitate transition into finding new opportunities for self-development, thus misfortunes are left in the past and become less salient.

6. Limitations and future directions

There are several limitations that need to be considered when interpreting the findings of the current study. This study was exclusively conducted with university-educated Filipino residents to provide a more conservative assessment, considering previous findings that higher education may regulate regret, and thus may likely serve as a buffer against depression. Hence, the results cannot be generalised to the entire Philippine population or to other populations. Examining this mediational model in less educated Filipinos or the general population of Filipinos could be a future research avenue. The use of a non-clinical sample also precludes interpretations that the relationships identified in the current study will also be found amongst individuals diagnosed with depression.

Further, although our results were consistent with theoretical models of depression, the cross-sectional design of the study means that we cannot infer causal relationships. Instead, it provides a framework which future researchers can use to determine the validity of this direction of causality as articulated by Epstude and Roese (2008). Past research on the reverse direction of causality has already demonstrated that depressed individuals are more regretful (Monroe et al., 2005) and that depressive states may exacerbate upward counterfactual thinking tendencies (Feng et al., 2015). On the other hand, there is a paucity of studies demonstrating that upward counterfactual thinking may lead to depression (Broomhall et al., 2017), hence the need for the current investigation. Future investigations using an experimental research design to examine our model may allow the drawing of causal inferences. Experimental research may also examine the possibility of a bi-directional feedback loop amongst variables, in which depression may increase the generation of self-referent upward counterfactuals, intensify feelings of regret, and lead to more self-referent upward counterfactuals, thereby increasing depression symptoms in a vicious cycle (Monroe et al., 2005).

The use of a single-item regret assessment may be viewed as a limitation in the current study because a longer regret scale may have captured individual facets of regret and allowed reliability to be assessed. However, a single-item regret measure has been commonly used in the counterfactual literature (e.g. Bonnefon & Jiehai, 2008; East et al., 2012; Newall et al., 2009; Towers et al., 2016). Single-item regret assessments have demonstrated convergent and divergent validity in previous research (e.g. Beike et al., 2009; East et al., 2012) and offer a viable solution to an observed problem with longer self-report regret scales that may be logistically difficult to administer (Buchanan, Summerville, Lehmann, & Reb, 2016), such as in the current study.

Our unexpected finding that other-referent upward counterfactuals were significantly associated with depressive symptoms in our Filipino sample is also worthy of future investigation, as this differs markedly from non-significant relationships previously observed in Western samples (Markman & Miller, 2006; Rye et al., 2008). The result of our *post hoc* analysis found that regret did not mediate this relationship, and therefore may not represent a crucial mechanism in the link between other- referent upward counterfactuals and depression amongst educated Filipinos. It is possible that harmonious interpersonal relationships associated with collectivism may play a role in this relationship, and thus, could be an informative avenue for future investigation.

The CTNES has been validated using Western samples. In this study, we validated the CTNES in a Filipino sample. We found that a three-factor model of the CTNES fits our data better than the original four-factor model, with no clear distinction found between self-referent upward and nonreferent upward counterfactuals. Consequently, we elected to discard the nonreferent upward items. Our finding does not suggest that the self-referent upward counterfactual items of the CTNES are not valid; rather, it suggests that the two constructs may have a conceptual overlap in a Filipino sample. This finding needs to be replicated and is consistent with the view that upward counterfactual constructs can be conflated (Broomhall et al., 2017). However, the CTNES questions that assess these two types of upward counterfactuals differ in theoretically relevant ways. The self-referent upward items reflect a maladaptive internal attributional style in the prediction of depression, whereas the nonreferent upward counterfactual items correspond to a global attributional style (Rye et al., 2008). Given that we were specifically examining self-blame in upward counterfactual thinking, it was not appropriate to include the nonreferent upward items. Most relevant to the "content-specific pathway" in behavioural change are self-referent upward counterfactuals because these thoughts specify mistakes that one should avoid making in the future, albeit at the expense of experiencing distress (Epstude & Roese, 2008; Roese & Epstude, 2017).

Demonstrating regret as a mediator in this model does not preclude the possibility that other variables may mediate the relationship between self-referent upward counterfactual thinking and depression. Future researchers may fruitfully explore other potential mediators. These may involve other counterfactual emotions in the form of disappointment, rejoicing or elation, which can be compared with the influence of regret – regarded as the primary counterfactual emotion (Lorini & Schwarzentruber, 2011). Also, we chose covariates that may serve as a buffer against depression, informed by the theory of Regret Regulation (Pieters & Zeelenberg, 2007; Zeelenberg & Pieters, 2007). However, future researchers could consider examining other possible covariates that may impact the proposed associations, such as hopelessness, which is believed to be the proximate cause of depressive symptoms (Abramson et al., 1989; Alloy, Abramson, Walshaw, & Neeren, 2006), and perceived future opportunities for change (Roese & Epstude, 2017). Controlling for hopelessness will tease apart the unique contribution of intense regret feelings in the association between self-referent upward counterfactuals and depression. With regards to future opportunities for change, determining if having available opportunities for corrective action may influence depression tendencies associated with upward counterfactual thinking is a future research avenue.

In conclusion, our results extend the counterfactual thinking literature by examining self-referential upward counterfactuals and regret about lost opportunities (Beike et al., 2009) in relation to depression. Specifically, we found that regret intensity mediated the association between tendencies to generate self-referent upward counterfactuals and depression. The current study also adds to the small number of studies about the relationship between upward counterfactual thinking and depression conducted in Asian samples, and may inform the choice of treatment strategies for depressed or vulnerable individuals who tend to generate highly frequent self-referent upward counterfactuals.

Funding
The authors received no direct funding for this research.

Competing interests
The authors declare no competing interest.

Author details
Anne Gene Broomhall[1]
E-mail: abroomha@myune.edu.au
Wendy J. Phillips[1]
E-mail: wendy.phillips@une.edu.au
[1] School of Behavioural, Cognitive and Social Sciences of University of New England, Armidale, NSW, 2351 Australia.

Notes

1. As the survey was anonymous, we were not able to identify participants who reported being severely depressed. However, in addition to the counselling service number provided, participants were also given the contact information of the authors should they need to discuss any concerns.
2. Given the significant negative associations of age with self-referent upward counterfactuals and regret, and negative associations of educational attainment with self-referent upward counterfactuals, regret and depression, we repeated the analysis with age and educational attainment as covariates. Mediation was also established when age and education were added to the model, $B = 0.02$ ($\beta = .09$), $SE = 0.01$, 95% CI = 0.00 to 0.04, $p < .001$. The individual contribution of education to the model was significant, $B = -0.14$ ($\beta = -.25$), $SE = 0.05$, $p < .05$, but age was not, $B = 0.01$ ($\beta = .08$), $SE = 0.01$, $p = .37$. Religiosity was not investigated as a covariate because it did not correlate significantly with self-referent counterfactuals, regret or depression.

References

Abramson, L. Y., Metalsky, G. I., & Alloy, L. B. (1989). Hopelessness depression: A theory-based subtype of depression. *Psychological Review, 96*(2), 358–372. doi:10.1037/0033-295X.96.2.358

Aherrera, J. M., Abrahan, L., Racaza, G., Train, C., & Jara, R. (2015). Depression and anxiety in adult Filipinos with congenital heart disease using the validated Filipino version of the hospital anxiety and depression scale (HADS). *Global Heart, 10*(2, Supplement), 1–10. doi:10.1016/j.gheart.2015.03.029

Akiyama, A., Numata, K., & Mikami, H. (2010). Importance of end-of-life support to minimize caregiver's regret during bereavement of the elderly for better subsequent adaptation to bereavement. *Archives of Gerontology and Geriatrics, 50*(2), 175–178. doi:10.1016/j.archger.2009.03.006

Alloy, L. B., Abramson, L. Y., Walshaw, P. D., & Neeren, A. M. (2006). Cognitive vulnerability to unipolar and bipolar mood disorders. *Journal of Social and Clinical Psychology, 25*(7), 726–754. doi:10.1521/jscp.2006.25.7.726

Alloy, L. B., Lipman, A. J., & Abramson, L. Y. (1992). Attributional style as a vulnerability factor for depression: Validation by past history of mood disorders. *Cognitive Therapy and Research, 16*(4), 391–407. doi:10.1007/BF01183164

Arbuckle, J. L. (2015). *IBM SPSS Amos 23 user's guide [Computer software and manual]*. New York, NY: IBM.

Beck, A. T. (1967). *Depression: Clinical, experimental, and theoretical aspects*. New York, NY: Harper & Row.

Beck, A. T. (1987). Cognitive models of depression. *Journal of Cognitive Psychotherapy: An International Quarterly, 1*, 5–37.

Beck, A. T., & Dozois, D. J. A. (2011). Cognitive therapy: Current status and future directions. *Annual Review of Medicine, 62*(1), 397–409. doi:10.1146/annurev-med-052209-100032

Beck, A. T., Rush, A. J., Shaw, B. F., & Emery, G. (1979). *Cognitive therapy of depression*. New York, NY: The Guilford Press.

Beck, A. T., & Weishaar, M. E. (2005). Cognitive Therapy. In R. J. Corsini & D. Wedding (Eds.), *Current Psychotherapies* (7th ed., pp. 238–268). Belmont, CA: Brooks/Cole.

Beike, D. R., Adams, L. P., & Wirth-Beaumont, E. T. (2007). Incomplete inhibition of emotion in specific autobiographical memories. *Memory, 15*(4), 375–389. doi:10.1080/09658210701276850

Beike, D. R., Markman, K. D., & Karadogan, F. (2009). What we regret most are lost opportunities: A theory of regret intensity. *Personality and Social Psychology Bulletin, 35*(3), 385–397. doi:10.1177/0146167208328329

Beike, D. R., & Wirth-Beaumont, E. (2005). Psychological closure as a memory phenomenon. *Memory, 13*(6), 574–593. doi:10.1080/09658210444000241

Bernardo, A. B. I. (2004). McKinley's questionable bequest: Over 100 years of English in Philippine education. *World Englishes, 23*(1), 17–31. doi:10.1111/j.1467-971X.2004.00332.x

Bernardo, A. B. I. (2007). Language in Philippine education: Rethinking old fallacies, exploring new alternatives amidst globalization. In T. R. F. Tupas (Ed.), *(Re)making society: The politics of language, discourse, and identity in the Philippines* (pp. 1–26). Quezon City: University of the Philippines Press.

Bernardo, A. B. I., Clemente, J. A. R., & Nalipay, M. J. N. (2016). What personal value types are associated with beliefs on the social value of religion? *Psychological Studies, 61*(3), 170–180. doi:10.1007/s12646-016-0359-5

Bernardo, A. B. I., & Estrellado, A. F. (2014). Measuring hope in the Philippines: Validating the short version of the locus-of-hope scale in Filipino. *Social Indicators Research, 119*(3), 1649–1661. doi:10.1007/s11205-013-0573-7

Bond, R., & Smith, P. B. (1996). Culture and conformity: A meta-analysis of studies using Asch's (1952b, 1956) line judgment task. *Psychological Bulletin, 119*(1), 111–137. doi:10.1037/0033-2909.119.1.111

Bonnefon, J.-F., & Jiehai, Z. (2008). The intensity of recent and distant life regrets: An integrated model and a large scale survey. *Applied Cognitive Psychology, 22*(5), 653–662. doi:10.1002/acp.1386

Bossuyt, E., Moors, A., & De Houwer, J. (2014). Exploring the relations between regret, self-agency, and the tendency to repair using experimental methods and structural equation modeling. *The Psychological Record, 64*(4), 841–857. doi:10.1007/s40732-014-0065-4

Branscombe, N. R., Wohl, M. J. A., Owen, S., Allison, J. A., & N'gbala, A. (2003). Counterfactual thinking, blame assignment, and well-being in rape victims. *Basic and Applied Social Psychology, 25*(4), 265–273. doi:10.1207/S15324834BASP2504_1

Broomhall, A. G., Phillips, W. J., Hine, D. W., & Loi, N. M. (2017). Upward counterfactual thinking and depression: A meta-analysis. *Clinical Psychology Review, 55*, 56–73. doi:10.1016/j.cpr.2017.04.010

Bruine de Bruin, W., Dombrovski, A. Y., Parker, A. M., & Szanto, K. (2016). Late-life depression, suicidal ideation, and attempted suicide: The role of individual differences in maximizing, regret, and negative decision outcomes. *Journal of Behavioral Decision Making, 29*, 363–371. doi:10.1002/bdm.1882

Buchanan, J., Summerville, A., Lehmann, J., & Reb, J. (2016). The Regret Elements Scale: Distinguishing the affective and cognitive components of regret. *Judgment and Decision Making, 11*(3), 275–286. Retrieved from journal.sjdm.org/15/15901/jdm15901.pdf

Byrne, R. M. J. (2016). Counterfactual thought. *Annual Review of Psychology, 67*(1), 135–157. doi:10.1146/annurev-psych-122414-033249

Callander, G., Brown, G. P., Tata, P., & Regan, L. (2007). Counterfactual thinking and psychological distress following recurrent miscarriage. *Journal of Reproductive and Infant Psychology, 25*(1), 51–65. doi:10.1080/02646830601117241

Carpenter, S. (2000). Effects of cultural tightness and collectivism on self-concept and causal attributions. *Cross-Cultural Research, 34*(1), 38–56. doi:10.1177/106939710003400103

Catellani, P., & Bertolotti, M. (2014). The effects of counterfactual defences on social judgements. *European Journal of Social Psychology, 44*(1), 82–92. doi:10.1002/ejsp.1995

Chase, H., Camille, N., Michael, A., Bullmore, E., Robbins, T., & Sahakian, B. (2010). Regret and the negative evaluation of decision outcomes in major depression. *Cognitive, Affective, & Behavioral Neuroscience, 10*(3), 406–413. doi:10.3758/CABN.10.3.406

Chen, S. X., Hui, N. H. H., Bond, M. H., Sit, A. Y. F., Wong, S., Chow, V. S. Y., ... Law, R. W. M. (2006). Reexamining personal, social, and cultural influences on compliance behavior in the United States, Poland, and Hong Kong. *The Journal of Social Psychology, 146*(2), 223–244. doi:10.3200/SOCP.146.2.223-244

Church, A. T. (1987). Personality research in a non-Western culture: The Philippines. *Psychological Bulletin, 102*(2), 272–292. doi:10.1037/0033-2909.102.2.272

Church, A. T., & Katigbak, M. S. (2000). Trait psychology in the Philippines. *American Behavioral Scientist, 44*(1), 73–94. doi:10.1177/00027640021956107

Contractor, S. H., & Kumar, P. (2013). The effects of personal agency on regret. *Journal of Behavioral Decision Making, 26*(3), 304–315. doi:10.1002/bdm.1760

Cristea, I. A., Huibers, M. J. H., David, D., Hollon, S. D., Andersson, G., & Cuijpers, P. (2015). The effects of cognitive behavior therapy for adult depression on dysfunctional thinking: A meta-analysis. *Clinical Psychology Review, 42*(Supplement C), 62–71. doi:10.1016/j.cpr.2015.08.003

Cruz, J. P., Colet, P. C., Qubeilat, H., Al-Otaibi, J., Coronel, E. I., & Suminta, R. C. (2016). Religiosity and health-related quality of life: A cross-sectional study on filipino christian hemodialysis patients. *Journal of Religion and Health, 55*(3), 895–908. doi:10.1007/s10943-015-0103-9

Cuijpers, P., Berking, M., Andersson, G., Quigley, L., Kleiboer, A., & Dobson, K. S. (2013). A meta-analysis of cognitive-behavioural therapy for adult depression, alone and in comparison with other treatments. *The Canadian Journal of Psychiatry, 58*(7), 376–385. doi:10.1177/070674371305800702

Cuijpers, P., Donker, T., Weissman, M. M., Ravitz, P., & Cristea, I. A. (2016). Interpersonal psychotherapy for mental health problems: A comprehensive meta-analysis. *American Journal of Psychiatry, 173*(7), 680–687. doi:10.1176/appi.ajp.2015.15091141

Cuijpers, P., Geraedts, A. S., van Oppen, P., Andersson, G., Markowitz, J. C., & van Straten, A. (2011). Interpersonal psychotherapy for depression: A meta-analysis. *American Journal of Psychiatry, 168*(6), 581–592. doi:10.1176/appi.ajp.2010.10101411

Datu, J. A. D., King, R. B., & Valdez, J. P. M. (2016). The benefits of socially-oriented happiness: Validation of the interdependent happiness scale in the Philippines. *Child Indicators Research, 9*(3), 631–649. doi:10.1007/s12187-015-9333-3

Davis, C. G., & Lehman, D. R. (1995). Counterfactual thinking and coping with traumatic life events. In N. J. Roese & J. M. Olson (Eds.), *What might have been: The social psychology of counterfactual thinking* (pp. 353–374). Mahwah, NJ: Lawrence Erlbaum Associates.

Davis, C. G., Lehman, D. R., Wortman, C. B., Silver, R. C., & Thompson, S. C. (1995). The undoing of traumatic life events. *Personality and Social Psychology Bulletin, 21*(2), 109–124. doi:10.1177/0146167295212002

de Guzman, M. L. R. (2013). A validation of the Hospital Anxiety and Depression Scale (HADS) in the medically ill. *Acta Medica Philippina, 47*(3), 53–62. Retrieved from actamedicaphilippina.com.ph/sites/default/files/fulltexts/vol-47-no-3-avalidation.pdf

Diedrich, A., Grant, M., Hofmann, S. G., Hiller, W., & Berking, M. (2014). Self-compassion as an emotion regulation strategy in major depressive disorder. *Behaviour Research and Therapy, 58*, 43–51. doi:10.1016/j.brat.2014.05.006

Diedrich, A., Hofmann, S. G., Cuijpers, P., & Berking, M. (2016). Self-compassion enhances the efficacy of explicit cognitive reappraisal as an emotion regulation strategy in individuals with major depressive disorder. *Behaviour Research and Therapy, 82*, 1–10. doi:10.1016/j.brat.2016.04.003

East, P. L., Chien, N. C., & Barber, J. S. (2012). Adolescents' pregnancy intentions, wantedness, and regret: Cross-lagged relations with mental health and harsh parenting. *Journal of Marriage and Family, 74*(1), 167–185. doi:10.1111/j.1741-3737.2011.00885.x

Ehring, T., Fischer, S., Schnülle, J., Bösterling, A., & Tuschen-Caffier, B. (2008). Characteristics of emotion regulation in recovered depressed versus never depressed individuals. *Personality and Individual Differences, 44*(7), 1574–1584. doi:10.1016/j.paid.2008.01.013

Ehring, T., Tuschen-Caffier, B., Schnülle, J., Fischer, S., & Gross, J. J. (2010). Emotion regulation and vulnerability to depression: Spontaneous versus instructed use of emotion suppression and reappraisal. *Emotion, 10*(4), 563–572. doi:10.1037/a0019010

Eisma, M. C., Schut, H. A., Stroebe, M. S., Boelen, P. A., van den Bout, J., & Stroebe, W. (2015). Adaptive and maladaptive rumination after loss: A three-wave longitudinal study. *British Journal of Clinical Psychology, 54*(2), 163–180. doi:10.1111/bjc.12067

Epstude, K., & Roese, N. J. (2008). The functional theory of counterfactual thinking. *Personality and Social Psychology Review, 12*(2), 168–192. doi:10.1177/1088868308316091

Feng, X., Gu, R., Liang, F., Broster, L. S., Liu, Y., Zhang, D., & Luo, Y. J. (2015). Depressive states amplify both upward and downward counterfactual thinking. *International Journal of Psychophysiology, 97*(2), 93–98. doi:10.1016/j.ijpsycho.2015.04.016

Fukushima, M., Sharp, S. F., & Kobayashi, E. (2009). Bond to society, collectivism, and conformity: A comparative study of Japanese and American college students. *Deviant Behavior, 30*(5), 434–466. doi:10.1080/01639620802296212

Gilbar, O., & Hevroni, A. (2007). Counterfactuals, coping strategies and psychological distress among breast cancer patients. *Anxiety, Stress, & Coping, 20*(4), 383–392. doi:10.1080/10615800701384439

Gilovich, T., & Medvec, V. H. (1995). The experience of regret: What, when, and why. *Psychological Review, 102*(2), 379–395. doi:10.1037//0033-295X.102.2.379

Gilovich, T., Medvec, V. H., & Kahneman, D. (1998). Varieties of regret: A debate and partial resolution. *Psychological Review, 105*(3), 602–605. doi:10.1037/0033-295X.105.3.602

Gore-Felton, C., Koopman, C., Power, R., Israelski, D. M., Durán, R., Porter, J., ... Palmer, L. (2008). Psychosocial factors associated with disclosure of HIV positive serostatus: Understanding the influence of depression and social support. *Journal of HIV/AIDS & Social Services, 7*(1), 83–98. doi:10.1080/15381500802093258

Greenberg, L. S. (2008). Emotion and cognition in psychotherapy: The transforming power of affect. *Canadian Psychology/Psychologie Canadienne, 49*(1), 49–59. doi:10.1037/0708-5591.49.1.49

Greenberg, L. S., & Watson, J. (2005). *Emotion-focused therapy of depression*. Washington, DC: American Psychological Association.

Harcourt, D., Russell, C., Hughes, J., White, P., Nduka, C., & Smith, R. (2011). Patient satisfaction in relation to nipple reconstruction: The importance of information provision. *Journal of Plastic, Reconstructive and Aesthetic Surgery, 64*(4), 494–499. doi:10.1016/j.bjps.2010.06.008

Hayes, A. F. (2013). Mediation Analysis. *Introduction to mediation, moderation, and conditional process analysis: A regression-based approach* (pp. 83–203). New York, NY: The Guilford Press.

Hollon, S. D., & Dimidjian, S. (2014). Cognitive and behavioral treatment of depression. In I. H. Gotlib & C. L. Hammen (Eds.), *Handbook of Depression* (3rd ed.). (pp. 513–531). New York, NY: The Guilford Press.

Howlett, J. R., & Paulus, M. P. (2013). Decision-making dysfunctions of counterfactuals in depression: Who might I have been? *Frontiers in Psychiatry, 4*(143), 1–13. doi:10.3389/fpsyt.2013.00143

Jokisaari, M. (2004). Regrets and subjective well-being: A life course approach. *Journal of Adult Development, 11*(4), 281–288. doi:10.1023/B:JADE.0000044531.11605.d5

Kissane, D. W., Patel, S. G., Baser, R. E., Bell, R., Farberov, M., Ostroff, J. S., ... Shah, J. P. (2013). Preliminary evaluation of the reliability and validity of the Shame and Stigma Scale in head and neck cancer. *Head and Neck, 35*(2), 172–183. doi:10.1002/hed.22943

Klerman, G. L., Weissman, M. M., Rounsaville, B., & Chevron, E. (1984). *Interpersonal psychotherapy for depression*. New York, NY: Basic Books.

Kline, R. B. (2005). *Principles and practice of structural equation modelling* (2nd ed.). New York, NY: The Guilford Press.

Kraines, M. A., Krug, C. P., & Wells, T. T. (2017). Decision justification theory in depression: regret and self-blame. *Cognitive Therapy and Research, 41*(4), 556–561. doi:10.1007/s10608-017-9836-y

Kray, L. J., Galinsky, A. D., & Markman, K. D. (2009). Counterfactual structure and learning from experience in negotiations. *Journal of Experimental Social Psychology, 45*(4), 979–982. doi:10.1016/j.jesp.2009.03.008

Kray, L. J., Galinsky, A. D., & Wong, E. M. (2006). Thinking within the box: The relational processing style elicited by counterfactual mind-sets. *Journal of Personality and Social Psychology, 91*(1), 33–48. doi:10.1037/0022-3514.91.1.33

Kray, L. J., George, L. G., Liljenquist, K. A., Galinsky, A. D., Tetlock, P. E., & Roese, N. J. (2010). From what might have been to what must have been: Counterfactual thinking creates meaning. *Journal of Personality and Social Psychology, 98*(1), 106–118. doi:10.1037/a0017905

Krieger, T., Altenstein, D., Baettig, I., Doerig, N., & Holtforth, M. G. (2013). Self-compassion in depression: Associations with depressive symptoms, rumination, and avoidance in depressed outpatients. *Behavior Therapy, 44*(3), 501–513. doi:10.1016/j.beth.2013.04.004

Krieger, T., Berger, T., & Holtforth, M. G. (2016). The relationship of self-compassion and depression: Cross-lagged panel analyses in depressed patients after outpatient therapy. *Journal of Affective Disorders, 202*(Supplement C), 39–45. doi:10.1016/j.jad.2016.05.032

Kring, A. M., & Werner, K. H. (2004). Emotion regulation and psychopathology. In P. Philippot & R. S. Feldman (Eds.), *The regulation of emotion* (pp. 359–385). Mahwah, NJ: Lawrence Erlbaum Associates.

Lafrance Robinson, A., McCague, E. A., & Whissell, C. (2014). "That chair work thing was great": A pilot study of group-based emotion-focused therapy for anxiety and depression. *Person-Centered & Experiential Psychotherapies, 13*(4), 263–277. doi:10.1080/14779757.2014.910131

Lam, W. W. T., Kwok, M., Chan, M., Hung, W. K., Ying, M., Or, A., ... Fielding, R. (2014). Does the use of shared decision-making consultation behaviors increase treatment decision-making satisfaction among Chinese women facing decision for breast cancer surgery? *Patient Education and Counseling, 94*(2), 243–249. doi:10.1016/j.pec.2013.11.006

Landman, J. (1995). Through a glass darkly: Worldviews, counterfactual thought, and emotion. In N. J. Roese & J. M. Olson (Eds.), *What might have been: The social psychology of counterfactual thinking* (pp. 233–258). Mahwah, N.J.: Lawrence Erlbaum Associates.

Landman, J., Vandewater, E. A., Stewart, A. J., & Malley, J. E. (1995). Missed opportunities: Psychological ramifications of counterfactual thought in midlife women. *Journal of Adult Development, 2*(2), 87–97. doi:10.1007/BF02251257

Lecci, L., Okun, M. A., & Karoly, P. (1994). Life regrets and current goals as predictors of psychological adjustment. *Journal of Personality and Social Psychology, 66*(4), 731–741. doi:10.1037/0022-3514.66.4.731

Ligo-Ralph, V. (1990). Some theses concerning the Filipino value system. *Philippine Quarterly of Culture and Society, 18*(3), 149–161.

Lipsitz, J. D., & Markowitz, J. C. (2013). Mechanisms of change in interpersonal therapy (IPT). *Clinical Psychology Review, 33*(8), 1134–1147. doi:10.1016/j.cpr.2013.09.002

Lorini, E., & Schwarzentruber, F. (2011). A logic for reasoning about counterfactual emotions. *Artificial Intelligence, 175*(3–4), 814–847. doi:10.1016/j.artint.2010.11.022

Luby, J., Belden, A., Sullivan, J., Hayen, R., McCadney, A., & Spitznagel, E. (2009). Shame and guilt in preschool depression: Evidence for elevations in self-conscious emotions in depression as early as age 3. *Journal of Child Psychology and Psychiatry, 50*(9), 1156–1166. doi:10.1111/j.1469-7610.2009.02077.x

Lynch, F. (1973). Social acceptance reconsidered. In F. Lynch & A. de Guzman II (Eds.), *IPC Papers No. 2. Four readings on Philippine values* (pp. 1–68). Quezon City: Ateneo de Manila University.

MacBeth, A., & Gumley, A. (2012). Exploring compassion: A meta-analysis of the association between self-compassion and psychopathology. *Clinical Psychology Review, 32*(6), 545–552. doi:10.1016/j.cpr.2012.06.003

Mandel, D. R. (2003). Effect of counterfactual and factual thinking on causal judgements. *Thinking & Reasoning, 9*(3), 245–265. doi:10.1080/13546780343000231

Mandel, D. R. (2005). Counterfactual and causal explanation. In D. R. Mandel, D. J. Hilton, & P. Catellani (Eds.), Routledge research international series in social psychology. *The Psychology of Counterfactual Thinking* (pp. 11–27). New York: Routledge.

Marasigan, L. S. (2015, August). *Philippines' slow but expensive internet servic*. Business Mirror. Retrieved from https://businessmirror.com.ph/phls-slow-but-expensive-internet-service-4/

Markman, K. D., Gavanski, I., Sherman, S. J., & McMullen, M. N. (1993). The mental simulation of better and worse possible worlds. *Journal of Experimental Social Psychology, 29*(1), 87–109. doi:10.1006/jesp.1993.1005

Markman, K. D., & Miller, A. K. (2006). Depression, control, and counterfactual thinking: Functional for Whom? *Journal of Social and Clinical Psychology, 25*(2), 210–227. doi:10.1521/jscp.2006.25.2.210

Markus, H. R., & Kitayama, S. (1991). Culture and the self: Implications for cognition, emotion, and motivation. *Psychological Review, 98*(2), 224–253. doi:10.1037//0033-295X.98.2.224

Martin, Y., Gilbert, P., McEwan, K., & Irons, C. (2006). The relation of entrapment, shame and guilt to depression, in carers of people with dementia. *Aging & Mental Health, 10*(2), 101–106. doi:10.1080/13607860500311953

Maximo, S. I., Berlanga, K. N. B., Aquisay, A. P. F., Valencia, M. C. P., & Daoen, R. T. (2012). Regrets and well-being of senior citizens. *International Journal of Behavioral Science, 7*(1), 29–46. doi:10.14456/ijbs.2012.2

Monroe, M. R., Skowronski, J. J., Macdonald, W., & Wood, S. E. (2005). The mildly depressed experience more post-decisional regret than the non-depressed. *Journal of Social and Clinical Psychology, 24*(5), 665–690. doi:10.1521/jscp.2005.24.5.665

Morris, M. W., & Moore, P. (2000). The lessons We (Don't) learn: Counterfactual thinking and organizational accountability after a close call. *Administrative Science Quarterly, 45*(4), 737–765. doi:10.2307/2667018

Morrison, M., Epstude, K., & Roese, N. J. (2012). Life regrets and the need to belong. *Social Psychological and Personality Science, 3*(6), 675–681. doi:10.1177/1948550611435137

Myers, A. L., McCrea, S. M., & Tyser, M. P. (2013). The role of thought-content and mood in the preparative benefits of upward counterfactual thinking. *Motivation and Emotion, 38*(1), 166–182. doi:10.1007/s11031-013-9362-5

Neely, M., Schallert, D., Mohammed, S., Roberts, R., & Chen, Y.-J. (2009). Self-kindness when facing stress: The role of self-compassion, goal regulation, and support in college students' well-being. *Motivation & Emotion, 33*(1), 88–97. doi:10.1007/s11031-008-9119-8

Neff, K. D. (2003a). The development and validation of a scale to measure self-compassion. *Self & Identity, 2*(3), 223–250. doi:10.1080/15298860390209035

Neff, K. D. (2003b). Self-compassion: An alternative conceptualization of a healthy attitude toward oneself. *Self and Identity, 2*(2), 85–101. doi:10.1080/15298860309032

Neff, K. D., Ya-Ping, H., & Dejitterat, K. (2005). Self-compassion, achievement goals, and coping with academic failure. *Self & Identity, 4*(3), 263–287. doi:10.1080/13576500444000317

Newall, N. E., Chipperfield, J. G., Daniels, L. M., Hladkyj, S., & Perry, R. P. (2009). Regret in later life: Exploring relationships between regret frequency, secondary interpretive control beliefs, and health in older individuals. *The International Journal of Aging & Human Development, 68*(4), 261–288. doi:10.2190/AG.68.4.a

Osorio, A., López-del Burgo, C., Carlos, S., Ruiz-Canela, M., Delgado, M., & de Irala, J. (2012). First sexual intercourse and subsequent regret in three developing countries. *Journal of Adolescent Health, 50*(3), 271–278. doi:10.1016/j.jadohealth.2011.07.012

Paulhus, D. L. (1991a). *Assessing self-deception and impression management in self-reports: The Balanced Inventory of Desirable Responding, Version 6*. Unpublished manual, University of British Columbia.

Paulhus, D. L. (1991b). Measurement and control of response bias. In J. P. Robinson, P. Shaver, & L. S. Wrightsman (Eds.), *Measures of personality and social psychological attitudes* (pp. 17–59). San Diego, CA: Academic Press. https://doi.org/10.1016/B978-0-12-590241-0.50006-X

Phillips, W. J., Hine, D. W., & Thorsteinsson, E. B. (2010). Implicit cognition and depression: A meta-analysis. *Clinical Psychology Review, 30*(6), 691–709. doi:10.1016/j.cpr.2010.05.002

Pieters, R., & Zeelenberg, M. (2007). A theory of regret regulation 1.1. *Journal of Consumer Psychology, 17*(1), 29–35. doi:10.1207/s15327663jcp1701_6

Pos, A. E., & Greenberg, L. S. (2007). Emotion-focused therapy: The transforming power of affect. *Journal of Contemporary Psychotherapy, 37*(1), 25–31. doi:10.1007/s10879-006-9031-z

Preacher, K. J., & Hayes, A. F. (2008). Asymptotic and resampling strategies for assessing and comparing indirect effects in multiple mediator models. *Behavior Research Methods, 40*(3), 879–891. doi:10.3758/brm.40.3.879

Quelhas, A. C., Power, M. J., Juhos, C., & Senos, J. (2008). Counterfactual thinking and functional differences in depression. *Clinical Psychology & Psychotherapy, 15*(5), 352–365. doi:10.1002/cpp.593

Reker, G. T., & Woo, L. C. (2011). Personal meaning orientations and psychosocial adaptation in older adults. *SAGE Open, 1*(1), 1–10. doi:10.1177/2158244011405217

Robbins, J. E., & Stanley, C. T. (2012). Minimizing regrets in college athletes: An intervention approach. *International Journal of Sport and Exercise Psychology, 10*(3), 186–197. doi:10.1080/1612197X.2012.672010

Roese, N. J. (1994). The functional basis of counterfactual thinking. *Journal of Personality and Social Psychology, 66*(5), 805–818. doi:10.1037/0022-3514.66.5.805

Roese, N. J., & Epstude, K. (2017). The functional theory of counterfactual thinking: New evidence, new challenges, new insights. *Advances in Experimental Social Psychology, 56*, 1–79. doi:10.1016/bs.aesp.2017.02.001

Roese, N. J., Epstude, K., Fessel, F., Morrison, M., Smallman, R., Summerville, A., ... Segerstrom, S. (2009). Repetitive regret, depression, and anxiety: Findings from a nationally representative Survey. *Journal of Social and Clinical Psychology, 28*(6), 671–688. doi:10.1521/jscp.2009.28.6.671

Roese, N. J., & Hur, T. (1997). Affective determinants of counterfactual thinking. *Social Cognition, 15*(4), 274–290. doi:10.1521/soco.1997.15.4.274

Roese, N. J., & Morrison, M. (2009). The psychology of counterfactual thinking. *Historical Social Research / Historische Sozialforschung, 34*(2 (128)), 16–26. doi:10.2307/20762352

Roese, N. J., & Olson, J. M. (1997). Counterfactual thinking: The intersection of affect and function. *Advances in Experimental Social Psychology, 29*, 1–59. doi:10.1016/S0065-2601(08)60015-5

Roese, N. J., & Olson, J. M. (2007). Better, stronger, faster: self-serving judgment, affect regulation, and the optimal vigilance hypothesis. *Perspectives on Psychological Science, 2*(2), 124–141. doi:10.2307/40212193

Roese, N. J., & Summerville, A. (2005). What we regret most... and why. *Personality and Social Psychology Bulletin, 31*(9), 1273–1285. doi:10.1177/0146167205274693

Roese, N. J., Summerville, A., & Fessel, F. (2007). Regret and behavior: Comment on Zeelenberg and Pieters. *Journal of Consumer Psychology, 17*(1), 25–28. doi:10.1207/s15327663jcp1701_5

Rye, M. S., Cahoon, M. B., Ali, R. S., & Daftary, T. (2008). Development and validation of the counterfactual thinking for negative events scale. *Journal of Personality Assessment, 90*(3), 261–269. doi:10.1080/00223890701884996

Saffrey, C., Summerville, A., & Roese, N. J. (2008). Praise for regret: People value regret above other negative emotions. *Motivation and Emotion, 32*(1), 46–54. doi:10.1007/s11031-008-9082-4

Sanna, L. J., Meier, S., & Turley-Ames, K. J. (1998). Mood, self-esteem, and counterfactuals: Externally attributed moods limit self-enhancement strategies. *Social Cognition, 16*(2), 267–286. doi:10.1521/soco.1998.16.2.267

Sanna, L. J., & Turley-Ames, K. J. (2000). Counterfactual intensity. *European Journal of Social Psychology, 30*(2), 273–296. doi:10.1002/(SICI)1099-0992(200003/04)30:2<273::AID-EJSP993>3.0.CO;2-Y

Sanna, L. J., Turley-Ames, K. J., & Meier, S. (1999). Mood, self-esteem, and simulated alternatives: Thought-provoking affective influences on counterfactual direction. *Journal of Personality and Social Psychology, 76*(4), 543–558. doi:10.1037/0022-3514.76.4.543

Schmidt, R. E., Renaud, O., & Van Der Linden, M. (2011). Nocturnal regrets and insomnia in elderly people. *The International Journal of Aging & Human Development, 73*(4), 371–393. doi:10.2190/AG.73.4.f

Schwartz, B., Ward, A., Monterosso, J., Lyubomirsky, S., White, K., & Lehman, D. R. (2002). Maximizing versus satisficing: Happiness is a matter of choice. *Journal of Personality and Social Psychology, 83*(5), 1178–1197. doi:10.1037/0022-3514.83.5.1178

Seligman, M. E. P. (1975). *Helplessness: On depression, development, and death*. New York, NY: Freeman/Times Books/Holt.

Shaver, K. G., & Drown, D. (1986). On causality, responsibility, and self-blame: A theoretical note. *Journal of Personality and Social Psychology, 50*(4), 697–702. doi:10.1037/0022-3514.50.4.697

Sheehan, J., Sherman, K. A., Lam, T., & Boyages, J. (2007). Association of information satisfaction, psychological distress and monitoring coping style with post-decision regret following breast reconstruction. *Psycho-Oncology, 16*(4), 342–351. doi:10.1002/pon.1067

Sirois, F. M., Monforton, J., & Simpson, M. (2010). "If only i had done better": Perfectionism and the functionality of counterfactual thinking. *Personality and Social Psychology Bulletin, 36*(12), 1675–1692. doi:10.1177/0146167210387614

Smallman, R. (2013). It's what's inside that counts: The role of counterfactual content in intention formation. *Journal of Experimental Social Psychology, 49*(5), 842–851. doi:10.1016/j.jesp.2013.05.004

Smallman, R., & McCulloch, K. C. (2012). Learning from yesterday's mistakes to fix tomorrow's problems: When functional counterfactual thinking and psychological distance collide. *European Journal of Social Psychology, 42*(3), 383–390. doi:10.1002/ejsp.1858

Smallman, R., & Roese, N. J. (2009). Counterfactual thinking facilitates behavioral intentions. *Journal of Experimental Social Psychology, 45*(4), 845–852. doi:10.1016/j.jesp.2009.03.002

Smarr, K. L., & Keefer, A. L. (2011). Measures of depression and depressive symptoms: Beck Depression Inventory-II (BDI-II), Center for Epidemiologic Studies Depression Scale (CES-D), Geriatric Depression Scale (GDS), Hospital Anxiety and Depression Scale (HADS), and Patient Health Questionnaire-9 (PHQ-9). *Arthritis Care and Research, 63*(S11), S454–S466. doi:10.1002/acr.20556

Stewart, A. J., & Vandewater, E. A. (1999). "If I had it to do over again..": Midlife review, midcourse corrections, and women's well-being in midlife. *Journal of Personality and Social Psychology, 76*(2), 270–283. doi:10.1037/0022-3514.66.4.731

Stroebe, M., Stroebe, W., van de Schoot, R., Schut, H., Abakoumkin, G., & Li, J. (2014). Guilt in bereavement: The role of self-blame and regret in coping with loss. *PLoS ONE, 9*(5), 1–9. doi:10.1371/journal.pone.0096606

Tay, S. H., Cheung, P. P. M., & Mak, A. (2015). Active disease is independently associated with more severe anxiety rather than depressive symptoms in patients with systemic lupus erythematosus. *Lupus, 24*(13), 1392–1399. doi:10.1177/0961203315591026

Teasdale, J. D. (1988). Cognitive vulnerability to persistent depression. *Cognition and Emotion, 2*(3), 247–274. doi:10.1080/02699938808410927

Teigen, K. H., & Jensen, T. K. (2011). Unlucky victims or lucky survivors? Spontaneous counterfactual thinking by families exposed to the tsunami disaster. *European Psychologist, 16*(1), 48–57. doi:10.1027/1016-9040/a000033

Terry, M. L., & Leary, M. R. (2011). Self-compassion, self-regulation, and health. *Self and Identity, 10*(3), 352–362. doi:10.1080/15298868.2011.558404

Tilghman-Osborne, C., Cole, D. A., Felton, J. W., & Ciesla, J. A. (2008). Relation of guilt, shame, behavioral and characterological self-blame to depressive symptoms in adolescents over time. *Journal of Social and Clinical Psychology, 27*(8), 809–842. doi:10.1521/jscp.2008.27.8.809

Timulak, L. (2014). Witnessing clients' emotional transformation: An emotion-focused therapist's experience of providing therapy. *Journal of Clinical Psychology, 70*(8), 741–752. doi:10.1002/jclp.22109

Torges, C. M., Stewart, A. J., & Nolen-Hoeksema, S. (2008). Regret resolution, aging, and adapting to loss. *Psychology and Aging, 23*(1), 169–180. doi:10.1037/0882-7974.23.1.169

Towers, A., Williams, M. N., Hill, S. R., Philipp, M. C., & Flett, R. (2016). What makes for the most intense regrets? Comparing the effects of several theoretical predictors of regret intensity. *Frontiers in Psychology, 7*(1941), 1–8. doi:10.3389/fpsyg.2016.01941

Vally, Z., & Maggott, C. (2015). Evaluating the outcome of cultural adaptations of cognitive-behavioural therapy for adult depression: A meta-analysis of treatment studies in developing countries. *International Journal for the Advancement of Counselling, 37*(4), 293–304. doi:10.1007/s10447-015-9244-5

van Tol-Geerdink, J. J., Leer, J. W. H., Wijburg, C. J., van Oort, I. M., Vergunst, H., van Lin, E. J., ... Stalmeier, P. F. M. (2015). Does a decision aid for prostate cancer affect different aspects of decisional regret, assessed with new regret scales? A randomized, controlled trial. *Health Expectations, 19*, 459–470. doi:10.1111/hex.12369

Weissman, M. M., Markowitz, J. C., & Klerman, G. L. (2007). *Clinician's quick guide to interpersonal psychotherapy*. New York, NY: Oxford University Press. https://doi.org/10.1093/med:psych/9780195309416.001.0001

White, K., & Lehman, D. R. (2005). Looking on the bright side: Downward counterfactual thinking in response to negative life Events. *Personality and Social Psychology Bulletin, 31*(10), 1413–1424. doi:10.1177/0146167205276064

Wisco, B. E. (2009). Depressive cognition: Self-reference and depth of processing. *Clinical Psychology Review, 29*(4), 382–392. doi:10.1016/j.cpr.2009.03.003

Wrosch, C., Bauer, I., & Scheier, M. F. (2005). Regret and quality of life across the adult life span: The influence of disengagement and available future goals. *Psychology and Aging, 20*(4), 657–670. doi:10.1037/0882-7974.20.4.657

Zahn, R., Lythe, K. E., Gethin, J. A., Green, S., Deakin, J. F. W., Young, A. H., & Moll, J. (2015). The role of self-blame and worthlessness in the psychopathology of major depressive disorder. *Journal of Affective Disorders, 186*, 337–341. doi:10.1016/j.jad.2015.08.001

Zeelenberg, M. (2007). Emotional consequences of alternatives to reality: Feeling is for doing. *Behavioral and Brain Sciences, 30*(5–6), 469–470. doi:10.1017/S0140525X07002762

Zeelenberg, M., & Pieters, R. (2007). A theory of regret regulation 1.0. *Journal of Consumer Psychology, 17*(1), 3–18. doi:10.1207/s15327663jcp1701_3

Zeelenberg, M., & van Dijk, E. (2005). On the comparative nature of regret. In D. R. Mandel, D. J. Hilton, & P. Catellani (Eds.), Routledge research international series in social psychology. *The psychology of counterfactual thinking* (pp. 147–161). New York: Routledge.

Zeelenberg, M., van Dijk, E., Pieters, R., & van den Bos, K. (2002). The inaction effect in the psychology of regret. *Journal of Personality and Social Psychology, 82*(3), 314–327. doi:10.1037//0022-3514.82.3.314

Zeigarnik, B. (1927). On finished and unfinished tasks. In W. D. Ellis (Ed.), *A source book of Gestalt psychology* (pp. 300–314). New York: Harcourt Brace.

Zhang, J. W., & Chen, S. (2016). Self-compassion promotes personal improvement from regret experiences via acceptance. *Personality and Social Psychology Bulletin, 42*(2), 244–258. doi:10.1177/0146167215623271

Zigmond, A. S., & Snaith, R. P. (1983). The hospital anxiety and depression scale. *Acta Psychiatrica Scandinavica, 67*(6), 361–370. doi:10.1111/j.1600-0447.1983.tb09716.x

8

Perception of vulnerability in young females' experiences of oral sex: Findings from the focus group discussions

Elena Sovetkina[1]*, Marjorie Weiss[2] and Bas Verplanken[1]

*Corresponding author: Elena Sovetkina, Department of Psychology, University of Bath, Claverton Down, Bath BA2 7AY, UK
E-mail: elena.c.sovetkina@bath.edu

Reviewing editor: Justin Hackett, California University of Pennsylvania, USA

Abstract: The current study examined the issue of vulnerability in oral sex as perceived by female university students. Five focus group discussions were conducted with an aim to look at different sides of young females' experiences of fellatio and cunnilingus. The study revealed that vulnerability in oral sex was perceived by females as physical and emotional, and was further amplified by sociocultural and gender power pressures. Perception of vulnerability reflected the transition stage in females' efforts to resolve gender-structured oral sex dilemma. Findings have implications for educators and healthcare providers who aim to protect young females' physical and mental health.

Subjects: Social Sciences; Behavioral Sciences; Health and Social Care

Keywords: adolescent sexuality; qualitative studies; sex/gender roles; sexual health promotion

1. Introduction

The results of the UK national surveys on sexual behaviour (McManus et al., 2004; Mercer et al., 2009; Wellings et al., 2001) demonstrated that oral sex is becoming increasingly popular amongst adolescents and young adults. Nevertheless, the amount of research on their oral sex experiences is

ABOUT THE AUTHOR

Elena Sovetkina obtained her PhD (2016) from the University of Bath, UK. She is stage 1 health psychologist and an experienced health counsellor. Her research interests include self-control and risk-taking behaviour, health-related behaviour and motivation, social and cultural contexts of sexual activity of young people. Specifically, she is interested in medical sociology, epidemiology and in research exploring the link between oral sex behaviour and HPV-related oropharyngael cancer. The research reported in this paper was a part of her PhD project on the role of self-control in young people's oral sex behaviour and psychological well-being.

PUBLIC INTEREST STATEMENT

High level of young people involvement in oral sex is becoming a reality of modern life. This study aims to look at female university students' experiences of oral sex through their own lenses to explore what fuels their perception of vulnerability in oral sex. Five focus group discussions conducted for this study revealed that this vulnerability was perceived by female students as physical and emotional. They reported that their experiences of oral sex were affected on personal and relationship levels. Body image self-consciousness, lack of self-confidence contributed to the impact of media pressure regulating their physical appearance and performance in oral sex. This pressure was perceived by them directly and through males' behaviour and expectations. Young females' perception of vulnerability was further amplified by sociocultural gender roles stereotypes and reflected the transition stage in their efforts to adjust to the realities of gender-structured adults' sexual life.

relatively sparse and represented by mostly quantitative studies. The current paper aims to address this gap in knowledge by exploring the young females' oral sex experiences qualitatively.

Psychology literature indicates that majority of adolescents got engaged in oral sex because they perceive oral sex as a recreational activity that provide them with an opportunity for *risk-free sex*, in terms of health, social and emotional consequences (Bersamin, Walker, Waiters, Fisher, & Grube, 2005; Kaestle & Halpern, 2007; Lindberg, Jones, & Santelli, 2008; McKay, 2004; Prinstein, Meade, & Cohen, 2003; Uecker, Angotti, & Regnerus, 2008). Research on *hooking up*, as a distinct social form of behaviour on college campuses in the USA, revealed that parental discouragement of relationships emerged as an important predictor for oral sex *hook-ups* on college campuses (e.g. Fielder & Carey, 2010; Paul, McManus, & Hayes, 2000). It also appeared that parental discouragement also predicted the number of oral sex partners amongst college male students: the stronger was students' perception of parental discouragement of relationships, the greater the number of oral sex partners they reported (Owen & Fincham, 2011).

2. Polarity of oral sex experiences

Decades of research on sexual behaviour has revealed that oral sex can hold different meanings for males and females (e.g. Boyce et al., 2006; Ott, Millstein, Ofner, & Halpern-Felsher, 2006; Patrick & Lee, 2010) and can be associated with both positive and negative emotional outcomes (Chambers, 2007; Malacad & Hess, 2010). These outcomes have been linked to the motives behind young people's engagement in sexual activity: the approach motives and intrinsic motivation (e.g. seeking physical pleasure, enhanced relationship intimacy and shared pleasure) were associated with more positive outcomes, while avoidance motives and extrinsic motivation (e.g. preventing relationship conflict or partner disappointment, coping with negative emotions, responding to external pressures) were associated with more negative outcomes (e.g. Ott et al., 2006; Patrick & Lee, 2010). As young females were found to be more influenced by social and relationship pressure regarding their engagement in sex than young males, the association between extrinsic motives and their sexual behaviour proposed to be especially significant for them (e.g. Schatzel-Murphy, Harris, Knight, & Milburn, 2009; Tolman, 2012).

As attributed to oral sex, positive emotional outcomes, for both young males and females, were associated with oral sex in love or in relationships. They were grouped around the concept of mutual pleasure for both recipient and performer. Practicing oral sex in casual, non-committed relationships tend to produce a completely different spectre of emotional outcomes, which differ by gender. As a rule, young males reported being more satisfied with themselves as a result of having casual oral sex, as this gained them popularity amongst their peers, whereas young females were more likely than male adolescents to report negative social and emotional consequences from engagement in casual sex. In contrast to male adolescents, young females practising casual oral sex often felt as being used by their sexual partners; they also reported less pleasure and less satisfaction, lower sexual self-esteem, feelings of anxiety and being guilty for their sexual behaviour (e.g. Brady & Halpern-Felsher, 2007; Halpern-Felsher, Cornell, Kropp, & Tschann, 2005; Sanchez, Moss-Racusin, Phelan, & Crocker, 2011).

Negative or positive consequences of young females' oral sex experiences appeared to vary for cunnilingus and fellatio. Bay-Cheng and Fava's study (2011) found a relation between initiation of cunnilingus and sexual motives: females who initiated cunnilingus at younger ages demonstrated higher levels of engaging in sexual intercourse for personal gratification and in order to feel assertive, agentic and skilful. Amongst young women with cunnilingus experience, more sexually assertive young women (i.e. more able to advocate for their own sexual interests) also appeared to have more lifetime cunnilingus partners.

Contrary to cunnilingus experience, narratives of girls' fellatio experiences consist of talks on coercion, shame, guilt and ignorance (e.g. Tolman, Futch, & Burns, 2009). Research on early sexual activity suggested that higher levels of interpersonal sensitivity in adolescent girls (i.e. feelings of personal inadequacy and devalued self-worth) was related to initiating fellatio at younger age, and early experiences of fellatio increased their vulnerability in other domains and compromised their psychological functioning (e.g. Kaltiala-Heino, Kosunen, & Rimpelä, 2003; Meier, 2007).

It was also suggested that young females' lack of confidence and low self-esteem, as related to oral sex behaviour, may hold a potential link to the wide-spread in Western culture "standards" of females' bodily appearance, reflecting in huge media pressure for females to be thin (e.g. Wiederman, 2000). The range of physical and behavioural problems, associated with this sociocultural pressure, includes disordered eating, unbalanced diet regimes and increase in females' body image concerns and in body-shaping behaviours (e.g. Dittmar, 2005). In context of sexual behaviour, body image self-consciousness found to be concurrent with low sexual self-esteem, and subsequently, difficulties in negotiating sexual behaviour and, as a result, in increased depression in young females (e.g. Cash & Pruzinsky, 2002; Tiggemann, 2005; Wiederman & Hurst, 1998). It is highly possible that body image self-consciousness could be even more salient feature of females' experiences of oral sex.

Finally, the evidence from qualitative studies on sexuality perception indicates that negative or positive aspects of young females' oral sex experiences are likely to mirror sociocultural representations of oral sex that exist within culture and society, and are based on a combination of personal, relationship and social factors (Braun & Clarke, 2006).

3. Intersection of gender and class in sexual behaviour

Within contemporary gender theory's construct of young adulthood sexuality, both negative and positive psychological health outcomes of sexual behaviour are often considered through the concept of gender and in context of sexual interaction.

Research on gender and power arrangements in society suggested that gender beliefs, as a social structure, are embedded at multiple levels of society (Connell, 1987; Ridgeway & Correll, 2004; Sewell, 1992), including perceptions of individual selves, sociocultural organisational arrangements, and social and sexual interactions. According to this perspective, the power of gender beliefs influences individuals by "programming" the ways of how they see them in social and sexual interactions and by holding others accountable to this perception (e.g. Ridgeway, 2009).

In sexual behaviour, gender beliefs generated a powerful set of public beliefs about women's sexuality and sexual double standards: males are expected to desire and pursue sexual behaviour regardless of context, whereas female are expected to avoid casual sex and have sex only in love and in relationships (Risman & Schwartz, 2002). As part of their gender socialisation, adolescent girls are taught to be passive and to refrain from exhibition of their own sexual desire; they also expected to manage social pressure regarding their sexuality from their peer group (Impett, Schooler, & Tolman, 2006; Tolman, Striepe, & Harmon, 2003).

In oral sex, gender beliefs situate males as mainly recipients and females as mainly performers of oral sex on males. Sexual double standards in oral sex are further stretched to the societal and personal acceptance of appropriateness different types of oral sex for each gender. Any experiences of oral sex are universally seen to be appropriate to and benefit to young males. Conversely, young females who engaged in oral sex with males are very often stigmatised as "sluts" by their female peers for giving oral sex to males.

Merging together two systems of inequality in the sexual area, it was argued that like gender, social class beliefs can also possess a power to structure social and personal beliefs about appropriate sexual behaviour. In modern western society, the *self-development imperative* (i.e. social expectation to defer family formation until the later age to focus on education and career investment) makes casual sexual interactions on university campuses (hooking up) more appealing life-stage sexual activity for both genders than committed relationships (e.g. Arnett, 2004; Rosenfeld, 2007).

For young females, this intersection of gender and social class in area of sexual behaviour may produce a conflict between gendered beliefs (that they should avoid casual sex outside committed relationships) and social class beliefs (that they should delay relationship while pursuing educational and career goals) (Hamilton & Armstrong, 2009). This structural contradiction resulted in the rise of a strategic approach to sex and relationship, which provided female students with ambivalent sexual experiences. The necessity to utilise university's hook-up culture as a delay strategy made young females to face a challenge to elaborate their own ways of resolving this structural dilemma for themselves. As oral sex seems to be a part of this sexual hook-up's university culture, positive or negative emotions, accompanying young females' experiences of oral sex, can be seen as the indication of how well they can manoeuvre between structures constraining their sexual experiences in a complex arena of contemporary sexual behaviour, and how well they manage to establish themselves within this culture.

4. The current study

In the current study, we were interested in the further ways of how intersection of structured gender and class beliefs can guide and influence oral sex experiences of females' university students. Thus, our investigation was designed to look at different sides of young females' perception of their oral sex experiences through their own lenses, and was aimed to elucidate how gender and power arrangements in society could affect oral sex interactions between young heterosexual males and females.

By initiating discussions in focus groups about both fellatio and cunnilingus experiences and listening to our respondents' voices, we sought our female participants to elaborate their own understanding of power in oral sex on different structural levels (the individual, interactional, social environmental), and then identify any possible emotional and physical issues associated with their oral sex experiences, at each level. We also asked them to provide the possible explanations about the nature of their feelings. We wanted to know when, how and why any of these feelings get attached to their oral sex experiences and to which of their own personal characteristics, relationship interactions and characteristics of their social environment they were attributed to by our female respondents. Equally, we wanted to hear how they manage to resolve their oral sexual dilemmas, and how they utilise their structural positioning in resolving these dilemmas.

Although the use of focus groups for such a sensitive topic as oral sex experiences may have the potential to affect participants' privacy and to decrease the quality of disclosure obtained from the focus group members, the interactive nature of group discussion can provide the conditions under which female participants feel comfortable to discuss some most intimate and troubling them sexual issues and sexual experiences of their lives, and may enhance the quality of data obtained (e.g. Frith, 2000).

The choice of focus group for this study over interviewing each of young women individually provided us with some important advantages. Focus group discussions allow us to undercover and to explore various definitions and understandings of oral sex held by participants; to collect and to observe interactions between participants during discussion about oral sex, and to study how the consensus is achieved or conflict handled within a group setting (e.g. Morgan & Spanish, 1984). This method also offered us the opportunity to clarify questions and minimise misunderstandings, encourage females to address sensitive issue of engagement in oral sex in a supportive environment and allow collecting the data that provides explanations as well as descriptions (e.g. Krueger, 1998; Zeller, 1993).

5. Method

5.1. Procedures

The study was conducted as a part of larger project on oral sex behaviour in the one of the major universities on the South-West of the United Kingdom. Participation in the focus groups was on a volunteer basis and strictly anonymous. All participants were recruited by online advertising on internal students' university website, this method was chosen for ease of contact the population of interest. A total of five female focus groups were run; the smallest group comprised from three participants, the largest group—from six participants. To promote valuable discussion, groups were organised based on different levels of oral sex experience and the type of feedback on this experience, according to information from the demographic questionnaires. The focus groups took place in private non-formal locations at the university site so that participants feel more comfortable in providing their in-depth opinions.

All participants received the information sheet about the study and completed a consent form. Participants were given clear information about their right to withdraw from participating in the focus group at any time before the data will be processed and anonymised. The focus group discussions were led by a female facilitator (the researcher), and lasted from 90 min to 2 h, and were audio-taped and transcribed. Each participant received £10 for her participation.

At the beginning of the session the researcher set up the ground rules for the discussion and gave the instructions to participants. To encourage focus group discussion, stimulus material was prepared which consisted of a short presentation with a selection of anonymous students' responses to the previous researchers' oral sex survey questions about their reasons for being involved in oral sex. The researcher then asked participants to explicate how these came to be, or what the stories may be behind these data. In accordance with the concept of collective interrogations (i.e. exploration of the intellectual and political possibilities of focus groups), the researcher let the subject of oral sex to travel between personal experiences and combined imagination. This method allows participants to be active subjects of research and provides them with the opportunity to make inquiry and speak for ambiguity.

5.2. Data analysis

The research used a narrative approach and thematic analysis (Hollway & Jefferson, 2000) to analyse data from this focus groups. The researcher and the second coder read through the transcripts from each focus group separately. In accordance with methodological recommendations for qualitative research (e.g. Denzin & Lincoln, 2000) at the first stage the researcher conducted line-by-line open coding in order to establish the main themes and sub-themes. Then the researcher reviewed these preliminary coding themes and re-organised those sub-themes that were less meaningful to make them thematically coherent (Figure 1).

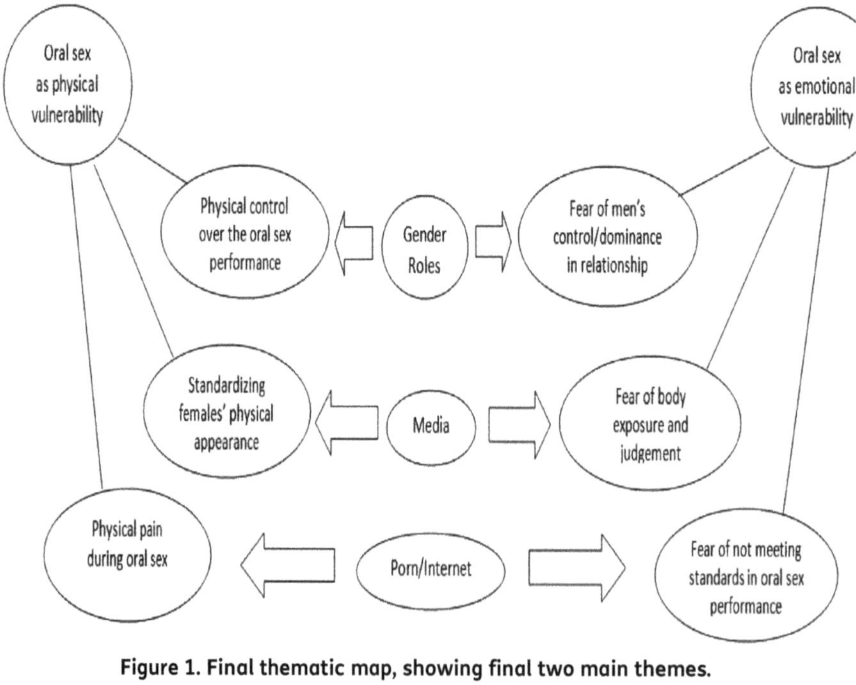

Figure 1. Final thematic map, showing final two main themes.

At the second stage, the researcher and second coder reviewed and revised the initial coding scheme. Both the researcher and second coder coded each focus group transcript individually, and then compared their results, gradually reaching agreement regarding the meaning of individual codes, their definitions and relation to one another, and also their applications to the coding themes (Table 1).

Based on what had been heard in each group, the researcher and the second coder designed a coding frame for the transcripts using themes of research interest. Once agreement was reached, the researcher revisited the transcripts and coded them using the final coding scheme. The second coder coded two out of five transcripts randomly chosen by the researcher. During this process, the researcher and second coder periodically discussed their coding strategy to ensure coding convergence on those transcripts that both of them had coded. Reliability was calculated amongst the two coders. In the final stage, the researcher matched the main themes and sub-themes across each group and separated them on the basis of whether they occurred in the story about oral sex experience or in general discussion.

In addition to coding themes, the researcher compared the course of discussion across focus groups. The format of the focus group interview research allowed participants to freely interact with each other in the course of discussion, questioning and challenging one another thereby deepening individual understandings and broadening meanings (Wilkinson, 1998).

6. Results

6.1. Characteristics of the study sample

In total, 24 female university students participated in the focus groups. Their age varied from 18 to 22 (*M* Age = 20). About 87.5% of participants (*N* = 21) identified themselves as white. Approximately 17% (*N* = 4) of female students reported to have an extensive experience of oral sex, while the remaining 83% (*N* = 20) reported rather moderate experience. Half of the participants indicated that they have performed oral sex in and outside relationships; about 42% of females (*N* = 10) said that they had oral sex only in relationships, while 8% (*N* = 2) had it solely outside relationships. Half of the female students reported to have a positive experience of oral sex, 25% (*N* = 6) had had neutral experiences, 21% (*N* = 5) could remember a mixture of experiences and 4% (*N* = 1) of females reported having a negative experience of oral sex.

6.2. Perception of vulnerability in oral sex: Power of socially arranged gender role's stereotypes and behaviour

The issue of the different purpose and meanings of oral sex inside and outside relationships was clearly made in each of the focus groups. While discussions developed, a clear distinction between giving and receiving oral sex was identified by all female respondents. The nature of this distinction was in females' personal perception of vulnerability in fellatio and in cunnilingus.

Females defined their vulnerability in oral sex as physical and emotional and related them to external (i.e. partners' characteristics) and internal (females' own characteristics) factors. *External factors* were associated with females' physical vulnerability in oral sex and were closely connected to an experience of distress from males' attempts to take physical control during fellatio and a physical pain/discomfort during cunnilingus. *Internal factors* were associated with females' emotional (psychological) vulnerability and were closely connected to the experience of distress about the perception of females' own physical appearance, and their perception of males taking control over the relationships. On many occasions physical vulnerability was accompanied by emotional vulnerability, as external and internal factors appeared to be inter-connected.

Table 1. The example of codes applied to a short segment of data (transcription)

	Data extract	Coded for
422	P3: I think its all because of all the porn out there [agreement by others] exposed to	
423	because the first guy that I had was he had never done anything sexual, even with	
424	regards to oral sex and he had given me oral sex and it felt so weird and it was exactly	influence of porn—feeling of oddness
425	like porn which is not what you are supposed to do	
426	P1: yes	
427	P3: it felt weird and painful for me because as I said I am really sensitive down there	
428	and he was being really ruff and he was sorry for being ruff, but he was sucking on my	not able to say no—negative experience
429	vagina and it felt so weird and it was not pleasurable, it was rather painful and since he	
430	was my friend but not in that bond emotionally and I did not feel comfortable enough to	
431	say like 'hey, what are you doing?' but it was a really negative experience because it	
432	was exactly as to what you would see in a porn movie	not able to say no—negative experience
433	P1: I think there is a confusion between porn being a film that is sort of exaggerated to	
434	make you feel turned on before you do your thing and people feel like that is what they	
435	should do in real life. when its not	
436	P3: yeah I think that like as with any other movie that porn should be regarded as	confusion between sex in porn and real life
437	entertainment and not real, because it's not real	
438	P1: because when you are 17, everything is real though and you have only ever	
439	experienced sex by watching a film and you can't really see what is real and what is not,	
440	its like a 17 year old man does that really?	
441	P3: I think that some more naive 17 year old might think that this is what sex is but that	
442	is not what is most normal and its not what women like sometimes, that is all they think	
443	that this is what a woman wants and they see this woman orgasming like 10 times in a	
444	movies [Laughter]. and they think, oh they must really like this and that they should do this since	influence of porn—boys got ideas from porn what women like
445	women like this	
446	P1: and that puts pressure on women to orgasm like 10 times [Common talk]	
447	P3: yeah exactly, for me like from oral sex I can only barely orgasm because I do enjoy	
448	it . but its just not that awesome for me ... so for me its actually a big accomplishment for	
449	me to orgasm from oral sex, but in porn movie, they like orgasm like 5 times from it, and	influence of porn—pressure on women to orgasm
450	I think that is what younger boys think that its supposed to be like that and when its not	

6.2.1. The theme of physical vulnerability in oral sex and the nature of psychological distress attached to it

Perception of physical vulnerability was organised around socially accepted stereotypes of appropriate gender roles and gender behaviour. It was related to males' attempts to take physical control during fellatio and a physical discomfort or pain during cunnilingus. Physical vulnerability was accompanied by females' feelings of emotional distress.

The males' tendency to take physical control during fellatio was perceived by our respondents as males' efforts to change the balance of power in oral sex in their own favour and attributed to the very nature of males' perception of sexuality:

Participant 3: Actually, my boyfriend told me that he kind of likes when I am a bit uncomfortable, and I had heard that from a lot of guys. It's kind of power thing but he didn't really mean that he wants to hurt me. I think that they just find it sexy when you are a bit uncomfortable. I think that it just has to do with their nature: they want to feel like they are powerful (FG4).

Participant 4: I think that men do feel empowerment when they are having oral sex with you, because they can move your head and stuff like that (FG3).

Participant 1: I hate if they start, like, thrusting it into your mouth and when they try to take control of the situation. I don't like that at all, its like, "No, I am in control!" (FG2).

Amongst the most unpleasant things in fellatio, perceived as males taking physical control over sexual activity, female students nominated males ejaculating in their mouth and expecting them to swallow their sperm, and physically pushing their heads down.

Female students emphasised that majority of boys were obtaining knowledge about oral sex from watching porn on the Internet:

Participant 1: Boys seeing porn on the internet and stuff and thinking really that is what sex is, but I suppose it's kind of like, I see it and I want to try it and stuff (PG1).

They regretted that the quality of this information from porn movies put young females in a very vulnerable position.

The experience of physical pain during cunnilingus was perceived by females' respondents as a sign of males' non-maturity and was attributed to the influence of porn.

The porn ideas about males' understanding of good cunnilingus performance, obtained from focus group discussions, can be divided on "the myths" how to give "good" oral sex to girls and on the myths that girls can have orgasm from oral sex numerous times.

The myths about the "technical" side of cunnilingus were discussed in accounts of females' experiences of physical pain and discomfort from this sexual activity. In many cases, the physical discomfort from cunnilingus was accompanied by psychological distress.

Participant 3: When I was 17 or 18, I went out with an idiot who thought that porn was normal sex. He had never done anything sexual, even with regards to oral sex and he had given me oral sex. It felt so weird and it was exactly like porn, which is not what you are supposed to do. It felt weird and painful for me because, as I said, I am really sensitive down there and he was being really rough, he was sorry for being rough but he was sucking on my vagina, it was not pleasurable, it was rather painful, and since he was my friend, but not in that bond emotionally, I did not feel comfortable enough to say, like, hey, what are you doing? But it was a really negative experience, because it was exactly as to what you would see in a porn movie (FG3).

The myths that girls can have orgasm from cunnilingus numerous times were also discussed in the light of its psychological pressure for females:

> Participant 3: From oral sex I can only barely orgasm, because I do enjoy it, but it's just not that awesome for me. So, for me it's actually a big accomplishment to orgasm from oral sex. But in porn movie they orgasm like 5 times from it, and I think that is what younger boys should think that it's supposed to be like that.
>
> Participant 1: And that puts pressure on women to orgasm like 10 times (FG4).

Our respondents argued that this pressure led them to worry about not meeting "the standards" and feeling guilty of not performing like in porn movies, and such as not fulfilling boys' expectations. At this point, perceptions of physical and psychological vulnerability were inter-connected.

> Participant 1: I feel a pressure to orgasm, because it's just such an effort to me. I feel like I have to orgasm, but then I feel like I cannot orgasm. So, sometimes I just say, oh I can't [lots of laughter], so by the time they realise all that it's gone, you know, particularly if I get stressed.
>
> Participant 3: I find the same thing with the pressure to orgasm, I do feel that pressure, because if the guy is down there for like 10 min and I am still not close to it, just feels like selfish, and then it feels like I am taking advantage of him, and I worry that they might feel inadequate down there (FG5).

These issues were so troublesome for girls that one of them finally noted that she could see the "hidden" boys' control over girls in these expectations: "it's kind of like he is controlling you in a way because you worry about it" (PG1).

6.2.2. The theme of emotional vulnerability in oral sex and the nature of psychological distress attached to it

Perception of emotional vulnerability was more complex. In first instance, it was organised around socially accepted stereotypes about females' physical appearance and, in this way, was related to females' problems with their self-esteem and sexual self-efficacy.

More deeply, females' emotional vulnerability reflected their difficulties in utilising their structural positioning as the means of resolving oral sex dilemma for themselves. The main sub-themes here were females' anxiety about not meeting males' sexual standards and their concerns of males' controlling and dominating them in relationship.

The general statement reflecting the issue of body image concerns, as it was expressed by one of our respondents, is provided below:

> Participant 1: mine (perception of vulnerability) are quite heavily based on feelings, so for me it can be painful not in a physical sense but in an emotional sense because of what they are going to be looking at me down there, and what if they find that I am unattractive down there? They are going to be right up against my vagina and look at other parts too, like they might find my stomach a bit too flabby for them at that angle? You know, it's more like that kind of vulnerable, so it's their opinion of me (FG3).

Talking about body image self-consciousness in context of females' experiences of cunnilingus, participants discussed the social pressure from media and porn in dictating young females the standards of their physical appearance. Participants noted that this made them feel self-conscious and reflect upon their body image satisfaction.

Participant 4: We have to be clean and all that, our legs and underarms. So, that has become another fact we have to worry about, because with some guys, that like this kind of thing, it's expected amongst all girls. There is more of the pressure, like on top of being pretty and skinny, to worry about.

Participant 6: I think that it makes you feel more like self-conscious about yourself and, I think, a lot of women have this sort of an illusional power of men.

Participant 1: You have to think about how you look, not just that area, but like flabby tummies and everything else, so it's not just that but it's the image on the whole.

Participant 2: Yeah, I feel really put off by receiving oral sex because I am like, what kind of angle are they getting down there from my face? [Laughter] You know, like double chin? (FG4)

Participant 2: I think that women are worried because they know that men watch a lot of porn and that, and women in porn have these designer vaginas, and I think that men expect that from us (FG5).

These body image concerns were agreed to play a major role in females' perception of vulnerability in cunnilingus. The best illustrations of this were found in talks about females' perception of being not physically fit enough (i.e. issue related to having cellulite etc.) and having body disfigurations.

Participant 1: um something that I could add to the whole confidence issue that we had been talking about ... on the left inside lip of my vagina I have got a birth mark which is basically its kind of blueish and its just a bit bumpy but um I remember that at one point I was so uncomfortable with myself just because I was like, oh my gosh, guys are going to see, that what are they going to think? Are they going to think that it's some kind of STD or whatever? I have been scared that people think that I am not clean, not in the sense that I don't wash, but in the sense like omg is that an STD? When its not, is just a birth mark (FG2).

The discussion about body image concerns, as applied to cunnilingus, made participants talk about such types of psychological vulnerability, as self-exposure and fear of judgement on the basis of their body image flaws:

Participant 1: Yeah, cause women are quite worried on men picking up on any of their flaws and, you know, she might have a bit of cellulite or, you know, maybe there is the whole thing about men don't liking pubic hair, as well, and that is whole another issue for women to deal with. Maybe women just feel worried about that men are going to see all of me now rather than just, you know, my personality, they are going to see everything.

Participant 2: I think because it is more intimate with oral, so they feel a lot more exposed so if you got any fears like that. But then again, that is probably also disturbance from body image problems from the media and pressure? (FG5)

Participants explicitly linked body image worries to the issue of "self-confidence" that they consider to be very important for both involvement in oral sex with males and declining the offer of oral sex from males.

They clearly attributed the lack of confidence to resist relationship pressure to get involved in oral sex to the potential danger for them to be controlled and dominated in relationships by males.

Participant 3: It would affect the rest of your life as well, so when they are like pressuring you to have oral sex and you don't want to, you would start thinking about other things that they do, like, if you both go out to dinner, he gets to choose what you eat and, like, when you are watching TV then he is the one who gets to choose, it just shows the way the pressure is more dominant! (PG1)

Participant 1: I think that is a point of concern because I feel like giving oral sex, that is the time that they have the power in the relationship sexually and I feel like there needs to be an even power exchange, umm, in the relationship. So, that is if that is taken away, that is a bit worrying.

Participant 4: Yeah, that is sort of like a slipperly slope really (FG5).

6.2.3. The challenge of overcoming vulnerability in oral sex: personal confidence to manipulate gender power

The issue of "self-confidence" appeared to have an outer lining for young females as related to their experience of both fellatio and cunnilingus, as they linked it with perception of males' physical and emotional control over them and over relationships. This, in turn, led them to experience a psychological distress attached to the perception of vulnerability in oral sex. The critical point here appeared to be females' capacity to say NO to unwanted oral sex, if a female liked the partner and wanted to have a relationship with him.

The females' opinions of how to overcome this challenge differentiated:

Opinion 1: Well, with my boyfriend at the beginning we did not have sex with each other, it was literally just foreplay and stuff and there were some times when I was like "I don't want to do it", but I really couldn't just, like, say No because then what else were we gonna do? It would just completely ruin the atmosphere, and the guy might get really offended and annoyed, which is why in the early stages of the relationship I just didn't say NO, like, how would he react if I say no? So, I just made the best effort not to say NO and just go with the flow (Participant 4, PG1).

Opinion 2: It depends on your confidence really, like if the guy is putting pressure on you to do something, then it is not ok, you should not be with someone whom makes you feel like that, and there are a lot of people in the world whom would feel pressured in all sorts of relationships, and they feel like they are just doing what is expected of them, but I think, it is just that confidence thing, like if you feel pressured then don't do it! (Participant 4, FG3).

In attempt to somehow counterbalance this pressure and emotionally to ease their psychological vulnerability, respondents across all groups promoted the idea that performing oral sex can give them some kind of manipulative power over males. This type of power was referred to as taking control over males' pleasure and orgasm; using oral sex to keep hold on their boyfriend, and using oral sex to get what they wanted or to impress their partner in order to be liked or loved.

The females' power to take control over boys' pleasure/orgasm was transformed into emotional satisfaction that girls gained from performing both fellatio and cunnilingus. Interestingly, the currents within this link seem to operate in two different ways: in performing fellatio girls felt powerful by making boys to orgasm, and in cunnilingus while faking orgasm girls felt powerful by making boys to believe in their power to make girls to orgasm.

Participant 1: I find that in the past I had been using oral sex to get something that I wanted and for getting men to like me not always but, I guess, it was a tool of manipulation for me. It's, um, if I am see someone and I quite like them, then I might go down on them because I want to maybe impress them or show that I am giving or a good lover? Or, yeah, I think that is probably what it is, I suppose, it is a power thing, you know, although you might be physically beneath them, you are kind of looking up at them, you have complete control of their genitals and you have control over their arousal, you know they are getting aroused over what you are doing, and it feels nice to know that. Even if you don't like them or if they don't like you, they are still being aroused by you (FG4).

Participant 2: It's kind of a curse really ... you know that you are not going to get there ... and feel like, like to stop, it's not going to happen, so you try to consider that, so it's just like to spare us both, so that is a bit of power as well, in a way, I think, because you are faking it to get some fun, so you are making them think otherwise. Yeah, so, that is the power, that one day you can be like "You know all them times? I faked it!" [Laughter amongst participants], so that is kind of power, I guess, isn't it? (FG1)

While the experiences of using oral sex as the tool of manipulation with the purpose of getting some benefits or to be liked/loved were associated with engagement in both fellatio and cunnilingus, the experiences of engagement in oral sex with the aim of keeping a hold on boyfriends or to make a relationship work were strongly associated with fellatio.

Participant 3: I think that it's again a power thing, and I know that a lot of women actually use oral sex as a way to keep hold of their boyfriend, and not break up with them.

Participant 1: This is sort of a way to show him that is what I can do to you, this is what you would be missing if you are not with me sort of thing. And then that is the way (of influence) that you could have on the decisions that he should have made (FG4).

In both cases, while discussing these experiences, participants demonstrated a full awareness of what they were doing and why they were doing this, and applied explicitly the term of "power" to such actions and situations.

In comparison with the experiences of females engaging in both fellatio and cunnilingus with the aim to exercise their power over male's pleasure and getting emotional satisfaction for themselves, the experiences of fellatio with the aim to keep relationship going were rather associated with females' perception of being powerless and insecurity in sexual relationship, and demonstrated their vulnerability in current relationship that appeared to come to life through the vehicle of oral sex. This conclusion was supported by the final comment made by one of the participants:

Participant 3: I think, if he does not want to be with you and you are only using oral sex as a way to keep hold of him, then you are only abusing yourself not them and that is only you, you are the only person that is going to be affected at the end, if that makes sense? (FG4)

7. Discussion

This focus group study explored female students' oral experiences and the ways of how power arrangements in society can influence the interactions during oral sex between young heterosexual male and female university students. We used a narrative approach and thematic analysis to uncover young females' strategies of making sense of their oral sex experiences, with the purpose to investigate how these experiences may affect their perception of oral sex.

7.1. The issue of power and vulnerability in oral sex

In general, all participants agreed that both males and females hold a particular power in oral sex interactions. Males' power was referred to as their ability to make females give them oral sex, to control females' sexuality and to make females worry about their sexual performance and their desirability for them. Females' power in oral sex was defined as controlling males' orgasms, and using oral sex performance as a tool of manipulating men. Females' stories varied depending on the purpose of this manipulation. One of the main aims of such manipulation, spoken about quite openly by female participants, was "to be liked by their partner", to be "different" (from other girls) and to be "special to the partner". At this point females' accounts of power and vulnerability were mutually dependent.

Our findings indicated that the stories behind this accounts of power and vulnerability were multilayered.

On the upper layer, they were grounded in the very way of how modern society coined the whole issue of oral sex, and reflected gender and power arrangements in sexual behaviour. Focus groups showed that this actual or perceived vulnerability was inter-connected with different types of pressures placed on young females. Firstly, it was the pressure from societal norms and societal expectations related to their sexual behaviour in general and to their oral sex behaviour in particular. Young females reported to be pressurised by societal expectation to engage in oral sex and to perform both types of oral sex. Secondly, this pressure was identified as the pressure associated with dynamic of negotiating sexual behaviour with their partners within sexual interactions or relationships, accounting for the attitudes, standards and desirable/non-desirable outcomes for both parties. On the individual level, young females reported that they felt pressurised by males not only on the basis of their judgements about their oral sex performance but also on the basis of their own ability to get an orgasm from oral sex. Finally, for some of them, these pressures were reported to further transform into the feelings of being controlled by males, as they made them worry about their sexual performance.

On the lower layer, young females perceived their vulnerability in oral sex as physical and emotional, and these two appeared to co-exist at the same time and for the same person. Physical vulnerability was referred to as a partner's level of knowledge of physiology in general and females' physiology in particular, and was closely associated with a dangerous tendency amongst young males to have porn movies as a source of their sex education. Emotional vulnerability referred to females' individual body image self-consciousness, their sexual self-esteem and their anxiety about being emotionally and physically controlled in sex by males. In many cases physical discomfort was found to be accompanied by emotional distress.

7.2. The issue of body image concerns in oral sex

Body image-related concerns were in the heart of young females' worries about engagement in oral sex. Most importantly, these concerns were also grounded in the same multileveled gender and sociocultural structure. The concerns of looking not fit/good enough and a fear to be negatively judged by their male partners on the basic of their body image flaws appeared to make girls feel extremely vulnerable in both a physical and emotional sense, especially at the beginning of the relationship. Physical vulnerability was referred to as not being fit enough physically (e.g. flabby tammy, skinny legs) and having some physical disfigurations (e.g. skin problems, birth marks); whereas emotional vulnerability was more associated with not looking pretty enough to a partner during sex (e.g. under a particular angle and in a particular position). Applied to the whole nature of oral sex, body image concerns were exacerbated by sociocultural pressure to look pretty and skinny and to perform in oral sex as porn star models.

One the one hand, the findings that many of our participants, who already looked skinny according to the modern fashion, were talking about their body image self-consciousness during oral sex may be considered as a sign of their personal lack of sexual self-efficacy that has little to do with society standards to be thin. This suggestion was supported by findings from Wiederman's (2000) study where young women who viewed themselves as good sex partner were found to be least concerned about their bodily appearance during physical intimacy.

On the other hand, it can indicate that young females with higher body image self-consciousness but similarly sized with their peers may have developed and applied to themselves the unrealistic standards for female attractiveness, taken from the popular media and porn. Therefore, their greater body image self-consciousness during oral sex could be a result of such extreme views on their bodily appearance and attractiveness (Fredrickson & Roberts, 1997; McKinley & Hyde, 1996).

Finally, although none of focus group participants revealed that body image issues have stopped them from performing fellatio, experiences of cunnilingus was much strongly affected by young females' body image self-consciousness. A fruitful path for future research will be in exploring the impact of females' body image concerns and the frequency of their habitual negative body image thinking on their engagement in cunnilingus and its emotional and mental health consequences.

Future work would be useful in exploring the degree of consciousness in this behaviour on these outcomes, as habitual behaviour is argued to be highly automatic.

7.3. The issue of personal confidence to overcome vulnerability in oral sex

The discourse of confidence was the thread that linked all participants' talk about their oral sex experiences. All of them emphasised the role of confidence and sexual self-efficacy in females' vulnerability attached to oral sex practice. Participants referred these confidence and sexual self-efficacy to females' ability to say "NO" to unwanted oral sex offers in the service of preserving relationship and to express their own desires to their partner. The discourse of "inauthenticity in relationship" (e.g. Tolman, Impett, Tracy, & Michael, 2006), known from a previous research, was clearly presented in stories of female students who find it difficult to communicate their own desires and therefore, who were willing "to sacrifice their sexual health in the service of preserving relationships" (Impett et al., 2006, p. 133). Thus, our findings were in accordance with findings from previous studies on self-efficacy in sexual relationship (e.g. Impett & Peplau, 2003; Impett et al., 2006). Although female participants particularly emphasised the importance of "confidence" in oral sex, majority of them talked about this issue in the manner which allow to suggest that they have already managed to sort it out for themselves, and mentioned it rather in context of some of their friends' current experiences.

At the same time, we heard the stories of very confident young females who appeared to be satisfied with performing both fellatio and cunnilingus. Some of them reported to give oral sex in order "to please their partner", and expressed a feeling of pride about their ability to do this to satisfy their men. Some of them considered their engagement in oral sex as a personal achievement, and clearly evaluated it as a personal success accompanied by the positive emotions. The positive emotional feelings were normally applied to female students' performance of fellatio in trustful and committed relationship.

The importance of females' confidence to manipulate power arrangements and thus, to overcome their personal vulnerability in oral sex was particularly salient in the discourse of "desire". In this study we had a single narrative of pure "desire" related to oral sex, from female participant who openly declared that she likes to give oral sex because of her personal perception of giving oral sex to men as an extremely submissive and arousing experience. This narrative was rather the exception than a norm for our focus groups. This female student appeared to sound like a woman who likes her looks and who was completely satisfied with her appearance and, subsequently, as a woman who feels particularly efficacious within an oral sex situation and when her body displayed, a situation where women are typically afford less power than men. This narrative can be interpreted as an example of the importance of accepting stereotypical gender roles in sexual behaviour for females' sexual desire and satisfaction. This story, taken in as a whole, also provided a strong link between female's body image satisfaction and their confidence and self-efficacy in oral sex.

Although the discourse of desire and pleasure was present in females' narratives about oral sex, this discourse was relatively rare. Typically, females reported positive emotional feelings from satisfying their male partners or overcoming the challenge of performing fellatio or cunnilingus rather than from getting a pleasure from fellatio or cunnilingus itself. At this point, our results were different from results of Bay-Cheng, Robinson, and Zucker (2009) study, in which experiences of cunnilingus in young females were associated with positive emotional reactions.

For many of our female respondents, gaining the confidence in themselves as related to their sexual behaviour appeared to be a turning point in their oral sex experiences. This confidence provided them with a power to navigate in the complex gender-structured waters of oral sex behaviour in a search for the means to exploit its structural vulnerabilities in the way that they can change the structure for themselves. Until this change occurred, gender beliefs and power arrangements in society were still perceived by them as a threat for their sexuality and they see them as a source of their vulnerability. Once this change has happened and secured, this very personal process of overcoming power pressures and such reducing their vulnerabilities in oral sex, constantly going on the background, made females feel more psychologically comfortable, confident and successful. Problems related to their body image satisfaction seemed to become not so salient to them anymore; they faded away as their confidence and self-acceptance were growing.

8. Limitations

The major limitation of this study was in excluding from analysis young males. Although being previously justified as purposeful approach in this study, the future research would greatly benefit from inclusion of male students in this type of research.

Secondly, we used a relatively small convenience sample of female university students. Similar to other focus group studies investigating sexual behaviour and assessment of sexual risks in young females (e.g. Bay-Cheng et al., 2009; Zeller, 1993), our sample was comprised of a group of 24 female students who expressed the interest in the topic of oral sex and who were confident enough to participate in focus groups on such a sensitive subject. Our justification of using such narrow sample was in that the nature of qualitative research allows the narrow focus on investigating life-lived experiences of individual or small groups of individuals representing the certain homogeneous population.

Next limitation of this study was that our focus groups included female students from multicultural background. As such, our results have to be applied with caution to the population of typical British young females; nevertheless, they can be reflecting the contingent of modern university students' female population in the country. Our focus groups were also mixed in terms of students' extent of oral sex experience, and this may have inhibited some females from fully expressing their views. In addition, in this study we did not differentiate female students' oral sex experiences on the basis on their age. Further research need to explore females' oral sex experiences in different age groups and perhaps in longitudinal studies to see how this perceived vulnerability can change over time.

The use of incentives can be also seen as a potential limitation on this study. Although the use of incentives to get participants in the research may hold implications for the quality of data obtained and can compromise the voluntariness of their informed consent (e.g. Head, 2009), in the current study offering money to female students was rather an indication of respect for their time and contribution that they made. The interest in the topic and the willingness to participate in this research on oral sex was surprisingly high.

It is also important to consider that this study was explicitly focused on heterosexual females. In this sense, the large area of oral sex in bisexual or homosexual relationship was not covered at all. In the same-gender or bisexual relationships, the perception and meanings of oral sex, as well as gender power pressure and sexual self-efficacy may vary and differ from our findings, thus, this will be a very interesting and potential avenue for future research.

9. Implications and conclusions

In the present study, we uncovered the story of young females' physical and emotional vulnerability as related to their oral sex experiences. This vulnerability, attributed to females' perception of gender power imbalance in oral sex, was found to be fuelled by power arrangements in modern society and females's confidence to challenge these gender beliefs and societal pressures.

Findings from this study demonstrated how pushing contemporary gender theory into the area of young people sexual behaviour can provide a key for uncovering gender inequality in young females' perception of their oral sex experiences and in explaining their vulnerability within this sexual behaviour.

The personal accounts describing the impact of gender and societal pressures on young females' vulnerability in oral sex, emerged from this paper, can contribute to a long line of research elucidating how power arrangements in society influence gender interactions between young heterosexual males and females. They can also add an interesting and important nuance to the whole story, illustrating the ways how young females manage to recognise and comprehend their positioning within socially structured gender beliefs in the area of oral sex behaviour, and then utilise them as a resource in resolving problems related to their experiences of oral sex.

The results of this study may have implications for educators and healthcare providers who aim to protect young females' physical and mental health. Once identified, the patterns of young females' physical and emotional vulnerability as related to their experiences of oral sex could be targeted in future sexual health interventions to derive enduring health-related benefits for adolescent females.

Ethical approval
University of Bath Psychology Ethics Committee (Ref: 14-020).

Funding
The authors received no direct funding for this research.

Competing interests
The authors declare no competing interest.

Author details
Elena Sovetkina[1]
E-mail: elena.c.sovetkina@bath.edu
Marjorie Weiss[2]
E-mail: b.verplanken@somewhere.com
Bas Verplanken[1]
E-mail: m.weiss@somewhere.com
[1] Department of Psychology, University of Bath, Claverton Down, Bath BA2 7AY, UK.
[2] Department of Pharmacy and Pharmacology, University of Bath, Claverton Down, Bath BA2 7AY, UK.

References
Arnett, J. J. (2004). *Emerging adulthood: The winding road from the late teens through the twenties.* New York, NY: Oxford.
Bay-Cheng, L. Y., & Fava, N. M. (2011). Young women's experiences and perceptions of cunnilingus during adolescence. *Journal of Sex Research, 48*(6), 531–542. https://doi.org/10.1080/00224499.2010.535221
Bay-Cheng, L. Y., Robinson, A. D., & Zucker, A. N. (2009). Behavioral and relational contexts of adolescent desire, wanting, and pleasure: Undergraduate women's retrospective accounts. *Journal of Sex Research, 46*(6), 511–524. https://doi.org/10.1080/00224490902867871
Bersamin, M. M., Walker, S., Waiters, E. D., Fisher, D. A., & Grube, J. W. (2005). Promising to wait: Virginity pledges and adolescent sexual behavior. *Journal of Adolescent Health, 36*(5), 428–436. https://doi.org/10.1016/j.jadohealth.2004.09.016
Boyce, W., Doherty-Poirier, M., MacKinnon, D., Fortin, C., Saab, H., King, M., & Gallupe, O. (2006). Sexual health of Canadian youth: Findings from the Canadian youth, sexual health and HIV/AIDS study. *The Canadian Journal of Human Sexuality, 15*(2), 59–68.
Brady, S., & Halpern-Felsher, B. L. (2007). versusAdolescents' reported consequences of having oral sex vs. vaginal sex. *Pediatrics, 119*, 229–236. https://doi.org/10.1542/peds.2006-1727
Braun, V., & Clarke, V. (2006). Using thematic analysis in psychology. *Qualitative Research in Psychology, 3*, 77–101. https://doi.org/10.1191/1478088706qp063oa
Burns, A., Futch, V. A., & Tolman, D. L. (2011). "It is like doing homework": Academic achievement discourse in adolescent girls' fellation narratives. *Sexuaity Research and Social Policy, 8*, 139–251.
Cash, T. F., & Pruzinsky, T. (Eds.). (2002). *Body images: A handbook of theory, research, and clinical practice.* New York, NY: Guilford.
Chambers, W. (2007). Oral sex: Varied Behaviors and perceptions in a college population. *Journal of Sex Research, 44*(1), 28–42. https://doi.org/10.1080/00224490709336790
Connell, R. W. (1987). *Gender and power: Society, the person, and sexual politics.* Stanford, CA: Stanford University Press.
Denzin, N. K., & Lincoln, Y. S. (Eds.). (2000). *Handbook of qualitative research.* Thousand Oaks, CA: Sage.
Dittmar, H. (2005). Introduction to the special issue: Body image - vulnerability factors and processes linking sociocultural pressures and body dissatisfaction. *Journal of Social and Clinical Psychology, 24*(6), 768–791.
Fielder, R. L., & Carey, M. P. (2010). Predictors and consequences of sexual 'hook-ups' among college students: a short-term prospective study. *Archives of Sexual Behavior, 39*, 1105–1119. https://doi.org/10.1007/s10508-008-9448-4
Fredrickson, B. L., & Roberts, T. (1997). Objectification theory: Towards understanding woman's lived experiences and mental health risks. *Psychology of Women Quarterly, 21*, 173–206. https://doi.org/10.1111/j.1471-6402.1997.tb00108.x
Frith, H. (2000). Focusing on sex: Using focus groups in sex research. *Sexualities, 3*(3), 275–297. https://doi.org/10.1177/136346000003003001
Halpern-Felsher, B. L., Cornell, J. L., Kropp, R. Y., & Tschann, J. M. (2005). Oral versus vaginal sex among adolescents: Perceptions, attitudes, and behaviour. *Pediatrics, 115*, 845–851. https://doi.org/10.1542/peds.2004-2108
Hamilton, L., & Armstrong, E. A. (2009). Gendered sexuality in young adulthood: Double binds and flawed options. *Gender & Society, 23*(5), 589–616. https://doi.org/10.1177/0891243209345829
Head, E. (2009). The ethics and implications of paying participants in qualitative research. *International Journal of Social Research and Methodology, 12*(4), 335–344. https://doi.org/10.1080/13645570802246724
Hollway, W., & Jefferson, T. (2000). *Doing qualitative research differently: Free associations, narrativa and the interview method.* London: Sage. https://doi.org/10.4135/9781849209007

Impett, E. A., & Peplau, L. A. (2003). Sexual compliance: Gender, motivational, and relationship perspectives. *Journal of Sex Research, 40*(1), 87–100. https://doi.org/10.1080/00224490309552169

Impett, E. A., Schooler, D., & Tolman, D. L. (2006). To be seen and not heard: Femininity ideology and adolescent girls' sexual health. *Archives of Sexual Behavior, 35*(2), 129–142. https://doi.org/10.1007/s10508-005-9016-0

Kaestle, C. E., & Halpern, C. T. (2007). What's love got to do with it? Sexual behaviors of opposite-sex couples through emerging adulthood. *Perspectives on Sexual and Reproductive Health, 39*(3), 134–140. https://doi.org/10.1363/3913407

Kaltiala-Heino, R., Kosunen, E., & Rimpelä, M. (2003). Pubertal timing, sexual behaviour and self-reported depression in middle adolescence. *Journal of Adolescence, 26*(5), 531–545. https://doi.org/10.1016/S0140-1971(03)00053-8

Krueger, R. A. (1998). *Analyzing & reporting focus group results.* Thousand Oaks, CA: Sage. https://doi.org/10.4135/9781483328157

Lindberg, L. D., Jones, R., & Santelli, J. S. (2008). Noncoital sexual activities among adolescents. *Journal of Adolescent Health, 43*, 231–238. https://doi.org/10.1016/j.jadohealth.2007.12.010

Malacad, B. L., & Hess, G. C. (2010). Oral sex: Behaviours and feelings of Canadian young women and implications for sex education. *The European Journal of Contraception and Reproductive Health Care, 15*(3), 177–185. https://doi.org/10.3109/13625181003797298

McClelland, S. I., & Fine, M. (2008). Writing on cellophane: Studying teen women's sexual desires; inventing methodological release points. In K. Gallagher (Ed.), *The methodological dilemma: Creative, critical and collaborative approaches to qualitative research* (pp. 232–260). London: Routledge.

McKay, A. (2004). Oral sex among teenagers: Research, discourse, and education. *Canadian Journal of Human Sexuality, 13*, 201–203.

McKinley, N. M., & Hyde, J. S. (1996). The objectified body consciousness scale: Development and validation. *Psychology of Women Quarterly, 20*, 181–215. https://doi.org/10.1111/j.1471-6402.1996.tb00467.x

McManus, S., Erens, B., Field, J., Johnson, A. M., Mercer, C.H., Wellings, K., ... Fenton, K. A. (2004) The National Survey of Sexual Attitudes and Lifestyles: Summary of key findings. *AIDS & Hepatitis Digest*, 99.

Meier, A. M. (2007). Adolescent first sex and subsequent mental health. *American Journal of Sociology, 112*(6), 1811–1847. https://doi.org/10.1086/512708

Mercer, C. H., Copas, A. J., Sonnenberg, P., Johnson, A. M., McManus, S., Erens, B., & Cassell, J. A. (2009). Who has sex with whom? Characteristics of heterosexual partnerships reported in the second National Survey of Sexual Attitudes and Lifestyles. *International Journal of Epidemiology, 38*, 206–214. https://doi.org/10.1093/ije/dyn216

Morgan, D. L., & Spanish, M. T. (1984). Focus groups: A new tool for qualitative research. *Qualitative Sociology, 7*, 253–270. https://doi.org/10.1007/BF00987314

Ott, M. A., Millstein, S. G., Ofner, S., & Halpern-Felsher, B. L. (2006). Greater expectations: Adolescents' positive motivations for sex. *Perspectives on Sexual and Reproductive Health, 38*(2), 84–89. https://doi.org/10.1363/3808406

Owen, J., & Fincham, F. D. (2011). Young adults' emotional reactions after hooking up encounters. *Archives of Sexual Behavior, 40*, 321–330. https://doi.org/10.1007/s10508-010-9652-x

Patrick, M. E., & Lee, C. M. (2010). Sexual motivations and engagement in sexual behavior during the transition to college. *Archives of Sexual Behavior, 39*(3), 674–681. https://doi.org/10.1007/s10508-008-9435-9

Paul, E. L., McManus, B., & Hayes, A. (2000). 'Hook-ups': Characteristics and correlates of college students' spontaneous and anonymous sexual experiences. *Journal of Sex Research, 37*, 76–88. https://doi.org/10.1080/00224490009552023

Prinstein, M. J., Meade, C. S., & Cohen, G. L. (2003). Adolescent oral sex, peer popularity, and perceptions of best friends' sexual behaviour. *Journal of Pediatric Psychology, 28*, 243–249. https://doi.org/10.1093/jpepsy/jsg012

Ridgeway, C. L. (2009). Framed before we know it: How gender shapes social relations. *Gender & Society, 23*, 145–160. https://doi.org/10.1177/0891243208330313

Ridgeway, C. L., & Correll, S. J. (2004). Unpacking the gender system: A theoretical perspective on gender beliefs and social relations. *Gender & Society, 18*, 510–531. https://doi.org/10.1177/0891243204265269

Risman, B., & Schwartz, P. (2002). After the Sexual revolution: Gender politics in teen dating. *Contexts, 1*, 16–24. https://doi.org/10.1525/ctx.2002.1.1.16

Rosenfeld, M. J. (2007). *The age of independence: Interracial unions, same sex unions and the changing American family.* Cambridge, MA: Harvard University Press.

Sanchez, D. T., Moss-Racusin, C. A., Phelan, J. E., & Crocker, J. (2011). Relationship contingency and sexual motivation in women: Implications for sexual satisfaction. *Archives of Sexual Behavior, 40*(1), 99–110. https://doi.org/10.1007/s10508-009-9593-4

Schatzel-Murphy, E. A., Harris, D. A., Knight, R. A., & Milburn, M. A. (2009). Sexual coercion in men and women: similar behaviors, different predictors. *Archives of Sexual Behavior, 38*(6), 974–986. https://doi.org/10.1007/s10508-009-9481-y

Sewell, W. H. (1992). A theory of structure: Duality, Agency, and transformation. *American Journal of Sociology, 98*, 1–29. https://doi.org/10.1086/229967

Tiggemann, M. (2005). Body dissatisfaction and adolescent self-esteem: Prospecive findings. *Body Image: An International Journal of Research, 2*, 129–135. https://doi.org/10.1016/j.bodyim.2005.03.006

Tolman, D. L. (2012). Female adolescents, sexual empowerment and desire: A missing discourse of gender inequity. *Sex Roles, 66*(11–12), 746–757. https://doi.org/10.1007/s11199-012-0122-x

Tolman, D. L., Futch, V., & Burns, A. (2009). *Narrating fellatio: Coercion, competence and contradictions.* Toronto: American Psychological Association.

Tolman, D. L., Impett, E. A., Tracy, A. J., & Michael, A. (2006). Looking good, sounding good: Femininity ideology and adolescent girls' metal health. *Psychology of Women Quarterly, 30*(1), 85–95. https://doi.org/10.1111/j.1471-6402.2006.00265.x

Tolman, D. L., Striepe, M. I., & Harmon, T. (2003). Gender matters: Constructing a model of adolescent sexual health. *Journal of Sex Research, 40*(1), 4–12. https://doi.org/10.1080/00224490309552162

Uecker, J. E., Angotti, N., & Regnerus, M. D. (2008). Going most of the way: "Technical virginity" among American adolescents. *Social Science Research, 37*(4), 1200–1215. https://doi.org/10.1016/j.ssresearch.2007.09.006

Wellings, K., Nanchahal, K., Macdowall, W., McManus, S., Erens, B., Mercer, C. H., ... Field, J. (2001). Sexual behaviour in Britain: Early heterosexual experience. *The Lancet, 358*(9296), 1843–1850. https://doi.org/10.1016/S0140-6736(01)06885-4

Wiederman, M. W. (2000). Womens' body image self-consciousness during physical intimacy with a partner. *Journal of Sex Research, 37*(1), 60–68. https://doi.org/10.1080/00224490009552021

Wiederman, M. W., & Hurst, S. R. (1998). Body size, physical attractiveness, and body image among young adult women: Relationship to sexual experience and sexual esteem. *Journal of Sex Research, 35*, 272–281. https://doi.org/10.1080/00224499809551943

Wilkinson, S. (1998). Focus groups in feminist research: Power, interaction and the co-construction of meaning. *Women's Studies International Forum, 21*(1), 111–125. https://doi.org/10.1016/S0277-5395(97)00080-0

Zeller, R. A. (1993). Focus group research on sensitive topics: Setting the Agenda without setting the Agenda. In D. Morgan (Ed.), *Successful focus groups* (pp. 167–183). Newbury Park, CA: Sage.

9

The relationship between EFL teachers' reflective practices and their teaching effectiveness: A structural equation modeling approach

Khalil Motallebzadeh[1], Fatemeh Ahmadi[1] and Mansooreh Hosseinnia[1*]

*Corresponding author: Mansooreh Hosseinnia, English Department, Torbat-e-Heydarieh Branch, Islamic Azad University, Torbat-e-Heydarieh, Iran
E-mail: mansoorehhossinnia@yahoo. com
Reviewing editor: Meihua Qian, Clemson University, USA

Abstract: The main purpose of this study is to investigate the relationship between English Foreign Language teachers' reflective practices and their teaching effectiveness. Moreover, years of experiences in teachers' reflective practices and their teaching effectiveness were explored. The participants comprised 115 EFL teachers teaching at different language institutes in several cities of Iran. Their selection was based on convenience sampling, and the participation was entirely voluntary. In this study, two instruments were used: the English language teaching reflection inventory and Effective teaching questionnaire. Pearson's correlation coefficient, independent sample *t*-test, and structural equation modeling (SEM) were run to analyze the causal relationships among the components. Results of structural equation modeling indicated that there was a positive significant relationship between the subscales of teachers' reflective practices and their teaching effectiveness. In addition, there was a strong positive and significant relationship between EFL teachers' level of teaching effectiveness and experience. Also, there was a weak positive and significant relationship between EFL teachers' level of teaching reflectiveness and experience. Finally, these findings were discussed with reference to the context of Iran.

ABOUT THE AUTHORS

Khalil Motallebzadeh is an associate professor at the Islamic Azad University (IAU) of Torbat-e-Heydarieh and Mashhad Branches, Iran. He is a widely published researcher in teacher education, language testing, and e-learning. He has been a visiting scholar at the University of Illinois at Urbana Champaign (UIUC) in 2007–2008. He is also an accredited teacher/master trainer of the British Council since 2008. He has represented Iran in Asia TEFL since 2009.

Fatemeh Ahmadi is a PhD student in TEFL, Teaching English as Foreign Language, at the Azad University of Torbat-e-Heydarieh, Iran. She is a EFL teacher in high school and he is also teaching English in University of Birjand, Iran.

Mansooreh Hosseinnia is a PhD student in TEFL, Teaching English as Foreign Language, at the Azad University of Torbat-e-Heydarieh, Iran. She is also teaching English in Azad University of Jajarm, Elmi karbordi University of Jajarm, and PNU University of Jajarm and Garmeh, Iran.

PUBLIC INTEREST STATEMENT

In teaching profession, teachers evaluate their teaching by means of some reflective practices to improve their teaching quality. Also, teaching effectiveness means meeting educational goals and plans and students' success. So, the main purpose of this study is to examine the relationship between English language teachers' reflective practices and their teaching effectiveness. With this aim, 115 English teachers teaching at different language institutes in several cities of Iran were selected. For assessing teachers' level of reflective practices and their teaching effectiveness, two questionnaires were used. After gathering the questionnaires, some statistical approaches were done. Finally, the results of those statistical approaches showed that there was a strong positive and significant relationship between EFL teachers' level of teaching effectiveness and experience.

Subjects: Educational Research; Teachers & Teacher Education; Educational Psychology

Keywords: teachers' reflective practices; effective teaching; EFL teacher

1. Introduction

In recent decades, there have occurred changes in teacher education attitudes. Teachers moved beyond methods with the aim of achieving better results (Salmani Nodoushan, 2011, p. 1). In ESL context, teachers and practitioners came to this conclusion that no method is best for every situation. Teachers are not any more passive transmitters of information, but they are active, critical thinker, and autonomous teachers. Teachers adapted themselves with post method pedagogies proposed by Kumaravadivelu (1994). ELT teachers (teachers who teach English language) started to examine and change their approaches, attitudes, behaviors in order to be more effective in their classrooms. Thus, teachers started to move beyond usual classroom circumstances and appraise outcomes of teachers' pedagogical decisions by watching and considering one's own instructing, and utilizing perception and reflection as a method for achieving change. This way to deal with instructing can be portrayed as "Reflective Teaching" (Richards, 2013, p. 1). Borg (2011) argues that the final aim of reflective teaching is improving teachers' teaching quality. Moussa-Inaty (2015) considers reflection as effective instruments for growth and intellectual development. Also, Motallebzadeh, Hosseinnia, and Domskey (2016) regards reflective teaching as a powerful tool for developing and empowering teachers.

It is supposed that being a reflective teacher influence in the amount of their teaching's effectiveness. Teaching effectiveness has been defined differently by different people in different contexts based on their aims and constructs. According to Borich (1994), for teaching effectiveness, a teacher should prefer teaching and effective learning, and teaching should be obvious, various, and promote the success amounts of students in order to achieve their educational aims. The truth of the matter is that we have sufficient knowledge about the components of effective teacher. In spite of the fact that specific investigations and models for teacher effectiveness have unobtrusive contrasts, every one of them concur that the check for teacher effectiveness is student learning (Barry, 2010, p. 3). Paolini (2015) believes that those teachers who have commitment to their profession and do educating as an art that needs qualification and expertise are in a high level of teaching effectiveness.

Many studies have been done to examine effectiveness of different types of reflective teaching tools. However, scare studies have been implemented for examining involvement of teachers in reflective practices as a whole. Also, Moradkhani, Raygan, and Moein (2017) mentioned that few studies have been done to explore the relationship of involvement teachers in reflective practices with enhancement of teachers' performance. So, in an attempt, they investigated the relationship between EFL teachers' reflective practices and self-efficacy. Their findings revealed that teachers' reflective practices had a significant positive effect on their self-efficacy. Therefore, because of scarcity of studies in this field, this study aimed to engage in this important issue from the point of view of its relationship with effective teaching. So, the main purpose of this study is to examine the relationship between EFL teachers' reflective practices and their teaching effectiveness.

2. Review of literature

2.1. Reflective teaching

Reflection refers to a kind of "mental processing" with a special aim that is related to complicated or unorganized notions (Moon, 1999, 2004). Richards (2013) defines reflection as a mechanism in which an experience is remembered, considered, and assessed, usually in relation to a broader aim. Tice (2004, p. 1) mentions reflective teaching means examining what you carry out in the classroom, thinking about its purpose, and thinking about if it effective—a process of self-observation and self-evaluation. Pollard and Collins (2005) remark that the notion of reflective teaching promotes the professional development and competency. It helps teachers to develop and improve themselves as a core of professional development. Teachers by doing reflective teaching can find their teaching strong points and weaknesses and can try to overcome them. Bartlett (1990) (as cited in Richards, 2013, p. 1) points out that being a reflective teacher requires moving beyond a basic concern with educational strategies and "how to" questions and asking "what" and "why" questions that consider instructions and managerial strategies not as means in themselves. In order to do reflective teaching, different reflective tools have been proposed by many researchers (Murphy, 2001, Tice, 2002) such as peer observation, video or audio recording, diary keeping, journal writing, and so on.

Many researchers have implemented different studies to examine effectiveness of different types of reflective teaching tools and techniques. Fatemipour (2013) in his study investigated effectiveness of different types of reflective teaching tools by means of a researcher-made questionnaire related to the teachers' perspectives. Their findings reveal that there were significant differences among the kind of data that different reflective tools obtained. They found that Teacher Diary was the most efficient tool. At the second place, Peer Observation was efficient. After peer observation, Students' Feedback was effective. And finally, audio recording was the least efficient tool. In another study, Motallebzadeh et al. (2016) reported on the attitudes of Iranian EFL teachers about the effects, strong points and weaknesses of peer observation. As a result of those viewpoints, it can be resulted that peer observation as a reflective instrument could significantly influence on Iranian EFL teachers' professional development. Lofthouse and Birmingham (2010) examined the effect of video-recording in the classrooms as a tool for professional development of teachers. Based on their findings, they found positive and substantial effects on using the video-recording by teachers in the classroom. Moussa-Inaty (2015) in an attempt examined the effect of some guidelines on reflective writing on a group of interns in the College of Education. According to their findings most interns selected to utilize the guiding questions when they try to write their reflections. There was also a significant positive effect on the use of those guiding questions on reflective writing.

2.2. Teaching effectiveness

Because teachers as the most important members of the society are responsible for having depositary of all the resources—the human intelligence and they are holding the luck of other individuals and the civilization in their hands, they have achieved an exclusive position in societies all over the world (Borkar, 2013).

According to Borkar (2013), the effectiveness of the educational system largely depends upon the effective teachers. Paolini (2015) mentioned that remarkable teachers are culturally keen, respectful, sensual and charming. They encourage students to work to their talents by setting high, yet reasonable prospects, focusing free communication, and asking challenging thinking problems that provoke discussion.

Barry (2010) argues that teaching effectiveness can be understood by examining what effective teachers know and do in their daily professional practice. Also, he (2010) adds that these require a deep understanding of topic, learning theory and learner distinctness, planning, classroom educational techniques, knowing individual learners, and evaluation of student understanding and skill with learning achievements. Also, according to Barry (2010) effective instructors are familiar with their students' reality, desires, and needs. They are familiar with their students' learning styles, their strengths and their weaknesses as learners. They are professionals in their subject matter ... but more essentially, effective teachers always consider their students' learning. Marsh and Roche (1997) argued about the evaluation of teaching effectiveness that teaching effectiveness can be assessed by current learners, past students, the instructor himself or herself, colleagues, managers, or trained observers. Instructors' self-evaluations are effective because they can be collected in all educational contexts.

During the recent decades, researchers have carried out much about teacher effectiveness. Chi, Yeh, and Wu (2014) in their study with the aim of investigating the effects of well-being, social support, principal leadership on teaching effectiveness, the mediating impact of well-being between social support and teaching effectiveness, and the moderating effect of principal leadership between social support and teaching effectiveness, found that (1) social support will positively and significantly affect teaching effectiveness, (2) social support will positively and significantly affect well-being, (3) well-being will positively and significantly affect teaching effectiveness, (4) principal leadership will positively and significantly affect teaching effectiveness, (5) well-being has mediating effect between social support and teaching effectiveness, and (6) principal leadership has no moderating effect between social support and teaching effectiveness. In another study, Reynolds, Ross, and Rakow (2002) made a comparison among Professional Development School (PDS) and non-PDS graduates in the United States in terms of retention in teaching, teaching effectiveness, and perceptions of professional preparation. According to their results, there were no significant differences in retention in teaching and effectiveness and small but significant differences favoring PDS over non-PDS teacher education programs. Kafi and Motallebzadeh (2015) in an attempt investigated the relationship between EFL teachers' effective teaching and the language learning motivation of Iranian EFL learners. They found a significant positive relationship between teachers' effective teaching and the L2 learners' language learning motivation.

As mentioned in review of literature part, no study has addressed the relationship between EFL teachers' reflective practices and their teaching effectiveness. The following research questions were posed and were investigated in the current study:

RQ1: Is there any significant relationship between EFL teachers' reflective practices and their teaching effectiveness?

RQ2: Is there any significant relationship between EFL teachers' level of teaching effectiveness and reflective Teaching in their years of experiences?

3. Methodology

3.1. Participants

The participants are 115 EFL teachers teaching at different language institutes in several cities of Iran. Their selection was based on convenience sampling and the participation was entirely voluntary. They were 50 females and 65 males whose age varied from 20 to 37 (M = 28.42, SD = 3.21) with 1 to 15 years of teaching experience (M = 8.24, SD = 2.79). The teachers had all majored in the various branches of English such as teaching, literature, and translation at B.A. or M.A. or PhD. This group of participants completed the English language teaching reflection inventory.

3.2. Instruments

In this study, two instruments were used: the English language teaching reflection inventory, and Effective teaching questionnaire by Umme Kulsum (2000).

3.2.1. The English language teaching reflection inventory

The English language teaching reflection inventory is designed by Akbari, Behzadpoor, and Dadvand (2010). This scale includes 29 items and assesses participants' reflective practices in five subscales. The first one is practical reflection (six items), which is exercised when teachers share teaching-related issues with their colleagues, observe other teachers' classes or have their peers observe their classes with the aim of making improvements in their instruction, and keep reflective journals about their class performance. The second subscale, cognitive reflection (six items), refers to teachers' conscious efforts to be engaged in professional development by, for example, attending conferences or reading professional journals. Affective reflection (three items) is the third subscale, comprising attempts that teachers make in order to gain a better understanding of students' background and elicit their ideas about various teaching tasks. Metacognitive reflection (seven items), which is the fourth subscale, encompasses three themes, i.e. teachers' personal beliefs about the nature of teaching, critical appraisal of their own performance, and interpretations of their own teachers' behavior. Finally, the last subscale, critical reflection (seven items), pertains to teachers' knowledge of the socio-political factors of teaching and the influence of these factors on the classroom context.

The scale should be responded based on a five-point Likert scale varying from (1) "never" to (5) "always". The scale has high reliability and validity indices (Akbari et al., 2010). The reliability coefficient was .911 for total reflective teaching, which shows the scale enjoys high reliability. The reliability coefficient for sub-scales was: Practical = .89, Cognitive = .83, Affective = .92, Metacognitive = .77, and Critical = .79.

3.2.2. Effective teaching questionnaire

Teacher effectiveness questionnaire was developed and validated by Umme Kulsum in 2000. It consisted of 60 items. The scale has five distinct areas that included classroom management, the preparation for teaching and planning, knowledge of subject matter, interpersonal relations, and teacher characteristics (Buela & Joseph, 2015). The reliability of this scale was calculated by Goed (2011) as .85.

3.3. Procedure

The data collection of this study took place in April and May 2017. This correlational study collected quantitative data through two questionnaires. The participants (EFL teachers) answered the reflective practices questionnaires in the presence of the researcher. The questionnaire took about 30-40 min. There was no limitation of time in doing. After a brief explanation of the purpose of the research, the teachers received the questionnaires. Moreover, the process of distribution of questionnaires was done via email. We explained the purpose of completing the questionnaire and asked them not to write a name on them. They were required to provide demographic information such as, gender and years of experience only. After gathering the data, they were calculated in SPSS software (24.0 version) and were analyzed by Structural equation modeling software by Amos software.

4. Results

In the present study, before analyzing, the data were screened and two missing data were estimated using "expectation maximization algorithm. Descriptive statistics of sub-factors of teachers" reflective practices and teaching effectiveness are presented in Table 1. Because the number of items was different in the various subscales of both questionnaires, an average item score was computed for each sub-construct, ranging from 1 to 5.

Results of correlations between five sub-factors of teachers' reflective practices and five sub-factors of teaching effectiveness are given in Table 2. As can be seen in Table 2, there is positive and significant correlation between total reflective practices and total teaching effectiveness ($r = .61$, $p < .05$). In addition, among five sub-factors of teachers' reflective practices, affective reflection has the highest correlation ($r = .62$, $p < .05$) and critical reflection has the lowest correlation ($r = .42$, $p < .05$) with total teaching effectiveness.

Table 1. Descriptive statistics of the variables

	N	Mean	Std. deviation
Practical	115	3.49	1.11
Cognitive	115	3.71	1.07
Affective	115	4.32	2.41
Metacog.	115	2.83	.98
Critical	115	3.47	1.22
Total Ref.	115	3.50	2.20
Cl. management	115	4.21	1.11
Preparation	115	3.98	2.02
Knowledge	115	4.19	1.75
Interpersonal rel.	115	3.99	1.12
Characteristics	115	4.25	.75
Total eff.	115	3.58	2.09

Table 2. Results of Pearson correlation

	Cl. management	Preparation	Knowledge	Interpersonal rel.	Characteristics	Total effectiveness
1. Practical	.25**	.63**	.30**	.41**	.35**	.50**
2. Cognitive	.22**	.41**	.56**	.35**	.15*	.47**
3. Affective	.40**	.55**	.62**	.73**	.23**	.62**
4. Metacog.	.46**	.40**	.45**	.35**	.37**	.45**
5. Critical	.19*	.31**	.32**	.51**	.11	.42**
6. Total reflective	.31**	.42**	.54**	.69**	.29**	.61**

*Correlation is significant at the level of .05.

**Correlation is significant at the level of .01.

In order to have a better understanding of the relationship between teachers' reflective practices and their teaching effectiveness, path analysis was used in which only single indicators are employed for each of the variables in the causal model. Path analysis is SEM with a structural model, but no measurement model. Figure 1 indicates the interrelationship among teachers' reflective practices and four sub-factors of teaching effectiveness. A number of fit indices were examined to evaluate the model fit. As the model shows, all the fit indices, CFI (.93), GFI (.95), and the chi-square/df ratio (2.256), except RMSEA (.097), lie within the acceptable fit thresholds based on Schreiber, Nora, Stage, Barlow, and King (2006). Hence, it can be concluded that the proposed model had an acceptable fit with the empirical data.

As indicated in Figure 1, all five dependent variables positively and significantly are predicated by reflective practices: classroom management ($\beta = .25, p < .05$), the preparation for teaching and planning ($\beta = .31, p < .05$), knowledge of subject matter ($\beta = .45, p < .05$), interpersonal relations ($\beta = .56$, $p < .05$), and teacher characteristics ($\beta = .21, p < .05$).

To answer the second research question aiming at examining relationship between EFL teachers' level of teaching effectiveness, reflective Teaching and their years of experiences Pearson correlation coefficient was performed. Table 3 shows the results of Pearson correlation between EFL teachers' level of teaching effectiveness and their years of experiences.

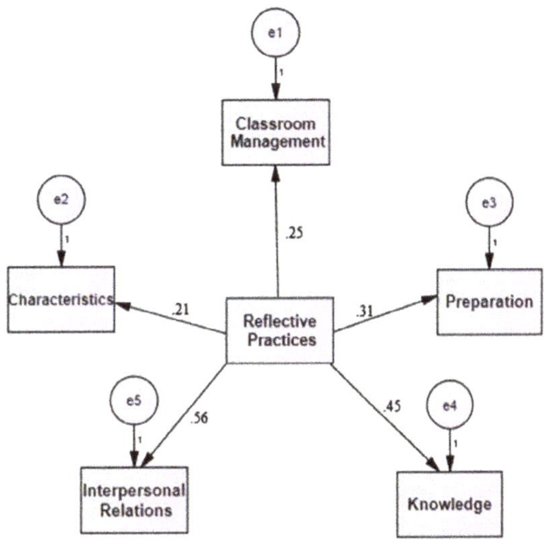

Figure 1. Interrelationship among teachers' reflective practices and their teaching effectiveness.

Table 3. The results of Pearson correlation between EFL teachers' level of teaching effectiveness and their years of experiences

	Cl. management	Preparation	Knowledge	Interpersonal rel.	Characteristics	Total effectiveness
Experience	.56**	.52**	.65**	.42**	.35**	.59**

**Correlation is significant at the level of .01.

Table 4. The results of Pearson correlation between EFL teachers' level of reflective teaching and their years of experiences

	Practical	Cognitive	Affective	Metacog	Critical	Total Ref.
Experience	.26**	.17*	.21**	.10	.05	.15*

*Correlation is significant at the level of .05.

**Correlation is significant at the level of .01.

As it can be seen in Table 3, there is a strong positive and significant relationship between EFL teachers' level of teaching effectiveness and experience ($r = .59, p < .05$).

Table 4 shows the results of Pearson correlation between EFL teachers' level of reflective teaching and their years of experiences.

As it can be seen in Table 4, there is a weak positive and significant relationship between EFL teachers' level of teaching reflectiveness and experience ($r = .15, p < .05$).

5. Conclusion and discussion

The objective of the present study was to investigate relationship between EFL teachers' reflective practices and their teaching effectiveness. Moreover, years of experiences in teachers' reflective practices and their teaching effectiveness were explored. For this purpose, two questions were posited: (1) "Is there any significant relationship between EFL teachers' reflective practices and their teaching effectiveness?" and (2) "Is there any significant relationship between EFL teachers' level of teaching effectiveness and reflective Teaching in their years of experiences?"

The first research question was addressed by examining the proposed model with SEM. The last research question was answered using Pearson correlation coefficient.

As the results indicated there were positive and significant correlation between total reflective practices and total teaching effectiveness. In other words, higher scores on teachers' reflective practices correlated with high effective teaching. In addition, among five sub-factors of teachers' reflective practices, Affective reflection has the highest correlation and Critical reflection has the lowest correlation with total teaching effectiveness.

To answer the second research question aiming at examining relationship between EFL teachers' level of teaching effectiveness, reflective Teaching and their years of experiences Pearson correlation coefficient was performed. According to the results that there was a strong positive and significant relationship between EFL teachers' level of teaching effectiveness and experience. Also, there was a weak positive and significant relationship between EFL teachers' level of teaching reflectiveness and experience.

This finding corroborates previous research (Akbari, 2007; Javadi & Khatib, 2014; Mahmoodi & Ghaslani, 2014). This finding is in line with the research evidence obtained in Cimer, Cimer, and Vekli (2013) who investigated the importance of reflection and reflective teaching for teachers in terms of their contribution to ensure effective teaching. They concluded that "since effective teaching involves more than reflection, reflection and reflective skills may not be the only factors to become effective teachers" (p. 133). Also, they recommended that "reflection should be incorporated into both pre- service and in-service teacher education courses for the purpose of growing effective teachers" (Cimer et al., 2013). In an attempt, Moradkhani et al. (2017) investigated the relationship between EFL teachers' reflective practices and self-efficacy. Their findings revealed that teachers' reflective practices had a significant positive effect on their self-efficacy. Ashraf and Hosseinnia (2017) in their study examined the relationship between professional ethics and teacher effectiveness. Their results have shown that there is a significant relationship between those two variables. In another study, Hosseinnia (2017) also found the significant relationship between emotional intelligence and teaching effectiveness. So, various factors have positive relationship with teaching effectiveness. Also, it has been revealed that some factors have negative relationship with teaching effectiveness. Javadi and Khatib (2014) investigated the relationship between reflective teaching and teachers' burnout. Their findings showed that teachers' reflection was significantly and inversely related to their feeling of burnout ($r = -80$, $p < .05$). Moreover, the Step-Wise Multiple Regression indicated that the components of burnout, i.e. emotional exhaustion, depersonalization, and reduced personal accomplishment can negatively predict teachers' reflection. Besides, Akbari (2007) declared that, level of teachers' reflective teaching practices changes their beliefs, values, and their personality and these changes can finally enhance their performance and decrease their level of burnout. In other words, teachers' reflective teaching practices can help them to perceive their own abilities and finally can prompt their personal accomplishment. Furthermore, EFL teachers can more reflect on their interaction with their students to enhance their interpersonal relationship. This can ultimately help them to increase their effectiveness in their classes.

Funding
The authors received no direct funding for this research.

Competing interests
The authors declare no competing interest.

Author details
Khalil Motallebzadeh[1]
E-mails: k.motalleb@iautorbat.ac.ir, Kmotallebz@gmail.com
Fatemeh Ahmadi[1]
E-mail: Fatemeh.ahmadi51@yahoo.com
Mansooreh Hosseinnia[1]
E-mail: mansoorehhossinnia@yahoo.com
[1] English Department, Torbat-e-Heydarieh Branch, Islamic Azad University, Torbat-e-Heydarieh, Iran.

References
Akbari, R. (2007). Reflections on reflective teaching: A critical appraisal of reflective practices in L2 teacher education. *System, 35*, 192–207. https://doi.org/10.1016/j.system.2006.12.008

Akbari, R., Behzadpoor, F., & Dadvand, B. (2010). Development of English language teaching reflection inventory. *System, 38*, 211e227.

Ashraf, H., & Hosseinnia, M. (2017). EFL teachers' commitment to professional ethics and their teaching's effectiveness: A relationship study. Manuscript submitted for publication.

Barry, R. A. (2010). *Teaching effectiveness and why it matters.* Marylhurst University and the Chalkboard Project.

Bartlett, L. (1990). Teacher development through reflective teaching. In J. C. Richards & D. Nunan (Eds.), *Second language teacher education* (pp. 2002–2214). New York, NY: Cambridge University Press.

Borg, S. (2011). *Language teacher education.* (J. Simpson, Trans, the Routledge handbook of applied linguistics). New York, NY: Routledge.

Borich, G. D. (1994). *Observation skills for effective teaching.* New York, NY: Macmillan.

Borkar, U. A. (2013). A study of teacher effectiveness of secondary school teachers in relation to teacher stress. *International Journal of Humanities and Social Science Invention, 2*(12), 13–16.

Buela, S., & Joseph, M. (2015). Relationship between personality and teacher effectiveness of high school teachers. *The International Journal of Indian Psychology, 3*(1). Retrieved from http://www.ijip.in

Chi, H., Yeh, H., & Wu, S. F. (2014). How well-being mediates the relationship between social support and teaching effectiveness. *Journal of Education and Learning, 3*(4), 117–130.

Cimer, A., Cimer, S. O., & Vekli, G. S. (2013). How does reflection help teachers to become effective teachers? *International Journal of Educational Research, 1*(4), 133–149.

Fatemipour, H. (2013). The Effectiveness of reflective teaching tools in English language teaching. *The Journal of Modern Thoughts in Education, 4*, 73–90.

Goed, S. (2011). Teacher effectiveness of school teachers in relation to their job satisfaction, personality and mental health. A thesis submitted to the faculty of education and information science Punjabi university, Patiala in partial fulfillment of the requirement for the degree of doctor of philosophy in education. Retrieved from http://hdl.handle.net/10603/10346

Hosseinnia, M. (2017). EFL teachers' emotional intelligence and their teaching's effectiveness: A relationship study. A presented article in 37th Annual Thailand TESOL International conference "ELT pathways to professional excellence", Bangkok.

Javadi, F., & Khatib, M. (2014). On the relationship between reflective teaching and teachers' burnout. *International Journal of Research Studies in Language Learning, 3*(4), 85–96.

Kafi, Z., & Motallebzadeh, K. H. (2015). Effective teaching and language learning motivation: A study on the interconnection. *Indonesian EFL Journal, 1*(2), 135–143.

Kulsum, U. (2000). *Tea cher Effectiveness Scal e (KTES).* Agra: National Psy chological Corporation.

Kumaravadivelu, B. (1994). The postmethod condition: (E) merging strategies for second/foreign language teaching.

TESOL Quarterly, 28(1), 27–48. https://doi.org/10.2307/3587197

Lofthouse, R., & Birmingham, P. (2010). The camera in the classroom: Video-recording as a tool for professional development of student teachers. *Tean Journal*. Retrieved May 3, 2016, from http://bit.ly/tyfJ5M

Mahmoodi, M. H., & Ghaslani, R. (2014). Relationship among Iranian EFL teachers' emotional intelligence, reflectivity and burnout. *Iranian Journal of Applied Language Studies, 6*(1), 90–116.

Marsh, H. W., & Roche, L. A. (1997). Making students' evaluations of teaching effectiveness effective. *The American Psychological Association, Inc, 52*(11), 1187–1197. https://doi.org/10.1037/0003-066X.52.11.1187

Moon, J. (1999). *Reflection in learning and professional development*. London: Kogan Page.

Moon, J. (2004). *A handbook of reflective and experiential learning: Theory and practice*. London: RoutledgeFalmer.

Moradkhani, S. H., Raygan, A., & Moein, M. S. (2017). Iranian EFL teachers' reflective practices and self-efficacy: Exploring possible relationships. *System, 65*, 1–14. https://doi.org/10.1016/j.system.2016.12.011

Motallebzadeh, K. H., Hosseinnia, M., Domskey, G. H. J. (2016). Peer observation: A key factor to improve Iranian EFL teachers' professional development. *Cogent Education, 4*, 1–12.

Moussa-Inaty, J. (2015). Reflective writing through the use of guiding questions. *International Journal of Teaching and Learning in Higher Education, 27*, 104–113.

Murphy, J. M. (2001). Reflective teaching in ELT. In M. Celce-Murcia (Ed.), *Teaching English as a second or foreign language* (3rd ed.). (pp. 499–514). Boston, MA: Heinle and Heinle.

Paolini, A. (2015). Enhancing teaching effectiveness and student learning outcomes. *The Journal of Effective Teaching, 15*(1), 20–33.

Pollard, A., & Collins, J. (2005). *Reflective teaching: Evidence-informed professional practice*. London: Continuum

Reynolds, A., Ross, S. M., & Rakow, J. H. (2002). Teacher retention, teaching effectiveness, and professional preparation: A comparison of professional development school and non-professional development school graduates. *Teaching and Teacher Education, 18*, 289–303. https://doi.org/10.1016/S0742-051X(01)00070-1

Richards, J. C. (2013). Towards reflective teaching. Journal of the teacher trainer: Back articles. *The Teacher Trainer Journal*. Retrieved May 3, 2016, from http://www.tttjournal.co.uk

Salmani Nodoushan, M. A. (2011). Reflective teaching in EFL classes: An overview. *Managers' Journal of School Educational Technology, 6*, 1–6.

Schreiber, J. B., Nora, A., Stage, F. K., Barlow, E. A., & King, J. (2006). Reporting Structural Equation Modeling and Confirmatory Factor Analysis Results: A Review. *The Journal of Educational Research, 99*(6), 323–338.

Tice, J. (2002). *Reflective teaching: Exploring our own classroom practice*. BBC/British Council Teaching English. Retrieved May 15, 2007, from http://www.teachingenglish.org.uk/think/methodology/reflection/shtml

Tice, J. (2004). Reflective teaching: Exploring our own classroom practice. *Teaching English Site, British Council*, 1–3. Retrieved May 3, 2016, from https://www.teachingenglish.org.uk

10

Chip on the shoulder? The hunchback heuristic predicts the attribution of anger to low status groups and calm to high status groups

Chuma Kevin Owuamalam[1*], Maas Misha'ari Weerabangsa[1], Jaya Kumar Karunagharan[1] and Mark Rubin[2]

*Corresponding author: Chuma Kevin Owuamalam, School of Psychology, University of Nottingham (Malaysia Campus), Jalan Broga, Semenyih 43500, Selangor, Malaysia
E-mails: chuma_owuamalam@ yahoo.co.uk, chuma.owuamalam@ nottingham.edu.my
Reviewing editor: Traci Craig, University of Idaho, USA

Abstract: Across societies, there is a tendency to associate members of low status groups with anger, and to associate members of high status groups with calm (i.e. the *hunchback heuristic*), but there is no empirical documentation for this phenomenon. Thus, in a pilot study ($N = 30$) we validated the stimuli that we generated to test the existence of a hunchback stereotype by distinguishing two interstatus contexts of skin-shade and race in terms of social status: Dark-skinned Indians (and Blacks) were perceived as lower in social status compared to light-skinned Indians (and Whites). Using a multi-method approach comprising an IAT-like protocol and explicit self-reports, Study 2 ($N = 80$) revealed that perceivers associated dark-skinned Indians with anger, and light-skinned Indians with calm: An effect that was explained by perceived social status. Study 3 ($N = 114$) corroborated the evidence from Study 2, but in the interstatus contexts of Blacks vs. Whites, and large men vs. slim men. Blacks (and large men) were associated with anger, and Whites (and slim men) were associated with calm. Additionally, Study 3 ruled out "racial prejudice" as an explanation for these trends. We conclude with an outline of the theoretical and practical implications of these findings.

ABOUT THE AUTHORS

Chuma Kevin Owuamalam is an assistant professor of social psychology at the University of Nottingham (Malaysia campus). His work centres on cognitions, emotions and behaviours associated with people's awareness of their own (and others') social status.

Maas Misha'ari Weerabangsa is a PhD student at the University of Nottingham. Her work centres on the lay hunchback heuristic of emotional attributions and she investigates this topic with Chuma Owuamalam.

Jaya Kumar Karunagharan holds an MSc in genetics and is currently a PhD student at the University of Nottingham. Jaya is interested in social anxieties within the classroom and examines this issue with Chuma Owuamalam. Jaya maintains an active interest in emotional regulation.

Mark Rubin is a senior lecturer in social psychology at the University of Newcastle, Australia. He is best known for his work on social identity and intergroup relations, including research on in-group identification, intergroup contact, perceived group variability and stereotyping.

PUBLIC INTEREST STATEMENT

In 2015, German Youtubers "Dit Is Normaal" disguised a copy of the Bible as the Qur'an and read some of its extreme contents to ordinary citizens at locations in Germany. They found that people were repulsed and viewed the excerpts they heard as extremely violent and barbaric, but softened their views when they learnt the verses were in fact from the Bible. Unbeknownst to these pranksters, their experiment unearthed what appears to be a fundamental heuristic that people use in their social judgements—the tendency to associate anger and violent conduct with low social status, and calm with high status. We refer to this phenomenon as the hunchback stereotype and provide the first rigorous test of its existence in a culture where the licence to display anger is presumed to be reserved for those in elevated positions. We further show that racial prejudice isn't necessarily responsible for this phenomenon.

Subjects: Behavioral Sciences; Politics & International Relations; Social Sciences

Keywords: hunchback stereotypes; Malaysia; identity; prejudice; social status

1. Introduction

People with this "chip on the shoulder" syndrome may react quietly with a "hurt feelings" attitude or maybe in a *violent burst of emotion.*

- Jim Lord (2016, our emphasis).

A "chip on the shoulder" is the expression often used to describe individuals with a sense of continuing frustration over mistreatment from others and, as the opening quote illustrates, people who feel this way are expected to vent their frustration via anger. Evidence abound regarding the widespread use of this assumption across societies, both in the West (e.g. the French's *avoir une crotte sur le cœur*) and also in the East (e.g. the Chinese 愤恨不平 [fèn fèn bù ping]; and the Indo-Malay idiom *sakit hati*; cf. Rees & Silove, 2011). Although these expressions are ostensibly used for people who are aggrieved in some way, there are indications that the link they make between frustration and proneness to anger is more often directed towards groups that occupy low social status or are dehumanised in some way. In the United Kingdom, for instance, youths from lower social class backgrounds are perceived as *chavs*—a term with connotations of disadvantage, frustration and violent conduct (Jones, 2012; Loughnan, Haslam, Sutton, & Spencer, 2014). Similarly, folk beliefs in parts of Western Africa assume that people with a *hunchback* (a dehumanised demographic; Akosah-Sarpong, 2008) are so afflicted due to cumulated frustration in a previous life, which predisposes them to outbursts of anger (Owuamalam, Weerabangsa, Mamdouh, Karunagharan, & Rubin, 2014). Even a Google search for "angry" with a wildcard returns several hits that more directly associate members of undervalued or stereotyped groups in society with anger: e.g. "the angry black woman", "the angry black man", "the angry feminist", "the angry wife", "angry nerd" and so on.

Inspired by the Western African lay beliefs about the hunched back, we use the term *hunchback stereotype* to describe the tendency for people to associate anger with low social status based on the presumption that members of such groups are likely to encounter more frustrating situations and are therefore more likely to vent this frustration. Extending this reasoning, then, people from privileged backgrounds may be associated with calm even in the face of adversity, because being calm is a demeanour thought to be necessary to achieve goals, and those in elevated positions should act in this way in order for their perceived competence to manifest (Tablante, Durante, & Fiske, in press).

Surprisingly, despite the anecdotal pointers to the existence of a hunchback stereotype as a fundamental heuristic in the judgements of the *anger* and *calm* of people with a low or high status, not a single empirical study has documented the reality of its existence. It is important to establish whether people use a hunchback heuristic in their inferences about which people are or aren't normally expressive of anger, because (a) anger is a threat inducing emotion, (b) people who feel threatened generally engage a defensive "fight" response and (c) a "fight" response can often have detrimental consequences for the intended targets of this behaviour, as seen in recent fatal shootings of young Black men in North America by law enforcement officers (CNN News Report, 2014; Lowery, 2016; McLaughlin, 2015).

1.1. Is there a basis for the hunchback stereotype?

Several theories exist on the basis of which one can infer the existence of a hunchback stereotype. According to the stereotype content model (SCM; Fiske, Cuddy, Glick, & Xu, 2002), lay perceivers often assign the "incompetence" label to members of low status groups due to a presumed inability to overcome difficulties and, by extension, those who are frustrated can be expected to vent this emotion: a conclusion that even the lay frustration-aggression theories put forward by Berkowitz (1989) and by Carlsmith, Wilson, and Gilbert (2008) agree with. Likewise, individuals who occupy a high social status are expected to be competent, even when faced with difficult situations and being calm (or cold) is thought to be a state necessary for the competence expected of them to shine through (cf. Tablante et al., in press). In short the SCM predicts the hunchback stereotype in relation to anger and calm attributions to low and high status groups, respectively.

Other theoretical formulations of status-based emotional expressivity, such as those proposed by Keltner, Gruenfeld, and Anderson (2003), also concur with the SCM, in that they explicitly associate negative emotions (e.g. anger) with low social status, and positive emotions (e.g. calm) with high social status. The reason for these associations is also traceable to the broad premise underlying the hunchback stereotype: members of low status groups encounter frustration more, while their higher status counterparts feel satisfied and content with the privileges bestowed by their elevated position. A proposition that resonates with the well-documented *halo effect* (Nisbett & Wilson, 1977): the tendency for people to associate undesirable traits to less attractive people (or those who are low in status) compared to their more attractive counterparts (or those who are high in status). Only that we extend this logic to the context of emotional attributions.

1.2. Are there reasons for these propositions?

The extant literature on anger attributions has focused largely on the racial context involving the relationship between Blacks (undervalued group) and Whites (advantaged group). Findings from these investigations show that people expect Blacks to be angrier than Whites (Hutchings & Haddock, 2008); are quicker to associate Blacks with threat compared to Whites (Correll, Urland, & Ito, 2006), even when these Black targets are merely children (Goff, Jackson, Di Leone, Culotta, & DiTomasso, 2014). Perceivers are also unable to distinguish angry and happy Black targets, despite a clear differentiation between happy and angry faces when the object of evaluation is White (Shapiro et al., 2009). Although these previous contributions are notable, they often allude to prejudice against Blacks as the primary (even sole) explanation for the association of the threat-inducing emotion of anger to Blacks relative to Whites despite the mixed evidence in the literature. For example, studies have shown that implicit racial biases predict the association of anger to Blacks (Ackerman et al., 2006)—and other racially threatening out-groups (e.g. Middle-Eastern Arabs) even at the neural level (Fleming, Bandy, & Kimble, 2010). However, a large-scale study comparing racial bias in fatal shootings across counties in the United States found that indicators of racial prejudice (e.g. racist norms, and racial assaults) were not reliable predictors of the differences in the greater threat appraisals (and consequent shooting) of ethnic minorities relative to Whites. Interestingly, Ross (2015) found that proxies of social status (such as the median income) were consistent and reliable predictors of racial bias in police shootings.

Notably, these previous studies fail to directly test the complementary assumption that higher status groups are associated with calm: assuming that calm is necessarily the opposite of anger, and that a positive effect on anger would always mean a negative effect on calm. Also, participants in majority of the studies within the "Black threat" paradigm conducted in the West (typically the US) are often Whites. Such a paradigm makes it likely that the effects observed in those studies could have resulted from the tendency to favour one's own group on evaluative judgements by excusing one's in-group from the image-tainting bestial (negative) emotions of anger (Tajfel, Billig, Bundy, & Flament, 1971). After all, evidence shows that bestial non-uniquely human emotions (like anger) are generally reserved for out-groups, not the in-group (Leyens et al., 2000).

To address these issues, we treated calm as a separate emotional dimension relevant to the hunchback stereotype because people can be angry, but could also chose to either restrain an expression of this emotion (i.e. calm) or to display it (i.e. rage) as the opening quote suggests. Specifically, we propose that the association of anger to low status is not restricted to the racial context of Blacks vs. Whites and, that lay perceivers would attribute anger to targets that signal a low status position and calm to targets that signal high status. Unlike the previous studies that have largely been conducted in the West, we situate our research in a different (collectivistic) cultural context in South-East Asia (Malaysia), testing the predictions derived from the hunchback stereotype in a third-party group that is unconnected to the interstatus context being evaluated.

The cultural dimension is important in the light of recent suggestions of a collectivistic cultural creed permitting only those with power and authority to display anger (Park et al., 2013). Thus, demonstrating that the hunchback heuristic is applicable even in a collectivistic culture would provide conclusive evidence of its existence rather than a biased test of it.

2. Study 1

This study was designed to generate stimuli that are fit for a rigorous test of the hunchback stereotype in the light of the methodological difficulties in previous research. For example, research on status-based emotional attributions has largely relied on an "imagination" paradigm in which participants are required to evaluate 'unseen' exemplars of high and low status group members based on a short written biography (e.g. Tiedens, Ellsworth, & Mesquita, 2000). Although this approach has the potential to produce strong "stereotype effects" due to the limited information on which perceivers are required to make their judgements, it nonetheless increases the possibility that judgements are based on category prototypes that may not adequately capture intra-category diversity. This makes it uncertain whether stereotypes that are tied to category prototypes also have a wider application to other members that do not neatly fit the "typical" member. Similarly, other approaches that have utilised a facial stimulus approach, using single images that are then manipulated to represent one group or the other (e.g. Fleming et al., 2010), do not address the diversity issue. Here, we adopt a multiple facial stimuli approach by generating a series of images for each category within the two interstatus contexts (skin-shade and race) to be sure that judgements are closer to the intended phenomenon in the real world.

Given the widespread preference for light skin compared to dark skin in South Asia and South-East Asia (Leong, 2006; Nadeem, 2014), we reasoned that people would accord high social status to those with a light skin than to those with a dark skin. This distinction is most prominent amongst the Indian ethnic group in Malaysia and we capitalised on this existing difference within the same racial group to control for possible differences due to inter-racial variability. We also selected a further interstatus context, concerning the historical relations between Blacks and Whites, in which the former social category is often perceived as undervalued relative to the latter one (Kluegel, 1990). Assuming our assumption that the social categories within these two interstatus contexts signal low and high status is correct, then light-skinned Indians should be seen as higher in status compared to dark-skinned Indians, and also Whites should be perceived as higher in status compared to Blacks. Given the present focus on facial images, we further reasoned that participants' status rankings would likely be based on the extent to which they consider the images to be attractive. Consequently, we anticipated that status judgements would be positively related to the degree to which they consider images within each category to be attractive.

2.1. Method

2.1.1. Ethics

The programme of research reported in this paper received ethics approval from the Science and Engineering Research Ethics Committee (SEREC) at the University of Nottingham's Malaysia campus. We adhered strictly to the ethical protocol enshrined in the British Psychological Society's directive for the conduct of research involving human subjects. All participants provided informed consent digitally via Qualtrics' online survey suite.

2.1.2. Participants

Thirty Malaysian students at the University of Nottingham's Malaysia campus who responded to an email advert that was sent via the students' mailing list took part in this study (10 were men and 20 were women, $M_{age} = 21.13$, $SD_{age} = 2.45$). Participants were compensated with RM5 (approximately US$1.5) for their time.

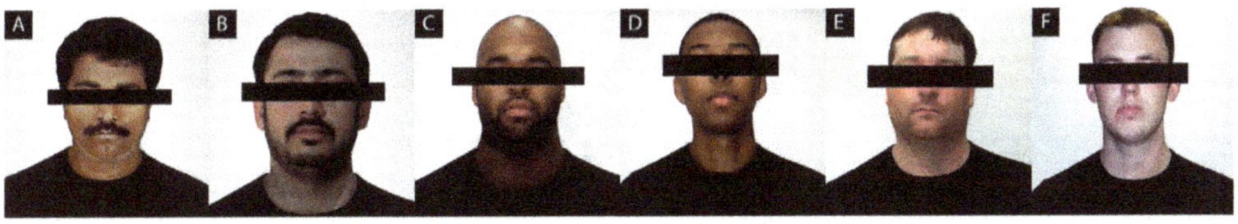

Figure 1. Examples of face stimuli: dark-skinned Indian (A), light-skinned Indian (B), large Black (C) and slim Black (D), and large White (E) and slim White (F).

2.1.3. Design, stimuli and procedure

Participants were exposed to seven images of dark-skinned Indians, seven images of light-skinned Indians, 10 images of Blacks and 10 images of Whites (e.g. see Figure 1). We generated images of dark- and light-skinned Indians online using the search word "Indian faces". The categorisation of the two Indian subgroups based on skin tone was then carried out by a trained research assistant of Indian origin. The Black and White facial stimuli were generated from a publicly available online databank (The Park Aging Mind Laboratory Face Database; Minear & Park, 2004). The images were then photo-edited into a flat grey background and "dressed" in plain black t-shirts in order to standardise clothing. Finally, to control for cross-gender effects, all the images that were presented to participants in the current and subsequent studies were those of men.

Participants were asked to provide repeated ratings of the perceived status and attractiveness for each facial stimuli on a seven-point scale (perceived social status: +3 = *high status*, −3 = *low status*; perceived attractiveness: +3 = *very attractive*, −3 = *not at all attractive*). Upon completion, participants were thanked and dismissed.

2.2. Results and discussion

2.2.1. Analytical strategy

First, we combined the status and attractiveness ratings within each category to obtain an index of perceived social status and, perceived attractiveness. For each interstatus context, we then calculated a paired *t*-test to establish the groups that participants considered to be relatively high or low in social status.

Results of this *t*-test corroborated our status assumptions across the two contexts and showed that light-skinned Indians were seen as higher in status than dark-skinned Indians ($\bar{d}$ = .95, *SE* = .15, 95% CI = [.645, 1.260], Cohen's *d* = 1.16). Similarly, Whites were perceived as higher in status compared to Blacks ($\bar{d}$ = .37, *SE* = .11, 95% CI = [.645, 1.260], Cohen's *d* = .61). Furthermore, although participants favoured light-skinned Indians compared to dark-skinned Indians in terms of perceived attractiveness ($\bar{d}$ = .62, *SE* = .13, 95% CI = [.358, .880], Cohen's *d* = .89), this difference was absent in the context of Black versus Whites ($\bar{d}$ = .05, *SE* = .13, 95% CI = [−.218, .318], Cohen's *d* = .07): suggesting that attractiveness may not be a strong determinant of social status in this context because these two (foreign) out-groups are remote from our Malaysian participants' everyday circles and hence the participants have little direct experience on the basis of which they could gauge their relative attractiveness. We offer this interpretation with caution, given the non-representativeness of the present sample.

To test the proposed link between social status and attractiveness in the current context of facial images, we regressed the perceived attractiveness scores on to the perceived social status scores. Results from this analysis showed a medium-to-strong positive relationship between perceived attractiveness and perceived social status for same category evaluations except for Whites (see Table 1). We reasoned, in retrospect, that the null pattern for Whites could have resulted because Malaysians generally perceive this group as higher in status given their colonial history with White Europeans. This tangible historical status, we reason, perhaps, overpowered a status assessment of this elite group based on superficial attributes (e.g. attractiveness). Thus, in our subsequent studies we focused on the light- vs. dark-skinned Indian context because it offers the clearest distinction between the two intergroup contexts in terms of both status and attractiveness.

Table 1. The relationship between attractiveness and social status perceptions across two interstatus contexts (Skin-shade and Race–Study 1)

Perceived status of ...	Perceived attractiveness							
	Dark-skinned Indians		Light-skinned Indians		Blacks		Whites	
	β (SE)	[95% CI]	β (SE)	[95% CI]	β (SE)	[95% CI]	β (SE)	[95% CI]
Same category	.599** (.19)	[.313, 1.098]	.392* (.25)	[.010, 1.021]	.599** (.24)	[.393, 1.367]	.088 (.38)	[−.606, .948]
Opposite category	.048 (.22)	[−.384, .513]	.081 (.22)	[−.349, .535]	−.161 (.25)	[−.774, .267]	.136 (.35)	[−.480, .974]
R^2	.38**		.18†		.34**		.03	

Note: Same or opposite category labels refer to the social category in the relevant column for each estimate.

†$p = .065$.

*$p \leq .050$.

**$p \leq .010$.

3. Study 2

In this study, we aimed to demonstrate that a flimsy status signal such as skin shade elicits greater attributions of anger to darker-skinned Indians and calm to lighter skinned Indians. Previous investigations have often focused on the emotional perceptions of members of groups that are involved in the interstatus context being evaluated (e.g. White participants making judgements of the emotional states of Whites vs. Blacks) with the potential for inter-category biases favouring one's own group relative to the out-group (Tajfel et al., 1971). This is important in the light of the literature on infrahumanisation showing a tendency for people to attribute bestial (often negative) emotions to out-groups while reserving uniquely human (often secondary positive emotions such as calm) to the in-group (Leyens et al., 2000). Therefore, in the current study we focused on the emotional attributions of a third-party group (Chinese Malaysians) who are unconnected to the social category (light- and dark-skinned Indians) that would constitute the subject of their anger and calm attributions.

Furthermore, to circumvent the issue of methodological consistency, especially given the mixed evidence often obtained in studies adopting a cognitive approach (e.g. the Implicit Association Task [IAT]-Greenwald, McGhee, & Schwartz, 1998) to those adopting a self-report approach, we combined both implicit and explicit measurements to be sure of the robustness of the predicted patterns. After all, different methods of accessing the same underlying psychological phenomenon should produce similar effects on the intended outcome (Jost et al., 2012). If the hunchback stereotype exists, then it should take people less time to respond to a category/emotion pairing that is congruent to (or agrees with) the hunchback stereotype than to a category/emotion pairing that isn't, because cognitive processing tends to be quicker when information pairs are consistent than when they are not (MacLeod, 1991). Thus, to find evidence for the existence of a hunchback stereotype at the implicit (unconscious) level, people should be quicker in responding to a hunchback congruent pairing in which a dark-skinned Indian is paired with the emotion word ANGER and a light-skinned Indian is paired with CALM, compared to a hunchback inconsistent pairing in which a dark-skinned Indian is paired with CALM and a light-skinned Indian is paired with ANGER. We expected this effect to occur because perceivers should take less time to *verify* representations that conform to established stereotypes relative to those that do not (see Carreiras, Garnham, Oakhill, & Cain, 1996).

On the explicit measures, we expected greater anger attributions to dark-skinned versus light-skinned Indians and, greater calm attributions to light-skinned versus dark-skinned Indians. Given the focus on facial images, combined with the positive link between status and attractiveness that we established in Study 1, we further anticipated a link between anger/calm attributions and perceived attractiveness: those images that elicit strong attractiveness should be associated with less anger and greater calm.

3.1. Method

3.1.1. Participants

Eighty Chinese Malaysian participants at the University of Nottingham's Malaysia campus were recruited opportunistically to take part in the study (41 men and 39 women; M_{age} = 20.89, SD = 1.58). They were offered candies as compensation for their time.

3.1.2. Design and procedure

The experiment was comprised of two parts: a cognition probe task (CPT) that is similar to the traditional IAT set-up, and an explicit self-report component in which participants completed repeated measurements of anger and calm for a series of light- and dark-skinned Indian faces.

3.1.2.1. Implicit CPT measure. A within-subject design was used in which hunchback congruity was experimentally manipulated by pairing a light-skinned Indian or dark-skinned Indian face with the emotion ANGER or CALM. In the hunchback-congruent condition, we paired a light-skinned Indian face with the emotion word CALM and dark-skinned Indian face with the emotion word ANGER. These pairings were reversed in the hunchback incongruent condition so that the light-skinned Indian was paired with ANGER and the dark-skinned Indian was paired with CALM. These stimuli pairs remained constant on the top left and top right corners of the screen throughout each block of trials (see Figure 2). At the centre of the screen, participants were presented with a fixation cross for 250 ms, followed by a probe word that either matched or did not match with either of the emotion words presented in the stimuli pairs (see Figure 2). Participants were to decide which emotion word the probe word matched. The dependent variable was the time it took for them to reach this decision, with longer response latencies indicating interference in cognitive processing. Thus, quicker response latencies in the hunchback congruent (relative to incongruent) condition will provide evidence for the presence of a heuristic associating light-skinned Indians with "calm" and dark-skinned Indians with "anger". If this hunchback heuristic does not exist, then there should not be any interference and participants should spend no more time in matching the probe words to the target emotions in the hunchback incongruent condition than they do in the hunchback congruent condition.

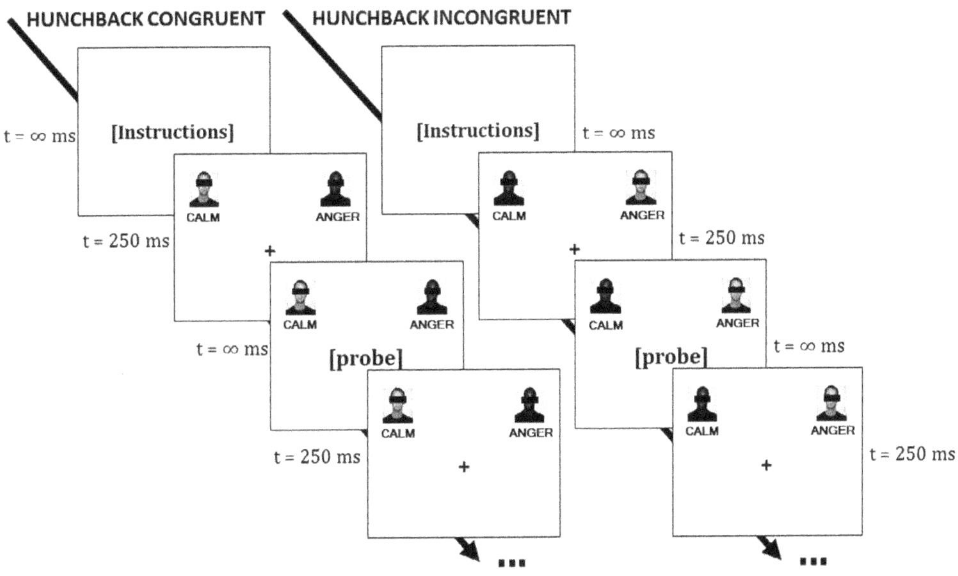

Figure 2. Flow chart of the experimental protocol for hunchback congruent and hunchback incongruent conditions.

3.1.2.2. Explicit (self-report) measures. We used a within-subjects design in which participants provided repeated anger and calm ratings in relation to light-skinned and dark-skinned Indian faces. The dependent variable was participants' responses to scale items for each light-skinned and dark-skinned Indian, which asked them how angry- and calm-looking each face was. Responses were provided on a seven-point scale (−3 = *not at all angry-looking*, +3 = *very angry-looking*; −3 = *not at all calm-looking*, +3 = *very calm-looking*). Participants also provided their judgements of the attractiveness of each target (−3 = *not at all attractive-looking*, +3 = *very attractive-looking*), assuming that more attractive faces signal higher social status (see Owuamalam, Wong, & Rubin, 2016 for a similar use of attractiveness as an index of social status in a face stimuli paradigm).

3.1.3. Stimuli and apparatus

We used the same 7 "light-skinned" and 7 "darker-skinned" Indian faces that we generated in Study 1, which were then photo-edited into a flat grey background and "dressed" in plain black t-shirts. One light-skinned and 1 dark-skinned Indian faces were used in the CPT protocol; the other six were used in the explicit self-report measurements. We used 20 probe-word stimuli (10 were anger-associated, and the other 10 were calm-associated, see Appendix A; Nelson, McEvoy, & Schreiber, 2004). The CPT protocol was presented using Psychopy 1.70 (Peirce, 2007), while the explicit self-report ratings were presented via Qualtrics—an online survey suite.

3.2. Results and discussion

3.2.1. Status awareness check

To establish that participants perceived light-skinned Indians in the current study as high in status (in terms of physical attractiveness), we ran a paired *t*-test in which the difference between perceived attractiveness for the two groups was calculated. Results corroborated the evidence in Study 1 and showed that light-skinned Indians were perceived to be higher in status (more attractive) than dark-skinned Indians, t (77) = −8.84, $p < .0001$, ($\bar{d}$ = .68, SE = .08, 95% CI = [.526, .833], Cohen's d = 1.00).

3.2.2. Implicit (CPT) data

Reaction times (RTs) were collated for the hunchback-congruent and hunchback-incongruent trials. We discarded corrupted data from four participants, and the error rate across all trials was low (≤20%). Therefore, we used for our analysis only the RTs in trials with correct responses. Figure 3(a) and (b) depict the trends for anger and calm associations, respectively.

Consistent with the hunchback stereotypes, results from a paired *t*-test revealed that participants were quicker in matching the probe-word with the target emotion when the category/emotion word pairings were hunchback congruent, compared to when the pairings were hunchback incongruent. This was true for anger associations, t (75) = −2.39, p = .019, ($\bar{d}$ = −216 ms, SE = −90.31 ms, 95% CI = [−396.100,−36.260], Cohen's d = .28), as it was for calm associations, t (75)=−2.58, p = .012, ($\bar{d}$ = −196.90 ms, SE = 76.26 ms, 95% CI = [−348.800, −44.940], Cohen's d = .30).

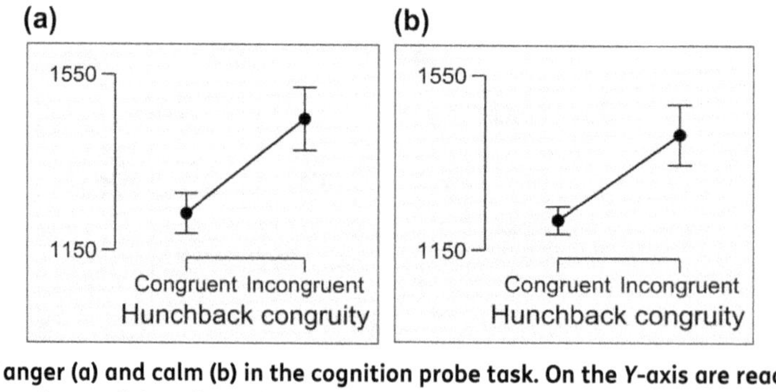

Figure 3. Implicit associations of anger (a) and calm (b) in the cognition probe task. On the *Y*-axis are reaction times (ms) and on the *X*-axis are the hunchback congruity conditions for each emotional probe.

Note: Error bars are standard errors (Study 2).

3.2.3. Explicit (self-report) data

Corroborating the evidence from the implicit measures, paired *t*-tests that we conducted on the anger and calm measures revealed patterns that were consistent with the hunchback stereotype (see Table 2). Dark-skinned Indians were perceived to be more angry-looking compared to light-skinned Indian faces (see Table 2). In contrast, light-skinned Indians were perceived as more calm-looking compared to dark-skinned Indians (see Table 2).

To establish that these effects were tied to status, we ran a series of regression analyses in which we examined whether or not our index of status (attractiveness) predicted attributions of anger and calm for each light and dark-skinned Indians. To be sure that the associations between status (attractiveness) and anger and calm attributions were systematic (and not opportunistic), we included in each model, the perceived attractiveness scores for the opposite social category. Assuming perceptions of status (attractiveness) explains the attributions of anger vs. calm to targets within each category, then one should observe that perceived attractiveness predicts greater anger and less calm attributions to dark-skinned Indians, while the perceived attractiveness of light-skinned Indians does not. We anticipated the reverse of this pattern for light-skinned Indians. Results from this analysis corroborated the hunchback stereotype and revealed that the less attractive the dark-skinned Indian faces were perceived to be, the more angry-looking and less calm-looking they were also thought to be. Similarly, for light-skinned Indians, the more attractive they were perceived to be, the less angry-looking and more calm they were thought to be (see Table 3). Thus even within each social category, markers of social status determine the extent to which people relied on the hunchback heuristic in their anger and calm attributions.

Taken jointly the evidence from the implicit CPT, the explicit self-report measures and the direct evidence linking emotional attributions to markers of social status show clear support for the existence of a hunchback stereotype. Despite this strong evidence, there are reasons to approach the interpretation of these findings with caution given alternative accounts relating to (a) context, and (b) a racial prejudice hypothesis.

In relation to context, the Indian ethnic group is immersed in Malaysian society, and as a result, it is entirely possible that attributions of calm and anger are based on *actual* negative contact experiences of our Chinese Malaysian participants with Indian Malaysians—not a hunchback heuristic. According to the lay attribution theory (Kruglanski, 1990), people judge others on the basis of the constancy of their behaviour across different contexts. As Chinese Malaysians are more likely to encounter Indians (compared to distal out-groups such as Blacks and Whites), it seems possible that their attributions could embody the reality of their frequent negative encounters with this

Table 2. The main effects of status category on anger and calm attributions to targets

		Dark-skinned Indians		**Light-skinned Indians**		**t-value**		**Cohen's d**		**[95% CI]**	
Study 2	Anger	.12 (.09)		−.69 (.09)		9.58***		1.09		[.640, .976]	
	Calm	−.04 (.08)		.78 (.08)		10.56***		1.20		[.667, .977]	
		Blacks	***Whites***	***F-value***	η^2_p	***[95% CI]***	***Large***	***Slim***	***F-value***	η^2_p	***[95% CI]***
Study 3	Anger	.65 (.08)	−.79 (.08)	189.43***	.63	[1.228, 1.641]	.46 (.31)	−.59 (.08)	124.87***	.53	[.862, 1.234]
	Calm	−.28 (.08)	.68 (.07)	119.66***	.51	[−1.137, −.788]	−.30 (.08)	.70 (.07)	152.80***	.58	[−1.158, −.838]

Note: Means are presented outside the parenthesis while the standard error associated with each mean are presented within curved parenthesis.

***$p \leq .001$.

Table 3. The relationship between perceived status (attractiveness) and attributions of anger and calm to dark- and light-skinned Indians (explicit measures, study 2)

Perceived attractiveness of ...	Emotional attributions							
	Dark-skinned Indians' anger		Light-skinned Indians' anger		Dark-skinned Indians' calm		Light-skinned Indians' calm	
	β (*SE*)	[95% CI]	*β* (*SE*)	[95% CI]	*β* (*SE*)	[95% CI]	*β* (*SE*)	[95% CI]
Same category	−.414** (.14)	[−.657, −.103]	−.418** (.13)	[−.624, −.096]	.410** (.12)	[.079, .562]	.286† (.13)	[−.021, .480]
Opposite category	.035 (.14)	[−.238, .300]	.094 (.22)	[−.189, .355]	−.117 (.12)	[−.323, .146]	.022 (.13)	[−.240, .276]
R^2	.15***		.13***		.11**		.09**	

Note: Same or opposite category labels refer to the social category in the relevant column for each estimate.
†$p = .072$.
*$p \leq .050$.
**$p \leq .010$.
***$p \leq .001$.

demographic rather than a reliance on the fundamental hunchback heuristic that we propose. This reason seems seductive especially in the light of the evidence that negative (but not positive) contact experiences are stronger predictors of unfavourable characterisation of out-groups—the *contact caveat* (see Barlow et al., 2012).

Second, and following on from the first, it is entirely possible that an orientation towards prejudice against dark-skinned Indians explains the link between perceived status and attributions of anger and calm in this study. Given the association between dark-skinned Indians and menial jobs relative to their lighter skinned counterparts that are often associated with affluence and the business class (Sandhu, 1993), and because people who do "dirty" work are often dehumanised (Volpato, Andrighetto, & Baldissarri, in press), it is possible that an orientation towards prejudice against dark-skinned Indians could also explain the attribution of negative emotions (anger) but not positive emotions (calm) to them.

Thus, in the next study, we used another interstatus context (Blacks vs. Whites) to circumvent the contact issue because (a) we have previously established that the interstatus distinction between Black and White is apparent to our Malaysian participants, and (b) encounters with these two out-groups are relatively infrequent in Malaysian society, therefore reducing the possibility that a hunchback pattern in this context could be explained by the frequency of negative contact. That is, assuming people infer the traits (calm and anger) of others entirely based on how frequent they have observed others' behaviour across situations, then such inferences should be harder to make the less frequent contact between people are.

In addition, we included a measure of an orientation towards prejudice in our next study to delineate the status-based hunchback heuristic that we propose from a racial prejudice account. If the effects in Study 2 were only due to prejudice, then an effect of perceived social status on anger and calm attributions that is mediated by the status signal (attractiveness) should cease to exist once the variance in anger and calm that is associated with a prejudice orientation is accounted for.

4. Study 3

We again used a multi-method approach combining implicit and explicit measures as we did in Study 2. Because stereotypes tend to be automatic judgements that are based on existing heuristics (Bargh, Chen, & Burrows, 1996), we reasoned, again, that perceivers should be quicker at matching words related to the emotions of anger and calm when they are exposed to a hunchback congruent pairing (i.e. a Black face/ANGER, and White face/CALM) compared to when they are exposed to a hunchback incongruent pairing (i.e. a White face/ANGER, and Black face/CALM). We expected the same patterns that we observed on the explicit measures in Study 2 to also manifest here.

Additionally, we embedded another social category within the images of Blacks and Whites which related to the perceived physical sizes of the targets in terms of whether they are large or slim. Previous research has demonstrated that large people are perceived to be lower in social status compared to thin people (Crandall & Schiffhauer, 1998; Durante, Fasolo, Mari, & Mazzola, 2014; Owuamalam, Wong, & Rubin, 2016). If the hunchback pattern is robust then its predictions should also apply to a status category based on physical size: larger targets should be seen as angrier looking than slim targets and, slim targets should be seen as calmer looking compared to large targets.

4.1. Method

4.1.1. Participants

One-hundred and fourteen Malaysians at the University of Nottingham's Malaysia campus took part in this study (36 were men and 78 were women; M_{age} = 19.40, *SD* = 1.39). They were recruited via an email advert that was sent using the students' mailing list at this university. Participants received either course credit or a payment of RM5 (approximately US$1.50) as compensation for their time.

4.1.2. Design and procedure

As in Study 2, the current experiment consisted of two parts: a cognition probe task (CPT) and an explicit self-reported rating of various outcomes including: anger and calm, and two correlates of anger, aggressiveness and dangerousness. The CPT was conducted before the explicit self-report task in order to reduce the salience of anger/calm associations, which might otherwise confound the CPT results.

4.1.2.1. Implicit (CPT) measure. We used an identical protocol to the one described in Study 2. Hunchback congruity was manipulated so that in the hunchback congruent condition, category/emotion-word pairings were White/CALM, Black/ANGER. In the incongruent condition, the pairings were reversed to White/ANGER, Black/CALM. The dependent measure, again, was the time (in ms) that it took participants to match a probe-word to the target emotion of ANGER and CALM while exposed to the hunchback congruent versus incongruent trials.

4.1.2.2. Explicit (self-report) measures. We used a 2 (racial status: Black versus White) × 2 (physical size: large versus slim) repeated measures design in which participants rated the emotions of the faces of Black and White large and slim men. The dependent variables were participants' responses to scale items that were displayed in random order on screen and that measured the perceived calm and anger of the target faces (for anger: −3 = *not at all angry-looking*, +3 = *very angry-looking;* and for calm: −3 = *not at all calm-looking*,+3 = *very calm-looking*). Participants then completed a perceived status measure on which they made judgements of the social standing of each target within a social category (−3 = *lowest status*, +3 = *highest status*). They also gave their judgements of the attractiveness of each target within each social category (−3 = *not at all attractive-looking*, +3 = *very attractive-looking*).

4.1.2.2.1. Orientation towards prejudice. Theorists have proposed that the tendency to support social hierarchies and/or to hold ideologies that accept the dominance of certain groups over others causes racial prejudice (Sidanius & Pratto, 2001). For this reason, we measured an orientation towards prejudice using an eight-item hierarchy version of the social dominance orientation (SDO) scale, which examines people's preference for unequal relations between groups. The more people subscribe to this ideology, then, the more likely this orientation towards prejudice should explain the association of anger to low status and calm to high status. An example of items on the SDO scale included "Some groups of people are just more worthy than others". The reliability of this scale was good, α = .82, 95% CI = [.759, .862].

On an exploratory basis, we also examined whether or not high status formal clothing (versus casual and hoodies) would soften the angry/aggressive perceptions of Black targets (Hayes, Lawless, & Baitinger, 2014). For this reason, some of the targets were photo-edited into formal suits (high status), and others into neutral clothing (plain t-shirt) or hoodies (low status). A hoodie was chosen as a low status clothing item given the association of this sort of clothing to gang subculture and violence (McLean, 2005).

4.1.3. Stimuli and apparatus

Participants were presented with eight emotionally neutral expression male face stimuli that we used in Study 1: four of these were images of Black men (2 large and 2 slim—see examples in Figure 1) and the other four were those of White men (2 large and 2 slim—see examples in Figure 1).

We used the same 20 probe-word stimuli that we used in Study 2 as synonyms of anger (10) and calm (10) in the current study. Although these probe-words produced the hunchback effects, there are still questions about whether the effects only relate to anger/calm associated probe-words, or whether the effects would emerge also on control probe-words that were unconnected to anger and calm. For this reason, we included 10 filler items (e.g. "define", "maximum", and "theory") that we used as controls, reasoning that the hunchback interference should be most visible when the probe-words were associated with the hunchback relevant emotions of anger and calm (see Appendix A for a fuller list of filler items). These additional filler items also allowed us to disguise the experimental hypothesis. As in Study 2, stimuli relating to the cognition probe task were presented via Psychopy 1.70 (Peirce, 2007) while the explicit self-report measures were presented via Qualtrics.

4.2. Results and discussion

4.2.1. Status awareness check

We computed the difference in perceived social status between race and size groups. As expected, a repeated *t*-test showed that our Malaysian participants perceived White targets to be higher in social status compared to Black targets ($t = 6.18$, $\bar{d} = .60$, $SE = .10$, $p < .0001$, 95% CI = [.408, 793], Cohen's $d = .58$). They also perceived slim targets to be higher in status than larger targets ($t = 9.75$, $\bar{d} = .84$, $SE = .09$, $p < .0001$, 95% CI = [.671, 1.013], Cohen's $d = .91$). However, further analysis revealed that the attire manipulation did not neatly differentiate the three attire groups in terms of status and this variable was dropped from a subsequent analysis as a result.

4.2.2. Implicit (CPT) data

We collated participants' reaction times in milliseconds for the congruent trials by computing the mean reaction times relating to anger/probe-word associations (anger-congruent) and calm/probe-word associations (calm-congruent). The same procedure was repeated for the incongruent trials, resulting in anger-associated and calm-associated incongruent reaction times.

In a small number of trials (<20% on average), the probe-word was not accurately matched to anger or calm. This error rate was equally distributed between the congruent and incongruent trials for anger ($\bar{d} = 6.03$, $SE = 4.80$, $p = .218$) and calm ($\bar{d} = 7.35$, $SE = 4.32$, $p = .098$). Therefore, for each participant, we discarded inaccurate trials, assuming that participants were not paying attention. Hence, we used only reaction times that were related to correct responses.

Figure 4(a) and (b) depicts the reaction latencies in the hunchback congruent vs. incongruent conditions for anger and calm. Consistent with the hunchback hypothesis and refuting a criticism based on the contact caveat (Barlow et al., 2012), results from a paired *t*-test revealed that participants were quicker in their anger associations in the hunchback congruent condition compared to the incongruent condition ($t = -5.76$, $\bar{d} = -191.68$ ms, $SE = 33.30$ ms, $p < .0001$, 95% CI = [−257.700, −125.706], Cohen's $d = .54$). We also investigated the calm associations and found that participants were also quicker in the congruent trials compared to the incongruent trials ($t = -2.12$, $\bar{d} = -107.63$ ms, $SE = 50.67$ ms, $p = .036$, 95% CI = [−208.000, -7.235], Cohen's $d = .20$). We did not find any significant differences between the hunchback congruent and incongruent conditions for the filler control

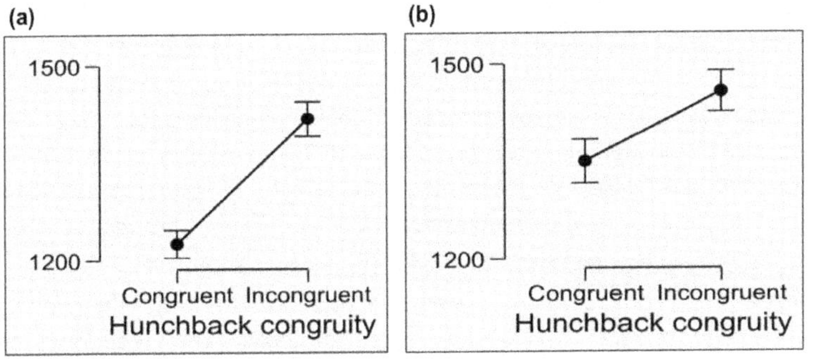

Figure 4. Implicit associations of anger (a) and calm (b) in the cognition probe task. On the Y-axis are reaction times (ms) and on the X-axis are the hunchback congruity conditions for each emotional probe.

Note: Error bars are standard errors (Study 3).

items ($t = -.85$, $\bar{d} = -41.55$ ms, $SE = 49.17$ ms, $p = .400$, 95% CI = [-139.000, 55.861], Cohen's $d = .08$). Hence, the predicted effects emerged only when people made attributions that were related to the hunchback emotions of calm and anger.

4.2.3. *Explicit (self-report) data*

We predicted a hunchback effect for the two categories of race and size. However, it is entirely possible that both status categories interact such that targets with "double devalued" social status (e.g. Blacks and large men) produce the strongest hunchback effect. For this reason, we performed a 2 (race: White vs. Black) × 2 (physical size: large vs. slim) repeated measures ANOVA separately for anger and calm evaluations.

4.2.3.1. Anger attributions. Consistent with the hunchback hypothesis, and again refuting a criticism based on the contact caveat (Barlow et al., 2012), there were main effects of race and physical size: Black targets were perceived to be more angry-looking than the White targets, and large targets were perceived to be more angry-looking than slim targets (see Table 2). These main effects were qualified by a two-way interaction between race and physical size, $F(1, 113) = 6.63$, $p = .004$, $\eta_p^2 = .07$. Simple effect analysis revealed that this interaction did not eliminate the hunchback effect within race or size groups: Large Black targets were perceived to be more angry-looking than large White targets ($\bar{d} = 1.19$, $SE = .14$, $p < .0001$, 95% CI = [.913, 1.473], $\eta_p^2 = .39$; see Figure 5(a)) and, slim Black targets were perceived as more angry-looking than slim White targets ($\bar{d} = 1.68$, $SE = .12$, $p < .0001$, 95% CI = [1.430, 1.921], $\eta_p^2 = .62$; see Figure 5(a)). Also, there was a significant physical size effect within each racial group: Large targets were consistently rated as more angry-looking compared to slim targets, both for Blacks ($\bar{d} = .81$, $SE = .12$, $p < .0001$, 95% CI = [.578, 1.036], $\eta_p^2 = .30$; see Figure 5(a)) and Whites ($\bar{d} = 1.29$, $SE = .13$, $p < .0001$, 95% CI = [1.024, 1.554], $\eta_p^2 = .45$; see Figure 5(a)).

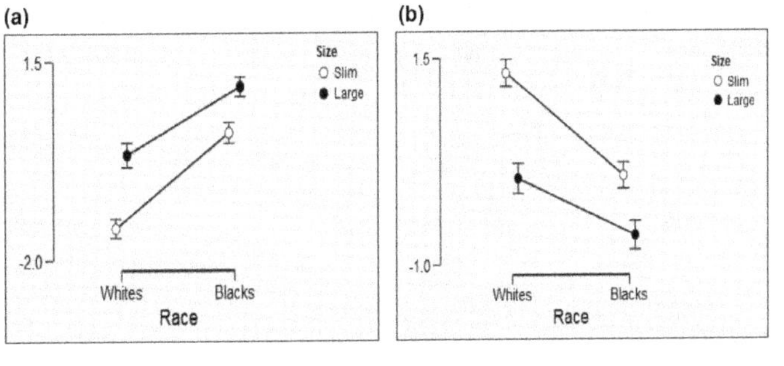

Figure 5. The interactive effect of race-based and size-based status on the attributions of anger (a) and calm (b) to targets. On the Y-axis are ratings of the relevant emotions and on the X-axis are the targets' social categories.

Note: Error bars are 95% confidence intervals (Study 3).

4.2.3.2. Calm attributions. Consistent with the hunchback hypothesis and contrary to a criticism based on the contact caveat (Barlow et al., 2012), there was a main effect of race in which White faces were perceived as more calm-looking than Black targets (see Table 2). There was also a main effect of size: Slim faces were perceived to be more calm-looking than large faces (see Table 2). Again, a race by physical size interaction emerged, $F(1, 113) = 10.32$, $p = .002$, $\eta_p^2 = .08$: Slim Whites were perceived as more calm-looking than slim Blacks ($\bar{d} = 1.24$, $SE = .12$, $p < .0001$, 95% CI = [1.014, 1.469], $\eta_p^2 = .51$; see Figure 5(b)), and large White men were seen as more calm-looking than large Black men ($\bar{d} = .68$, $SE = .13$, $p < .0001$, 95% CI = [.423, .945], $\eta_p^2 = .19$; see Figure 5(b)). When we investigated the simple effects of size within each racial group, we also found, consistent with the hunchback stereotype that, slim men were consistently viewed as more calm-looking than their larger counterparts and, this was true for Blacks ($\bar{d} = .72$, $SE = .11$, $p < .0001$, 95% CI = [.494, .945], $\eta_p^2 = .26$; see Figure 5(b)) as it was for Whites ($\bar{d} = 1.28$, $SE = .12$, $p < .0001$, 95% CI = [1.033, 1.520], $\eta_p^2 = .49$; see Figure 5(b)).

4.2.4. Do signals of social status predict anger and calm attributions?

To answer this question, first, we repeated the same regression as in Study 2, using perceived attractiveness to predict attributions of anger and calm. Corroborating the trends in Study 2, results in Table 4 show that perceived attractiveness of targets within each social category was associated with reduced perceptions of anger, but increased perceptions of calm. In other words, those targets that scored highly on the status signalling dimension of attractiveness were seen as more calm-looking, and less angry-looking, while the reverse was the case for their less attractive (low status) counterparts (see Table 4). We also found a pattern consistent with the hunchback stereotype when perceived attractiveness was substituted in the model with perceived social status: this was true for the Black vs. White interstatus context (see Table 5, Model 1), and also for the large vs. slim interstatus context (see Table 6, Model 1).

Recall that an assumption underlying the facial perception paradigm that we used across our studies is that perceived attractiveness is the metric that perceivers use to differentiate the facial images they saw into high and low social status. Thus, we reasoned that perceived attractiveness should be the conduit through which an effect of social status is passed on to anger/calm attributions. To be sure, we followed this reasoning with a mediational analysis, and specified a path from perceived social status to anger, calm and perceived attractiveness, and a further path from perceived attractiveness to anger and calm.

Results from this mediational analysis revealed two key findings. First, perceived attractiveness explained the link between perceived social status and anger/calm for the low status groups (see Tables 5 and 6, Model 1 for Blacks and large men). Consistent with the hunchback stereotype,

Table 4. The relationship between perceived attractiveness and attributions of anger and calm to blacks, whites, large and slim men (explicit Measures, Study 3)

Perceived attractiveness of …	Emotional attributions							
	β (*SE*)	[95% CI]	*β* (*SE*)	[95% CI]	*β* (*SE*)	[95% CI]	*β* (*SE*)	[95% CI]
Race	**Blacks' anger**		**Whites' anger**		**Blacks' calm**		**Whites' calm**	
Same category	−.384*** (.09)	[−.561, −.193]	−.203* (.10)	[−.383, −.007]	.325*** (.12)	[.142, .519]	.302** (.09)	[.100, .440]
Opposite category	.110 (.09)	[−.075, .289]	.088 (.10)	[−.104, .276]	.093 (.09)	[−.094, .280]	−.210* (.09)	[−.361, −.018]
R^2	.13***		.04		.14***		.09**	
Size	**Large men's anger**		**Slim men's anger**		**Large men's calm**		**Slim men's calm**	
Same category	−.371*** (.09)	[−.506, −.165]	−.200* (.10)	[−.391, −.001]	.431*** (.10)	[.236, .593]	.330*** (.09)	[.377, .831]
Opposite category	.018 (.09)	[−.164, .199]	.149 (.09)	[−.046, .321]	−.100 (.10)	[−.292, .087]	−.132 (.08)	[−.281, .052]
R^2	.13***		.04		.16***		.09**	

Note: Same or opposite category labels refer to the social category in the relevant column for each estimate.

*$p \leq .050$.

**$p \leq .010$.

***$p \leq .001$.

decreased levels of perceived social status were associated with decreased perception of attractiveness (β_{Blacks} = 30, 95% CI = [.116, .467]; $\beta_{large\ men}$ = .44, 95% CI = [.304, .676]), which in turn increased anger perceptions and reduced calm perceptions (see Tables 5 and 6, mediation model)—the opposite was true with increased levels of perceived social status.

Second, and consistent with the hunchback stereotype, signals of status in terms of perceived attractiveness explained the link between perceived social status and calm attributions to high status but only for slim targets and not for Whites. Increasing levels of social status were associated with greater perceptions of attractiveness of high status groups ($\beta_{large\ men.}$ = 34, 95 CI = [.191, .615];

Table 5. Regression analysis for the association between race-based status and attributions of anger and calm when attractiveness is a mediator (Study 3)

Predictors	Emotional attributions							
	Blacks' anger		Whites' anger		Blacks' calm		Whites' calm	
	β (SE)	[95% CI]	β (SE)	[95% CI]	β (SE)	[95% CI]	β (SE)	[95% CI]
Model 1 (status perception)								
Same category	−.226* (.09)	[−.405, −.047]	−.206* (.11)	[−.452, −.023]	.329*** (.09)	[.148, .506]	.312*** (.10)	[.144, .527]
Opposite category	.061 (.11)	[−.145, .289]	.069 (.09)	[.112, .242]	−.007 (.11)	[−.226, .208]	.131 (.08)	[−.041, .274]
R^2	.05*		.04†		.11**		.13***	
Model 2 (mediation)								
DE of attractiveness (Att)	−.293** (.09)	[−.474, −.113]	−.118 (.10)	[−.304, .071]	.304*** (.09)	[.126, .482]	.116 (.08)	[−.051, .283]
IE of status via Att	−.088 (.04)	[−.184, −.029]	−.041 (.04)	[−.125, .024]	.089 (.04)	[.031, .192]	.044 (.04)	[−.012, .134]

Notes: DE = direct effect, IE = indirect effect. In the mediation model 95% CI are bias corrected bootstrapped estimates based on 1,000 simulations. Same or opposite category labels refer to the social category in the relevant column for each estimate. We adjusted for orientation towards prejudice (SDO) in the mediation model.

†p = .051.

*p < .050.

**p < .010.

***p ≤ .001.

Table 6. Regression analysis for the association between size status and attributions of anger and calm when attractiveness is a mediator (Study 3)

Predictors	Emotional attributions							
	Large targets' anger		Slim targets' anger		Large targets' calm		Slim targets' calm	
	β (SE)	[95% CI]	β (SE)	[95% CI]	β (SE)	[95% CI]	β (SE)	[95% CI]
Model 1 (status perception)								
Same category	−.291** (.09)	[−.478, −.105]	−.183† (.11)	[−.413, .009]	.356*** (.10)	[.188, .570]	.404*** (.09)	[.232, .603]
Opposite category	.026 (.10)	[−.174, .230]	.136 (.10)	[−.057, .334]	.076 (.10)	[−.119, .294]	−.086 (.09)	[−.254, .089]
R^2	.08**		.04		.15***		.15***	
Model 2 (mediation)								
DE of attractiveness (Att)	−.269** (.09)	[−.443, −.095]	−.111 (.10)	[−.300 .079]	.270** (.09)	[.093, .447]	.182* (.08)	[.020, .343]
IE of status via Att	−.132 (.05)	[−.231, −.044]	−.030 (.03)	[−.099, .013]	.124 (.05)	[.033, .236]	.053 (.03)	[.013, .122]

Notes: DE = direct effect, IE = indirect effect. In the mediation model 95% CI are bootstrapped BCA based on 1,000 bootstrap simulations. Same or opposite category labels refer to the social category in the relevant column for each estimate. We adjusted for orientation towards prejudice (SDO) in the mediation model.

†p = .060.

*p < .050.

**p < .010.

***p < .001.

$\beta_{\text{slim men}} = .27$, 95 CI = [.096, .502]), which then explained the calm attributions to slim men but not for Whites (see Table 6, mediation model and also Figure 6). This process did not account for the anger attributions to either of the two high status groups (see Table 6, mediation model) and suggests that attractiveness as one signal of social status is unconnected to perceivers' anger attributions to high status groups in this context. The fact that the attractiveness route does not explain the calm attributions to White men, again, could imply that superficial markers of social status are unconnected to calm associations to a high status group whose elevated position is not in doubt. After all, Malaysia was colonised by the (White) British making it likely that status connotations for this known "high status" out-group are based not on superficial status signals (like attractiveness) but, perhaps, more in terms of the perceived superiority of Western values to which Malaysians aspire. Note that this assumption is corroborated by the significant direct effect of social status on anger and calm of both Whites and slim men (see Tables 5 and 6, Model (1). Given the lack of history with Blacks, it seems intuitive that superficial signals of social status (such as attractiveness) sway Malaysians' attributions of calm and anger to this less known demographic.

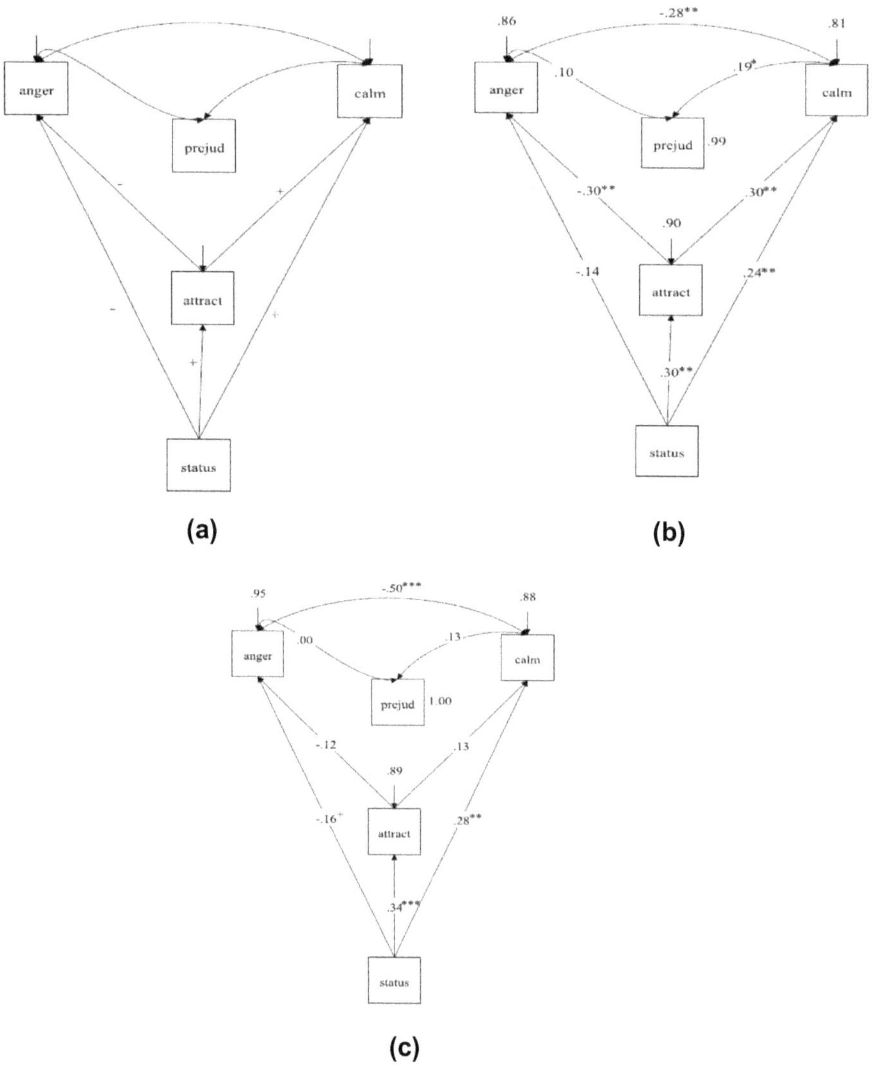

Figure 6. The conceptual status model (a) and the statistical models (b-c) depicting the effect of status on anger and calm attributions to Blacks (b) and Whites (c) when attractiveness is a mediator.

Notes: Attract = perceived attractiveness, prejud = orientation toward prejudice.

4.2.5. But how does the status model compare with a racial prejudice explanation?

We have resolved the issue over the contact caveat. But an alternative account to the pattern of anger/calm attributions that we observed is that an orientation towards racial prejudice is responsible for it: especially in the light of vicarious exposure to racial prejudice against Blacks via the media. A racial prejudice hypothesis would assume greater contempt towards devalued groups, consequently decreasing perceptions of attractiveness of Blacks and increasing attractiveness of Whites. Accordingly, such dislike should weaken the attributions of calm to Blacks while strengthening calm attributions to Whites. Prejudice should also correspondingly weaken an association of anger to Whites, but should reverse this trend for Blacks. This is presumably because those who orient towards racial prejudice might more readily associate stigmatised groups with negative attributes (e.g. anger) but associate their non-stigmatised counterparts with positive attributes (e.g. calm). We compared the adequacy of this racial prejudice model of anger/calm attributions (Figure 7(a)) to our preferred social status account (Figure 6(a)) for Blacks and Whites. In each model, we controlled for the alternative hypothesis, by correlating social status with the residuals of calm and anger in the prejudice model and, correlating prejudice with the residuals of anger and calm in the status model.

In particular, we examined both an unconstrained model in which the paths and associated covariances were free to vary, and compared this with a constrained alternative in which the paths from the focal predictors to the outcomes were fixed to assume a valence that one would expect if the predictions of either the status (Figure 6(a)) or prejudice (Figure 7(a)) hypotheses were correct. Specifically, in the status model for Blacks and Whites, we fixed the status → anger path to assume a value less than zero; the status → calm path to assume a value greater than zero and the status → attractiveness path to assume a value greater than zero.

In the racial prejudice models, the path from prejudice orientation → anger was fixed to assume a value greater than zero for Blacks (but less than zero for Whites) because people who orient towards racial prejudice should attribute socially undesirable emotions to the stigmatised groups, but not to their higher status counterparts. Similarly, the path from prejudice orientation → calm was fixed to a value less than zero for Blacks (but greater than zero for Whites) consistent with the prejudice hypothesis. Finally, the path from prejudice orientation → attractiveness was fixed to assume a value less than zero for Blacks (but greater than zero for Whites) because people who orient towards racial prejudice should be more attracted to the dominant group but less attracted to their subordinated stigmatised counterpart. These analyses were performed using the maximum likelihood estimation and in MPlus version 7 (Muthén & Muthén, 1998–2015).

Table 7 presents the model fit results for these path analyses. The status models fitted the data extremely well for Blacks and Whites according to all the conventional indices of model fitness (Hu & Bentler, 1999)[1]. In fact, the theoretically relevant paths in the constrained model were identical in valence to the unconstrained alternative for both Blacks and Whites, and unsurprisingly their model fit indices were the same, ΔAICs = .00 (see Table 7—upper panel for each racial group; and also Figure 6(b) and (c)). In sharp contrast, none of the racial prejudice models for Blacks and Whites fit the data well (see Table 7—lower panel for each racial group, and also Figure 7(b) and (c)). This was true not only for the constrained models, but also for their unconstrained alternative (see Figure 7 (b) and (c), and also Table 7—lower panel for each racial group). Interestingly, the prejudice model predicted greater (not reduced) expectations of calm for Blacks targets. In short, the status models fitted the data better than the prejudice models for Blacks and Whites (ΔAIC: Status $\text{model}_{\text{Blacks}}$ vs. Prejudice $\text{model}_{\text{Black constrained}}$ = 9.80; Status $\text{model}_{\text{Blacks}}$ vs. Prejudice $\text{model}_{\text{Black unconstrained}}$ = 15.15; Status $\text{model}_{\text{Whites}}$ vs. Prejudice $\text{model}_{\text{Whites constrained}}$ = 13.78; Status $\text{model}_{\text{Whites}}$ vs. Prejudice $\text{model}_{\text{Whites unconstrained}}$ = 13.78).[2]

In sum, the current study replicated and extended Study 2's findings on numerous fronts: (a) it presented direct and indirect evidence that status signals sway attributions of anger and calm in manners that are consistent with the hunchback stereotype; (b) it ruled out a criticism based on the

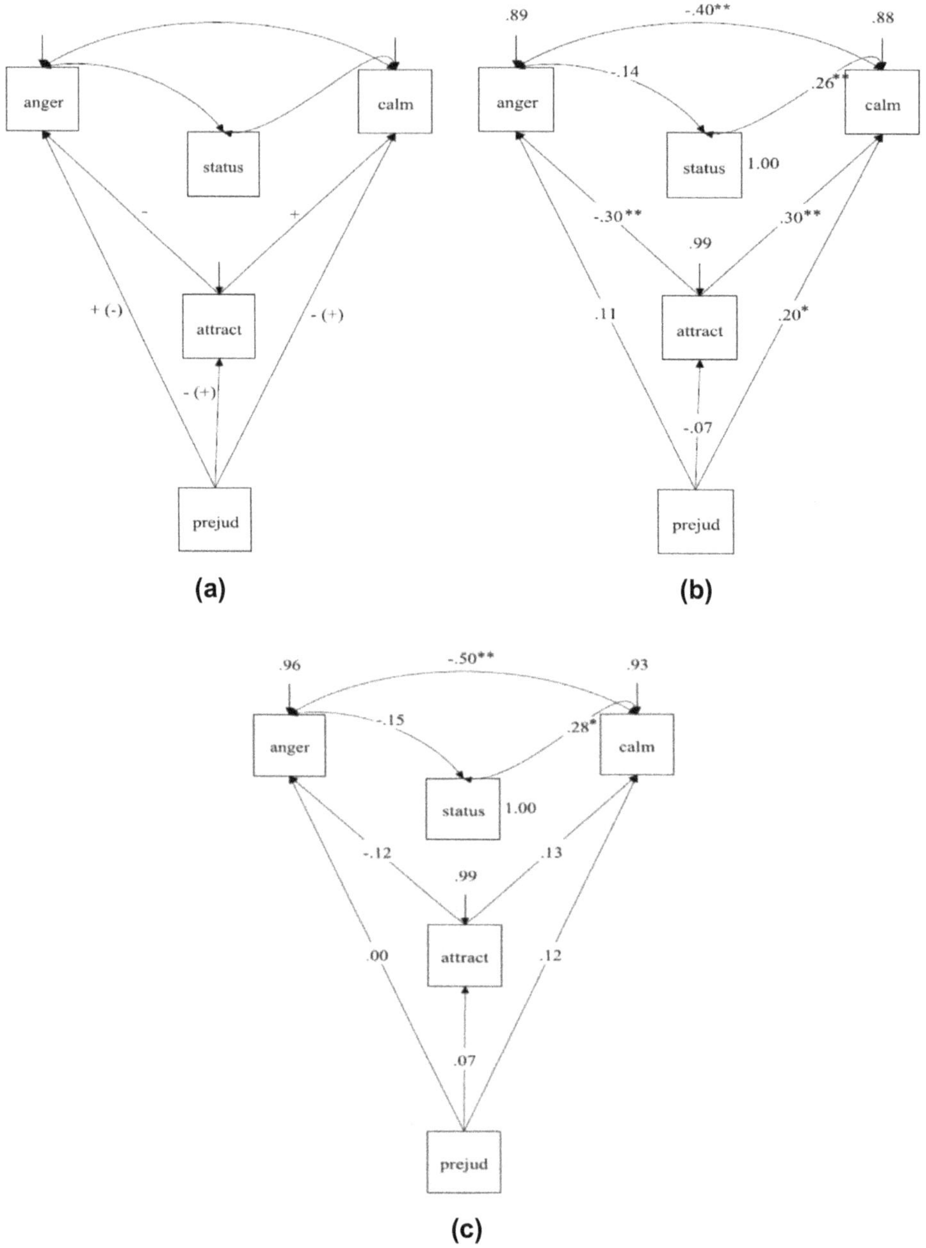

Figure 7. The conceptual prejudice model (a) and the statistical models (b–c) depicting the effect of orientation towards prejudice on anger and calm attributions to Blacks (b) and Whites (c) when attractiveness is a mediator. In Figure 7(a) the valence of paths from prejudice to anger and calm that are enclosed in parenthesis relates to Whites, while those outside parenthesis relates to Blacks.

Notes: Attract = perceived attractiveness, prejud = orientation towards prejudice.

contact caveat that the differential attributions of calm and anger could have been due to the frequency of actual negative encounters, insofar as identical results were obtained even for a low status group that our Malaysian participants were less experienced with (Blacks); (c) it ruled out an orientation towards racial prejudice as a plausible explanation for the trends in relation to the racial context of Blacks vs. Whites, (d) it showed that in the relatively mundane contexts of physical size or attractiveness, that use of the hunchback heuristic persists and finally (e) it showed that even within groups that are devalued, that signals of status (e.g. attractiveness) were sufficient to also prompt the use of the hunchback heuristic.

Table 7. Fit indices of theoretically relevant models in Study 3

	Model	χ^2 (*df*)	CFI	SRMR	RMSEA [90% CI]	AIC	ΔAIC
Blacks	Unconstrained status	.609 (2)	1.00	.018	< .001 [.000, .130]	1,247.950	.00
	Constrained status	.609 (2)	1.00	.018	< .001 [.000, .130]	1,247.950	
	Unconstrained prejudice	10.520** (2)	.868	.074	.193 [.090, .315]	1,257.750	5.347
	Constrained prejudice	15.867** (2)	.786	.087	.247 [.144, .366]	1,263.097	
Whites	Unconstrained status	.945 (2)	1.00	.025	< .001 [.000, .149]	1,251.227	.00
	Constrained status	.945 (2)	1.00	.025	< .001 [.000, .149]	1,251.227	
	Unconstrained prejudice	14.095** (2)	.804	.082	.230 [.127, .350]	1,265.002	.00
	Constrained prejudice	14.095** (2)	.804	.082	.230 [.127, .350]	1,265.002	

Notes: χ^2 = chi-square difference, *df* = degrees of freedom, CFI = comparative fit index, SRMR = squared root mean residual, RMSEA = root mean square error approximation, AIC = akaike information criterion. ΔAIC values for each contrast that is ≥ 10 are considered meaningful (Burnham & Anderson, 2004).
$^{**}p \leq .001$.

5. General discussion

The common wisdom is that threat perception and/or anger attributions to undervalued groups (particularly Blacks) are due to prejudice: individuals who orient towards prejudice generally perceive undervalued groups as being prone to the threat eliciting emotion of anger (see also Ross, 2015 for a similar discussion). Here we considered a more parsimonious status-based account: that a hunchback heuristic exists, which leads people to associate anger with low social status and calm with high social status. We reasoned that the hunchback stereotype would predict the expectations of anger and calm, respectively, from low and high status groups and found support for this proposition in a multi-method protocol comprising self-reports and a rigorous IAT-like implicit measure that taps unconscious cognitive associations. Our findings present a number of theoretical and practical opportunities.

5.1. Theoretical opportunities

While the predictions of the hunchback stereotype could be inferred from other theoretical accounts, it is important to distinguish between our approach and existing models of stereotyping. First, although the stereotype content model (SCM: Fiske et al., 2002) agrees with the hunchback stereotype in predicting the association of anger to low status and calm to high status, it is important to clarify that the SCM views these associations as being tied to trait incompentence, rather than a situation-related phenomenon that is tied to perceived frustration. That is, under the SCM framework people expect members of low status groups to be angry due to "trait" incompetence, and that this incompetence then frustrates the accomplishment of desired goals—making individual members of low status groups more likely to vent the frustration arising from their incompetence. The hunchback stereotype, by contrast, does not make any assumptions about traits. Rather, it supposes a generic tendency to associate people with low status with anger, because by definition, they are more likely to encounter frustration than their counterparts from privileged backgrounds. Creating conditions under which frustration is only attributable to internal (trait) versus external (situational) causes might be one fruitful way to differentiate as well as to integrate the SCM and the hunchback heuristic.

Second, the infrahumanisation theory (Leyens et al., 2000) with its emphasis on the attributions of uniquely human (often positive) emotions to one's in-group and bestial (often negative) emotions to out-groups seem similar to the hunchback stereotype—to the extent that people perceive their own groups as superior to out-groups. However, the problem with this reason is that people do not always see themselves as superior to out-groups. People may find it difficult, at times, to find an objective basis on which to claim superiority over a clearly higher status out-group—e.g. the context between Malaysia and the USA (Spears, Jetten, & Doosje, 2001). As the infrahumanisation approach is more suited to in-group vs. out-group dyads, its predictions therefore do not neatly extend to an interstatus dyad and presents opportunities for an extension of the hunchback framework to an inter*group* context.

Specifically, future research could aim to establish whether members of low status groups also use the hunchback heuristic in their attributions of anger and calm to the in-group vs. an out-group. As has been suggested by others (e.g. Spears et al., 2001), there often is an identity-based conflict within members of low status groups, between the need to service group interests, and a social reality that sets the boundaries for a group interested behaviour to manifest. While group interests might engender a tendency to *resist* an association of negative attributes to the in-group (such as the socially undesirable emotion of anger), it is entirely possible, on the other hand, that social reality could constrain the extent to which members of low status groups could claim positive attributes for their in-group (e.g. calm) relative to their higher status counterparts (see Spears et al., 2001; cf. Owuamalam, Rubin, & Issmer, 2016). Resolving this paradox warrants carefully unpacking the conditions under which the use of a group interested attribution strategy vs. an attribution strategy that yields to reality constraints is likely.

Third, there is also the outstanding issue of the cultural moderation hypothesis of status-based emotional expression put forward by Park et al. (2013). According to this perspective, a cultural creed exists in collectivistic cultures that permit only those in elevated positions of authority (i.e. high status groups) to express anger. Accordingly, people in collectivistic cultures expect members of high status groups to display anger because they are the ones to whom a licence is given to express this emotion. By extension, people in collectivistic cultures expect members of low status groups to be calm because their lack of authority denies them the licence to display anger. The problem with this proposition is that even in the collectivistic Malaysian culture, we found an association between low social status and anger, and between high social status and calm.

That said, the culture moderation hypothesis and the hunchback heuristic are not necessarily incompatible because we interpret the hunchback heuristic as a *fundamental heuristic* that people use in their social judgements, while the culture moderation hypothesis is ostensibly concerned with *norms* that may or may not proscribe reliance on the more fundamental heuristic. Thus, it is possible that in situations where such cultural norms are less salient (such as the mundane interstatus contexts that we used across our studies) that people may rely on the hunchback heuristic, while relying on norms in situations where the cultural norms prescribing the display of anger to those in elevated positions are more salient (e.g. managers vs. subordinates within an organisational context). This might help to explain the seemingly diverging evidence by Tiedens et al. (2000) to those reported by Park et al. (2013), which shows a similar tendency for people to expect anger from high status groups but within an *individualistic* culture and, in the cultural context of an organisation.

Finally, the gender paradox. Would the hunchback heuristic be applicable to the gender context where there are known norms that associate men with anger and aggression and women with calm and submission? We think the hunchback heuristic is potentially applicable even to the gender context, particularly in the light of the foregoing distinction between norms and fundamental heuristics. Accordingly, we reason that people with traditional beliefs about gender roles and norms may be more susceptible to adhering to societal norms that prescribe anger for men, and calm for women. Because we conceive the hunchback stereotype as a fundamental heuristic, we reasoned that those individuals who do not subscribe to traditional gender roles/norms may be more likely to resist normative associations of anger to men and calm to women, and might instead rely on the more hunchback heuristic. Not a single research has explored these novel propositions that are derivable via the lens of a hunchback heuristic, and we think it is a fruitful avenue for future research. Indeed, such a research programme, particularly in the gender context could help to understand the complexities of the *glass-ceiling/cliff* phenomenon (Baretto, Ryan & Schmitt, 2009). It is plausible that women do not get ahead not only because people at the upper echelons of an organisation subscribe to rigid gender role norms that prescribe calm and submissiveness for women, but because people who do not subscribe to these norms may be driven by the fundamental hunchback heuristic: expecting women to be *emotionally leaky* and therefore making them "unfit" for elevated positions requiring calm. Nonetheless, we offer these speculations with caution because they have yet to be documented.

5.2. Practical opportunities

The current findings have far-reaching applied implications. Firstly, in the aftermath of police shootings of Blacks in the US, debates hovered around the issue of racial prejudice against ethnic minorities as a possible (even sole) explanation for the fatalities. While we acknowledge that racial (implicit) prejudice may play a role in explaining some of these incidence (see Welch, 2007), our analysis concurs with Ross (2015) and suggests that an orientation towards racial prejudice may not be the only (even primary) factor in the anger (threat) attributions to low status groups (such as ethnic minorities). Here, we uncover a more fundamental hunchback heuristic that people use to infer the anger of (and therefore possible threat posed by) those who occupy a low status position, which is largely unrelated to an orientation towards racial prejudice. That these associations persist even at the unconscious level that are less susceptible to control, suggests that a fundamental process is at work: the hunchback heuristic. Our novel status-based account becomes even more appealing, particularly when a closer look at scenes of some of these shootings also reveals the involvement of minority police officers. In particular, the finding that people rely on status signals such as physical size (cf., the case of Michael Brown in the 2014 Ferguson shooting) and markers of social stigma (cf., the socially undesirable hoodie worn by Tamir Rice in the Cleaveland police shooting in 2014) in their attributions of anger underscores the complexity of threat perception. It further shows, consistent with our theorising, that perceived social status dictates who might (or might not) be a likely target of a threat-induced victimisation.

Second, the current findings have the potential to help understand the discourse around terrorism and law enforcement more broadly. Observers may perceive greater malice and violent intent from aggressive behaviour of members of low status groups compared to their counterparts from privileged higher status backgrounds. For example, the United States Federal Bureau of Intelligence (FBI) described the fatal shooting of African-Americans at a Church in Charleston South Carolina in 2015 that was perpetrated by Dylann Roof (who had ties to American white supremacists) as a "hate crime": A term that ostensibly carries less severe connotations compared to the 'terrorist' label that intensifies a perception of wanton violence (Berman, Izadi, & Lowery, 2015). Meanwhile, ethnic perpetrators of the San Bernardino, California shootings in 2015 faced terrorism-related charges by the FBI (Sarlin, 2015). Indeed, the motivations for both atrocities seemed political, but with starkly different outcomes for the perpetrators. Note that this trend is also compatible with a recent social experiment in which the German pranksters "Dit Is Normaal" demonstrated that extreme verses from the Bible were perceived to be obscene and violent when people were told that those verses were from the Qur'an. In this sense, the hunchback stereotype has implications for the judiciary: behaviours that may be excused by jurors when it comes from individuals with a high status background, may be attributed violent and therefore criminal intent if it came from people with a low status background. It is important for law enforcement officers and conflict arbiters to be familiar with the hunchback heuristic, and to put a check on it.

5.3. Limitations

Despite the overwhelming evidence for a hunchback heuristic in this investigation, sceptics might nonetheless argue that vicarious exposure to the "angry and aggressive Black stereotype" via media depictions of Black people in violent/aggressive roles is responsible for the attributions of anger, in particular, to Blacks. Even if cherry-picking evidence in this manner is tenable, such an explanation is unsatisfying because (a) the majority of actors in Western media depicting violence and aggression are Whites by virtue of their numeric dominance of the Western movie industry (Smith, Choueiti, & Pieper, 2014), (b) such tendency should be more apparent amongst people who orient towards racial prejudice—but evidence in Study 3 show that this isn't the case, that in fact such individuals expect Blacks to be calm and (c) the regularity of the hunchback pattern across the other interstatus contexts leads to the overwhelming conclusion that emotional attributions were tied to status than anything else.

Nonetheless, we acknowledge that we have used only a proxy of racial prejudice in the shape of an orientation towards acting in this way, and a specific operationalisation of an orientation towards prejudice that isn't exhaustive. Thus, it is entirely possible that a different operationalisation of an orientation towards racial prejudice could yield a prejudice effect. That being said, different theoretical operationalisations of a construct should yield empirically similar outcomes (see Jost et al., 2012 for a similar argument) and the fact that we find no evidence for a racial prejudice hypothesis using an explicit measure raises important questions which future investigations on this topic could aim to resolve. Similarly, it might be fruitful to investigate the patterns we show across these studies in a Western context where proximal contact with Blacks (and Whites) is more frequent.

6. Conclusion

We examined the existence of a hunchback stereotype—the idea that lay perceivers associate anger with low social status and calm with high social status. Using a multi-method approach, we found evidence of a hunchback stereotype across numerous interstatus contexts including: skin-shade, race, physical size and attractiveness. We found these associations in a collectivistic culture where there are suggestions of a cultural creed permitting only high status individuals to express anger, strengthening our view that the hunchback stereotype is a fundamental heuristic. Our analyses ruled out the possibility that frequent encounters with the demographies studied here could have explained our results. In particular, we ruled out a racial prejudice account and showed that the associations of anger to Blacks and calm to Whites are unlikely to result primarily from an orientation towards prejudice, but from a "chip on the shoulder-like" heuristic that we call the hunchback stereotype.

Acknowledgements

We are grateful to the European Association of Social Psychology for a Seedcorn grant to the first author. We would also like to thank Soumya Ramakrishna Bhat for her assistance in data collection and stimuli preparation. The views expressed in this paper are those of the authors alone and those not necessarily mean that the European Association of Social Psychology endorse them.

Funding

This work was funded by the European Association of Social Psychology.

Competing Interests

The authors declare no competing interests.

Author details

Chuma Kevin Owuamalam[1]

E-mail: chuma_owuamalam@yahoo.co.uk, chuma.owuamalam@nottingham.edu.my

ORCID ID: http://orcid.org/0000-0001-8219-7975

Maas Misha'ari Weerabangsa[1]

E-mails: khyx4mme@nottingham.edu.my, mishaari.weerabangsa@gmail.com

Jaya Kumar Karunagharan[1]

E-mail: jaya.kumar@nottingham.edu.my

Mark Rubin[2]

E-mail: mark.rubin@newcastle.edu.au

[1] School of Psychology, University of Nottingham (Malaysia Campus), Jalan Broga, Semenyih 43500, Selangor, Malaysia.

[2] Psychology, The University of Newcastle, Canberra, Australia.

Notes

1. According to Hu and Bentler (1999), good fitting models should have a comparative fit index (CFI) value close to .95; root mean square error of approximation (RMSEA) value close to .06; standardised root mean square residual (SRMR) value close to .08 and a non-significant chi-square value.
2. Because the hypothesised and alternative models are not nested, we used change in Akaike information criterion (ΔAIC) for model comparison. A lower AIC signals a better fit, and ΔAIC values ≥ 10 are regarded as meaningful (Burnham & Anderson, 2004).

References

Ackerman, J. M., Shapiro, J. R., Neuberg, S. L., Kenrick, D. T., Becker, D. V., Griskevicius, V., ... Schaller, M. (2006). They all look the same to me (unless they're angry): From out-group homogeneity to out-group heterogeneity. *Psychological Science, 17*, 836–840. http://dx.doi.org/10.1111/j.1467-9280.2006.01790.x

Akosah-Sarpong, K. (2008). *Essay/Ghana: The evil of the Bibiani Hunchback Ritual.* Modern Ghana. Retrieved 24th June 2016 from http://www.modernghana.com/news/179468/1/essayghana-the-evil-of-the-bibiani-hunchback-ritua.html

Bargh, J. A., Chen, M., & Burrows, L. (1996). Automaticity of social behavior: Direct effects of trait construct and stereotype activation on action. *Journal of Personality and Social Psychology, 71*, 230. doi:10.1037/0022-3514.71.2.230

Barlow, F. K., Paolini, S., Pedersen, A., Hornsey, M. J., Radke, H. R., Harwood, J., ... Sibley, C. G. (2012). The contact caveat: negative contact predicts increased prejudice more than positive contact predicts reduced prejudice. *Personality and Social Psychology Bulletin, 38*, 1629–1643. doi:10.1177/0146167212457953

Barreto, M. E., Ryan, M. K., & Schmitt, M. T. (2009). *The glass ceiling in the 21st century: Understanding barriers to gender equality*. Washington DC: American Psychological Association. http://dx.doi.org/10.1037/11863-000

Berkowitz, L. (1989). Frustration^aggression hypothesis: Examination and reformulation. *Psychological Bulletin, 106*, 59. doi:10.1037/0033-2909.106.1.59

Berman, M., Izadi, E., & Lowery, W. (2015). *At least 14 people killed, 17 injured in mass shooting in San Bernardino, Calif.; two suspects killed in shootout with police*. Retrieved August 3, 2016, from https://www.washingtonpost.com/news/post-nation/wp/2015/12/02/police-in-san-bernadino-calif-responding-report-of-shooting/?utm_term=.cd8af822b859

Burnham, K. P., & Anderson, D. R. (2004). Multimodel inference: Understanding AIC and BIC in model selection. *Sociological Methods Research, 33*, 261–304. http://dx.doi.org/10.1177/0049124104268644

Carlsmith, K. M., Wilson, T. D., & Gilbert, D. T. (2008). The paradoxical consequences of revenge. *Journal of Personality and Social Psychology, 95*, 1316–1324. doi:10.1037/a0012165

Carreiras, M., Garnham, A., Oakhill, J., & Cain, K. (1996). The use of stereotypical gender information in constructing a mental model: Evidence from English and Spanish. *The Quarterly Journal of Experimental Psychology Section A, 49*, 639–663. http://dx.doi.org/10.1080/713755647

CNN News Report. (August, 2014). *Missouri governor imposes curfew in Ferguson, declares emergency*. Retrieved 17th August 2014 from http://edition.cnn.com/2014/08/16/us/missouri-teen-shooting/index.html

Correll, J., Urland, G. R., & Ito, T. A. (2006). Event-related potentials and the decision to shoot: The role of threat perception and cognitive control. *Journal of Experimental Social Psychology, 42*, 120–128.

Crandall, C. S., & Schiffhauer, K. L. (1998). Anti-Fat prejudice: Beliefs, values, and American culture. *Obesity Research, 6*, 458–460. doi:10.1002/j.1550-8528.1998.tb00378.x

Durante, F., Fasolo, M., Mari, S., & Mazzola, A. F. (2014). Children's attitudes and stereotype content toward thin, average-weight, and overweight peers. *SAGE Open, 4*, 2158244014534697. doi:10.1177/2158244014534697

Fiske, S. T., Cuddy, A. J., Glick, P., & Xu, J. (2002). A model of (often mixed) stereotype content: Competence and warmth respectively follow from perceived status and competition. *Journal of Personality and Social Psychology, 82*, 878–902. doi:10.1037/0022-3514.82.6.878

Fleming, K. K., Bandy, C. L., & Kimble, M. O. (2010). Decisions to shoot in a weapon identification task: The influence of cultural stereotypes and perceived threat on false positive errors. *Social Neuroscience, 5*, 201–220. doi:10.1080/17470910903268931

Goff, P. A., Jackson, M. C., Di Leone, B. A. L., Culotta, C. M., & DiTomasso, N. A. (2014). The essence of innocence: Consequences of dehumanizing black children. *Journal of Personality and Social Psychology, 106*, 526. doi:10.1037/a0035663.

Greenwald, A. G., McGhee, D. E., & Schwartz, J. L. (1998). Measuring individual differences in implicit cognition: The implicit association test. *Journal of Personality and Social Psychology, 74*, 1464. doi:10.1037/0022-3514.74.6.1464

Hayes, D., Lawless, J. L., & Baitinger, G. (2014). Who cares what they wear? Media, gender, and the influence of candidate appearance. *Social Science Quarterly, 95*, 1194–1212. doi:10.1111/ssqu.12113

Hu, L., & Bentler, P. M. (1999). Cutoff criteria for fit indexes in covariance structure analysis: Conventional criteria versus new alternatives. *Structural Equation Modeling: A Multidisciplinary Journal, 6*, 1–55. http://dx.doi.org/10.1080/10705519909540118

Hutchings, P. B., & Haddock, G. (2008). Look black in anger: The role of implicit prejudice in the categorization and perceived emotional intensity of racially ambiguous faces. *Journal of Experimental Social Psychology, 44*, 1418–1420. doi:10.1016/j.jesp.2008.05.002

Jones, O. (2012). *Chavs: The demonization of the working class* (2nd ed.). London: Verso Books.

Jost, J. T., Chaikalis-Petritsis, V., Abrams, D., Sidanius, J., van der Toorn, J., & Bratt, C. (2012). Why Men (and Women) do and don't rebel: Effects of system justification on willingness to protest. *Personality and Social Psychology Bulletin, 38*, 197–208. doi:10.1177/0146167211422544

Keltner, D., Gruenfeld, D. H., & Anderson, C. (2003). Power, approach, and inhibition. *Psychological Review, 110*, 265. doi:10.1037/0033-295X.110.2.265

Kluegel, J. R. (1990). Trends in Whites' explanations of the Black-White gap in socioeconomic status, 1977-1989. *American Sociological Review, 55*, 512–525. http://dx.doi.org/10.2307/2095804

Kruglanski, A. W. (1990). Lay epistemic theory in social-cognitive psychology. *Psychological Inquiry, 1*, 181–197. doi:10.1207/s15327965pli0103_1

Leong, S. (2006). Who's the fairest of them all? Television ads for skin-whitening cosmetics in Hong Kong. *Asian Ethnicity, 7*, 167–181. doi:10.1080/14631360600736215

Leyens, J. P., Paladino, P. M., Rodriguez-Torres, R., Vaes, J., Demoulin, S., Rodriguez-Perez, A., & Gaunt, R. (2000). The emotional side of prejudice: The attribution of secondary emotions to ingroups and outgroups. *Personality and Social Psychology Review, 4*, 186–197. doi:10.1207/S15327957PSPR0402_06

Lord, J. (2016). *Life Lesson #45: Get the chip off your shoulder.* Retrieved June 18, 2016 from http://thecharacternetwork.org/life-lesson-45-get-the-chip-off-your-shoulder/

Loughnan, S., Haslam, N., Sutton, R. M., & Spencer, B. (2014). Dehumanization and social class. *Social Psychology, 45*, 54–61. doi:10.1027/1864-9335/a000159

Lowery, W. (2016). *Study finds police fatally shoot unarmed black men at disproportionate rates.* Retrieved June 15, 2016, from https://www.washingtonpost.com/national/study-finds-police-fatally-shoot-unarmed-black-men-at-disproportionate-rates/2016/04/06/e494563e-fa74-11e5-80e4-c381214de1a3_story.html

MacLeod, C. M. (1991). Half a century of research on the Stroop effect: An integrative review. *Psychological Bulletin, 109*, 163. doi:10.1037/0033-2909.109.2.163

McLaughlin, E. C. (2015). *There aren't more police shootings, just more coverage.* Retrieved June 15, 2016, from http://edition.cnn.com/2015/04/20/us/police-brutality-video-social-media-attitudes/

McLean, G. (2005). *In the hood. The Guardian.* Retrieved from http://www.theguardian.com/politics/2005/may/13/fashion.fashionandstyle

Minear, M., & Park, D. C. (2004). A lifespan database of adult facial stimuli. *Behaviour research methods, instruments, & computers*, 36, 630–633. Retrieved from http://agingmind.utdallas.edu/facedb/view/neutral-faces. doi:10.3758/BF03206543

Muthén, L. K., & Muthén, B. O. (1998–2015). *Mplus User's Guide.* (7th ed.). Los Angeles, CA: Muthén & Muthén.

Nadeem, S. (2014). Fair and anxious: on mimicry and skin-lightening in India. *Social Identities, 20*, 224–238. doi:10.1080/13504630.2014.881282

Nelson, D. L., McEvoy, C. L., & Schreiber, T. A. (2004). The University of South Florida free association, rhyme, and word fragment norms. *Behaviour Research Methods, Instruments, & Computers, 36*, 402–407. doi:10.3758/BF03195588

Nisbett, R. E., & Wilson, T. D. (1977). The halo effect: Evidence for unconscious alteration of judgments. *Journal of Personality and Social Psychology, 35*, 250–256. doi:10.1037/0022-3514.35.4.250

Owuamalam, C., Weerabangsa, M., Mamdouh, M., Karunagharan, J. K., & Rubin, M. (2014). *A mixed-method investigation of the hunchback hypothesis of emotional expressivity among members of low status groups*. figshare. https://dx.doi.org/10.6084/m9.figshare.1149979.v3

Owuamalam, C. K., Rubin, M., & Issmer, C. (2016). Reactions to group devaluation and social inequality: A comparison of social identity and system justification predictions. *Cogent Psychology, 3*, doi:10.1080/23311908.2016.1188442

Owuamalam, C., Wong, K. X., & Rubin, M. (2016). Chubby but cheerful? Investigating the compensatory judgments of high, medium, and low status weight groups in Malaysia. *Cogent Psychology, 3*, doi:10.1080/23311908.2016.1188441

Park, J., Kitayama, S., Markus, H. R., Coe, C. L., Miyamoto, Y., Karasawa, M., ... Ryff, C. D. (2013). Social status and anger expression: The cultural moderation hypothesis. *Emotion, 13*, 1122. doi:10.1037/a0034273

Peirce, J. W. (2007). PsychoPy—Psychophysics software in Python. *Journal of Neuroscience Methods, 162*, 8–13. doi:10.1016/j.jneumeth.2006.11.017

Rees, S., & Silove, D. (2011). Sakit hati: A state of chronic mental distress related to resentment and anger amongst West Papuan refugees exposed to persecution. *Social Science & Medicine, 73*, 103–110. doi:10.1016/j.socscimed.2011.05.004

Ross, C. T. (2015). A multi-level Bayesian analysis of racial bias in police shootings at the county-level in the United States, 2011–2014. *PLOS ONE, 10*, e0141854. doi:10.1371/journal.pone.0141854

Sandhu, K. S. (1993). The coming of Indians to Malaysia. In K. S. Sandhu & A. Mani (Eds.), *Indian Communities in Southeast Asia* (First Reprint 2006, pp. 151–189). Singapore: Institute of Southeast Asian Studies.

Sarlin, B. (2015). *Nine dead in Charleston church massacre*. Retrieved August 03, 2016, from http://www.msnbc.com/msnbc/charleston-police-church-shooting

Shapiro, J. R., Ackerman, J. M., Neuberg, S. L., Maner, J. K., Becker, D. V., & Kenrick, D. T. (2009). Following in the wake of anger: When not discriminating is discriminating. *Personality and Social Psychology Bulletin, 35*, 1356–1367. doi:10.1177/0146167209339627

Sidanius, J., & Pratto, F. (2001). *Social dominance: An intergroup theory of social hierarchy and oppression*. Cambridge: Cambridge University Press.

Smith, S., Choueiti, M., & Pieper, K. (2014). Race/ethnicity in 600 popular films: Examining on screen portrayals and behind the camera diversity. *Media, Diversity, & Social Change Initiative*. Retrieved 25th January 2016 from http://annenberg.usc.edu/pages/~/media/MDSCI/Racial%20Inequality%20in%20Film%202007-2013%20Final.ashx

Spears, R., Jetten, J., & Doosje, B. (2001). The (Il) legitimacy of ingroup bias-From social reality to social resistance. In J. T Jost & B. Major (Eds.), *The psychology of legitimacy: Emerging perspectives on ideology, justice, and intergroup relations* (pp. 332–362). New York, NY: Cambridge University Press.

Tablante, C. B., Durante, F., & Fiske, S. T. (in press). Poor but warm, rich but cold (and competent): Social classes in the stereotype content model. *Journal of Social Issues* (forthcoming issue).

Tajfel, H., Billig, M. G., Bundy, R. P., & Flament, C. (1971). Social categorization and intergroup behaviour. *European Journal of Social Psychology, 1*, 149–178. http://dx.doi.org/10.1002/(ISSN)1099-0992

Tiedens, L. Z., Ellsworth, P. C., & Mesquita, B. (2000). Sentimental stereotypes: Emotional expectations for high-and low-status group members. *Personality and Social Psychology Bulletin, 26*, 560–575. doi:10.1177/0146167200267004

Volpato, C., Andrighetto, L., & Baldissarri, C. (in press). Perceptions of low-status workers and the maintenance of the social-class status quo. *Journal of Social Issues* (forthcoming issue).

Welch, K. (2007). Black criminal stereotypes and racial profiling. *Journal of Contemporary Criminal Justice, 23*, 276–288. doi:10.1177/1043986207306870

Appendix A

List of word stimuli used in Studies 2 and 3.

Table A1. Emotion-associated probes in Studies 2 and 3

Calm-associated	Anger-associated	Non-associated (filler)
Passive	Fierce	Activity
Relax	Vent	Junior
Tame	Violent	Quarter
Still	Revenge	Zipper
Peace	Irritate	Define
Peaceful	Tantrum	Maximum
Patience	Jealousy	Theory
Subtle	Aggravate	Genuine
Patient	Mean	Nitrogen
Soothe	Frustrate	Wonderful

Note: Calm and anger columns in Studies 2 and 3, and non-associated column in Study 3.

11

Appearance issues, depression, and disordered eating among college females

Priscilla N. Gitimu[1*], Molly M. Jameson[2], Tacibaht Turel[1], Rachel Pohle-Krauza[1], Jeanine Mincher[1], Zara Rowlands[1] and Janice Elias[1]

*Corresponding author: Priscilla N. Gitimu, Human Ecology Department, Youngstown State University (YSU), One University Plaza, Youngstown, OH 44555, USA
E-mails: pngitimu@ysu.edu, priscillagitimu@gmail.com
Reviewing editor: Traci Craig, University of Idaho, USA

Abstract: The purpose of this study was to examine how various appearance issues and depression may relate to disordered eating among female college students. The appearance issues analyzed in this study were: level of body dissatisfaction, body mass index (BMI), social appearance anxiety (SAA), and social-cultural attitudes toward appearance. The questionnaire was distributed to volunteer students during regularly scheduled classes. Students, both study participants and non-participants, were furnished with information on where to get help if they had concerns about disordered eating behavior, appearance-related anxiety, or depression. Participants were 370 female undergraduate students enrolled at one Midwestern University in the United States. This study provided statistical evidence that college females at risk of acquiring an eating disorder had significantly larger differences between their current body shape and their ideal body shape, scored significantly higher in the sociocultural attitudes toward appearance, had more SAA, and depress ion compared to those less at risk of acquiring an eating disorder. However, the BMI of college females at risk of acquiring an eating disorder did not differ significantly from the BMI of college female students less at risk. This study contributes to a better understanding of disordered eating and how it relates to appearance issues, and depression.

ABOUT THE AUTHORS

All authors, except one, are professors at Youngstown State University, in Youngstown, Ohio, USA. This study is the synergy of seven faculty who aspire to make valuable contribution in understanding how appearance and depression may influence disordered eating behavior among college females.

Priscilla Gitimu and Taci Turel are both associate professors of Fashion Studies, and they have an in-depth knowledge of body image and appearance issues. Molly Jameson is Assistant Professor of Psychology at the University of Northern Colorado, and has in-depth understanding of statistics and psychological issues and measures.

Rachel Pohle-Krauza, Jeannine Mincher, and Zara Rowlands are all Associate Professors of Nutrition and they have in-depth knowledge on disordered eating and eating disorders.

Janice Elias is a Family and Consumer Sciences professor with background in gender studies and in psychological and cultural aspects of appearance.

PUBLIC INTEREST STATEMENT

A 2015 "Choose Beautiful Dove Campaign" revealed that 96% of the women surveyed would not use the word "beautiful" to describe themselves! (Stampler, 2015). One's opinions of what constitutes a beautiful appearance are often based on unrealistic media images. This study scrutinized how anxiety about one's appearance and unhappiness is associated with unhealthy eating habits among college females. Identifying and curbing unhealthy eating behavior, before it leads to an eating illness, is crucial.

Various appearance concerns among students at risk of acquiring an eating disorder were compared with those not at risk. The study shows evidence that college females at risk of acquiring an eating disorder were more discontent about their body shape and size, more anxious about their appearance in a social setting, more influenced by society's standards of beauty, and were unhappy compared to those less at risk of acquiring an eating disorder.

Subjects: Behavioral Sciences; Gender Studies - Soc Sci; Health & Development; Mental Health; Psychological Disorders; Psychological Disorders - Adult; Psychological Science; Social Sciences; Sociology; Women's Studies

Keywords: appearance issues; depression; disordered eating; college females; appearance anxiety

1. Introduction

One's beliefs in what constitutes a beautiful appearance develop in the context of several sociocultural factors, such as unrealistic media images of female attractiveness (Clay, Vignoles, & Dittmar, 2005) that promote singular ideals of beauty. There is extensive evidence that sociocultural pressure and appearance insecurity can predispose one to disordered eating behavior (Clay et al., 2005; Thompson, van den Berg, Roehrig, Guarda, & Heinberg, 2004; Tiggermann, Verri, & Scaravaggi, 2005; White & Halliwell, 2010). Social appearance anxiety (SAA) is a significant predictor of appearance dissatisfaction, disordered eating behavior, and concerns about shape and weight (Levinson & Rodebaugh, 2012). Additionally, depression is a significant predictor of disordered eating behavior, and the incidence is high among women (Liechty & Lee, 2013).

It is crucial to identify and curb disordered eating behavior before it leads to an eating disorder. Eating disorders are a set of severe illnesses in which one is excessively concerned about body shape, appearance and weight, and as a result, is immersed in extreme dieting habits which prevent sufficient food intake. Before one fits the diagnostic criteria of the *Diagnostic and Statistical Manual of Mental Disorders* (DSM) (American Psychiatric Association, 2013) for an eating disorder, one may engage in a disordered eating behavior, which encompasses unhealthy eating habits that may include restrictive dieting, skipping meals, or compulsive overeating. (Fitzsimmons-Craft, Ciao, & Accurso, 2016).

The purpose of this study was to examine how appearance issues and depression relate to disordered eating among female college students. Appearance issues are the stimuli that cause individuals to view their physical looks negatively. The appearance issues analyzed in this study were level of body dissatisfaction, body mass index (BMI), SAA, and social-cultural attitudes toward appearance.

1.1. Theoretical perspective

The current study looked at appearance issues, depression, and disordered eating through the lenses of three theories and their modern day interpretations: social comparison theory by Festinger (1954), self-discrepancy theory (Higgins, 1987), and the normative discontent theory (Rodin, Silberstein, & Striegel-Moore, 1984).

1.1.1. Social comparison theory

The social comparison theory (Festinger, 1954) conveys a base for the discourse factors that impact women's appearance issues and disordered eating behavior. The social comparison theory proposes that humans always strive to improve their lives and they do so by comparing themselves with other individuals. The theory discriminates between downward and upward comparisons. The downward comparison is when the comparison is with one considered lower than oneself. Hence, the downward comparison becomes a source of inspiration and feeling superior to others. The upward comparison is when the appraisal is based on a higher standard than the individual's. Thus, the upward comparison can lead to one feeling inferior. Upward comparison can be useful if used for self-improvement, but if the upward standard is unattainable, then it leads to frustration and even to feelings of anxiety and depression.

According to Festinger (1954), individuals are more likely to compare themselves with similar others. Regarding appearance, however, women often compare themselves with unrealistic images of other women portrayed in the media. Appearance-based social comparison may lead to appearance-based anxiety and even depression as well as a disordered eating behavior as one attempts to approximate the superior standard portrayed in media and in the culture (Myers, Ridolfi, Crowther, & Ciesla, 2012).

1.1.2. Self-discrepancy theory

Jung-Hee, Lennon, and Rudd (2001) suggest application of the self-discrepancy theory (Higgins, 1987) in understanding more about females and appearance issues. According to the self-discrepancy theory, differences may exist between the actual (real) and the ideal (desired) appearance. These discrepancies may lead to an unfavorable mental state, which again may lead to a decline in recognition of apparent self-discrepancies. When the discrepancy is large, it may yield to a mental condition such as depression (Higgins, 1987). The more a woman has perceptual discrepancy between actual and ideal appearance, the greater is her risk of body dissatisfaction, disordered eating behaviors, and depression (Cash, Wood, Phelps, & Boyd, 1991).

1.1.3. Normative discontent theory

The normative discontent theory proposes that dissatisfaction with one's weight has become so widespread among females that feeling negatively about one's appearance is alleged to be the "norm" rather than the exception (Tantleff-Dunn, Barnes, & Larose, 2011). The theory has been used by researchers to explain the phenomenon in which women generally have overwhelming body dissatisfaction (Rodin et al., 1984). Since the cultural thin ideal for women is achieved by only a small percentage of women, many women acquire a discrepancy between their actual appearance and the ideal appearance. The media images in the culture have provided a backdrop from which appearance is assessed.

1.2. Pertinent literature

1.2.1. Body dissatisfaction

According to Wood-Barcalow, Tylka, and Augustus-Horvath (2010), individuals have a favorable body image (perception of their appearance) when they possess an appreciation and respect for how their body looks. Women who possess a positive body image resist internalization of negative media information, are less prone to disordered eating behavior, have better self-esteem and social support, and delight in bodily activity (Wood-Barcalow et al., 2010).

A study by Wendell, Masuda, and Le (2012) proposed that rigid body image has associations with disordered eating behavior. An understanding of the appearance flexibility concept may be useful in handling disordered eating behavior complications. Vartanian and Dey (2013) reasoned that poor self-concept contributed to appearance issues because it increased women's susceptibility to thin internalization and appearance comparison propensities. In a study by Ahern, Bennett, and Hetherington (2008), females who had an established intellectual schema that associated being thinner with positive attributes reported more disordered eating behavior symptoms. They found that thin internalization significantly correlated with body dissatisfaction, drive for thinness, and restrained eating.

1.2.2. Body mass index

Regardless of a woman's body size and BMI, the tendency to practice restrictive dieting has been found to be the same (Hill, Masuda, & Latzman, 2013; Robinson, Kosmerly, Mansfield-Green, & Lafrance, 2013; Tod, Edwards, & Hall, 2013). This phenomenon concurs with the normative discontent theory (Cash & Henry, 1995). On the other hand, in other studies, BMI was a significant predictor of body dissatisfaction, with a higher BMI projecting greater dissatisfaction (Gardner, Brown, & Boice, 2012; Xu et al., 2010). According to Ferreira, Pinto-Gouveia, and Duarte (2013), disordered eating behavior does not necessarily result directly from dissatisfaction with one's current weight. Rather, it is the perception of a low social status based primarily on physical appearance that makes one vulnerable to an eating disorder. Therefore, prospective research, like the current study, ought to investigate the roles of body dissatisfaction and BMI in the development of eating disorders.

1.2.3. Sociocultural attitudes toward appearance

Sociocultural pressures regarding ideal body types are important influences on appearance dissatisfaction and the use of body change behaviors (Xu et al., 2010). The social comparison theory proposes that people have a tendency to compare themselves to others, especially to those they consider superior, which explains why females self-compare with ultra-thin models. This upward comparison often produces negative feelings, especially for those who are heavier than the model (Homan, McHugh, Wells, Watson, & King, 2012; Swami, Taylor, & Carvalho, 2011; Thompson et al., 2004; Xu et al., 2010). For example, an analysis of tweets before and after a Victoria's Secret fashion show evidenced upward social comparison to the models. The tweets contained thoughts about appearance, disordered eating behavior, weight, desire for food, and thoughts about self-harm (Chrisler, Fung, Lopez, & Gorman, 2013).

Body dissatisfaction and/or disordered eating behavior have also been linked to watching television (Schooler & Trinh, 2011) and Internet addiction (Rodgers, Melioli, Laconi, Bui, & Chabrol, 2013). Reading of fashion magazines was shown to have an impact on internalization of the thin ideal, but not necessarily an impact on body dissatisfaction and disordered eating behavior. The authors suggest that family structure, eating environment, and cultural norms are additional factors that may impact vulnerability or resistance to media images (Tiggermann et al., 2005).

Intervention programs ought to challenge the desire to be thin while incorporating the desire to be fit, considering the fact that exposure to fit models does not increase body dissatisfaction (Homan et al., 2012). Disordered eating behavior interventions should encourage females to acquire meaningful autonomy, so as to have rational and minimal pressure. Autonomy as a strategy can encourage females to internalize healthy eating, instead of a thin ideal, and will consequently ensure lasting benefits to their appearance and eating habits (Mask & Blanchard, 2011).

Exposure to healthy images and accurate information about media images may have a positive influence on one's body image (Owen & Spencer, 2013). Wood-Barcalow et al. (2010) purport that women with healthy body images shield themselves from media by having an understanding that media images are often computer-modified, unattainable, impractical, and atypical.

Body dissatisfaction has been strongly predicted by two aspects of the Sociocultural Attitudes Toward Appearance Questionnaire (SATAQ-3): (1) pressure (pressure from various media to strive for ideals of attractiveness) and (2) internalization-general (the support and acceptance of media messages concerning unrealistic esthetic ideals) (Thompson et al., 2004). Additional research like this current study is needed to further examine the particular processes by which sociocultural pressures influence one's appearance.

1.2.4. SAA and depression

SAA is a dread that one will be undesirably evaluated based on one's appearance (Hart et al., 2008). SAA differs from social physique anxiety (Martin Ginis, Murru, Conlin, & Strong, 2011) because the latter is concerned with self-evaluation of one's body form and structure, e.g. body size. SAA is a broader domain that integrates all of one's appearance and is not restricted to physique (Levinson & Rodebaugh, 2012; Martin Ginis et al., 2011). SAA is a significant predictor for appearance dissatisfaction, disordered eating behavior, and concerns about shape and weight (Levinson & Rodebaugh, 2012). According to Rosser, Moss, and Rumsey (2010), individuals with high levels of concern over their physical appearance also perceive more components of their environment as appearance-related and negative.

There are common associations between depression and disordered eating behavior (Fink, Bodell, Smith, & Joiner, 2013; Liechty & Lee, 2013; Ostrovsky, Swencionis, Wylie-Rosett, & Isasi, 2013; Robinson et al., 2013). Individuals who displayed high anxiety had a self-worth that relied more on appearance, had numerous appearance dialog, as well as disordered eating behavior patterns, the most frequent being binge eating (Bardone-Cone, Brownstone, Higgins, Fitzsimmons-Craft, & Harney, 2013).

This link between anxiety and disordered eating behavior has implications for interventions in that a therapist can focus on the anxiety and probably prevent development of eating disorders (Levinson & Rodebaugh, 2012). Emotional difficulties combined with a higher BMI have been related to higher dieting tendencies. Individuals were likely to participate in restrained and disordered eating behavior in an attempt to alleviate unregulated distress (Robinson et al., 2013; Swami et al., 2011). The strong association between depression and disordered eating behavior implies that teaching skills for managing negative emotions may possibly be an effective aid for the prevention of disordered eating behavior (Liechty & Lee, 2013).

1.2.5. Disordered eating vs. eating disorders

It is important to note that disordered eating is defined as a wide range of irregular eating behaviors that do not warrant a diagnosis of a specific eating disorder. Persons who have disordered eating may have characteristics that overlap a medically diagnosed eating disorder. While failure to fulfill all of the criteria for these may not qualify for a formal eating disorder diagnosis, the affected individual still does not have a healthy relationship with food and body weight, may suffer depression (Puccio, Fuller-Tyszkiewicz, Ong, & Krug, 2016) and other emotional and physical risks (Fairweather-Schmidt, Lee, & Wade, 2015).

The Diagnostic and Statistical Manual of Mental Disorders (DSM-5) (American Psychiatric Association, 2013) has highly specific criteria that patients must fulfill in order to receive formal diagnoses for an eating disorder, which would include anorexia nervosa, bulimia nervosa, binge eating disorder, or eating disorder not otherwise specified. The United States officially recognizes the DSM-5 for use in identifying codes for International Statistical Classifications of Diseases, which are used for health care reimbursement, underscoring the need for specificity in diagnoses.

1.2.6. Eating attitude test (EAT)-26

The eating attitude test (EAT) is one of the most widely used measures for evaluating eating behaviors. The EAT-26 has demonstrated sufficient internal consistency and test–retest reliability. For example, the EAT-26 has demonstrated an internal consistency ranging from 0.76 to 0.92 (Ahmadi, Moloodi, Zarbaksh, & Ghaderi, 2014). The EAT-26 scale has been correlated with other scales to assist in establishing validity, particularly in regard to its usefulness in identifying eating disorders (ED). Although many studies examine a variety of variables and their association with EAT-26, depression scores (as evidenced by the Beck Depression Inventory (BDI)) appear to be the most commonly utilized. Research has revealed a significant positive relationship between depressive symptoms (using BDI) and eating disorders as demonstrated by positive/higher scores (using EAT-26) (Ahmadi et al., 2014; Erol, Toprak, & Yazici, 2006; Juarasico, Perone, & Timko, 2011; Kaplan, 2006; Thompson, 2016).

In a congruent study, individuals who exhibited frequent disordered eating also displayed high anxiety, combined with appearance-dependent self-worth, and frequent appearance conversations (Bardone-Cone et al., 2013). Likewise, MacNeill and Best (2015) demonstrated that EAT-26 scores correlated with discontent appearance (marked difference between perceived current body size and ideal body size). The study also reported that those with higher body dissatisfaction tended to report a smaller ideal body size when viewing body figures. Similarly, in the Andreea-Elena (2015) study, EAT-26 exhibited significant correlations between the risk of eating disorders and all facets of social-cultural attitudes concerning appearance. Other studies have demonstrated a relationship between disordered eating behaviors (as measured by EAT-26) in college women and social physique anxiety (which is related to SAA) (Lanfranchi, Maïano, Morin, & Therme, 2015; White & Warren, 2014).

1.3. Hypotheses

This study was guided by five hypotheses and one major research question:

Hypotheses:

H1: College females at risk of acquiring an eating disorder (EAT-26 score ≥ 20) will have significantly larger difference between their ideal body shape and their current body shape, as measured by the Stunkard Body Figural Scale (SBFS), compared to the students who are at less risk of acquiring an eating disorder (EAT-26 score < 20).

H2: The mean BMI of college females at risk of acquiring an eating disorder (EAT-26 score ≥ 20) will not differ significantly from the mean BMI of college female students at less risk of acquiring an eating disorder (EAT-26 score < 20).

H3: College females at risk of acquiring an eating disorder (EAT-26 score ≥ 20) will score significantly higher in sociocultural attitudes towards appearance as measured by the Sociocultural Attitudes Toward Appearance Questionnaire (SATAQ-3) compared to college female students at less risk of acquiring an eating disorder (EAT-26 score < 20).

H4: College females at risk of acquiring an eating disorder (EAT 26 score ≥ 20) will have significantly higher SAA as measured by the Social Appearance Anxiety Scale (SAAS) compared to college female students at less risk of acquiring an eating disorder (EAT-26 < 20).

H5: College females at risk of acquiring an eating disorder (EAT-26 score ≥ 20) will have significantly higher depression as measured by the BDI compared to college female students at less risk of acquiring an eating disorder (EAT-26 < 20).

1.3.1. The culminating inquiry

Which of the variables (appearance issues, depression) considered in this study is the greatest predictor of risk for disordered eating behavior?

2. Materials and methods

The *ex post facto* research design was used; hence, there was no treatment of the variables, but attempts were made to understand the cause, or reason, for existing differences in the behavior or status of groups of individuals (Tuckman, 1999). In this study, the researchers investigated how appearance issues and depression related to disordered eating behavior among female college students.

The researchers obtained human subjects' approval from the institutional review board of their university before collecting any data. After obtaining informed consent from the participants, investigators distributed the questionnaires to volunteer students during regularly scheduled classes. Students, both study participants and non-participants, were furnished with information on where to get help if they had concerns about disordered eating behavior, appearance-related anxiety or depression. Participants were recruited from undergraduate students enrolled at one Midwestern University in the United States. Subjects were not offered any compensation for participating in the study.

The questionnaire was composed of five scales plus demographic items (i.e. age, gender, major, ethnicity, level of education, current and desired weight, and height). The first scale was the Stunkard Body Figure Scale (SBFS) by Stunkard, Sorensen, and Schulsinger (1983). This survey is widely used in research regarding body dissatisfaction. For this particular study, participants were asked to compare a set of nine drawings of increasing body size and to circle their perceived current body shape and ideal body shape (desired body shape). Body-shape drawings were assigned a series of ascending scores, and "body dissatisfaction" was calculated based on the difference between the number of the current shape and the number of the ideal shape. If the difference between the number of the current shape and the number of the ideal shape was greater than zero, then the individual had some level of body dissatisfaction; a larger differential was indicative of high body dissatisfaction.

The SBFS has a concurrent validity of .99, a test-retest reliability of the current size of 0.90 and 0.88 for ideal size (Gardner & Brown, 2010).

The second scale was the EAT-26 by Garner, Olmsted, Bohr, and Garfinkle (1982). It has been used extensively in research as a reliable measure of identifying the presence of symptoms that are consistent with either a possible eating disorder or disordered eating behavior. Individuals who score 20 or greater (EAT-26 ≥ 20) are considered to be at risk of having an eating disorder (Garner et al.). When used clinically, the EAT-26 is interpreted continuously, but in non-clinical samples such as in the current study, it is appropriate to dichotomize participants into at-risk and not at-risk for group comparisons (Anstine & Grinenko, 2000; Jones, Bennett, Olmsted, Lawson, & Rodin, 2001). The EAT-26 scale comprises four dimensions, which include dieting, bulimia, food preoccupation, and oral control. An example of a question in EAT-26 is "I have gone on eating binges where I feel that I may not be able to stop." Each item is rated on a scale of 0–3 as follows: never = 0, rarely = 0, sometimes = 0, often = 1, usually = 2, and always = 3. Only item 25 was reverse coded.

The third scale was the Social-cultural Attitudes Toward Appearance Questionnaire (SATAQ-3) validated by Thompson et al. (2004). SATAQ-3 is a measure of one's agreement with societal appearance standards (Calogero, Davis, & Thompson, 2004). The SATAQ-3 subscales have exhibited excellent convergent validity with measures of body image and eating disturbance (Thompson et al., 2004). SATAQ-3 has also exhibited strong psychometric properties in a sample of Caucasian, African-American, Asian, and Hispanic college women from the USA. SATAQ-3 showed excellent reliability, reporting Cronbach's alpha values for the total score of .97 for all four groups (Warren, Rakhkovskaya, & Gleaves, 2013). The SATAQ-3 is a 30-item questionnaire that assesses four aspects of media influence on individuals. The four subscales are: (1) internalization-general (the support and acceptance of media messages concerning unrealistic esthetic ideals); (2) Internalization-Athlete (approval and acceptance of an athletic body ideal); (3) Pressure (apparent pressure from various media to strive for ideals of attractiveness); (4) Information (the level to which various media are reflected as a significant source of information about appearance). The subscales of the SATAQ-3 have been considerably associated with appearance disorder (Thompson et al., 2004). An example of a question in SATAQ-3 is "I compare my appearance to the appearance of TV and movie stars." Participants responded to each question using a five-point scale (5 = definitely agree, 4 = mostly agree, 3 = neither agree nor disagree, 2 = mostly agree, 1 = definitely disagree). Higher scores on the SATAQ-3 indicate that there are higher levels of involvement in social-cultural attitudes toward appearance.

The fourth scale was SAAS by Hart et al. (2008). SAAS is a distinctive predictor and a psychometrically valid assessment of SAA regarding one's overall appearance (Hart et al., 2008). The SAAS was created to assess anxiety about being undesirably assessed by others based on one's overall appearance, including body shape. SAAS assesses feelings of unattractiveness, an obsession with being overweight, and the belief that one's looks are fundamentally imperfect and socially intolerable. The SAAS has an established high test-retest reliability and internal consistency. An example of a question in SAAS is "I am frequently afraid I would not meet others' standards of how I should look." Participants responded to each question using a five-point scale (5 = extremely, 4 = very, 3 = moderately, 2 = slightly, 1 = not at all). Higher scores on the SAAS indicate higher levels of SAA.

The original psychometric work designated SAAS as a single-factor scale and SAAS exhibited excellent internal consistency, test-retest reliability, and convergent validity (Hart et al., 2008). Levinson and Rodebaugh (2011) offered supplemental support for the use of the SAAS as a valid measure of SAA. In Hart et al. (2008), SAAS scores were positively related to depression as measured by BDI. Nevertheless, in the Levinson and Rodebaugh (2011) study, SAAS scores were not significantly correlated with BMI.

The fifth instrument was the BDI. The BDI is used to evaluate cognitive indicators of depression. BDI is a widely used measure of depression with an internal consistency of $\alpha = .88$ for nonclinical populations (Beck, Steer, & Garbin, 1988). Scores on this self-reported, 21-item scale range from 0 to

Table 1. Demographic and descriptive information for sample

	Total sample	At-risk	Not at-risk
Total N	342	65	277
Race			
Caucasian	276	59 (21%)	217 (79%)
African-American	46	4 (9%)	42 (91%)
Hispanic	6	0 (0%)	6 (100%)
Asian	3	0 (0%)	3 (100%)
Native American	1	0 (0%)	1 (100%)
Other	11	3 (27%)	8 (73%)
Age			
18–22 years	236	51 (12%)	185 (78%)
23–30 years	65	7 (11%)	58 (89%)
31–40 years	17	2 (12%)	15 (88%)
41–50 years	6	0 (0%)	6 (100%)
50 and over	11	2 (18%)	9 (82%)
Body satisfaction *	102	11 (11%)	91 (89%)
Body dissatisfaction *	240	54 (22%)	186 (78%)

*Body satisfaction and dissatisfaction were determined by the Stunkard Body Figural Scale.

63, with a score of 10 used to discriminate between asymptomatic and symptomatic individuals. Each item on the BDI scale is framed within a range of 0–3: 0 = I do not feel sad; 1 = I feel sad; 2 = I am sad all the time and I can't snap out of it; 3 = I am so sad or unhappy that I can't stand it. Participants are directed to select only the most representative response.

Finally, logistic regression was conducted to examine which of the appearance issues significantly contributed to the model fit and therefore had greatest prediction of disordered eating behavior.

The total sample included 370 undergraduate women from a mid-sized Midwestern State University in the US. After removing data from participants who did not complete all scales, the final sample included 342 female college students between the ages of 18–66 (M = 22.96; SD = 8.96). Participants were drawn from all levels of preparation, with attempts made to equally sample freshman (27.6% of sample), sophomore (27.6%), junior (26.8%), and senior (16.5%) students. A complete description of participant characteristics is available in Table 1.

3. Results

Prior to running analyses for the purpose of hypothesis testing, internal consistency analyses were conducted on all scales used. All measures had strong or excellent internal consistency (see Table 2 for Cronbach's alpha for all scales); further, examination of the "alpha if item deleted" analyses of all scales reveals that no items are serving as a drag on reliability. Therefore, the results of all subsequent inferential analyses can be considered robust.

Table 2. Internal consistency of scales

Scale	Number of items	Cronbach's alpha
EAT-26	26	.87
SATAQ	30	.95
SAAS	16	.97
BDI	21	.92

3.1. Body dissatisfaction and BMI

A large number of the participants, 68.6% ($N = 254$), reported an ideal body shape smaller than their current body shape, and of these 21.3% ($N = 54$) reported EAT-26 scores that would characterize them as at-risk for acquiring an eating disorder (i.e. scores of 20 or higher). Furthermore, an independent sample *t*-test revealed that women with body dissatisfaction (as measured by having a smaller ideal body shape than current body shape) were significantly more likely to be at-risk for disordered eating behavior than women with body satisfaction, t (116) = −2.91, $p = .004$, $d = .37$. According to Cohen (1992), this effect size is approaching moderate, indicating that the differences in appearance between women at-risk and those not at-risk for developing an eating disorder are meaningful. Levene's test reported unequal variances ($F = 40.97$, $p < .001$), so degrees of freedom were adjusted from 342 to 116.

These results support H1: college females at risk of acquiring an eating disorder (EAT-26 score ≥ 20) had a significantly larger difference between their ideal body shape and their current body shape, as measured by the SBFS, compared to the students who are at less risk of acquiring an eating disorder (EAT-26 score < 20).

Independent sample *t*-test results indicated no significant difference in the BMI of college females at-risk of acquiring an eating disorder and those not at-risk of acquiring an eating disorder, t (335) = −0.69, $p = .49$, ns. The average BMI of women not at-risk was 24.94 (SD = 7.28), while the average BMI of women at-risk was 25.64 (SD = 7.63). These results support H2: the mean BMI of college females at risk of acquiring an eating disorder (EAT-26 score ≥ 20) did not differ significantly from the mean BMI of college female students at less risk of acquiring an eating disorder (EAT-26 score < 20).

3.2. Sociocultural attitudes toward appearance

To explore the differences between those at-risk and those not at-risk for acquiring an eating disorder on their sociocultural attitudes toward appearance, an independent sample *t*-test was conducted for the SATAQ Total score, as well as for each of the four subscale scores (Internalization-General, Internalization-Athlete, Pressure, and Information). For the SATAQ Total, women at-risk for acquiring an eating disorder had significantly higher scores than women not at-risk, t (316) = −6.06, $p < .001$, $d = .84$. This effect size is large, indicating a significant magnitude of difference between the groups. Examination of the subscale scores shows that women at-risk for acquiring an eating disorder scored significantly higher on all subscales of the SATAQ than women not at-risk for acquiring an eating disorder. These results support H3: college females at risk of acquiring an eating disorder (EAT-26 score ≥ 20) scored significantly higher on the Sociocultural Attitudes Toward Appearance Questionnaire compared to college female students at less risk of acquiring an eating disorder (EAT-26 score < 20).

3.3. SAA and depression

To examine SAA between the women at-risk and not at-risk for acquiring an eating disorder, an independent sample *t*-test was conducted. The results of this test indicate that women at-risk for acquiring an eating disorder have significantly higher SAA than women not at-risk, t (81) = −5.30, $p < .001$, $d = .79$. Again, this effect size is large, indicating a substantial difference between the two groups. Levene's test reported unequal variances ($F = 18.30$, $p < .001$), so degrees of freedom were adjusted from 342 to 81. These results support H4: college females at risk of acquiring an eating disorder (EAT-26 score ≥ 20) had a significantly higher SAA compared to college female students at less risk of acquiring an eating disorder (EAT-26 < 20).

Women at-risk for acquiring an eating disorder reported significantly higher levels of depression than women not at-risk, t (78) = −3.87, $p < .001$, $d = .59$. Those at-risk had a mean BDI score of 13.3 (SD = 10.77), while women not at-risk for developing an eating disorder had a mean score on the BDI of 7.59 (SD = 8.31). The magnitude of the difference between the two groups is moderate (Cohen, 1992), indicating noticeable differences in depression levels between the two groups. Levene's test

Table 3. Descriptive and inferential statistics for participants at-risk and participants not at-risk for disordered eating

		M	SD	*t*-value	*p*-value	Cohen's *d*
EAT-26 total	At-risk	29.15	9.65			
	Not at-risk	7.33	4.68			
Body dissatisfaction (current body size-ideal body size)	At-risk	1.45	1.42	−2.91	.004	.37
	Not at-risk	0.87	1.22			
BMI	At-risk	25.64	7.63	−0.69	0.49	NA
	Not at-risk	24.94	7.28			
SATAQ total	At-risk	103.21	22.25	−6.06	<.001	.84
	Not at-risk	83.63	24.5			
SATAQ internalizing subscale-general	At-risk	30.55	9.18	−5.06	<.001	.69
	Not at-risk	24.58	8.15			
SATAQ internalizing subscale-athlete	At-risk	18.43	5.16	−5.19	<.001	.70
	Not at-risk	14.9	4.87			
SATAQ pressure subscale	At-risk	25.88	6.57	−7.15	<.001	1.00
	Not at-risk	19.18	6.78			
SATAQ information subscale	At-risk	27.77	8.71	−2.82	.005	.37
	Not at-risk	24.72	7.56			
SAAS	At-risk	46.69	20.06	−5.30	<.001	.79
	Not at-risk	32.68	14.89			
BDI	At-risk	13.33	10.77	−3.87	<.001	.59
	Not at-risk	7.59	8.31			

again reported unequal variance ($F = 8.85$, $p = .003$), so degrees of freedom were adjusted from 311 to 78. These results support H5: college females at risk of acquiring an eating disorder (EAT-26 score ≥ 20) had a significantly higher depression compared to college female students at less risk of acquiring an eating disorder (EAT-26 < 20).

See Table 3 for all descriptive and inferential statistical information.

4.4. The culminating inquiry

Prior to analyzing the culminating inquiry, correlations between all study variables were analyzed. As seen in Table 4, EAT-26 scores were significantly correlated with all study variables except participants' BMI. In fact, most study variables were significantly and moderately correlated with one another.

Table 4. Correlation analyses among all variables

	1	2	3	4	5	6
1. EAT-26	1	.017	.458**	.375**	.346**	.321**
2. BMI	–	1	.458**	−.069	.176**	.093*
3. Body dissatisfaction	–	–	1	.200**	.316**	.206**
4. SATAQ	–	–	–	1	.485**	.351**
5. SAAS	–	–	–	–	1	.565**
6. BDI	–	–	–	–	–	1

*Level of Significant at $p < .05$.

**Level of Significant at $p < .01$.

Table 5. Logistic regression analysis

Predictor	β	SE β	Wald's χ^2	df	p	Odds ratio
Constant	−5.37	.966	30.937	1	<.001	.005
Model 1						
Body dissatisfaction	.478	.466	1.051	1	.305	1.613
BMI	−.013	.024	.319	1	.572	.987
Sociocultural attitudes toward appearance	.028	.009	10.088	1	.001	1.029
Social appearance anxiety	.027	.012	5.122	1	.024	1.028
Depression	.014	.019	.594	1	.441	1.015

Among the four appearance issues and depression considered in this study, which was the greatest predictor of disordered eating behavior? To examine the quality of these factors as predictors of disordered eating behavior in female college students, a logistic regression was completed. The dichotomized risk of disordered eating behavior as measured by EAT-26 scores and categorized as at-risk or not at-risk according to said scores was the outcome, and body dissatisfaction, BMI, scores on the SATAQ, scores on the SAAS, and scores on the BDI were predictor variables. Results of this regression analysis indicate that the combination of these variables is a strong predictor of disordered eating behavior. The Hosmer and Lemeshow goodness-of-fit test indicates a non-significant statistic (χ^2 (8) = 10.56, p = .226), suggesting that the model estimates fit the data well. Furthermore, the classification table indicates that this model would correctly predict a female's risk for disordered eating behavior 83.6% of the time. Additional examination of the logistic regression revealed that two of the five predictors are significantly contributing to this model fit. Namely, participants' scores on the SATAQ; the measure of sociocultural attitudes toward appearance, and scores on the SAAS; the measure of SAA were significant predictors of female college students' risk for disordered eating behavior. The other predictors did not significantly add to the model. See Table 5 for full logistic regression statistics.

4. Discussion

This study examined depression and four appearance issues and how they relate to disordered eating among female college students. The results from this study gave evidence that college females at risk of disordered eating behavior differed significantly from those less at risk in body dissatisfaction, social-cultural attitudes, SAA, and depression, but not in BMI. About 70% of participants reported an ideal body shape smaller than their current body shape, indicating that most participants had some level of body dissatisfaction. More precisely, the present study found that for college females at risk of acquiring an eating disorder, the difference between current body shape and ideal body shape was significantly larger than for those less at risk of acquiring an eating disorder. However, Ferreira and colleagues (2013) cautiously noted that the dissatisfaction with one's current weight did not lead to disordered eating behavior, but that it is the label of an inferior social status centered entirely on bodily appearance that may be linked with disordered eating behavior.

This study found that the BMI of college females at risk of acquiring an eating disorder does not differ significantly from the BMI of college female students less at risk of acquiring an eating disorder. This finding differed from the studies by Gardner et al. (2012) and Xu et al. (2010), which indicated that BMI was a significant predictor of body dissatisfaction, with a higher BMI projecting greater body dissatisfaction. There is the possibility that the self-report for the BMI in the current study may account for the failure to find positive BMI findings reported in other studies. Rather, the current study concurred with studies (Hill et al., 2013; Robinson et al., 2013) which contended that, regardless of a woman's BMI, the tendency to diet was the same for all women. The current study findings also support the normative discontent theory, which claims that it is common for women to be discontent about their weight despite their BMI (Cash & Henry, 1995). Our study reveals that while discontentment (i.e. body dissatisfaction) is "normative" and an important hazard for eating disorder risk, it alone does not predict disordered eating behavior. Our results indicate that contentment (i.e. body satisfaction) is also common as approximately one-third of our participants report satisfaction with their body. However, though the normative discontent theory views body dissatisfaction as prominent in women, it does not prohibit the use of other important variables such as weight, body dissatisfaction, and dieting behaviors in seeking to understand individuals who are at risk.

The present study found that college females at risk of acquiring an eating disorder scored significantly higher in the sociocultural attitudes toward appearance compared to college females less at risk of acquiring an eating disorder. Notably, this finding concurs with the White and Halliwell (2010) study that claims that there is extensive knowledge that social-cultural pressures and appearance issues can lead to disordered eating behavior. Similarly, several studies have endorsed that thin internalization due to sociocultural influence significantly correlated with body dissatisfaction, drive for thinness, and restrained eating (Ahern et al., 2008; Griffiths et al., 2000; Swami et al., 2011; Thompson et al., 2004). The current study findings support the social comparison theory that people tend to compare themselves with others, especially those they consider superior (upward comparison) (Homan et al., 2012). On the contrary, Mask and Blanchard (2011) noted some females displayed an autonomous perception, which aided as a defensive factor from the media examples of thinness. Additionally, Homan et al. (2012) argued that not all media had negative impact on body dissatisfaction; for instance, exposure to sports media is linked with more positive feelings about the body.

The current study results indicate that college females at risk of acquiring an eating disorder had significantly higher SAA compared to college female students less at risk of acquiring an eating disorder. This finding concurs with studies by Levinson and Rodebaugh (2012) and Ostrovsky et al. (2013), which claimed that SAA is a significant predictor of appearance dissatisfaction, disordered eating behavior, and concerns about shape and weight.

The present study also found that college females at risk of acquiring an eating disorder had significantly higher depression compared to college female students less at risk of acquiring an eating disorder. Congruently, Liechty and Lee (2013) found that depression was a significant predictor of disordered eating behavior. Similarly, Robinson et al. (2013) claimed that individuals participated in restrained and disordered eating behavior in an attempt to alleviate unregulated distress. The current study findings are comparable with Fink et al. (2013) who found common associations between depression, anxiety sensitivity, and disordered eating behavior symptoms.

Finally, logistic regression revealed that two of the five factors investigated, namely, scores on the SATAQ: the measure of sociocultural attitudes toward appearance, and scores on the SAAS: the measure of appearance anxiety, were significant predictors of female college students' risk for disordered eating behavior. The other predictors did not significantly add to the model, suggesting that the combination of adherence to sociocultural attitudes and having high appearance anxiety best predicts female college students' disordered eating behavior. This finding regarding the influence of sociocultural attitudes supplements previous evidence that sociocultural pressure can predispose to disordered eating behavior (Clay et al., 2005; Thompson et al., 2004; Tiggermann et al., 2005; White & Halliwell, 2010). The role of SAA in predicting risk for disordered eating behavior is consistent with Levinson and Rodebaugh (2012) who found that social anxiety, which is found to be a predictor of SAA (Hart et al., 2008; Levinson & Rodebaugh, 2011), and eating disorders tended to coexist. This study adds unique information in that our sample was not singularly affected by sociocultural attitudes or SAA, but by the combination of the two constructs, and further refines the link between SAA and eating disorders by showing more precisely that SAA was an important predictor.

4.1. Practical implications

This study provides a basis for practical suggestions that practitioners can employ to identify appearance apprehensions that relate to disordered eating among college females. BMI was not shown to differ significantly between those at risk for disordered eating behavior and those less at risk. Therefore, it is important to educate instructors, advisors, health professionals, and others who interact with college females that women with a healthy body weight can nevertheless be at risk for the development of an eating disorder.

Since sociocultural attitudes toward appearance and SAA were shown to be the two best predictors of disordered eating behavior risk, efforts that focus on those two appearance issues may be the most effective in prevention. The effort to change sociocultural attitudes as transmitted by the media is a broad approach to prevention, whereas the connection between SAA and eating disorders has implications for interventions with individuals.

In an ideal world, the media could promote a positive appearance by using models that more accurately represent the assortment of shapes and sizes among females in society (Diedrichs & Lee, 2010). There should be campaigns, slogans, and deliberate efforts in society to ascribe value to women on attributes other than physical appearance, such as character. In Western cultures, girls' self-images decline considerably during mid-adolescence, hence the need to start early education interventions that help girls critique rather than internalize unrealistic media images (Clay et al., 2005) and form their own more flexible physical goals. It is important to encourage individuals to be autonomous in their absorption of negative social-cultural attributes portrayed in the media as recommended by Mask and Blanchard (2011). There should be an emphasis that the media images are often unrealistic and unattainable. Practitioners can help clients reduce appearance-related thoughts and conversations which may cause SAA (Bardone-Cone et al., 2013).

4.2. Limitations

The current study's sample is composed of mostly white females and this limits its generalizability. This limitation leads to the suggestion that future studies should preferably look at other specific racial groups or compare various racial groups. Secondly, self-report was relied upon to appraise the study variables; hence, some of the responses could have been biased. Future studies could employ other techniques (e.g. observation, or experimental techniques) to more fully understand the interplay of these constructs to disordered eating behavior. Additionally, since the BMI in the current study was self-reported, this could have led to the failure to find a relationship between BMI and eating disorder risk.

5. Conclusion

This study makes a valuable contribution in understanding how various appearance apprehensions and depression may influence disordered eating behavior among college females. The findings of this study can be beneficial for deterrence of disordered eating among female college students so that prevention and timely intervention can be possible before the disordered eating develops into an eating disorder.

Funding

The authors received no direct funding for this research.

Competing Interests

The authors declare no competing interest.

Author details

Priscilla N. Gitimu[1]
E-mail: pngitimu@ysu.edu
ORCID ID: http://orcid.org/0000-0002-2044-3613
Molly M. Jameson[2]
E-mail: Molly.Jameson@unco.edu
Tacibaht Turel[1]
E-mail: tturel@my.ysu.edu
Rachel Pohle-Krauza[1]
E-mail: rjpohlekrauza@ysu.edu
Jeanine Mincher[1]
E-mail: jlmincher@ysu.edu
Zara Rowlands[1]
E-mail: zcshah@ysu.edu
Janice Elias[1]
E-mail: jaelais@ysu.edu
[1] Human Ecology Department, Youngstown State University (YSU), One University Plaza, Youngstown, OH 44555, USA.
[2] School of Psychological Sciences, University of Northern Colorado, Greeley, CO 80639, USA.

References

Ahern, A. L., Bennett, K. M., & Hetherington, M. M. (2008). Internalization of the ultra-thin ideal: Positive implicit associations with underweight fashion models are associated with drive for thinness in young women. *Eating Disorders, 16*, 294–307. doi:10.1080/10640260802115852

Ahmadi, S., Moloodi, R., Zarbaksh, M., & Ghaderi, A. (2014). Psychometric properties of the eating attitude test-26 for female Iranian students. *Eating & Weight Disorders, 19*, 183–189. doi:10.1007/s40519-014-0106-7

American Psychiatric Association. (2013). *Diagnostic and statistical manual of mental disorders: DSM-5*. Washington, DC: Author.

Andreea-Elena, M. (2015). The risk of eating disorders in adolescence and its association with the impact of the sociocultural attitudes towards appearance (International Conference Psi World 2014, 5th ed.). *Procedia-Social and Behavioral Sciences, 187*, 153–157. doi:10.1016/j.sbspro.2015.03.029

Anstine, D., & Grinenko, D. (2000). Rapid screening for disordered eating in college-aged females in the primary care setting. *Journal of Adolescent Health, 26*, 338–342. doi:10.1016/S1054-139X(99)00120-2

Bardone-Cone, A., Brownstone, L., Higgins, M., Fitzsimmons-Craft, E., & Harney, M. (2013). Anxiety, appearance contingent self-worth, and appearance conversations with friends in relation to disordered eating: Examining moderator models. *Cognitive Therapy & Research, 37*, 953–963. doi:10.1007/s10608-013-9520-9

Beck, A. T., Steer, R. A., & Garbin, M. G. (1988). Psychometric properties of the beck depression inventory: Twenty-five years of evaluation. *Clinical Psychology Review, 8*, 77–100. doi:10.1016/0272-7358(88)90050-5

Calogero, R. M., Davis, W. N., & Thompson, J. K. (2004). The sociocultural attitudes toward appearance questionnaire (SATAQ-3): Reliability and normative comparisons of eating disordered patients. *Body Image, 1*, 193–198. doi:10.1016/j.bodyim.2004.01.004

Cash, T. F., & Henry, P. E. (1995). Women's body images: The results of a national survey in the U.S.A. *Sex Roles, 33*, 19–28. doi:10.1007/bf01547933

Cash, T., Wood, K., Phelps, K., & Boyd, K. (1991). New assessments of weight-related body image derived from extant instruments. *Perceptual and Motor Skill, 73* 253–241. doi:10.2466/pms.1991.73.1.235

Chrisler, J., Fung, K., Lopez, A., & Gorman, J. (2013). Suffering by comparison: Twitter users' reactions to the Victoria's Secret Fashion Show. *Body Image, 10*, 648–652. doi:10.1016/j.bodyim.2013.05.001

Clay, D., Vignoles, V. L., & Dittmar, H. (2005). Body image and self-esteem among adolescent girls: Testing the influence of sociocultural factors. *Journal of Research on Adolescence, 15*, 451–477. doi:10.1111/j.1532-7795.2005.00107.x

Cohen, J. (1992). A power primer. *Psychological Bulletin, 112*, 155–159. doi:10.1037/0033-2909.112.1.155

Diedrichs, P., & Lee, C. (2010). GI Joe or average Joe? The impact of average-size and muscular male fashion models on men's and women's body image and advertisement effectiveness. *Body Image, 7*, 218–226. doi:10.1016/j.bodyim.2010.03.004

Erol, A., Toprak, G., & Yazici, F. (2006). Psychological and physical correlates of disordered eating in male and female Turkish college students. *Psychiatry and Clinical Neurosciences, 60*, 551–557. doi:10.1111/j.1440-1819.2006.01557.x

Fairweather-Schmidt, A. K., Lee, C., & Wade, T. D. (2015). A longitudinal study of mid age women with indicators of disordered eating. *Developmental Psychology, 51*, 722–729. doi:10.1037/dev0000011

Ferreira, C., Pinto-Gouveia, J., & Duarte, C. (2013). Physical appearance as a measure of social ranking: The role of a new scale to understand the relationship between weight and dieting. *Clinical Psychology & Psychotherapy, 20*, 55–66. doi:10.1002/cpp.769

Festinger, L. (1954). A theory of social comparison processes. *Human Relations, 7*, 117. doi:10.1177/001872675400700202

Fink, E., Bodell, L., Smith, A., & Joiner, T. (2013). The joint influence of disordered eating and anxiety sensitivity on the acquired capability for suicide. *Cognitive Therapy & Research, 37*, 934–940. doi:10.1007/s10608-012-9502-3

Fitzsimmons-Craft, E. E., Ciao, A. C., & Accurso, E. C. (2016). A naturalistic examination of social comparisons and disordered eating thoughts, urges, and behaviors in college women. *International Journal of Eating Disorders, 49*, 143–152, 10 p. doi:10.1002/eat.22486

Gardner, R. M., & Brown, D. L. (2010). Review: Body image assessment: A review of figural drawing scales. *Personality and Individual Differences, 48*, 107–111. doi:10.1016/j.paid.2009.08.017

Gardner, R., Brown, D., & Boice, R. (2012). Using amazon's mechanical turk website to measure accuracy of body size estimation and body dissatisfaction. *Body Image, 9*, 532–534. doi:10.1016/j.bodyim.2012.06.006

Garner, D. M., Olmsted, M. P., Bohr, Y., & Garfinkle, P. E. (1982). The eating attitude test: Psychometric features and clinical correlates. *Psychological Medicine, 12*, 871–878. doi:10.1017/s0033291700049163

Griffiths, R. A., Mallia-Blanco, R., Boesenberg, E., Ellis, C., Fischer, K., Taylor, M., & Wyndham, J. (2000). Restrained eating and sociocultural attitudes to appearance and general dissatisfaction. *European Eating Disorders Review, 8*, 394–402. doi:10.1002/1099-0968(200010)8:5<394:AID-ERV358>3.0.CO;2-B

Hart, T. A., Flora, D. B., Palyo, S. A., Fresco, D. M., Holle, C., & Heimberg, R. G. (2008). Development and examination of the social appearance anxiety scale. *Assessment, 12*, 48–59. doi:10.1177/1073191107306673

Heinberg, L. J. (2004). Theories of body image disturbance: Perceptual, developmental, and sociocultural factors. In J. K. Thompson (Ed.), *Body image, eating disorders, and obesity: An integrative guide for assessment and treatment* (pp. 27–47). Washington, DC: American Psychological Association.

Higgins, E. T. (1987). Self-discrepancy: A theory relating self and affect. *Psychological Review, 94*, 319–340. doi:10.1037/0033-295x.94.3.319

Hill, M. L., Masuda, A., & Latzman, R. D. (2013). Body image flexibility as a protective factor against disordered eating behavior for women with lower body mass index. *Eating Behaviors, 14*, 336–341. doi:10.1016/j.eatbeh.2013.06.0

Homan, K., McHugh, E., Wells, D., Watson, C., & King, C. (2012). The effect of viewing ultra-fit images on college women's body dissatisfaction. *Body Image, 9*, 50–56. doi:10.1016/j.bodyim.2011.07.006

Jones, J. M., Bennett, S., Olmsted, M. P., Lawson, M. L., & Rodin, G. (2001). Disordered eating attitudes and behaviours in teenaged girls: A school-based study. *Canadian Medical Association Journal, 165*, 547–522.

Juarasico, A., Perone, J., & Timko, C. (2011). Moderators of the relationship between body image and dissatisfaction and disordered eating. *Eating Disorders, 19*, 346–354. doi:10.1080/10640266.2011.584811

Jung-Hee, J., Lennon, S. J., & Rudd, N. A. (2001). Self-schema or self-discrepancy? Which best explains body image? *Clothing and Textiles Research Journal, 19*, 171–184. doi:10.1177/0887302X0101900403

Kaplan, S. (2006). *Intra-personal correlates of disordered eating patterns in college students* (Thesis). Bowling Green State University, Bowling Green, OH.

Lanfranchi, M., Maïano, C., Morin, A., & Therme, P. (2015). Social physique anxiety and disturbed eating attitudes and behaviors in adolescents: Moderating effects of sport, sport-related characteristics, and gender. *International Journal of Behavioral Medicine, 22*, 149–160, 12 p. doi:10.1007/s12529-014-9406-6

Levinson, C. A., & Rodebaugh, T. L. (2011). Validation of the social appearance anxiety scale: Factor, convergent, and divergent validity. *Assessment, 18*, 350. doi:10.1177/1073191111404808

Levinson, C., & Rodebaugh, T. (2012). Social anxiety and eating disorder comorbidity: The role of negative social evaluation fears. *Eating Behaviors, 13*, 27–35. doi:10.1016/j.eatbeh.2011.11.006.

Liechty, J. M., & Lee, M. (2013). Longitudinal predictors of dieting and disordered eating among young adults in the U.S. *International Journal of Eating Disorders, 46*, 790–800. doi:10.1002/eat.22174

MacNeill, L. P., & Best, L. A. (2015). Perceived current and ideal body size in female undergraduates. *Eating Behaviors, 18*, 71–75. doi:10.1016/j.eatbeh.2015.03.004

Martin Ginis, K., Murru, E., Conlin, C., & Strong, H. (2011). Construct validation of a state version of the social physique anxiety Scale among young women. *Body Image, 8*, 52–57. doi:10.1016/j.bodyim.2010.10.001

Mask, L., & Blanchard, C. (2011). The effects of "thin ideal" media on women's body image concerns and eating-related intentions: The beneficial role of an autonomous regulation of eating behaviors. *Body Image, 8*, 357–365. doi:10.1016/j.bodyim.2011.06.003

Myers, T. A., Ridolfi, D. R., Crowther, J. H., & Ciesla, J. A. (2012). The impact of appearance-focused social comparisons on body image disturbance in the naturalistic environment: The roles of thin-ideal internalization and feminist beliefs. *Body Image, 9*, 342–351. doi:10.1016/j.bodyim.2012.03.005

Ostrovsky, N., Swencionis, C., Wylie-Rosett, J., & Isasi, C. R. (2013). Social anxiety and disordered overeating: An association among overweight and obese individuals. *Eating Behaviors, 14*, 145–148. doi:10.1016/j.eatbeh.2013.01.009

Owen, R., & Spencer, R. (2013). Body ideals in women after viewing images of typical and healthy weight models. *Body Image, 10*, 489–494. doi:10.1016/j.bodyim.2013.04.005

Puccio F., Fuller-Tyszkiewicz, M., Ong, D., & Krug, I. (2016). A systematic review and meta-analysis on the longitudinal relationship between eating pathology and depression. *International Journal of Eating Disorders* [Epub ahead of print]. doi:10.1002/eat.22506

Robinson, L. A., Kosmerly, S., Mansfield-Green, S., & Lafrance, G. (2013). Disordered eating behaviours in an undergraduate sample: Associations among gender, body mass index, and difficulties in emotion regulation. *Canadian Journal of Behavioral Science/Revue Canadienne Des Sciences Du Comportement, 46*, 320–326. doi:10.1037/a0031123

Rodgers, R. F., Melioli, T., Laconi, S., Bui, E., & Chabrol, H. (2013). Internet addiction symptoms, disordered eating, and body image avoidance. *Cyberpsychology, Behavior & Social Networking, 16*, 56–60. doi:10.1089/cyber.2012.1570

Rodin, J., Silberstein, L. R., & Striegel-Moore, R. H. (1984). Women and weight: A normative discontent. In T. B. Sonderegger (Ed.), *Nebraska symposium on motivation: Psychology and gender*. (pp. 267–307). Lincoln, NE: University of Nebraska Press.

Rosser, B., Moss, T., & Rumsey, N. (2010). Attentional and interpretative biases in appearance concern: An investigation of biases in appearance-related information processing. *Body Image, 7*, 251–254. doi:10.1016/j.bodyim.2010.02.007

Schooler, D., & Trinh, S. (2011). Longitudinal associations between television viewing patterns and adolescent body satisfaction. *Body Image, 8*, 34–42. doi:10.1016/j.bodyim.2010.09.001

Stampler, L. (2015). Here's what happens when women decide to call themselves beautiful. *Time.Com*. Retrieved from Vocational and Career Collection.

Stunkard, A. J., Sorensen, T., & Schulsinger, F. (1983). Use of the Danish adoption register for the study of obesity and thinness. In S. Kety (Ed.), *The genetics of neurological and psychiatric disorders* (pp. 115–120). New York, NY: Raven Press.

Swami, V., Taylor, R., & Carvalho, C. (2011). Body dissatisfaction assessed by the photographic figure rating scale is associated with sociocultural, personality, and media influences. *Scandinavian Journal of Psychology, 52*, 57–63. doi:10.1111/j.1467-9450.2010.00836.x

Tantleff-Dunn, S., Barnes, R. D., & Larose, J. G. (2011). It's not just a "woman thing:" The current state of normative discontent. *Eating Disorders, 19*, 392–402. doi:10.1080/10640266.2011.609088

Thompson, S. R. (2016). Ethics in sports medicine. *Clinics In Sports Medicine, 35*, 840–844. doi:10.1016/S0278-5919(15)00141-6

Thompson, J. K., van den Berg, P., Roehrig, M., Guarda, A. S., & Heinberg, L. J. (2004). The sociocultural attitudes towards appearance scale-3 (SATAQ-3): Development and validation. *International Journal of Eating Disorders, 35*, 293–304. doi:10.1002/eat.10257

Tiggermann, M., Verri, A., & Scaravaggi, S. (2005). Body dissatisfaction, disordered eating, fashion magazines, and clothes: A cross-cultural comparison between Australian and Italian young women. *International Journal of Psychology, 40*, 293–302. doi:10.1080/00207590444000311

Tod, D., Edwards, C., & Hall, G. (2013). Drive for leanness and health-related behavior within a social/cultural perspective. *Body Image, 10*, 640–643. doi:10.1016/j.bodyim.2013.05.002

Tuckman, B. W. (1999). *Conducting educational research* (5th ed.). Fort Worth, TX: Harcourt Brace College Publishers.

Vartanian, L., & Dey, S. (2013). Self-concept clarity, thin-ideal internalization, and appearance-related social comparison as predictors of body dissatisfaction. *Body Image, 10*, 495–500. doi:10.1016/j.bodyim.2013.05.004

Warren, C., Rakhkovskaya, L., & Gleaves, D. (2013). Score reliability and factor similarity of the sociocultural attitudes towards appearance questionnaire-3 (SATAQ-3) among four ethnic groups. *Journal of Eating Disorders, 1*(14), 1–8. doi:10.1186/2050-2974-1-14

Wendell, J., Masuda, A., & Le, J. (2012). The role of body image flexibility in the relationship between disordered eating cognitions and disordered eating symptoms among non-clinical college students. *Eating Behaviors, 13*, 240–245. doi:10.1016/j.eatbeh.2012.03.006

White, J., & Halliwell, E. (2010). Examination of a sociocultural model of excessive exercise among male and female adolescents. *Body Image, 7*, 227–233. doi:10.1016/j.bodyim.2010.02.002

White, E. K., & Warren, C. S. (2014). The influence of social anxiety on the body checking behaviors of female college students. *Body Image, 11*, 458–463. doi:10.1016/j.bodyim.2014.07.008

Wood-Barcalow, N., Tylka, T., & Augustus-Horvath, C. (2010). But i like my body: Positive body image characteristics and a holistic model for young-adult women. *Body Image, 7*, 106–116. doi:10.1016/j.bodyim.2010.01.001

Xu, X., Mellor, D., Kiehne, M., Ricciardelli, L., McCabe, M., & Xu, Y. (2010). Body dissatisfaction, engagement in body change behaviors and sociocultural influences on body image among Chinese adolescents. *Body Image, 7*, 156–164. doi:10.1016/j.bodyim.2009.11.003

12

An exploration of the relationships between gratitude, life satisfaction, and importance of helping others among a representative sample of the adult population of Mexico

Rogelio Puente-Díaz[1]* and Gustavo Meixueiro[1]

*Corresponding author: Rogelio Puente-Díaz, Department of Business Economics, Universidad Anáhuac México Norte, Av. Lomas de Anáhuac 46, Col. Lomas de Anáhuac, Huixquilucan, Estado de México C.P. 52786, Mexico
E-mail: rogelio.puente@anahuac.mx
Reviewing editor: Shane Bench, Washington State University, USA

Abstract: We used a representative sample of the adult population of Mexico to examine the influence of gratitude on life satisfaction and importance given to helping others. Questionnaires were administered by a trained interviewer in a face-to-face format outside the participants' home. Path analysis, treating the variables as observed, was used to test our hypotheses. Results showed that gratitude had a positive relationship with life satisfaction while controlling for financial satisfaction. Similarly, gratitude was positively related to importance given to helping others. For the most part, the positive influence of gratitude on life satisfaction and importance given to helping other remained significant at different income levels. The implications of the results were discussed.

Subjects: Applied Social Psychology; Positive Psychology; Social Psychology

Keywords: gratitude; life satisfaction; helping others; representative samples; income levels

1. Introduction

Adam Smith, in his theory of moral sentiments (Smith, 1976/1790), was one the first scholars to take a serious look at the emotion of gratitude. Psychology has recently shown more enthusiasm for understanding the positive aspects of life (Fredrickson, 2013), including an examination of gratitude and its consequences. Across different investigations, gratitude has been related to higher levels of well-being (Wood, Froh, & Geraghty, 2010) and prosocial behavior (McCullough, Kimeldorf, & Cohen, 2008). However, one of the shortcomings of these empirical investigations is that most of them have used samples of convenience: college students (see Chan, 2013; Szcześniak & Soares, 2011 for some exceptions). The excessive use of samples of college students has been criticized recently (Henrich, Heine, & Norenzayan, 2010), suggesting the need to conduct research with more diverse samples.

ABOUT THE AUTHOR

Rogelio Puente-Díaz is the José Cuervo professor of marketing at Universidad Anahuac México Norte. Rogelio conducts research on creativity, context effects, and gratitude. Results from this investigation are part of research program that seeks to examine the positive consequences of gratitude and its implications for life satisfaction, the generation of novel and useful ideas, and prosocial behavior.

PUBLIC INTEREST STATEMENT

Public opinion research has recently paid closer attention to the predictors of life satisfaction since results from empirical investigations are often used to make policy decisions by government officials. Yet, this research often neglects conducting investigations with participants from developing countries or participants from low-income levels. Our investigation tries to address these limitations.

Hence, the purpose of the present investigation is twofold. First, we want to examine the influence of gratitude on life satisfaction and importance given to helping others among a robust, representative sample of the adult population of Mexico. Second, we want to examine if the influence of gratitude on life satisfaction and importance given to helping others is moderated by income level. We first discuss the theoretical work and empirical findings on gratitude and its positive consequences and then propose why it is important to establish the robustness of these findings among more diverse segments of the population.

2. Gratitude

Gratitude is conceptualized as an emotion and a life orientation in which individuals appreciate and notice positive aspects in their lives (Wood et al., 2010). Gratitude emerges when one recognizes another agent as a source of one's positive aspects in life. The broaden-and-build theory of positive emotions suggests that positive emotions such as gratitude broaden thought repertories and build personal resources (Fredrickson, 2013). When one is grateful, then, there is a tendency to broaden one's mindset and acknowledge, among other aspects, the role of important others in life. Similarly, gratitude helps build durable resources for well-being such as intrinsic motivation and purposefulness (Froh & Bono, 2008).

Since gratitude is an orientation toward appreciating and noticing the positive aspects of life, it has been hypothesized to be related to variables reflecting this positive outlook such well-being and its components: life satisfaction and positive and negative affect (Sheldon & Kashdan, 2011; Wood et al., 2010). A recent review of the relationship between well-being and gratitude supports this conclusion (Wood et al., 2010). However, many of the reviewed investigations had limitations. Out of all the studies reviewed, only two used robust samples (Park, Peterson, & Seligman, 2004; Peterson, Ruch, Beermann, & Park, 2007), and as far as we know, not a single investigation used representative samples of the population. The use of convenience samples, especially the use of participants from Western, Educated, Industrialized, Rich, and Democratic (WEIRD) societies, has been criticized (Henrich et al., 2010).[1] We are not implying that the positive influence of gratitude on well-being might not hold with more diverse samples. Yet, this is something that should be put to empirical scrutiny rather than something to be taken as given.

With regards to prosocial behavior, it is suggested that gratitude serves as a motivator of prosocial behavior (McCullough et al., 2008). Specifically, gratitude is more than a positive emotion because it also involves acknowledging and appreciating that one is a recipient of good "things" in life. It is precisely these acknowledgment and appreciation what motivate people to behave and act prosocially (McCullough, Kilpatrick, Emmons, & Larson, 2001).

Several correlational and experimental studies have found support for the proposed link between gratitude and different forms of prosocial behavior (Bartlett & DeSteno, 2006; DeSteno, Bartlett, Baumann, Williams, & Dickens, 2010; Froh, Sefick, & Emmons, 2008; McCullough, Emmons, & Tsang, 2002; Naito, Wangwan, & Tani, 2005; Tsang, 2006). Even though the findings from these investigations have been valuable in increasing our understanding of how gratitude influences prosocial behavior, they have had the same limitation of using primarily samples of convenience.

Even though our criticism about the excessive use of samples of college students from Western countries is valid, this does not mean that the examination of gratitude, satisfaction with life, and prosocial behavior with diverse samples has been completely neglected. For example, one investigation with school teachers from Hong Kong found a positive relationship between gratitude and satisfaction with life (Chan, 2013). Another investigation with Italian residents also found a positive relationship between life satisfaction and gratitude (Szcześniak & Soares, 2011). Similarly, another investigation with Chinese students found a positive relationship between gratitude and helping behavior (Li & Chow, 2015). Hence, there seems to be some empirical support for the generalizability of the positive influence of gratitude on life satisfaction and importance given to helping other among more diverse samples. Yet, the use of more diverse samples has been more the exception than the rule.

As explained before, we are also interested in testing if income moderates the relationships between gratitude, life satisfaction, and importance given to helping others. Even though the examination of the moderating influence of income on the relationships between gratitude, satisfaction with life, and importance given to helping others is more exploratory in nature, there is some evidence suggesting that individuals belonging to the highest social class tend to show less empathy and compassion than the lower class counterparts (Kraus, Piff, Mendoza-Denton, Rheinschmidt, & Keltner, 2012). Whether this reduced empathy and compassion influence the relationship between gratitude and satisfaction with life or gratitude and importance given to helping others is something that needs to be empirically examined. Hence, we test for the moderating influence of income.

In sum, the influence of gratitude on well-being and prosocial behavior has not been examined with representative samples of the population, which limits our ability, for example, to investigate if the positive effects of gratitude are moderated by income level. Thus, we want to address this limitation using a representative sample of the adult population of Mexico, which includes, among others, people whose monthly income is $100 dollars or less. For our investigation, we have two research hypotheses and one research question:

(1a) Gratitude would have a positive relationship with life satisfaction.
(1b) Gratitude would have a positive relationship with importance given to helping others.
(2) Are these relationships moderated by income level?

3. Participants and sampling design

Participants were 1,200 (591 females and 609 males; ages 18–89, $M = 42.53$ years and SD = 16.30) residents of Mexico. We used a stratified two-stage cluster sample design. In the first step, we randomly selected Primary Sampling Units (PSUs) which in this case were the electoral sections created by the institution that organizes all the elections in Mexico (INE). In the second stage, we randomly selected houses and one individual from each house who was 18+ years of age and had a voting ID. Interviews were conducted in both rural and urban areas. The sample was representative of the adult population of Mexico in terms of age, sex, and income levels.

4. Measures

The questionnaire included, among other questions measuring political attitudes, two questions to assess gratitude taken from the Gratitude Scale (McCullough et al., 2002). The questions were: (1) I have so much in life to be thankful for and I am grateful to a wide variety of people. Both questions were measured in a scale of 1 (strongly disagree) to 5 (strongly agree). The wording of the life and financial satisfaction questions were taken from the World Values Survey (World Values Survey Association, 2009). Both items had a scale from 1 "Completely Unsatisfied" to 10 "Completely Satisfied." The life satisfaction item was phrased as "Considering all things, how satisfied are you with your life?" The financial satisfaction question was worded as "How satisfied are you with the financial situation of your house?" Lastly, the willingness to help question was phrased as: In your personal life, how important is it to help others? and used a scale from 1 (Not important) to 4 (Very important). We acknowledge that it would have been ideal to use the full gratitude scale or a more robust satisfaction with life scale, yet in studies with large and representative samples, it is not uncommon to use single items to measure psychological variables (Strack & Schwarz, 2007). Lastly, participants reported their monthly income by choosing one of the following alternatives:[2] $100 or less, $101–$300, $301–$500, $501–$1,000, and $1,001 or more.

5. Procedure

Questionnaires were administered by a trained interviewer in a face-to-face format outside the participants' home. This is a typical way of collecting data in public opinion research in Mexico since it is a more reliable way of obtaining representative samples of the population than doing telephone or Internet interviews. It took between 20 and 25 min to complete the questionnaires.

6. Results

Before testing our hypotheses, we wanted to examine differences in gratitude and importance given to helping others as a function of income level. We calculated the mean for the two gratitude questions ($r = .33$ between both gratitude items). For gratitude, results showed a significant effect of income level, F (3, 1,024)[3] = 5.18, $p < .05$, $\eta^2 = .02$. Tukey post hoc comparisons showed that participants from the lowest income level had the lowest levels of gratitude, yet the effect size was small. Conversely, results for the variable importance given to helping others showed that income level did not have a significant effect, F (3, 1,024) < 1.

We used path analysis to test the influence of gratitude on importance given to helping others and life satisfaction, while controlling for the known effects of financial satisfaction on life satisfaction (Schimmack, 2007). We used the Robust Diagonally Weighted Least Square (DWLS) estimation with LISREL 9.1 to model non-normally distributed data in all our analyses. We report a combination of absolute and incremental fit index (IFI): Satorra-Bentler χ^2, Root Mean Square Error of Approximation (RMSEA), and IFI.

We first report the results for the model with the whole sample. Results showed that the model fit was good $\chi^2 = 3.26$, $p = .20$ (df = 2), RMSEA = .02, and IFI = .99. Examination of individual parameters revealed that gratitude had significant effects on life satisfaction and importance given to helping others, $\gamma = .14$, $p < .001$; $\gamma = .33$, $p < .001$, respectively. The influence of financial satisfaction on life satisfaction was also significant, $\gamma = .41$, $p < .001$. Squared multiple correlations for the endogenous variables were, respectively, life satisfaction (0.21) and importance given to helping others (.11).

Results for the model with participants reporting monthly income levels of \$100 American dollars or less showed that the model fit was good $\chi^2 = 2.69$, $p = .26$ (df = 2), RMSEA = .01, and IFI = .99. Examination of individual parameters revealed that gratitude had significant effects on life satisfaction and importance given to helping others, $\gamma = .23$, $p = .01$; $\gamma = .46$, $p < .001$, respectively. The influence of financial satisfaction on life satisfaction was also significant, $\gamma = .40$, $p < .001$. Squared multiple correlations for the endogenous variables were, respectively, life satisfaction (.25) and importance given to helping others (.21).

Results for the model with participants reporting monthly income levels between \$101 and \$300 American dollars showed that the model fit was good $\chi^2 = 1.98$, $p = .37$ (df = 2), RMSEA = .01, and IFI = .99. Examination of individual parameters revealed that gratitude had significant effects on life satisfaction and importance given to helping others, $\gamma = .13$, $p = .01$; $\gamma = .34$, $p < .001$, respectively. The influence of financial satisfaction on life satisfaction was also significant, $\gamma = .38$, $p < .001$. Squared multiple correlations for the endogenous variables were, respectively, life satisfaction (.18) and importance given to helping others (.12).

Results for the model with participants reporting monthly income levels between \$301 and \$500 American dollars showed that the model fit was good $\chi^2 = 1.36$, $p = .51$ (df = 2), RMSEA = .001, and IFI = .99. Examination of individual parameters revealed that gratitude had significant effects on life satisfaction and importance given to helping others, $\gamma = .21$, $p < .001$; $\gamma = .26$, $p < .001$, respectively. The influence of financial satisfaction on life satisfaction was also significant, $\gamma = .34$, $p < .001$. Squared multiple correlations for the endogenous variables were, respectively, life satisfaction (.19) and importance given to helping others (.07).

Results for the model with participants reporting monthly income levels between \$501 and \$1,000 and \$1,001+[4] American dollars showed that the model fit was good $\chi^2 = 2.28$, $p = .32$ (df = 2), RMSEA = .03, and IFI = .99. Examination of individual parameters revealed that gratitude did not have a significant effect on life satisfaction, $\gamma = .02$, $p = .55$. Conversely, gratitude had a significant effect on importance given to helping others; $\gamma = .24$, $p < .001$, respectively. The influence of financial satisfaction on life satisfaction was also significant, $\gamma = .54$, $p < .001$ (for a summary of results for all models, see Table 1). Squared multiple correlations for the endogenous variables were, respectively, life satisfaction (.29) and importance given to helping others (.06).

Table 1. Descriptive statistics and gamma coefficients for all models

	Income level				
	Total	$100 or less	$101–$300	$301–$500	$500–$1,000 and $1,000+
Sample size	1,025	190	370	254	211
Mean/Standard Deviation gratitude	4.40 (.76)	4.23 (.89)	4.41 (.75)	4.44 (.68)	4.52 (.70)
Mean/Standard Deviation importance given to helping others	3.43 (.76)	3.42 (.81)	3.41 (.79)	3.42 (.79)	3.47 (.75)
Mean/Standard Deviation life satisfaction	8.63 (1.52)	8.36 (1.82)	8.54 (1.67)	8.64 (1.38)	8.86 (1.18)
Mean/Standard Deviation financial satisfaction	7.05 (2.29)	6.09 (2.84)	6.88 (2.22)	7.31 (1.94)	7.78 (1.97)
Influence of gratitude on life satisfaction	.14*	.23*	.13*	.21*	.02
Influence of gratitude on importance given to helping others	.33*	.46*	.34*	.26*	.24*
Influence of financial satisfaction on life satisfaction	.41*	.40*	.38*	.34*	.54*

*Significant at the .05 level.

7. Discussion

The purpose of the present investigation was to examine the influence of gratitude on life satisfaction and importance given to helping others among a representative sample of the adult population of Mexico. We found support for the hypothesized positive relationships between gratitude and life satisfaction and gratitude and importance given to helping others. Thus, our results are consistent with the literature on gratitude, well-being, and prosocial behavior (Sheldon & Kashdan, 2011; Wood et al., 2010). For the most part, the hypothesized correlations did not change as a function of income level. We believe it was important to empirically test if the proposed relationships between gratitude and life satisfaction and importance given to helping others held among representative samples of the population.

Even though one can be grateful about different things besides financial resources, one cannot ignore that income is related to a wide variety of important life outcomes such as health, life expectancy, job stability, perceived autonomy, among others, which might represent "things" to be grateful for (Kraus et al., 2012; Rojas, 2010). Thus, it was important to examine and establish that even under difficult economic conditions and its related consequences, being grateful is related to higher levels of life satisfaction and helping intentions. Establishing the positive consequences of being grateful among representative sample of the population provides more robust evidence about the universality of some psychological constructs such as gratitude. It also provides evidence about the ability that humans have to experience positive psychological states even under difficult circumstances.

The non-significant relationship between gratitude and life satisfaction among members from the highest income level was somewhat unexpected. We are hesitant to make any conclusions based on a single study. However, future research might want to examine if gratitude and its positive effects are significantly reduced among people whose basic needs are met. For example, a recent investigation found that individuals with fewer financial resources showed more compassion than individuals with more financial resources (Stellar, Manzo, Kraus, & Keltner, 2011). Similarly, another investigation found that individuals with fewer financial resources showed higher levels of prosocial behavior in terms of helping others and giving charity than individuals with more financial resources (Piff, Kraus, Côté, Cheng, & Keltner, 2010). Hence, there seems to be some empirical evidence suggesting differences between individuals with more/less financial resources or higher/lower socioeconomic status in variables relevant for our investigation. Future research with representative samples should continue exploring the relationships between gratitude, life satisfaction, and different forms of prosocial behavior.

7.1. Limitations and future directions

Our investigation had several limitations. First, we used a standard questionnaire to assess gratitude, life satisfaction, and helping intentions and test, quantitatively, for the proposed relationships. Yet, a qualitative approach could shade light on some very important aspects of gratitude. For example, with a monthly income of $100 dollars, a family cannot fulfill its basic needs. Thus, it would be interesting to conduct in-depth interviews and ethnographic observations to investigate how gratitude operates under these difficult economic conditions. Further research might want to use mixed designs to examine gratitude among different segments of the population.

A second, somewhat related, limitation is that we did not use the complete gratitude scale or a more robust life satisfaction questionnaire. It is often the case that public opinion research uses single items to measure psychological variables in order to manage the trade-off between the quality of information and time constraints (Strack & Schwarz, 2007). Future research might want to use more robust scales to examine the influence of gratitude on different psychological outcomes among more representative samples. Last, we used a cross-sectional research design which limited our ability to directly test for the directionality of our proposed effects. Hence, we could not directly test if the directionality went from gratitude to life satisfaction or from life satisfaction to gratitude, to mention one example.

In sum, our investigation was able to provide further evidence about the positive influence of gratitude on life satisfaction and helping intentions. We were able, in our opinion, to address one of the limitations of the current state of knowledge in gratitude and in psychological research in general: the excessive use convenience samples, especially the use of participants from WEIRD societies (Henrich et al., 2010). We encourage researchers to continue seeking opportunities to test some of the proposed positive consequences of gratitude among more robust and diverse samples.

Funding

The authors received no direct funding for this research.

Competing Interests

The authors declare no competing interest.

Author details

Rogelio Puente-Díaz[1]

E-mail: rogelio.puente@anahuac.mx

Gustavo Meixueiro[1]

E-mail: rogelio_p@yahoo.com

[1] Department of Business Economics, Universidad Anáhuac México Norte, Av. Lomas de Anáhuac 46, Col. Lomas de Anáhuac, Huixquilucan, Estado de México C.P. 52786, Mexico.

Notes

1. We do not try to claim that all investigations on gratitude and life satisfaction have been conducted with college students from Western countries. We just would like to propose that the use of diverse samples has been more the exception than the rule. We thank one of reviewers for pointing this out.
2. The question was asked in Mexican pesos but we report the results in American dollars for the sake of clarity.
3. We had some missing data and we used list-wise deletion to handle it. Given the nature of the questions asked, we have no reason to believe that nature of the missing values was not random.
4. We collapsed the last two income categories in order to have a larger sample size.

References

Bartlett, M. Y., & DeSteno, D. (2006). Gratitude and prosocial behavior: Helping when it costs you. *Psychological Science, 17*, 319–325. http://dx.doi.org/10.1111/j.1467-9280.2006.01705.x

Chan, D. W. (2013). Subjective well-being of Hong Kong Chinese teachers: The contribution of gratitude, forgiveness, and the orientations to happiness. *Teaching and Teacher Education, 32*, 22–30. http://dx.doi.org/10.1016/j.tate.2012.12.005

DeSteno, D., Bartlett, M. Y., Baumann, J., Williams, L. A., & Dickens, L. (2010). Gratitude as moral sentiment: Emotion-guided cooperation in economic exchange. *Emotion, 10*, 289–293. http://dx.doi.org/10.1037/a0017883

Fredrickson, B. L. (2013). Positive emotions broaden and build. In E. A. Plant & P. G. Devine (Eds.), *Advances in experimental social psychology* (Vol. 47, pp. 1–53). San Diego, CA: Academic Press.

Froh, J. J., & Bono, G. (2008). The gratitude of youth. In S. J. Lopez (Ed.), *Positive psychology: Exploring the best in people*, (Vol. 2, pp. 55–78). Westport, CT: Greenwood.

Froh, J. J., Sefick, W. J., & Emmons, R. A. (2008). Counting blessings in early adolescents: An experimental study of gratitude and subjective well-being. *Journal of School Psychology, 46*, 213–233. http://dx.doi.org/10.1016/j.jsp.2007.03.005

Henrich, J., Heine, S. J., & Norenzayan, A. (2010). The weirdest people in the world? *Behavioral and Brain Sciences, 33*, 1–75.

Kraus, M. W., Piff, P. K., Mendoza-Denton, R., Rheinschmidt, M. L., & Keltner, D. (2012). Social class, solipsism, and contextualism: How the rich are different from the poor. *Psychological Review, 119*, 546–572. http://dx.doi.org/10.1037/a0028756

Li, K.-K., & Chow, W.-Y. (2015). Religiosity/spirituality and prosocial behaviors among Chinese Christian adolescents: The mediating role of values and gratitude. *Psychology of*

Religion and Spirituality, 7, 150–161. http://dx.doi.org/10.1037/a0038294

McCullough, M. E., Kilpatrick, S. D., Emmons, R. A., & Larson, D. B. (2001). Is gratitude a moral affect? *Psychological Bulletin, 127*, 249–266. http://dx.doi.org/10.1037/0033-2909.127.2.249

McCullough, M. E., Emmons, R. A., & Tsang, J. (2002). The grateful disposition: A conceptual and empirical topography. *Journal of Personality and Social Psychology, 82*, 112–127. http://dx.doi.org/10.1037/0022-3514.82.1.112

McCullough, M. E., Kimeldorf, M. B., & Cohen, A. D. (2008). An adaptation for altruism? The social causes, social effects, and social evolution of gratitude. *Current Directions in Psychological Science, 17*, 281–285. http://dx.doi.org/10.1111/cdir.2008.17.issue-4

Naito, T., Wangwan, J., & Tani, M. (2005). Gratitude in university students in Japan and Thailand. *Journal of Cross-Cultural Psychology, 36*, 247–263. http://dx.doi.org/10.1177/0022022104272904

Park, N., Peterson, C., & Seligman, M. E. P. (2004). Strengths of character and well-being. *Journal of Social and Clinical Psychology, 23*, 603–619. http://dx.doi.org/10.1521/jscp.23.5.603.50748

Peterson, C., Ruch, W., Beermann, U., & Park, N. (2007). Strengths of character, orientations to happiness, and life satisfaction. *The Journal of Positive Psychology, 2*, 149–156. http://dx.doi.org/10.1080/17439760701228938

Piff, P. K., Kraus, M. W., Côté, S., Cheng, B., & Keltner, D. (2010). Having less, giving more: The influence of social class on prosocial behavior. *Journal of Personality and Social Psychology, 99*, 771–784. http://dx.doi.org/10.1037/a0020092

Rojas, M. (2010). Mejorando los programas de combate a la pobreza en México: Del ingreso al bienestar [Improving programs to combat poverty in Mexico: From income to well-being]. *Perfiles Latinoamericanos, 18*, 35–59.

Schimmack, U. (2007). The structure of subjective well-being. In R. Larsen & M. Eid (Eds.), *The science of subjective well-being* (pp. 97–123). New York, NY: Guilford.

Sheldon, K. M., & Kashdan, T. B. (2011). Why gratitude enhances well-being: What we know, what we need to know. In K. Sheldon, T. Kashdan, & M. F. Steger (Eds.), *Designing positive psychology* (pp. 248–262). New York, NY: Oxford University. http://dx.doi.org/10.1093/acprof:oso/9780195373585.001.0001

Smith, A. (1976/1790). *The theory of moral sentiments* (6th ed.). Oxford: Clarendon Press.

Stellar, J., Manzo, V., Kraus, M. W., & Keltner, D. (2012). Class and compassion: Socioeconomic factors predict responses to suffering. *Emotion, 12*, 449–459. http://dx.doi.org/10.1037/a0026508

Strack, F., & Schwarz, N. (2007). Asking questions: Measurement in the social sciences. In M. Ash & T. Sturm (Eds.), *Psychology's territories: Historical and contemporary perspectives from different disciplines* (pp. 225–250). Mahwah, NJ: Erlbaum.

Szcześniak, M., & Soares, E. (2011). Are proneness to forgive, optimism and gratitude associated with life satisfaction? *Polish Psychological Bulletin, 42*, 20–23.

Tsang, J.-A. (2006). Gratitude and prosocial behavior: An experimental test of gratitude. *Cognition & Emotion, 20*, 138–148.

Wood, A. M., Froh, J. L., & Geraghty, A. W. A. (2010). Gratitude and well-being: A review and theoretical integration. *Clinical Psychology Review, 30*, 890–905. http://dx.doi.org/10.1016/j.cpr.2010.03.005

World Values Survey Association. (2009). *World Values Survey 1981–2008 (Official Aggregate v.20090901)*. Madrid: Aggregate File Producer: ASEP/JDS. Retrieved from www.worldvaluessurvey.org

13

The influence of political candidates' facial appearance on older and younger adults' voting choices and actual electoral success

Robert G. Franklin Jr.[1]* and Leslie A. Zebrowitz[2]

*Corresponding author: Robert G. Franklin Jr., Department of Psychology, Anderson University, 316 Boulevard, Anderson, SC 29625, USA.
E-mail: rfranklin@andersonuniversity. edu

Reviewing editor: Traci Craig, University of Idaho, USA

Abstract: Younger adults (YA) judgments of political candidates' competence from facial appearance accurately predict electoral success. Whether this is true for older adults (OA) has not been investigated despite the fact that OA are more likely to vote than YA and may respond differently to particular facial qualities. We examined whether OA and YA ratings of competence, trustworthiness, attractiveness, and babyfaceness of opposing candidates in US Senate elections independently predicted their own vote choices and actual election outcomes. OA and YA ratings of attractiveness, competence, and trustworthiness positively predicted their choices, but the effect of competence was weaker for OA. Babyfaceness negatively predicted OA, but not YA, choices. OA and YA competence ratings equally predicted the actual election winners, while OA, but not YA, attractiveness ratings did so. Trustworthy and babyface ratings did not predict actual winners. These findings have implications for understanding age differences in candidate preferences and the prediction of election outcomes.

Subjects: Lifespan Development; Non-verbal Communication; Political Psychology; Social Psychology

Keywords: facial appearance; competence; trustworthiness; voting behavior; babyfaceness; attractiveness

ABOUT THE AUTHORS

Robert G. Franklin, Jr. is an Assistant Professor of Psychology at Anderson University, in Anderson SC. He is interested in researching how facial appearance has broader implications in social interactions. This includes examining age differences in face perception and how those differences affect older and younger adults in their social interactions.

Leslie A. Zebrowitz is the Manuel Yellen Professor of Social Relations and Professor of Psychology at Brandeis University in Waltham, MA. She has published widely on the topic of social perception, and her book, (*Reading Faces: Window to the Soul?*) provides a systematic account of the tendency to judge people by their appearance, offering an in-depth analysis of two appearance qualities that influence impressions of others (babyfaceness and attractiveness) as well as a theoretical explanation of these impressions and their social outcomes.

PUBLIC INTEREST STATEMENT

This research examines whether there are age differences in voting behavior based on facial appearance. Research shows that people tend to vote for more competent-looking individuals in elections but this research has not examined specific age groups. Since there are differences in how older adults judge personality traits from faces, we examined whether this would affect how they evaluated potential candidates based on facial appearance alone. We found that older adults still chose more competent-looking candidates, but they did not prefer them as strongly as younger adults. Older adults also preferred more mature-looking candidates whereas younger adults did not prefer more mature or more babyish-looking candidates. These findings show that aging can lead to changes in what facial characteristics voters prefer which may play an important role in understanding age differences in voting behavior.

1. Introduction

Facial appearance plays an important role in individual preferences for political candidates. One critical limitation of this research is that it has examined only younger adults (YA) despite the fact that older adults (OA) are a key segment of the electoral process in the United States. Indeed, they vote at a much higher rate than other age groups across a variety of different democracies, even despite physical limitations that may make voting difficult (Binstock, 2006; Goerres, 2007). The importance of OA voting behavior has led candidates and researchers to invest considerable resources in issues important to OA and OA voting preferences. While much is known about OA voting tendencies, it is not known whether OA will be swayed by facial characteristics in the same manner as YA. The aim of the present study was to fill this gap in the literature.

2. Influence of candidates' facial appearance on voting behavior

In order to examine age as a potential moderator for the relationship between facial appearance and voting behavior, it is necessary to review the literature examining how facial appearance can affect voting behavior. Facial appearance plays a considerable role in determining YA voting preferences. Just a single image of a candidate from a campaign flyer is enough to convey an image of the candidate's competence, integrity, and fitness for office and can sway participants' choices for hypothetical elections (Rosenberg, Bohan, McCafferty, & Harris, 1986; Rosenberg & McCafferty, 1987). Moreover, facial appearance ratings made by YA also predict actual election results. For example, naïve participants' ratings of perceived competence based on facial appearance alone predicted electoral success in US Senate and House elections, with the more competent appearing candidate winning approximately 70% of elections. Judgments of competence are predictive even when viewing faces for only 100 ms, indicating the robustness of this effect (Olivola & Todorov, 2010).

Despite evidence indicating the reliability of facial ratings in predicting election outcomes, it is less clear which appearance qualities predict electoral success. Work by Todorov and colleagues found that competence ratings predicted success in US elections (Ballew & Todorov, 2007; Hall, Goren, Chaiken, & Todorov, 2009; Todorov, Mandisodza, Goren, & Hall, 2005). Another influence on electoral outcomes is a preference for more attractive candidates (Rosenberg, Kahn, & Tran, 1991). This may be an example of the attractiveness halo effect, or the general preference to see attractive individuals as possessing other positive attributes, such as being more socially adept or competent. Such a halo effect may lead to an association between attractiveness and competence, as in one study, attractiveness mediated the link between competence and vote share (Verhulst, Lodge, & Lavine, 2010). However, Todorov et al. (2005) found that attractiveness and looking competent were independent predictors of electoral success.

Other first impressions from faces also have been found to predict electoral success. Rule et al. (2010) examined perceptions of traits conveying power (dominance and facial maturity) and warmth (likeability and trustworthiness) as predictors of electoral success for US and Japanese politicians. They found that greater perceived power of candidates by both Japanese and US participants predicted US electoral success, whereas greater perceived warmth by both Japanese and US participants predicted Japanese electoral success. Thus, although both Japanese and US participants' trait ratings reliably predicted electoral success, looking powerful (maturefaced and dominant) was an asset in US elections while looking warm (likeable and trustworthy) was an asset in Japan. Although another study of US elections found that babyfaceness was unassociated with electoral success (Olivola & Todorov, 2010), a study of Finnish parliamentary elections found that higher babyfaceness predicted electoral success for male candidates, but not female candidates (Poutvaara, Jordahl, & Berggren, 2009). Since babyfaceness has been associated with greater perceived warmth and honesty as well as lower dominance and shrewdness (see Montepare & Zebrowitz, 1998 for a review), the Finnish election results may be due to preferences for the former traits in Scandinavian culture, which, like Japan, tends to value interpersonal harmony to a greater degree than does US culture (Thomsen, Sidanius, & Fiske, 2007). This account can explain why babyfaceness only influenced the electoral success of male candidates, as women are both more babyfaced than men and also viewed as more warm and trustworthy, thus diminishing the degree to which babyfaceness would augment the perception of those traits in women (Brownlow & Zebrowitz, 1990; Zebrowitz, 1997).

3. Aging, and facial qualities influencing voting behavior

Research indicating that cultural factors affect which traits are associated with electoral success has implications for age differences in the traits that predict voting preferences. Hess and colleagues (Hess & Auman, 2001; Hess, Osowski, & Leclerc, 2005) have found that OA tend to value morality-based traits, such as honesty, to a greater degree than do YA, whereas YA value competence-based traits, such as intelligence, when evaluating others. Extrapolating to the political domain, OA may value trustworthiness in politicians more than YA do, with the reverse for valuation of competence. If so, then OA voting preferences may be more positively influenced by the perceived trustworthiness of candidates than are YA preferences, with the reverse for the influence of perceived competence. Insofar as trustworthiness has more influence on voting preferences for OA than YA, babyfaceness, which is positively associated with trustworthiness, should also have a more positive influence for OA than YA. These results would parallel the preferences of voters from cultures that place a high value on interpersonal harmony vs. those that do not (Poutvaara et al., 2009; Rule et al., 2010). Finally, YA and OA impressions of attractiveness and competence from facial appearance may both accurately predict actual US election outcomes, as these facial qualities have reliably predicted electoral success in previous studies, and OA–YA ratings of them show significant agreement (Franklin & Zebrowitz, 2013; Zebrowitz & Franklin, 2014; Zebrowitz, Franklin, Hillman, & Boc, 2013).

4. Present study

We evaluated the degree to which OA and YA perceptions of US Senatorial candidates' competence, trustworthiness, attractiveness, and babyfaceness predicted the same participants' voting preferences. Further, we examined the degree to which these perceptions predicted actual electoral outcomes. We tested four hypotheses.

(1) Compared with YA, the voting preferences of OA would be less positively influenced by their assessments of the candidates' competence and more positively influenced by their assessments of the candidates' trustworthiness.

(2) Insofar as babyfaceness is positively associated with perceived trustworthiness, it should have a more positive influence on voting preferences of OA than YA.

(3) Both OA and YA impressions of competence would predict actual electoral outcomes.

(4) Both OA and YA impressions of attractiveness would predict their own voting preferences and actual electoral outcomes.

5. Method

5.1. Participants

Twenty-one Caucasian YA participants (8 men), aged 18–24 (M = 19.9, SD = 1.3), were recruited from a university and completed the study for course credit. Seventeen Caucasian OA participants (5 men), aged 68–90, (M = 78.7, SD = 6.7), were recruited from the local community by calling participants from a database of volunteers 65 years and older. OA participants were paid $25 for completing the study. One additional OA (male) was dropped because he accurately recognized politicians from more than half of the elections, whereas all the other participants accurately recognized at most two politicians. OA were screened using the Mini-Mental State Examination, in order to screen for dementia (Folstein, Folstein, & McHugh, 1975). All participants scored in the normal range, above 26 out of 30 (M = 28.7, SD = 1.53).

5.2. Stimuli

We selected stimuli based on elections for the 2010 and 2012 US Senate races. In order to minimize the degree to which participants recognized any candidates, we removed elections for elections in local media markets as well as elections containing candidates who were previously part of presidential primary elections (e.g. John McCain and Rick Perry). In addition, we removed elections where candidates were not opposed by a major party candidate. This yielded a total of 54 elections.

Faces were selected from Internet sources and we attempted to use official campaign portraits where available. If these were not available, we used images selected to be as close to campaign portraits as possible. Images were cropped to 300 × 300 pixel size (6.7 cm) and backgrounds were removed and replaced with a standard taupe background.

5.3. Dependent measures

5.3.1. Face ratings

Participants made four evaluations of candidates in each pair. First, they were asked to choose which of the two candidates was more competent, trustworthy, attractive, and babyfaced.[1] Next, they were asked to indicate how much more of that attribute they thought that candidate had on a seven-point scale, with 1 indicating a little more, 4 indicating somewhat more, and 7 indicating much more. Following these trait ratings, participants chose which candidate they would vote for in a hypothetical election.

In the analysis, these ratings were scored from −7 to +7. For each pair of politicians, one was arbitrarily assigned to the positive end of the scale and one assigned arbitrarily to the negative end of the scale. Thus, if a person rated the politician assigned to the negative end of the scale to be much more competent than the one assigned to the positive end of the scale, the rating would be scored as −7. Likewise, if a person rated the politician arbitrarily assigned to the positive end of scale as somewhat more competent than the one assigned to the negative end of the scale, the rating would be scored as +4.

5.3.2. Control measures

Measures of vision, affect, and cognitive function were administered to assess age differences. Results are consistent with previous studies of community-dwelling OA, demonstrating the representativeness of our sample (see Table 1). As none of the control measures significantly predicted the dependent measures, they will not be discussed further.

5.4. Procedure

After obtaining informed consent, participants completed a rating task where they were shown photographs of pairs of politicians and were asked to rate them on various attributes. Participants rated each pair of candidates relative to the other candidate. Participants were told that these were real politicians running for office and that if at any point in the study they recognized any of the

Table 1. Scores on control measures between OA and YA participants

Measure	Older adults		Younger adults		t-value	p-value
	M	SD	M	SD		
Snellen visual acuity (denominator)	33.89	12.9	24.79	15.1	1.97	0.057
Mars letter contrast sensitivity	1.54	0.17	1.73	0.06	4.51	<0.001
Benton facial recognition test	44.4	4.42	47	4.59	1.72	0.094
Pattern comparison test	27.4	5.34	41.4	7.34	6.62	< 0.001
Shipley vocabulary test	35.2	4.25	32.9	3.05	1.82	0.079
Mind in eye test	21.38	4.62	26.31	5.39	2.78	0.009
BCST correct responses	28.41	10	36.8	4.57	3.18	0.004
Level of education*	4.88	1.53	2.37	0.5		

*Level of Education was coded for highest level attained: 1—no high school diploma, 2—high school diploma, 3—some college, 4—Bachelor's degree, 5—some graduate work, 6—Master's degree, 7—Doctorate degree.

politicians, they were to write down who that politician was. Since none of the participants retained in the study recognized more than two politicians, we included all the elections in the analysis.

Participants evaluated the politicians on four dimensions presented in one of two orders, (trustworthy, competent, attractive, and babyfaced or competent, trustworthy, babyfaced, and attractive). Each trait rating used the following format. Participants saw the two faces of the politicians on the computer screen, with one politician randomly placed on the left and indicated as Politician X and the other politician on the right of the screen and indicated as Politician Y. Participants were asked to choose which politician was more of the trait adjective (e.g. more trustworthy). Participants had as long as they needed to make this choice. After making this choice, participants were then presented with a rating scale, stating that "you chose Candidate (X or Y) as more trustworthy. Please indicate the degree to which you feel Candidate (X or Y) is more trustworthy than the other candidate". Participants rated all of the pairs of politicians using this format for one trait adjective before moving to the next trait adjective. Following the trait ratings, participants chose which candidate they would vote for by making a dichotomous choice between the two candidates, using the same format as above.

6. Results

6.1. Overview of analysis

We used a series of multilevel models to assess how participants' rating of traits and facial appearance predicted their own voting preferences as well as the actual election results. Since each rating rated each pair of candidates relative to one another, we scored ratings from −7 to 7. As discussed above, we arbitrarily assigned one candidate to the negative half of the scale and one to the positive half of the scale. The trait ratings for each candidate were scored from −7 to +7, with −7 indicating the highest rating for the candidate assigned to the negative half of the scale, whereas +7 indicated the highest rating for the candidate assigned to the positive half of the scale.

Using these variables, we computed two series of models. The first used each participant's trait and appearance ratings to predict which candidate the participant chose to vote for in each election, with a score of 0 assigned to votes for the candidate on the negative side of the scale and 1 to votes for the candidate on the positive side of the scale. The second series of models used the same trait and appearance ratings to predict the percentage of votes received by the candidate assigned to the positive side of the scale. The percentage of votes received was computed after excluding all votes for any other candidates than the ones pictured. To account for both subject-level and election-level variance, participant and election were included as random effects in the models predicting participants' voting preferences, with election-level factors nested within subject-level factors. However, election was not included as a random effects variable in models predicting actual vote share since it was co-linear with the dependent variable of vote outcome.

6.2. Relationships among the ratings

Table 2 shows the correlations among the mean four face ratings separately for OA and YA as well as the inter-age correlations. Correlations were computed by taking the mean ratings for each election across participants separately for OA and YA participants. As expected, attractiveness ratings were positively correlated with ratings of competence and trustworthiness for raters of both ages. In addition, ratings of competence and trustworthiness were highly correlated. Contrary to expectation, babyface ratings were not significantly correlated with any of the other measures for either OA or YA. Finally, OA and YA showed strong agreement for all four ratings. We also computed correlations between the ratings and the difference in age between the two politicians in each election for the 48 elections where age data were readily available for both candidates. Age was negatively correlated with ratings of babyfaceness for OA and YA raters. However, age was negatively correlated with attractiveness ratings by YA but was not significantly correlated with attractiveness ratings by OA.

Table 2. Correlations among face ratings averaged across raters. Part A shows correlations within rater age with older adult raters above the diagonal and younger adult raters below the diagonal. Part B shows correlations between older and younger adult raters

Part A					
	Competence	Trustworthiness	Attractiveness	Babyfaceness	Face age
Competence	–	0.721***	0.626***	−0.279*	0.134
Trustworthiness	0.619***	–	0.756***	−0.050	0.060
Attractiveness	0.606***	0.642***	–	0.214	−0.227
Babyfaceness	−0.155	0.075	0.272*	–	−0.344*
Face age	0.068	−0.096	−0.402**	−0.305*	–
Part B					
Younger adult	Older adult				
	Competence	Trustworthiness	Attractiveness	Babyfaceness	
Competence	0.700***	0.617***	0.689***	−0.084	
Trustworthiness	0.480***	0.705***	0.721***	0.115	
Attractiveness	0.301*	0.499***	0.809***	0.310*	
Babyfaceness	−0.252+	−0.053	0.174	0.849***	

Note: DF = 52 for all correlations except correlations with face age, with DF = 48.

$^{+}p < 0.1$.

$^{*}p < 0.05$.

$^{**}p < 0.01$.

$^{***}p < 0.001$.

6.3. Facial ratings predicting participants' own voting preferences

6.3.1. Trait impressions (Hypotheses 1)

To examine the influence of perceived competence and trustworthiness on participants' voting preferences, we tested a series of stepwise multilevel logistic models. The first step tested whether perceived competence and trustworthiness ratings predicted participants' voting preferences and whether these effects were moderated by rater age (see Table 3, left). The results revealed that both perceived trustworthiness and competence predicted participants' voting choices. An interaction between rater age and voting preference for competence ratings revealed that competence was a stronger predictor of the voting preferences of YA than OA, as predicted by Hypothesis 1. However, contrary to prediction, the effect of trustworthiness was not moderated by rater age.

Table 3. Multilevel models for face ratings as predictors of participants' own electoral preferences, with and without attractiveness and babyfaceness in the model

	Step 1				**Step 2**			
	M	***SE***	**t**	***P***	***M***	***SE***	**t**	***P***
Intercept	−0.01	0.10	−0.10	0.92	0.03	0.08	0.31	0.75
Rater age	0.18	0.11	1.62	0.108	0.22	0.12	1.85	0.064
Competence	0.28	0.02	12.21	<0.001	0.26	0.02	11.02	<0.001
Trustworthiness	0.22	0.02	9.43	<0.001	0.18	0.02	7.62	<0.001
Competence × rater age	−0.07	0.03	−2.23	0.026	−0.07	0.03	−2.06	0.04
Trustworthiness × rater age	−0.03	0.03	−0.81	0.41	−0.03	0.03	−1.05	0.296
Attractiveness					0.18	0.03	5.79	<0.001
Attractiveness × rater age					0.02	0.03	0.68	0.51
Babyfaceness					0.01	0.02	0.50	0.614
Babyfaceness × rater age					−0.06	0.03	−1.89	0.059

The second step of the analysis added attractiveness and babyfaceness to examine whether controlling for these qualities affected the predictive influence of perceived trustworthiness and competence. The results revealed that controlling for these traits did not substantially reduce the predictive power of competence or trustworthiness, nor did it substantially alter the competence by rater age interaction. When controlling for attractiveness and babyfaceness, YA showed a stronger competence effect ($\beta = 0.259$, $SE = 0.023$, $p < 0.001$) than OA ($\beta = 0.184$, $SE = 0.021$, $p < 0.001$) (see Figure 1).

6.3.2. Appearance qualities (Hypothesis 2)

Step 2 of the analysis further showed that, with all other facial qualities controlled, attractiveness positively predicted voting preferences for both OA and YA, as predicted, and this preference was not moderated by rater age. Babyfaceness had no overall effect on electoral preference. However, there was a marginally significant rater age × babyfaceness interaction. OA showed a negative association between babyfaceness and the candidate for whom they would choose to vote, which is contrary to Hypothesis 2, ($\beta = -0.056$, $SE = 0.022$, $p = 0.011$) while YA showed no relationship ($\beta = 0.008$, $SE = 0.023$, $p = 0.72$ (see Figure 2).

6.4. Facial ratings predicting actual electoral success (Hypotheses 3 and 4)

6.4.1. Trait impressions (Hypothesis 3)

Stepwise regressions examining whether facial qualities predicted electoral success used the same approach described above with the dependent variable changed to vote share. Higher perceived competence predicted greater electoral success, as predicted, and this effect was not moderated by rater age (see Table 4). Greater perceived trustworthiness was not associated with greater electoral success. Including attractiveness and babyfaceness at Step 2 did not alter these results.

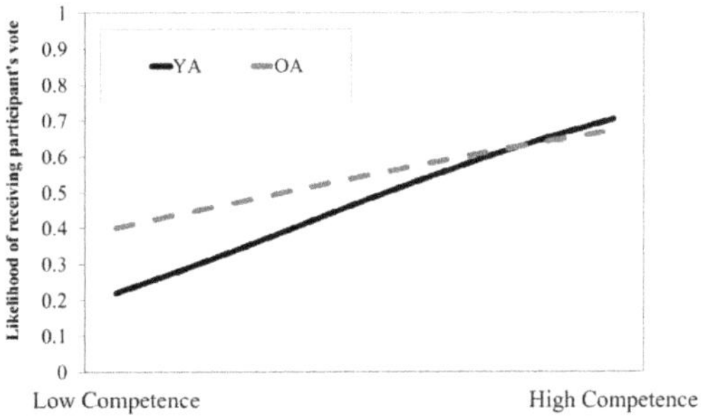

Figure 1. The interaction between competence and rater age predicting participants' vote preferences.

Notes: Values are plotted based on Step 2 in Table 3. Values for competence are plotted at −7 for low competence and +7 for high competence.

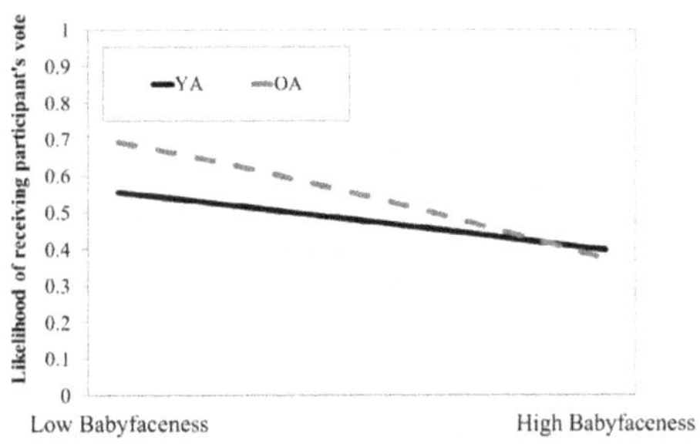

Figure 2. The interaction between rater age and babyfaceness ratings predicting participants' vote preferences.

Notes: Values are plotted based on Step 2 in Table 3. Values for babyfaceness are plotted at −7 for low babyfaceness and +7 for high babyfaceness.

Table 4. Multilevel models for face ratings as predictors of candidates' actual electoral success with and without attractiveness and babyfaceness in the model

	Step 1				Step 2			
	M	*SE*	t	P	*M*	*SE*	t	P
Intercept	50.25	0.35	140.5	<0.001	50.24	0.36	140.2	<0.001
Rater age	−0.07	0.54	0.14	0.89	−0.05	0.54	0.10	0.92
Competence	0.27	0.10	2.61	0.009	0.34	0.11	3.14	0.002
Trustworthiness	0.03	0.11	0.27	0.79	0.09	0.11	0.82	0.41
Competence × rater age	0.00	0.14	0.02	0.98	−0.10	0.15	0.64	0.52
Trustworthiness × rater age	0.00	0.15	0.01	0.99	−0.09	0.16	0.55	0.58
Attractiveness					−0.22	0.11	2.04	0.042
Attractiveness × rater age					0.29	0.15	1.94	0.053
Babyfaceness					0.09	0.10	0.94	0.35
Babyfaceness × rater age					−0.15	0.14	1.12	0.26

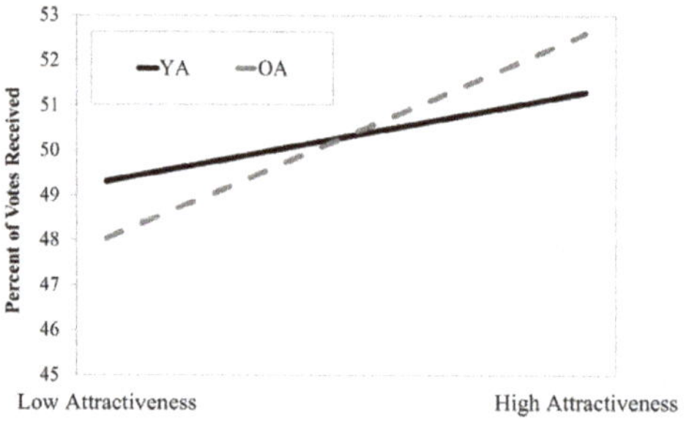

Figure 3. The interaction between rater age and attractiveness predicting percentage of actual election votes received by a candidate.

Notes: Values are plotted from the regression in Step 2 of Table 4. Values for attractiveness are plotted at −7 for low attractiveness and +7 for high attractiveness.

6.4.2. Appearance qualities (Hypothesis 4)

Step 2 of the analysis further revealed that, with all other facial qualities controlled, babyfaceness had no effect on electoral success. However, greater attractiveness predicted worse electoral success with a significant rater age × attractiveness interaction that reflected a marginally significant positive influence on electoral success for OA attractiveness ratings ($\beta = 0.162$, $SE = 0.088$, $p = 0.062$), but no significant effect for YA ratings ($\beta = -0.052$, $SE = 0.095$, $p = 0.58$) (Figure 3). The counter-intuitive negative main effect of attractiveness on electoral success resulted from controlling for the interaction between rater age and attractiveness. If the model is run with all factors except for the interaction between rater age and attractiveness, the main effect of attractiveness is not significant, $\beta = -0.067$, $SE = 0.074$, $t = 0.66$, $p = 0.37$

7. Discussion

The present study investigated OA and YA impressions of US Senatorial candidates' facial appearance as predictors of their candidate preferences and the candidates' electoral success. We found that both OA and YA impressions of candidates' attractiveness, competence, and trustworthiness predicted their personal voting choices. Confirming our first hypothesis, judgments of competence were stronger positive predictors of YA than OA voting intentions. However, contrary to our second hypothesis, judgments of babyfaceness were negative predictors of OA with no effect on YA preferences. The effects of each of these appearance qualities held true with the other appearance qualities controlled. Confirming our third hypothesis, actual electoral success was predicted by both OA and YA judgments of competence, replicating previous research that examined only YA ratings (Todorov et al., 2005). The strength of this effect did not vary by rater age and it held true with the other appearance qualities controlled. On the other hand, OA, but not YA, judgments of attractiveness positively predicted electoral success, which only partially supports our fourth hypothesis.

The finding that OA were less influenced by facial competence in their voting decisions is consistent with evidence that OA value competence-based traits to a lesser degree than do YA (Hess & Auman, 2001; Hess et al., 2005) and indicate that OA may be seeking different qualities in their politicians than are YA. Hess et al. also found that OA value morality-based traits more so than competence-based traits, but we found no age differences in the degree to which looking trustworthy predicted voting choices.

Evidence to support the argument that age differences in the influence of perceived competence on voting preferences reflect differences in the valuation, rather than the assessment of that trait is provided by the strong OA and YA agreement in competence ratings, consistent with OA-YA agreement in ratings of competence from facial appearance in other studies (e.g. Zebrowitz et al., 2013). Thus, although OA and YA see competence similarly in faces, OA voting preferences suggest that they may care less about this trait.

It is also possible OA use competence to a lesser degree than YA when making voting decisions because they are less swayed by the type of heuristic processing which may lead to YA preferring competent-looking politicians. OA are more involved and knowledgeable about the political process when compared to YA (Goerres, 2007), and as such may be more likely to desire different traits in potential politicians. Those traits may not fit the general ratings of competence that YA prefer. This is a hypothesis which warrants future investigation.

When examining the appearance qualities of attractiveness and babyfaceness, we found that OA and YA personal candidate preferences showed equal attractiveness halo effects, or the degree to which attractiveness correlates with other positive social cues such as competence. This is consistent with evidence that OA and YA have shown similar halo effects in trait impressions from faces in previous research (Larose & Standing, 1998; Zebrowitz & Franklin, 2014) as well as in the present study, where attractiveness was positively correlated with rated competence and trustworthiness (see Table 2). However, an interaction between babyfaceness and participant age revealed that OA showed a preference for more mature-faced candidates whereas YA did not, an age difference that was sustained when controlling for the other ratings. This pattern of results was contrary to the prediction that OA would prefer more babyfaced candidates, due to higher valuation of trustworthiness. However, babyfaceness was not significantly related to impressions of trustworthiness or other face ratings by either OA or YA, an unexpected result that may be due to the negative correlation between babyfaceness and perceived age, as discussed below.

As greater perceived dominance has been the strongest correlate of facial maturity in previous research (Montepare & Zebrowitz, 1998), it is possible that OA valued facial maturity to a greater degree than do YA due to its association with dominance. Research has shown that dominance is another facial characteristic that is related to voting behavior. Specifically, Riggio and Riggio (2010) found that facial dominance may serve as a cue to competence and influences voting behavior in lab studies. Since our study did not examine preferences for dominance per se, additional research is necessary to determine whether OA lesser preference for more babyfaced candidates reflects a preference for more dominant-looking politicians.

It is also possible that OA valued more mature-faced candidates because OA preferred older-looking candidates and babyface ratings served as a proxy for the age of candidates. This may be the case since participants rated the candidates' babyfaceness absent instructions to make their ratings of each face relative to others of the same age, which differs from instructions in previous research when faces varied in actual age (Zebrowitz, Olson, & Hoffman, 1993). In fact, there was a moderate negative correlation between politicians' actual age and babyface ratings (see Table 2). There also was strong OA and YA agreement in babyface ratings, which indicates that the differences in their voting preferences reflect differences in their valuation of candidates' facial maturity rather than in its assessment. This may reflect the fact that mature-looking candidates are more similar to OA participants than YA participants and OA participants prefer more mature-looking candidates because of this self-similarity. An OA preference for older-looking candidates would be consistent with research showing preferences for people similar to oneself (e.g. Bailenson, Garland, Iyengar, & Yee, 2006). This is a hypothesis warranting future investigation.

Whereas OA ratings of competence were less predictive of their own voting choices than were YA ratings, OA and YA competence ratings were equally predictive of actual electoral success. These findings are consistent with previous research showing that OA trait impressions from faces are just as accurate at predicting actual traits as are ratings by YA (Boshyan, Zebrowitz, Franklin, McCormick, & Carre, 2014; Zebrowitz et al., 2014). On the other hand, only OA attractiveness ratings were predictive of electoral success, an unexpected finding that may have implications for the prediction of future election outcomes.

Although we have no certain explanation for the greater prediction of candidates' electoral success by OA than YA attractiveness ratings, it is noteworthy that OA attractiveness ratings also better predicted the choices of voters of all ages in the present study. Specifically, OA attractiveness ratings predicted OA and YA vote choices with equal strength, respective rs (52) = 0.827 and 0.788, age difference $z = 0.57$, $p = 0.56$, whereas YA attractiveness ratings were marginally less predictive of OA than YA vote choices, respective rs (52) = 0.521 and 0.734, age difference $z = 1.82$, $p = 0.068$. The fact that YA attractiveness ratings were weaker predictors of OA vote choices can explain their weaker prediction of outcomes in actual elections, where OA vote at higher rates than do YA (Binstock, 2006). The question remains as to why OA attractiveness ratings are more robust. One possibility is that they are less biased by negative reactions to older faces. Consistent with this suggestion, OA attractiveness ratings in the present study were not significantly influenced by candidate age, whereas YA attractiveness ratings showed a significant negative relationship to age (see Table 2). Similarly, other research has found that when participants were asked to rate the attractiveness of large sets of older or younger faces as compared with others of the same age, YA nevertheless rated older faces as significantly less attractive than younger faces, while OA did not (Zebrowitz & Franklin, 2014). These results suggest that YA are less sensitive to relatively high attractiveness in older faces, which may render their ratings less diagnostic of the voting preferences of OA in actual election outcomes.

8. Conclusions and future directions

OA form an important and growing voting population and understanding influences on OA voting preferences is crucial to predicting future electoral results. Although both OA and YA candidate preferences were influenced by how competent, trustworthy, and attractive the contenders look, perceived competence had a weaker effect on OA preferences, consistent with other evidence that OA value competence-based traits to a lesser degree than do YA. Facial maturity ratings had a positive effect only on OA preferences, which may reflect more positive responses to more dominant-looking or older candidates. Finally, only OA attractiveness ratings predicted actual electoral success, which may reflect less biasing effects of candidate age on OA ratings.

These findings have significant implications for age differences in voting behavior as well as predicting election outcomes. Specifically, these findings are relevant in examining what characteristics are preferred by different segments of the voting public. As politicians target different advertisements to different demographics, it is important to highlight facial appearance characteristics to certain populations which would be most swayed by this characteristic. For instance, our findings indicating OA prefer less babyish-looking politicians would suggest that babyfaced politicians should try to minimize their babyish features in advertisements targeted toward OA. Likewise, politicians could enhance their competence more prominently in advertisements targeting YA.

Future research is necessary to examine what variables may underlie the age-related differences we find here. For instance, as mentioned earlier, differences in political knowledge may cause OA participants to see the political process differently and thus be drawn to different facial characteristics. Further, other age groups, such as middle-aged individuals, need to be examined to fully understand how aging moderates the relationships examined here. In addition, future directions also involve examining how other individual differences may moderate the relationship between candidate appearance and voting behavior. For instance, it is possible that political ideology and/or party affiliation may lead to preferences for different facial appearance candidates. Further, certain personality types may be drawn to competence or trustworthiness in candidates. These are questions for future research.

Funding
This research was funded by the National Institute of Aging [grant number AG38375].

Competing interests
The authors declare no competing interest.

Author details
Robert G. Franklin Jr.[1]
E-mail: rfranklin@andersonuniversity.edu
Leslie A. Zebrowitz[2]
E-mail: zebrowit@brandeis.edu
[1] Department of Psychology, Anderson University, 316 Boulevard, Anderson, SC 29625, USA.
[2] Department of Psychology, Brandeis University, 410 South Street MS 062, Waltham, MA 02454, USA.

Note
1. It should be noted that previous research not only has shown a strong consensus in judging all these qualities from faces, but also babyface ratings have been validated by facial measurements showing that people judged as more babyfaced have more babyfaced features, such as larger eyes and rounder faces. The consensus judgments of babyfaceness also have been validated by computer modeling. We are using rated babyfaceness in the present study both to be consistent with our other predictors that cannot be measured and also because rated babyfaceness has been shown to predict many significant social outcomes (see Zebrowitz & Montepare, 2008, for a review).

References
Bailenson, J. N., Garland, P., Iyengar, S., & Yee, N. (2006). Transformed facial similarity as a political cue: A preliminary investigation. *Political Psychology, 27*, 373–385. http://dx.doi.org/10.1111/pops.2006.27.issue-3
Ballew, C. C., & Todorov, A. (2007). Predicting political elections from rapid and unreflective face judgments. *Proceedings of the National Academy of Sciences, 104*, 17948–17953. http://dx.doi.org/10.1073/pnas.0705435104
Binstock, R. H. (2006). Older people and political engagement: From avid voters to 'cooled-out marks'. *Generations, 30*, 24–30.
Boshyan, J., Zebrowitz, L. A., Franklin, Jr., R. G., McCormick, C. M., & Carre, J. (2014). Age similarities in recognizing threat from faces and diagnostic cues. *Journal of Gerontological Sciences B, 69*, 710–718. doi:10.1093/geronb/gbt054.
Brownlow, S., & Zebrowitz, L. A. (1990). Facial appearance, gender, and credibility in television commercials. *Journal of Nonverbal Behavior, 14*, 51–60. http://dx.doi.org/10.1007/BF01006579
Folstein, M. F., Folstein, S. E., & McHugh, P. R. (1975). "Mini-mental state". *Journal of Psychiatric Research, 12*, 189–198. http://dx.doi.org/10.1016/0022-3956(75)90026-6
Franklin, Jr. R. G., & Zebrowitz, L. A. (2013). Older adults' trait impressions of faces are sensitive to subtle resemblance to emotions. *Journal of Nonverbal Behavior, 37*, 139–151. http://dx.doi.org/10.1007/s10919-013-0150-4
Goerres, A. (2007). Why are older people more likely to vote? The impact of ageing on electoral turnout in Europe. *The British Journal of Politics & International Relations, 9*, 90–121.
Hall, C. C., Goren, A., Chaiken, S., & Todorov, A. (2009). Shallow cues with deep effects: Trait judgments from faces and voting decisions. In E. Borgida, C. Federico, & J. L. Sullivan (Eds.), *The political psychology of democratic citizenship* (pp. 73–99). New York, NY: Oxford University Press. http://dx.doi.org/10.1093/acprof:oso/9780195335453.001.0001
Hess, T. M., & Auman, C. (2001). Aging and social expertise: The impact of trait-diagnostic information on impressions of others. *Psychology and Aging, 16*, 497–510. http://dx.doi.org/10.1037/0882-7974.16.3.497
Hess, T. M., Osowski, N. L., & Leclerc, C. M. (2005). Age and experience influences on the complexity of social inferences. *Psychology and Aging, 20*, 447–459. http://dx.doi.org/10.1037/0882-7974.20.3.447
Larose, H., & Standing, L. (1998). Does the halo effect occur in the elderly? *Social Behavior and Personality: An International Journal, 26*, 147–150. http://dx.doi.org/10.2224/sbp.1998.26.2.147
Montepare, J. M., & Zebrowitz, L. A. (1998). Person perception comes of age: The salience and significance of age in social judgments. In M. P. Zanna (Ed.), *Advances in experimental social psychology* (Vol. 30, pp. 93–163). San Diego, CA: Academic Press.
Olivola, C. Y., & Todorov, A. (2010). Elected in 100 milliseconds: Appearance-based trait inferences and voting. *Journal of Nonverbal Behavior, 34*, 83–110. http://dx.doi.org/10.1007/s10919-009-0082-1
Poutvaara, P., Jordahl, H., & Berggren, N. (2009). Faces of politicians: Babyfacedness predicts inferred competence but not electoral success. *Journal of Experimental Social Psychology, 45*, 1132–1135. http://dx.doi.org/10.1016/j.jesp.2009.06.007
Riggio, H. R., & Riggio, R. E. (2010). Appearance-based trait inferences and voting: Evolutionary roots and implications for leadership. *Journal of Nonverbal Behavior, 34*, 119–125. doi:10.1007/s10919-009-0083-0
Rosenberg, S. W., Bohan, L., McCafferty, P., & Harris, K. (1986). The image and the vote: The effect of candidate presentation on voter preference. *American Journal of Political Science*, 108–127. http://dx.doi.org/10.2307/2111296
Rosenberg, S. W., Kahn, S., & Tran, T. (1991). Creating a political image: Shaping appearance and manipulating the vote. *Political Behavior, 13*, 345–367.

http://dx.doi.org/10.1007/BF00992868
Rosenberg, S. W., & McCafferty, P. (1987). The image and the vote manipulating voters' preferences. *Public Opinion Quarterly, 51*, 31–47. http://dx.doi.org/10.1086/269012
Rule, N. O., Ambady, N., Adams, Jr. R. B., Ozono, H., Nakashima, S., Yoshikawa, S., & Watabe, M. (2010). Polling the face: Prediction and consensus across cultures. *Journal of Personality and Social Psychology, 98*, 1–15. http://dx.doi.org/10.1037/a0017673
Thomsen, L., Sidanius, J., & Fiske, A. P. (2007). Interpersonal leveling, independence, and self-enhancement: A comparison between Denmark and the US, and a relational practice framework for cultural psychology. *European Journal of Social Psychology, 37*, 445–469. http://dx.doi.org/10.1002/ejsp.v37:3
Todorov, A., Mandisodza, A. N., Goren, A., & Hall, C. C. (2005). Inferences of competence from faces predict election outcomes. *Science, 308*, 1623–1626. http://dx.doi.org/10.1126/science.1110589
Verhulst, B., Lodge, M., & Lavine, H. (2010). The attractiveness halo: Why some candidates are perceived more favorably than others. *Journal of Nonverbal Behavior, 34*, 111–117. http://dx.doi.org/10.1007/s10919-009-0084-z
Zebrowitz, L. A. (1997). *Reading faces: Window to the soul?* Boulder, CO: Westview Press.
Zebrowitz, L. A., & Franklin, Jr. R. G. (2014). The attractiveness halo effect and the babyface stereotype in older and younger adults: Similarities, own-age accentuation, and the older adult positivity effect. *Experimental Aging Research, 40*, 1–19.
Zebrowitz, L. A., & Montepare, J. M. (2008). Social psychological face perception: Why appearance matters. *Social and Personality Psychology Compass, 2*, 1497–1517. http://dx.doi.org/10.1111/j.1751-9004.2008.00109.x
Zebrowitz, L. A., Olson, K., & Hoffman, K. (1993). Stability of babyfaceness and attractiveness across the life span. *Journal of Personality and Social Psychology, 64*, 453–466. http://dx.doi.org/10.1037/0022-3514.64.3.453
Zebrowitz, L. A., Franklin, R. G., Hillman, S., & Boc, H. (2013). Older and younger adults' first impressions from faces: Similar in agreement but different in positivity. *Psychology and Aging., 28*, 202–212. http://dx.doi.org/10.1037/a0030927
Zebrowitz, L.A., Franklin, Jr. R.G., Boshyan,J., Luevano,V., Agrigoroaei,S., Milosavljevic, B., & Lachman, M.E. (2014). Older and younger adults' accuracy in discerning health and competence in older and younger faces. *Psychology and Aging, 29*, Special section: Social perception and aging, 454–468.

Permissions

All chapters in this book were first published in CS&N, by Cogent OA; hereby published with permission under the Creative Commons Attribution License or equivalent. Every chapter published in this book has been scrutinized by our experts. Their significance has been extensively debated. The topics covered herein carry significant findings which will fuel the growth of the discipline. They may even be implemented as practical applications or may be referred to as a beginning point for another development.

The contributors of this book come from diverse backgrounds, making this book a truly international effort. This book will bring forth new frontiers with its revolutionizing research information and detailed analysis of the nascent developments around the world.

We would like to thank all the contributing authors for lending their expertise to make the book truly unique. They have played a crucial role in the development of this book. Without their invaluable contributions this book wouldn't have been possible. They have made vital efforts to compile up to date information on the varied aspects of this subject to make this book a valuable addition to the collection of many professionals and students.

This book was conceptualized with the vision of imparting up-to-date information and advanced data in this field. To ensure the same, a matchless editorial board was set up. Every individual on the board went through rigorous rounds of assessment to prove their worth. After which they invested a large part of their time researching and compiling the most relevant data for our readers.

The editorial board has been involved in producing this book since its inception. They have spent rigorous hours researching and exploring the diverse topics which have resulted in the successful publishing of this book. They have passed on their knowledge of decades through this book. To expedite this challenging task, the publisher supported the team at every step. A small team of assistant editors was also appointed to further simplify the editing procedure and attain best results for the readers.

Apart from the editorial board, the designing team has also invested a significant amount of their time in understanding the subject and creating the most relevant covers. They scrutinized every image to scout for the most suitable representation of the subject and create an appropriate cover for the book.

The publishing team has been an ardent support to the editorial, designing and production team. Their endless efforts to recruit the best for this project, has resulted in the accomplishment of this book. They are a veteran in the field of academics and their pool of knowledge is as vast as their experience in printing. Their expertise and guidance has proved useful at every step. Their uncompromising quality standards have made this book an exceptional effort. Their encouragement from time to time has been an inspiration for everyone.

The publisher and the editorial board hope that this book will prove to be a valuable piece of knowledge for researchers, students, practitioners and scholars across the globe.

List of Contributors

Nicola S. Schutte and John M. Malouff
Psychology, University of New England, Armidale, Australia

Lucia Mannetti, Ambra Brizi and Ilaria Bufalari
Department of Social and Developmental Psychology, University of Rome La Sapienza, Via dei Marsi 78, 00185 Roma, Italy

Jocelyn Belanger
New York University, Abu Dhabi, United Arab Emirates

Cecilie Gaziano
Research Solutions, Inc., 4511 Fremont Avenue South, Minneapolis, MN 55419-4744, USA

Fabian O. Ugwu
Department of Psychology, Federal University Ndufu-Alike, Ikwo Nigeria, Abakiliki, Nigeria

Lawrence O. Amazue and Nneoma G. Onyedire
Faculty of the Social Sciences, Department of Psychology, University of Nigeria, Nsukka, Nigeria

Hazel Spears
Center for Health Behavior and Communication Research, Annenberg School for Communication, University of Pennsylvania, 3901 Walnut Street Suite 503, Philadelphia, PA 19104, USA
Department of Social and Behavioral Sciences, Cheyney University of Pennsylvania, Cheyney, PA, USA

John B. Jemmott III
Center for Health Behavior and Communication Research, Annenberg School for Communication, University of Pennsylvania, 3901 Walnut Street Suite 503, Philadelphia, PA 19104, USA
Department of Psychiatry, Perelman School of Medicine, University of Pennsylvania, 3901 Walnut Street, Philadelphia, PA 19104, USA

G. Anita Heeren
Health Services, St. Joseph's University, Philadelphia, PA, USA

Frank Reichert
Faculty of Education, The University of Hong Kong, Room 217, 2/F, Runme Shaw Building, Pok Fu Lam Road, Hong Kong, Hong Kong SAR

Anne Gene Broomhall and Wendy J. Phillips
School of Behavioural, Cognitive and Social Sciences of University of New England, Armidale, NSW, 2351 Australia

Elena Sovetkina and Bas Verplanken
Department of Psychology, University of Bath, Claverton Down, Bath BA2 7AY, UK

Marjorie Weiss
Department of Pharmacy and Pharmacology, University of Bath, Claverton Down, Bath BA2 7AY, UK

Khalil Motallebzadeh, Fatemeh Ahmadi and Mansooreh Hosseinnia
English Department, Torbat-e-Heydarieh Branch, Islamic Azad University, Torbat-e-Heydarieh, Iran

Chuma Kevin Owuamalam, Maas Misha'ari Weerabangsa and Jaya Kumar Karunagharan
School of Psychology, University of Nottingham (Malaysia Campus), Jalan Broga, Semenyih 43500, Selangor, Malaysia

Mark Rubin
Psychology, The University of Newcastle, Canberra, Australia

Priscilla N. Gitimu, Tacibaht Turel, Rachel Pohle-Krauza, Jeanine Mincher, Zara Rowlands and Janice Elias
Human Ecology Department, Youngstown State University (YSU), One University Plaza, Youngstown, OH 44555, USA

Molly M. Jameson
School of Psychological Sciences, University of Northern Colorado, Greeley, CO 80639, USA

Rogelio Puente-Díaz and Gustavo Meixueiro
Department of Business Economics, Universidad Anáhuac México Norte, Av. Lomas de Anáhuac 46, Col. Lomas de Anáhuac, Huixquilucan, Estado de México C.P. 52786, Mexico

Robert G. Franklin Jr.
Department of Psychology, Anderson University, 316 Boulevard, Anderson, SC 29625, USA

Leslie A. Zebrowitz
Department of Psychology, Brandeis University, 410 South Street MS 062, Waltham, MA 02454, USA

Index

CPSIA information can be obtained
at www.ICGtesting.com
Printed in the USA
LVHW062020100122
708212LV00002B/346

9 781647 283667